CRAFTING QUALITATIVE RESEARCH

CRAFTING QUALITATIVE RESEARCH

WORKING IN THE
POSTPOSITIVIST TRADITIONS

PUSHKALA PRASAD

M.E.Sharpe
Armonk, New York
London, England

Copyright © 2005 by M.E. Sharpe, Inc.

Library of Congress Cataloging-in-Publication Data

Prasad, Pushkala.
Crafting qualitative research : working in the postpositivist traditions / by Pushkala Prasad.
   p. cm.
Includes bibliographical references and index.
ISBN 0-7656-0789-1 (cloth : alk. paper) — ISBN 0-7656-0790-5 (pbk. : alk. paper)
  1. Qualitative research. 2. Qualitative research—Methodology. I. Title.

H62.P651 2005
001.4′2—dc22

                                                                 2004023624

Printed in the United States of America

The paper used in this publication meets the minimum requirements of
American National Standard for Information Sciences
Permanence of Paper for Printed Library Materials,
ANSI Z 39.48-1984.

BM (c)	10	9	8	7	6	5	4	3	2	1
BM (p)	10	9	8	7						

Contents

Acknowledgments

This book is the direct outcome of several years of teaching qualitative research methods at the doctoral level. The course was first developed and offered at the Faculty of Management at the University of Calgary in Canada, where I benefited tremendously from the participation and feedback of my doctoral students. Many of them also worked closely with me either on their own theses, or on other research projects, and constantly urged me to convert my lecture notes into a book. I have taken their advice seriously and owe them all a huge debt of gratitude for their unstinting encouragement, their warm appreciation for all my pedagogic efforts, and above all, for their friendship and emotional support during some difficult professional circumstances. It is with much affection and thanks that I dedicate this book to Judy Birdsell, Michael Rouse, Tim Hynes, Gloria Miller, Charlotte Echtner, Alex Harrison, Jeff Everett, Connie Friesen, and Kariann Aarup.

Many colleagues at the University of Calgary contributed directly or indirectly to this project. Abhijit Gopal and Brad Jackson were enthusiastic participants in many of my doctoral seminars, giving willingly of their time and interest. Dean Neu and Alison Taylor were quiet and steadfast pillars of strength in all my five years in Calgary, while Wilf Zerbe and Julie Rowney were invariably models of collegial encouragement and support. Our good friend and neighbor, Morny Joy, listened to all my woes, and inspired me with her intellectual strength and amazing productivity. I also would like to thank my erstwhile colleagues in what used to be called General Studies—especially Barbara Crow, David Mitchell, Brian Rusted, and David Taras—for repeatedly recognizing and appreciating my efforts in making management research more interdisciplinary.

Although this book indeed grew out of my years of teaching at the University of Calgary, it was almost entirely written after I joined Skidmore College in the United States in 2000. Here I have gained enormously from the sheer interdisciplinarity of the college's culture as well as the discussions and warm encouragement of friends and colleagues, notably Adrienne Zuerner, Roy Rotheim, Paty Rubio, Ella Lepkowska White, Viviana Rawgil, Jordana Dym, and Sujani Reddy. I would also like to acknowledge with appreciation a grant from Skidmore College that facilitated the completion of this manuscript. My position as the Zankel Chair Professor of Management for Liberal Arts students also facilitated and encouraged the interdisciplinarity that is a core element of this book. I thank Arthur Zankel for his vision in endowing this position and his warm support of my scholarly and pedagogic efforts at Skidmore College.

Other friends and colleagues across the globe read and commented on sections of this manuscript while it was in progress. My thanks to Eileen Fischer, Ulla Johansson, Kate Kearins, Maureen Scully, and Ralph Stablein. I am also deeply thankful for the enduring friendship and faith in my abilities shown by Mike Elmes, Mike and Pat Cavanaugh, Carol Batker, Ashwin Joshi, Kiran Mirchandani, and Sue Rosenberg.

During the entire process of writing this book, I have incessantly consulted and argued with my cherished life companion, my husband, Anshu Prasad, who remains my harshest critic and most ardent supporter. Without question, this book bears a huge imprint of his thinking and his advice. With all my heart, I thank him for his intellectual counsel, his delightful (if periodic) cooking, and our endless conversations over coffee in the mornings and single malts at night. Throughout this period, our beloved cat companion, Derri, has helped me keep the academic world in perspective with his acts of mischief and his constant play.

And finally, my thanks also to Ben Wilkinson who helped me with formatting the manuscript, to Nancy Walker who helped me with the figures, and most of all to Harry Briggs at M.E. Sharpe for his initial encouragement and subsequent editorial help and guidance.

CRAFTING QUALITATIVE RESEARCH

1

Qualitative Research as Craft

Postpositivist Traditions and Research Styles

The so-called qualitative turn that has overtaken the social sciences in the last twenty-five years has yielded both a rich body of research using nonstatistical methods and a substantive amount of methodological advice on how to engage in qualitative inquiry. Together, these writings offer a dazzling array of methodological choices to tackle a multitude of research questions and problems. Yet, the task of producing high-quality research outside the positivist tradition can still seem as daunting as ever. One can even speculate that the immense diversity of qualitative options available to researchers can be somewhat overwhelming on occasion.

At the very least, any reference to qualitative research conjures up images of diverse perspectives, techniques, and styles of presentation. Ethnography, narrative analysis, participant observation, deconstruction, and focus group interviews, to name a few, are all subsumed under this label. Does qualitative research imply a state of mind, the use of specific field methods, or the employment of certain data collection and writing conventions? The fact that the answer to all of these questions is "yes" does not make the practice of qualitative research any easier.

The only certainty to emerge out of the recent proliferation of writings on qualitative research is that it is far from being a uniform set of techniques or procedures for collecting and analyzing data. Diverse strands of qualitative research are influenced by different scholarly disciplines (e.g., literary theory and anthropology), and different ontological and epistemological assumptions (e.g., phenomenology and feminism) that transcend disciplinary boundaries. The result is a complex (and frequently bewildering) amalgamation of metaphors, paradigms, techniques, and procedures that are primarily united by their nonstatistical orientation, all falling under the rubric of qualitative research.

The resulting confusion, especially for the novice qualitative researcher, is not surprising. Not only are clear-cut guidelines hard to come by, but the variation in the usage of specific terms such as ethnography and textual analysis can be considerable. The situation is not helped by the presence of similar-sounding commonly used terms such as structuralism and structuration, or ethnography and ethnomethodology, all of which carry very different connotations to different sets of researchers. For those of us who are interested in applying qualitative methods to study businesses, organizations, public policy, and managerial practices, there is also a heightened sense of uncertainty in using methods that seem to "belong" to outside disciplines such as sociology, anthropology, and communication studies.

What is needed is an appreciation of the intricate terrain we call qualitative research with all its ambiguities, tensions, and interlinkages without resorting to too many oversimplifications. Also needed is an ability to navigate this terrain in order to generate research that is both relevant and of high scholarly quality. The primary goal of this book is to untangle some of these complex methodological interconnections and to distinguish between different ways of conducting qualitative work from the standpoints of different *traditions*. The choice of the term *tradition* is central to this project and will be discussed extensively later in this chapter.

Dilemmas in Conducting Qualitative Research

Qualitative researchers are often pulled in conflicting and less-than-meaningful directions. Strongest of all is the enduring attraction of positivism that continues to influence the assumptions and values of several qualitative researchers even when they are not working with numerical data or statistical procedures. In fact, a substantial body of research in the social sciences, especially in management, organization, and business studies, suffers from various forms of positivist anxiety that is manifested in an eagerness to measure up to conventional positivist standards. Such work is best described as constituting a form of *qualitative positivism* (Prasad & Prasad, 2002a). In brief, qualitative positivism employs nonquantitative methods of data collection such as interviews and observation within conventional positivist assumptions about the nature of social reality and the production of knowledge. For the most part, qualitative positivism adopts a relatively commonsensical and realist approach to ontological and epistemological issues. Reality is assumed to be concrete, separate from the researcher, and understandable through the accurate use of "objective" methods of data collection. Many conventional case studies (e.g., Burgelman, 1994) are rooted either explicitly or implicitly within the assumptions of qualitative positivism.

Positivism retains its intellectual hold over many qualitative researchers because of its provenance in the models of the natural sciences that are still perceived (in some quarters) as the only legitimate mode of conducting scientific inquiry. However, as Max Weber (1949) observed, it is useful to understand the differences between the natural and the social sciences before firmly concluding how science is to be conducted. The first—*Naturwissenschaften* or the science of the natural world—emerges out of the traditions of the "hard" sciences that examine natural or biological phenomena. The second— *Geisteswissenschafte*—is the tradition producing knowledge about the cultural/social world. According to Weber (1949), *Naturwissenschaften* remains the main inspiration for positivism in the social sciences, even though it is *Geisteswissenschaften* that is the more appropriate tradition in which to locate the study of human action and interaction.

There are several reasons for Weber's conclusion. First, as Weber (1949), Bernstein (1985), and others argued, the assumptions guiding positivism derive from the study of largely inanimate or biological phenomena that lack the capacity for self-reflection and cultural production. By contrast, the social sciences are inevitably concerned with social, economic, and cultural worlds that are constituted by the human capacity for meaningful understanding and action. According to Flyvbjerg (2001), this human capacity for interpretation incessantly thwarts the social science dream of becoming the mirror image of the natural sciences. Furthermore, such a dream is not merely impossible, it is also pointless inasmuch as positivism is ill equipped to answer many questions of interest to social science. These include questions such as why organizational reform efforts are frequently met with resistance; which cultural features are most responsible for the collapse of corporate ethics; or how organizations socialize their members. In essence, the *Geisteswissenschaften* tradition that draws from history, philosophy, jurisprudence, rhetorics, and literary theory may well be far more suited to answering questions that deal with organizations and social processes.

If positivism is unable to offer meaningful guidelines for qualitative researchers, where can they find their methodological inspiration? In their efforts to bypass positivism, some researchers adopt an excessively casual approach to data collection and analysis, arguing that a completely open-ended and open-minded stance is the best way to conduct qualitative inquiry. The primary motto of this group appears to be "anything goes." Theoretical preconceptions are studiously avoided, and little effort is made to develop a sharp research focus grounded in theory. The implicit assumption here is that sustained encounters with the field will, on their own, guarantee the emergence of sound qualitative findings.

Although some researchers may well serendipitously arrive at this desired place, such a lackadaisical approach is not likely to advance our understanding of social phenomena in meaningful ways. The absence of theoretical grounding, the lack of a theoretically driven focus, the failure to develop careful and well-structured methodologies, and an unawareness of the fundamental assumptions underpinning one's fieldwork are more likely to result in a piece of work that is closer to a shabby and pedestrian form of journalism. Such studies can do little more than report and categorize the results of interviewing and observation. They are likely to produce "literal translations" (Stablein, 1996, 513) of empirical situations that are relatively simplistic and unsurprising descriptions of social processes.[1]

In sum, neither positivism nor an atheoretical version of exploratory research can provide useful guidelines for qualitative researchers. The tenets of positivism are somewhat inadequate for the understanding of complex, nuanced, and context-dependent social processes. A completely open-ended approach, on the other hand, is careless in its neglect of theoretical foundations and in its failure to acknowledge its own meta-theoretical assumptions. In the next section, it is suggested that proficient qualitative research can only develop within reputed and inspiring intellectual *craft traditions*. Such research is at once theoretically grounded and methodologically rigorous (even if its rigor takes different forms from that which is to be found in positivist research). Before we proceed with examining such work, we need to appreciate what is meant by suggesting that the research process is best understood as a craft.

Qualitative Research as Craft: Research Traditions and Styles

The case for qualitative research being regarded as a form of proficient craftwork has many advocates. Some argue that all genres of scientific inquiry have strong elements of craftwork, whereas others hold that nonpositivist inquiry is more artistic and craftsman-like than scientific on account of its affinities with narrative genres such as history, literature, and philosophy. Both positions possess considerable merit.

The first position attained prominence with the lively debates in the philosophy and sociology of science that were precipitated by Thomas Kuhn's (1970) fundamental questioning of the notion that scientific knowledge was the result of a slow and steady process of incremental accumulation. Since then, countless commentators have undermined the belief that scientific method strictly follows the logical principles of deduction, induction, and falsification (Feyrabend, 1987; Lakatos, 1965). A substantial body of work convincingly asserts that the actual mundane practice of science bears little resemblance to the formal models of scientific procedure (Latour, 1987). In particular, increasingly apparent are the messy, random, and creative elements in science, as well as the key role of constructs and interpretive frames in coming up with scientific categories. Stablein (1996) even proposes that many scholars would now conclude that scientists *invent* rather than discover the empirical world. If this is indeed the case, scientific practice itself (and by extension, the application of positivism in the social sciences) can no longer be understood as a rigid adherence to scientific protocol. Instead, science in practice becomes an inventive form of craftsmanship that is constantly engaged in adjusting and reconfiguring scientific protocols to meet the vagaries of each unique empirical situation.

The second position, best exemplified by Flyvbjerg (2001), relies on Aristotle's (1976) discussion of intellectual virtues to contend that the qualitative branches of the social sciences are much closer to ideals of craft than to conventional scientific models. Flyvbjerg sees positivism as corresponding to Aristotle's notion of *episteme,* which is only one of the intellectual virtues elaborated in his *Nicomachean Ethics.* Episteme is concerned with the production of knowledge that has universal application and is invariable across time and space. Episteme is guided by analytical rationality and corresponds closely to the modern ideal of science that grew out of Enlightenment thinking. Positivism, which is virtually identical to epistemic thinking, has gradually come to be regarded as the only legitimate way of doing science.

Flyvbjerg (2001), however, also points out that in the Aristotelian mindset, epistemic knowledge production is only one way of doing science. *Techne,* which is a far more suitable model for qualitative research, is another way and is influenced by notions of artisanship and craftwork. Since qualitative research is more concerned with process, context, and intricate detail, it can draw meaningful inspiration from techne rather than from episteme. Techne is best summarized by Flyvbjerg (2001, 56) himself, who notes that *"Techne* is thus craft and art, and as an activity it is concrete, variable and context-dependent. The objective of *techne* is the application of technical knowledge and skills according to a pragmatic instrumental rationality."

Thus, whether one believes qualitative research belongs to the genre of episteme or to techne, there is no getting away from its practice as craft. This entire book is premised on the assumption of qualitative research as craft. Working at a craft requires the development and perfection of skills and expertise that are usually handed down through several generations. Craftwork also involves the disciplined creativity that results in a tangible and well-made product—in this case, the piece of research. Knowledge of methods and theoretical paradigms alone is therefore insufficient for engaging in the craft of research. Of much more value is the notion of an intellectual *tradition.* Although working within a tradition involves the understanding of one's own paradigm and preferred method, it is also much more than paradigm or method.

Different orientations toward research and knowledge have been identified with the help of the term, *paradigm.* First popularized by Thomas Kuhn (1970) and later by Burrell and Morgan (1979), paradigm is often used to designate a shared set of ontological and epistemological assumptions that unites a community of scholars and prescribes specific guidelines for conducting research. Researchers often describe themselves as working in the ethnographic paradigm or the radical humanist paradigm. The term *paradigm,* however, can frequently be somewhat misleading, presenting a false sense of commonality among a group of researchers. In the material world of actual research practice, the tidy abstraction of the paradigm as a hermetic domain of shared assumptions and world-views quickly begins to give way to the messy reality of contested ideas, multiple ongoing influences, and constant experimentation.

The concept of *method* refers in general to the appropriate use of techniques of data collection and analysis. Discussions of method typically focus on interview protocols, observational formats, and variants of document analyses. For methods to prove insightful, however, more than knowledge of technique is required. Methods themselves are linked to larger paradigmatic issues and are often appropriated in diverse ways within the same and different paradigms.

Traditions, as we have already noted, are somewhat more complex. Traditions govern every sphere of craftwork—in music, art, literature, architecture, and filmmaking. One can work in the baroque, jazz, surrealist, art deco, or film noir traditions. Each tradition develops its own distinct *style* of producing the novel, film, artwork, or musical score. These styles tend to be influenced by prominent figures, central assumptions, and emergent conventions. Qualitative research is no different and can also be regarded as a craft drawing on a specific intellectual tradition. A research tradition (Hamilton, 1993; Jacob, 1987) is best conceptualized as a complex ensemble of assumptions, world-views, orientations, procedures, and practices. A scholarly or intellectual tradition intimates an entire *way of conducting scholarship* rather than merely offering a choice of technique or a uniform set of assumptions. Understanding different traditions of scholarship can help researchers identify the match between their own intellectual preferences and a particular mode of inquiry so that they can develop a research style that is personally meaningful and simultaneously meets the standards of a wider academic community.

The idea of an intellectual tradition therefore subsumes both method and paradigm while at the same time offering much more. Traditions are constantly in the process of being created and passed on by communities of practice. They are therefore never as clearly specified or as neat as research methods or paradigms. To Hamilton (1993), traditions resemble "messy social movements" rather than pristine sets of rules handed down from one generation of scholars to another. "Traditions can be invented, established, ransacked, corrupted and eliminated . . . the history of traditions is as much a narrative of diaspora as it is a chronicle of successful parallel cohabitation" (Hamilton, 1993, 62). Becoming familiar with the different qualitative traditions can give researchers a better understanding of the entire spectrum of choices available to them and a stronger sense of the distinctions between variants of qualitative research. Given the wide range of traditions present in the qualitative terrain (e.g., ethnography, semiotics, critical theory, and symbolic interaction), such an awareness is increasingly becoming more necessary. One of the book's goals, therefore, is to highlight the main features of each tradition with detailed implications for the design, conduct, and presentation of research.

The majority of qualitative orientations found in the social sciences and humanities, however, are best described as postpositivistic by inclination. In other words, they tend to approach questions of social reality and knowledge production from a more problematized vantage point, emphasizing the constructed nature of social reality, the constitutive role of language, and the value of research as critique. As stated earlier, postpositivism is far from being a single invariant tradition. Sometimes also referred to as the narrative tradition, it includes (among others) a number of diverse genres such as dramatism, hermeneutics, critical theory, semiotics, and poststructuralism— all of which are primarily united in their rejection of prominent positivist assumptions. At the same time, these traditions develop somewhat unique conventions regarding the conduct of research, despite many interlacing congruencies and influences. The focus of this book is exclusively on the postpositivist traditions rather than on the entire spectrum of qualitative ones.

About the Book

The book provides a detailed overview of the major postpositivist traditions and focuses on four comprehensive meta-traditions (or traditions with a capital T): (1) the interpretive, (2) structuralist, (3) critical, and (4) "post" traditions. Within each broad tradition, a number of subtraditions are outlined and described. For example, within the interpretive tradition, it is possible to identify the subtraditions of symbolic interaction, hermeneutics, ethnography, ethnomethodology, and dramatism. Although all of these subtraditions share the fundamental intellectual orientations of interpretive or social constructionist philosophy, they diverge in their empirical preoccupations, the development of certain key concepts, their preferences for some modes of data collection, and their writing and presentation styles. Over time, each of these traditions has produced certain shared (to a large extent) conventions about the conduct and presentation of research, resulting in a distinctive scholarly style that tends to be associated with them. The hermeneutic tradition, for instance, uses the notion of "text" to study the social world, whereas dramaturgy employs that of the stage or "theater" for the same purpose. Not surprisingly perhaps, the hermeneutic tradition shows a strong preference for the analysis of documents, whereas researchers in the dramaturgical tradition tend to favor observation. Yet both traditions are committed to similar assumptions about the socially constructed nature of reality that are at the core of the interpretive tradition. Often, owing to unique historical circumstances, each tradition can develop along different lines within the same basic ontological and epistemological parameters.

The book offers a detailed exposition of each tradition in order to provide readers with a vivid sense of how research is conducted within them. The intent is not to provide rules and formulas as much as to give readers a "feel" for actual research practices within a living tradition. In all, thirteen different traditions are covered. Each chapter examines central concepts, key intellectual figures, and crucial debates within a selected tradition. Conventions governing the conduct of research and overall research directions are discussed, as are appropriate ways of designing research projects, gathering data, and presenting the research for multiple audiences. In addition, the chapters report, analyze, and comment on a number of existing conceptual and empirical writings in each tradition, with a strong emphasis on fieldwork in management, public administration and policy, consumer research, organization studies, the sociology of work, and related areas. Although every attempt has been made to maintain a consistent organizational scheme for all chapters, readers will note that some chapters deviate from the overall pattern of the book. Some chapters, for instance, devote an entire section to current debates and developments, whereas others do not. In writing the book, it quickly became apparent that the sheer diversity of the traditions did not permit each chapter to follow an identical format. Hence, each chapter is designed to address the more central questions raised within each tradition.

The book does not promise to turn the reader into an overnight "expert" or "maestro researcher" in any or all of the traditions. What it will do is to give the reader a comfortable familiarity with working in them. Our main objective is to provide a detailed map of postpositivist qualitative research and help readers metaphorically (a) decide which destination they would like to travel to, (b) figure out how to get there, and (c) have an understanding of what might be expected in the course of such a journey. To illustrate, readers drawn to semiotics should be prepared to develop an understanding of linguistic analysis and to work substantially with "texts" of all kinds. Those wanting to work in the ethnographic tradition, on the other hand, will require some level of mastery over cultural analysis and should be prepared to spend considerable periods of time in the field.

The book also attempts to address the issues surrounding research standards and scholarly expectations in each tradition. Researchers working in many genres of postpositivism are often asked how their work meets conventional criteria of reliability and validity employed to judge positivist research. Two broad responses are typically encountered in this area. The first is predominantly defensive, calling for an outright rejection of all questions of criteria as belonging solely to the positivist tradition. The second is overly acquiescent—seeking to tailor postpositivist work in order to meet the criteria laid down by positivism. Both responses are somewhat counterproductive, for they do not contribute to enhancing the *craftsmanship* of the actual research process.

Meeting research standards is obviously a crucial matter, and one that is best accomplished through learning to work within any intellectual tradition. All traditions are deeply concerned about the quality of research that is produced out of them. Many traditions, however, do not regard reliability and validity as touchstones by which their research should be judged. Reliability and validity remain important to qualitative positivism because they are compatible with the ontological and epistemological assumptions undergirding it. They are far less important to something like the ethnographic tradition that places tremendous importance on the presentation of research in the form of a coherent and plausible narrative (Czarniawska, 1998; Van Maanen, 1988). The main point here is that an understanding of standards comes with an awareness of a tradition and cannot be arbitrarily imposed from outside it. The book's discussion of actual empirical research pieces in multiple traditions makes this notion much easier to appreciate.

The final chapter takes up the question of innovation and improvisation within and between the traditions. Obviously, although each tradition follows certain conventions, none of them is completely sealed off from diverse influences, or from each other. Traditions also continually change and evolve, triggering discontinuities with older conventions and alliances with newer ones. Researchers in any tradition are always part of this simultaneous process of adhering to conventions and creating new ones. The book opens up avenues for such discussions as well.

Note

1. Although it is tempting to dismiss these casual qualitative efforts as being merely *journalistic,* it is also worth noting that some investigative reports by journalists are of a higher quality than many qualitative research pieces published in leading journals. This is because some journalistic accounts convey an impressive understanding of history and context, and are careful in framing the data with which they are working. Eric Schlosser's (2000) *Fast Food Nation,* for instance, displays a theoretical soundness (without being theoretically heavy-handed) and offers remarkable insights into the workings of the beef industry and the culture of food consumption in the United States.

I

The Interpretive Traditions

All interpretive traditions emerge from a scholarly position that takes *human interpretation* as the starting point for developing knowledge about the social world. In contrast to positivist traditions, which are drawn from the philosophy of Descartes, interpretive traditions are rooted in the thinking of Immanuel Kant and are part of what is sometimes referred to as the German idealist tradition. Many of Kant's ideas were later further elaborated by Edmund Husserl (1960), the prominent German philosopher-mathematician whose philosophy of *phenomenology*, at some level, undergirds all interpretive research in the social sciences.

For Husserl and the German idealists, "reality" exists not in some tangible, identifiable outside world but in human consciousness itself. In other words, what is of paramount importance is how we order, classify, structure, and interpret our world, and then act upon these interpretations. Phenomenology assumes that the experience of any reality is possible only through interpretation. For instance, an oblong piece of wood on four legs is easily identifiable as a table used for eating, writing, and so on, within our own cultural context. To someone arguably from a social milieu that is completely unfamiliar with our understanding of tables, it could be interpreted as something to be used for resting, dancing upon, and the like. The main point here is not to deny the "table" its ontological existence, but to show that even its material reality comes into being through acts of social interpretation and meaningful sense making.

A second example may help to further illustrate this point. The town of Banff in the Canadian Rockies is dominated by the craggy peaks of "Sleeping Buffalo." To most of us, Sleeping Buffalo is a mountain—to be climbed, gazed upon in admiration, and photographed. To the original native inhabitants who lived there long before the European presence, Sleeping Buffalo was exactly that—Sleeping Buffalo, a godlike awesome being demanding considerable reverence and respect. The rather obvious point here is that what we experience as a mountain might as easily be experienced as a deity or a supernatural being in another time–space context. The "reality" of both situations is *socially constructed* through acts of interpretation. For phenomenologists, therefore, it is these interpretive acts that constitute valid targets of scholarly inquiry.

In the late nineteenth and twentieth centuries, phenomenology was extensively appropriated and developed by leading Western intellectual figures including Alfred Schutz, Hans-Georg Gadamer, and George Herbert Mead. Moreover, several prominent social scientists, notably Max Weber (1949) and Berger and Luckman (1967), have systematically translated the philosophic components of phenomenology into a usable framework for understanding the social and cultural world. As phenomenology has traveled with the help of several mediators through diverse academic disciplines, it has stimulated the growth of major scholarly traditions that share fundamental interpretive ideas and assumptions, and have yet developed in unique and distinctive ways. Five interpretive traditions are discussed here. They are (1) symbolic interaction, (2) dramaturgy and dramatism, (3) hermeneutics, (4) ethnomethodology, and (5) ethnography. Figure PI.1 traces some of the ways in which these prominent traditions are related to one another

What tenets do these diverse traditions share? In essence, all of them are firmly built on *interpretive* notions that take acts of subjective meaning very seriously (Holstein and Gubrium, 1993). Although interpretive traditions uniformly subscribe to the belief that our worlds are socially created, they also assert that these constructions are possible only because of our ability to attach meanings to objects, events, and interactions. Thus, for instance, the wearer of a white coat is likely to be identified as a member of the medical profession, a brisk manner tends to be interpreted as signifying efficiency, and a proclivity to punctuality tends to convey an impression of diligence. In all of these cases, actions and objects are not only identified as constituting a particular phenomenon on their own, but are also interpreted as standing for something else. In other words, all of them are meaningful in some way or another. It is this inherent human capacity for meaningful social construction that interpretivists term as being *subjective* since it departs from the idea of a fixed external reality.

It is the goal of all interpretive traditions to understand these processes of subjective reality construction in all walks of social life. This is often referred to as the principle of *verstehen* (Weber, 1949) whereby understanding meaning and intentionality is emphasized over and above causal explanations. As a result, the preferred subject matter is the everyday lifeworld or *lebenswelt* in which individuals make sense of the phenomena they encounter and order them into taken-for-granted realities.

Another common feature of the interpretive traditions is the emphasis placed on the *social* dimensions of reality construction. That is, even while we are individually engaged in acts of sense making, these acts are significantly mediated by the cognitive schema and language that we obtain from our wider societies. Thus, although an infinite number of personal interpretations are

Figure Pl.1   The Interpretive Traditions: Immanuel Kant

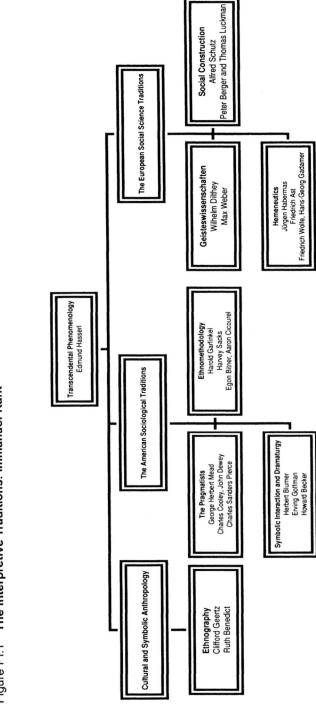

technically possible in a given situation, our tendency is to resort to fewer but more commonly shared ones. The sight of several children seated behind rows of desks and being talked to by an adult is likely to be interpreted as a classroom by most observers, even though other interpretations are possible. In actual social practice, therefore, subjectivity becomes somewhat limited, with individuals tacitly moving toward common agreements and understandings of reality. It is this tendency to arrive at common constructions and shared interpretations of reality that phenomenologists refer to as *intersubjectivity* (Berger & Luckman, 1967; Holstein & Gubrium, 1993) and that is the core concern of the interpretive traditions.

Intersubjective interpretations are central to human lives because they are so often concretized and fixed so firmly in our consciousness that they become taken-for-granted and eventually acquire a kind of "natural" existence. This process of treating social constructions as if they were objective and immutable facts of life is referred to as *reification* (Berger & Luckman, 1967). Reifications are crucial because they can turn us into prisoners of our own social constructions. Some common, powerful reifications include notions of intelligence, ideas of female/male abilities, and leadership styles in organizations. Although all of these are socially constructed, we tend to treat them as if they were natural and enduring phenomena. One of the most evocative definitions of reification is provided by Berger and Luckman (1967, 89) in their landmark treatise, *The Social Construction of Reality:*

> Reification is the apprehension of human phenomena as if they were things, that is non-human or possibly supra-human terms . . . reification is the apprehension of the products of human activity as if they were something else than human products— such as facts of nature, results of cosmic laws, or manifestations of divine will. Reification implies that man is capable of forgetting his own authorship in the human world, and further that the dialectic between man the producer, and his products is lost to consciousness. The reified world is, by definition, a dehumanized world. It is experienced by man as a strange facticity, an *opus alienum* over which he has no control rather than as the *opus proprium* of his own productive activity.

The constant unpeeling of reifications is one of the goals of interpretive scholars and researchers.

These ideas of social construction, *verstehen*, intersubjectivity, and reification are all integral to the different interpretive traditions covered in this book. Yet each tradition appropriates and extends these central tenets quite uniquely. As phenomenology spread into different cultures and academic disciplines, its core ideas have been shaped to suit the needs and research interests of various scholarly communities. Phenomenology eventually influenced American pragmatism, European hermeneutics, and segments of cultural anthropology, albeit in different ways and to somewhat different degrees.

Not surprisingly, it has spawned diverse traditions in sociology, communication, religious studies, and anthropology, each of which has, in turn, been shaped by prominent intellectual figures such as George Herbert Mead, Erving Goffman, and Hans-Georg Gadamer. Above all, as interpretive ideas have met the material interests of research practitioners, they have been modified and elaborated in distinctively creative ways. Anthropologists, for instance, have used interpretivism as a basis for understanding unfamiliar cultures by entering the subjective worlds of their natives, whereas symbolic interactionists have employed it to show how realities are negotiated out of the multiple social constructions in any situation.

At the same time, the different interpretive traditions have also been influenced by the broader cultural and subcultural milieus in which they are located. Not surprisingly, perhaps, the American traditions incorporate a stronger level of individualism into their research focus while the European hermeneutic traditions are more concerned with historical influences on subjectivity. Within the ethnographic tradition, anthropologists emphasize the value of interpretation for exploring diverse cultures, whereas sociologists make equally skillful uses of interpretation for studying the mundane aspects of everyday life. The following chapters will examine five selected interpretive traditions in detail, highlighting the directions they have taken as communities of practice engaged in crafting research.

2

Symbolic Interactionism

Searching for Self and Meaning

Symbolic interactionism (SI) is a distinctly American variant of interpretive scholarship, showing significant influences of pragmatist thinking and steadily developing as an applied sociological tradition at the University of Chicago. Intellectually, SI is the offspring of German phenomenology (Husserl, 1960; Simmel, 1950) and American pragmatism, emerging largely out of the ideas of George Herbert Mead (1934; 1977) and Charles Horton Cooley (1918). The American influences are most striking in SI's emphasis on individual sense making, expressed through its detailed development of the role of the *self* in the construction of reality. In fact, Martindale (1981) characterizes SI as a genre of research and thinking that emphasizes the creation of meaning in social situations, with the point of gravity being located in the self or personhood.

Symbolic interactionism owes much to the sociologist, Herbert Blumer, who not only gave it its name, but also promoted its use in sociology at the University of Chicago, ultimately leading to its close identification with the Chicago School. In essence, Blumer (1969) translated many of Mead's and Cooley's complex philosophic concepts in ways that made them accessible to social researchers. Several of Blumer's own ideas were later further elaborated by Stryker (1968), Rock (1979), Hewitt (1988), Maines (1988), and others, who jointly contributed to the establishment of SI as a respectable (if somewhat less prominent) tradition in American sociology. In the last twenty years, SI has been taken up by researchers in many other fields, including organization studies (Prasad, 1993; Vaught & Wiehagen, 1991), marketing (Solomon, 1983), and information systems (Gopal & Prasad, 2000). In many ways, SI's attraction lies in its relatively easy-to-grasp notions and in its easily discernible linkages to individual behavior in social situations. SI also tends to attract researchers inclining toward social psychological explanations of the world.

Philosophic Influences on Symbolic Interactionism

No intricate understanding of SI is possible without some appreciation of Mead's philosophic influences on it. While subscribing to several phenomenological tenets including a belief in the social construction of reality, Mead's writings on the mind and the self (1934; 1977) have provided a more *cognitive* layer that is now widely recognized as the hallmark of symbolic interactionism. Mead's fundamental contribution lies in his understanding of the *self* and its implications for meaningful social action. For Mead, the human capacity to objectify oneself, that is, to "see" oneself in social situations, is key to understanding the process of sense making and reality construction. These self-images that accompany us at all times, become, in Mead's view, the central point from which all interpretations are then carried out.

Mead (1934), therefore, is concerned with the more individual dimensions of interpretation, even while accepting the broader interpretive premise about shared reality constructions. According to Mead, individuals and society do not enjoy an ontological independence—that is, they are not separate from one another. Even the self (in the form of self-images) is a social construction, learned from a very young age through messages from the immediate community (family, neighborhood, school, etc.) or what Mead refers to as the "Generalized Other" (Mead, 1977). Through the interactions between individuals and society, people develop the capacity to view themselves as others see them, and hence begin to build what Cooley (1918) calls the "looking-glass self." Put differently, we can see our entire lives and actions through metaphorical mirrors that reflect our actions and personalities, and help us comprehend how others may see us.

The centrality of the self in Mead's philosophy leads to the development of another crucial concept, that is, that of *role-taking*. The human tendency to constantly see oneself in social situations also implies that we consciously decide how to act and behave in them. Such conscious action is facilitated by an understanding of the *roles* that we are expected to play and that others play. Mead (1977) even goes as far as to argue that people shape and classify the phenomenological world into roles, which in turn, offer guidelines for behavior and action. With the help of roles and self-images, individuals make sense of any social situation and articulate for themselves (and others) their own place in it. This specific process of sense making that is referred to as the "definition of the situation" has become one of the building blocks of SI.

Mead's theorizing on the interactive relationship between self and society was of particular significance to the American intellectual milieu of the late nineteenth century because it provided a refreshing alternative to the popular behaviorist thinking of the time, which overwhelmingly emphasized the reflexive nature of all living beings. In contrast, Mead and the American pragmatists emphasized the *conscious* and reflective nature of humans, and repeatedly stressed the importance of the social self in understanding human action. Ultimately, it was this knowing, reflective, and social dimension of human nature that was taken up by Blumer in the development of SI as a tradition of social inquiry.

Central Concepts in Symbolic Interactionism

Herbert Blumer, who is commonly regarded as the principal architect of SI, was responsible for developing a micro-sociological tradition based on Mead's and Cooley's ideas of individual and social meaning construction. SI is not exclusively concerned with the study of symbols as much as with the study of human meaning, which is seen as emerging out of symbolic realms and related meaningful action. The approach rests on the belief that objects and events have no intrinsic meaning apart from those assigned to them by individuals in the course of everyday social interaction. Indeed, this simultaneous emphasis on meaning and action is reflected in the term *symbolic interaction* itself. Blumer's (1969) three fundamental assumptions drawn from Mead's theory of mind, self, and society are worth repeating here because they constitute the bedrock of symbolic interactionist thinking. First, human beings act toward objects on the basis of the meaning that these objects hold for them. Second, the meaning of such objects arises out of the social interactions one has with the larger society. And third, these meanings are not completely predetermined but are constantly being modified through a series of individual interpretations. Based on these assumptions, SI also centers on the following concepts that strongly influence research carried out in this tradition.

The Symbolic Character of Everyday Life

In essence, SI posits that all social phenomena are symbolic—that is, objects, events, and actions always hold meanings for different individuals. A book not only is something to be read, but also symbolizes knowledge and wisdom; a skyscraper is not merely a place of work, but can also be a symbol of modern architecture and corporate lifestyles. Peoples' relationships with both books and skyscrapers are based on meanings they hold for them. For fields like consumer research, this notion is particularly significant since meaning drives the consumption of certain objects on account of their symbolic value (Solomon, 1983). As Pfeffer (1981) acutely pointed out, every aspect of organizational life is equally symbolic. Office rituals, organizational policies, managerial styles, and new technologies are all meaningful in the sense that they evoke a variety of emotions and responses to them. As a result, they are also constantly interpreted and made sense of by managers, employees, customers, and others who come into contact with the organization. For symbolic interactionists, organizational phenomena only come to life in and through these interpretations and have little existential standing outside them.

Roles, Identities, and Multiple Realities

Given the centrality of the self in the SI tradition, a further assumption is that self-images influence the process by which people assign meaning to objects and events, and mediate their eventual choices of meaningful action. As pointed out earlier, these self-images are strongly tied to different roles taken on by individuals in society. Not only do we constantly take on different roles, but we also organize our experiences of the world from the standpoint of these roles (Blumer, 1969; Gopal & Prasad, 2000). The role refers to socially defined expectations of behavior for individuals in particular social positions, be it a manager, a consumer, an accountant, a parent, or a woman (Colton, 1987). Ultimately, the roles we take on provide us with a complex amalgamation of identities that also become the source of our constructions of reality (Blumer, 1969; Shibutani, 1967; Stryker, 1968). In other words, one's identity as a caring parent or as a knowledgeable consumer will strongly influence one's sense making of any object, action, or circumstance.

For symbolic interactionists, these identities themselves are far from being rigidly fixed and permanent. Different social situations will witness the prominence of some identities over others. At work, for instance, one's dominant identity-in-use is likely to be one of competent manager, loyal union member, and so on, while in one's neighborhood, a stronger ethnic identity may gain salience. Furthermore, the connotations of these identities and the meaning of the roles they generate can also change over time. The fluidity and multivocality of these identities also imply that socially constructed realities are likely to be characterized by multiple and changing meanings rather than fixed and shared ones. This is a point of departure for SI from the European phenomenological tradition, which tends to more strongly emphasize the intersubjective and shared aspects of reality construction. SI, on the other hand, is definitely more concerned with the multiplicity of realities within any situation.

Negotiated Orders

Given SI's strong emphasis on individual sense making and multiple realities, one might easily ask—how is any agreement about social reality ever reached? The answer, from the SI tradition, is that this takes place through the endless negotiations (implicit and explicit) between different groups and individuals in any local social situation (Shibutani, 1967; Strauss et al., 1963). All social realities are therefore negotiated orders—built on multiple realities that are tacitly adjusted and refined to comprise the day-to-day reality that individuals can agree upon. The concept of negotiated orders stresses the *constructed* nature of social reality to an enormous degree. This construction/ negotiation process, moreover, though emerging out of individual sense making, is fundamentally social and interactive in nature. Our understanding of important social realities such as schooling systems, organizational policies, and guidelines of professional conduct, is negotiated with others on an ongoing basis in different everyday situations. Many so-called social structures that we often see as being fixed and immutable are really products of ongoing social negotiations and are, therefore, more amenable to change than we might believe.

Research in the Symbolic Interactionist Tradition

Anyone choosing to work in the SI tradition has to be interested in the meaningfulness of ordinary lives in everyday local situations such as family, work, school, and neighborhood. Symbolic interactionists seek an intimate understanding of social situations largely from the standpoint of participants themselves. One of the earliest studies of managers in this tradition is Melville Dalton's (1959) classic—*Men Who Manage: Fusions of Feeling and Theory in Administration,* an in-depth examination of the world of managers in which the researcher tried to get as close as possible to this world and to interpret it from the viewpoint of managers themselves. Dalton's (1959) study is a refreshing contrast to most writings about management at that time. It is one of the earliest attempts to understand the process of management being inextricably tied to managerial interpretations of various organizational roles such as line and staff positions, and foremen. Dalton's work is also remarkable for its portrayal of the "informal" organization as constituting the essence of organizational life and influencing formal policy and salary decisions.

The most mundane aspects of our social world are of interest to symbolic interactionists; yet this interest is really in uncovering the meanings that these seemingly mundane phenomena hold for different people. Research in the SI tradition is explicitly designed to extract the multiplicity of meanings in any social situation. Take Prasad's (1993) study of work computerization in a Health Maintenance Organization (HMO). While focusing on the introduction of new information technology, the study painstakingly examined the rich symbolism of computerization that was experienced by different individuals in the HMO. Prasad's (1993) symbolic interactionist orientation thus helps us appreciate the subjective computer—that is, the computer not as an objective, instrumental technology, but as a cultural and symbolic artifact constructed out of a diversity of local meaning and interpretations. Her study shows that to the people in the organization, the computers were much more than pieces of equipment. They represented desirable levels of professionalism and superior intelligence, and in some cases they also symbolized the darker side of robotization and organizational turmoil. Symbolic interactionist influences on the study are also evident in the researcher's exploration of different self-images and their connection to the symbolic world of computerization. For instance, she links the strong symbols of the professionalism associated with computerization to certain employee identities, showing how working with computers was repeatedly interpreted as being "professional" by some occupational groups whose sense of self-worth was tied to the so-called professionalization of their work.

The importance of SI's emphasis on multiple meanings for consumer research is recognized by Solomon (1983) who asserts that market researchers do not have an adequate appreciation of the symbolic nature of products and their consumption. Not many consumer or market researchers, however, have taken this notion very seriously. One of the few symbolic interactionist studies in this area is Colton's (1987) work on leisure and recreational tourism where he shows that concepts such as leisure and recreation themselves are ongoing socially defined categories that can vary significantly from one local situation to another. Consumer research and tourism marketing can benefit enormously from the SI tradition, which could explain the appeal of products ranging from toothbrushes to luxury cruises in symbolic terms.

Research in the SI tradition can do more than elaborate on the multiple realities present in any social situation. Its recognition of the centrality of roles in human sense making can shed some useful insights into different organizational processes. A case in point is Vaught and Wiehagen's (1991) study of a prolonged mine fire in which some miners abandoned their co-workers in their attempts to escape. Within the occupational subculture of mining, such behavior is widely regarded as uncharacteristic in its violation of the "sacred" miners' code of sticking together in times of crises. By closely exploring the more specific nature of roles and relationships within the mine prior to the fire, Vaught and Wiehagen (1991) offer interesting explanations as to why some of the miners felt that escaping on their own was reasonably acceptable behavior. Their study also discusses some of the survivor rationalizations of this behavior as attempts to align self-images with actions taken during the fire.

Working in the SI tradition also implies paying close attention to process. Symbolic interactionists are compelled to look at how certain realities are produced. In this, they are driven by their own beliefs in the salience of roles and identities, as well as the German phenomenological emphasis on *vergesellschaftung*, or the process of collective interactive association (Simmel,

1950). For the researcher, this translates into a constant watchfulness to ensure that the fluidity and dynamic nature of our everyday worlds are not lost. An example can be found in the concept of organizational culture. For a symbolic interactionist, it is important to recognize that organizational cultures are negotiated on a regular basis rather than to regard them as stable structures. Moulettes and Prasad (2001) study of corporate cross-cultural encounters in an American takeover of a Swedish company is a good example of such work. Questioning the stable and essential presence of national cultures behind the organizational ones, they show how organization members employ different assumptions about American and Swedish cultures to negotiate a "blended" organizational culture at work.

Despite many of the differences in the studies discussed in this section, they all share an interest in entering the everyday worlds of the people they are looking at and in understanding these worlds from the perspectives of the individuals who inhabit them. The methods favored in this tradition are thus overwhelmingly those of observation and interviews. Observation in the SI tradition, moreover, is not of the detached kind but is much more *participative* in nature. The researcher tries (as far as possible) to enter the *lebenswelt* or everyday lifeworld of the people being studied in order to comprehend their own processes of sense making. Long hours are spent in the organization or relevant community getting to know the inhabitants, learning their vocabulary and habits, and understanding what is important and meaningful to them. In this respect, the observation methods of SI bear a striking similarity to those of cultural ethnography, except that symbolic interactionists adopt a more fluid view of culture and are more directly interested in the impact of self-images, roles, and identities on local sense making. They often use the term, *ethnography* to refer to their own data collection methods, even though they remain less preoccupied with culture per se and more interested in the self than traditional ethnographers in anthropology.

Symbolic interactionists also use interviews quite intensively, usually alongside participant observation rather than as a standalone method of data collection. Within this tradition, interviews are typically in-depth and meaning-centered. In other words, they ask fewer questions about "what" is or was taking place and more questions about "how" interviewees make sense of specific situations. Symbolic interactionist interviews also try to substantially explore issues of self-identity by asking subjects how they see themselves and others in different social situations. Often, interviews in this tradition can be relatively open-ended, giving the respondents considerable control over the direction of the interview itself.

Once data analysis begins, SI adopts a somewhat open-ended stance. To begin with, studies in this tradition are invariably inductive, posing broad research questions and refraining from introducing too many theoretical propositions at the start of the study. SI is far more comfortable with generating theory out of research findings than going in with a set of clear conceptual relationships that need to be confirmed. To some extent, therefore, SI bears a strong resemblance to grounded theory (Glaser & Strauss, 1967), the extremely popular methodological approach favoring a far more nontheoretical bent. Many proponents of grounded theory including Anselm Strauss himself began their academic careers as symbolic interactionists. It should be noted, however, that there are some important differences between the two traditions. With all of its openness to empirical situations, SI remains strongly committed to social construction from the standpoint of multiple roles, self-images, and identities. Grounded theorists, on the other hand, frequently favor a much more positivist set of ontological assumptions, believing in the existence of a much more concrete reality that ultimately anchors or "grounds" all research efforts.

Debates and New Directions in Symbolic Interactionism

Much of what is appealing about SI also makes it vulnerable to somewhat sharp criticisms from diverse theoretical positions. First of all, its insistence on seeing the self as a bedrock for understanding sense making is criticized for being far too individualistic and for ignoring many of the restrictive pressures on society. It is true that although Mead went to considerable pains to emphasize the influence of the "Generalized Other" on individual constructions of reality, in practice, the SI tradition tends to distinctly privilege the self over society. At times this results in an overly voluntaristic view of all social phenomena, attributing far more agency to individual actors than might be warranted.

SI's vision of "the self" is not without detractors either. A common contention is that SI looks exclusively at the conscious, thinking, and reflective self. From a more Freudian perspective, the irrational and unconscious self is completely missing from the symbolic interactionist picture, yielding a somewhat incomplete view of social interactions. Moreover, it is sometimes also argued that SI's preoccupation with individual sense making blinds it to the influence of power relations in our everyday cognitive lives. It must be admitted that researchers in the SI tradition do seem allergic to issues of power and dominance in social relations, going to some length to avoid even mentioning them. Through their consistent neglect of power dynamics, SI might well present an overly optimistic view of social interactions where roles and self-images are *chosen* rather than imposed and where the individual capacity to effect social change might well be overestimated.

By virtue of its ontological and epistemological position, the symbolic interactionist tradition is best equipped for an understanding of the micro and local world of organizations, community, consumption, and the like, and not for an understanding of broader social and cultural patterns. Although this in itself might appear as a limitation, symbolic interactionists would be unlikely to see it this way, for the validity of the entire scholarly project rests on their ability to provide meaningful discussions of local sense-making processes.

The SI tradition itself has seen some interesting shifts and changes over the past few years, shedding its image as the respectable "loyal opposition" (Mullins, 1973) to mainstream sociology and showing an increased willingness to incorporate newer and more radical forms of thinking into its scholarly agenda. Fine (1992) even argues that it might be more useful to think of SI as having entered a "Post-Blumerian Age" in which directions from older macro-sociologies (such as structuralism) and newer, more "postmodern" or "poststructural" ones are eagerly being added to the existing legacies of Blumer and Mead. As Fine (1992, 120) also observes, "although interactionism once had the somewhat deserved reputation of parochialism, today, interactionists are among the most promiscuous in their willingness to thrash in any theoretical bedding they can find."

One of the more interesting intellectual partnerships being forged in recent years is between SI and structuralism, a merger that finds expression in Howard Becker's (1982) *Art Worlds*. Becker takes the structures and conventions that govern the production and evaluation of art very seriously, but he examines them in the context of social worlds where conventions mingle with interpersonal interactions and identities to produce the larger symbolic world of art. Becker's work is an interesting attempt to understand an institutional world from a micro sense-making perspective.

Another direction, rejuvenated in the SI tradition by voices from poststructuralism, takes a stronger interest in everyday language. Although language has always occupied a position of central importance in Mead's philosophy, it was pushed more into the background in Blumer's (and his followers') approach. More recently, researchers working in the SI tradition have renewed the idea that language and interpretation are intimately related, and that self-identities are produced in and through language. This alliance between SI and a poststructural linguistic turn is best illustrated by Prasad and Prasad's (2000) study of employee resistance to technological change. This study shows how employee resistance as a category of social action is actually produced through retrospective accounts and the labeling of specific incidents and behaviors. For instance, in the organization that they looked at, a number of seemingly innocuous activities (such as misfiling data and interruptions at training sessions) were later reconstituted as resistance through the multiple claims and attributions made by different employees and managers. In addition, the study reveals how employee reframing of their actions as "resistant" was important for maintaining of their own identities as responsible, autonomous adults in an organizational situation that neither respected nor listened to them.

Although many of these newer intellectual directions have made SI more interesting and innovative, post-Blumerian symbolic interactionism also might be in some danger of losing its distinctive appeal (Fine, 1992). The more that SI freely mingles with other, more strident traditions, the more it is likely to sacrifice its uniqueness and become lost in another theoretical paradigm. The question for the future is whether the symbolic interactionist tradition will return to its "pristine" Blumerian state or develop along its contemporary more hybrid form.

Figure 2.1 **Highlights of the Symbolic Interactionist Tradition**

Philosophic influences: Phenomenology, American pragmatism
(George Herbert Mead)

Major figures: Herbert Blumer, Sheldon Stryker, Howard
Becker, Anselm Strauss, Shibutani, John
Hewitt

Central concepts
- The symbolic *Lebenswelt*
- Multiple social realities
- Role-taking and identity
- *Vergesellschaftung*
- Negotiated orders

Key practices
- Attention to process over outcome
- Participative (rather than detached) observation
- Interviews geared to understanding identity
- Divergence from grounded theory in its more constructionist
  orientation

Exemplary research
- *Art Worlds* (Becker, 1982)
- "Understanding GDSS in Symbolic Context" (Gopal & Prasad, 2000)
- "Stretching the Iron Cage" (Prasad & Prasad, 2000)
- "Escape from a Mine Fire" (Vaught & Wiehagen, 1991)

3

Hermeneutics

The Interpretation of Texts

The notion of hermeneutics remains extraordinarily pervasive in qualitative research, often being used interchangeably with that of interpretation. Jurgen Habermas (1972) is largely responsible for this ever since his widely used categorization of three types of knowledge (analytic, hermeneutic, and critical) roughly equated hermeneutics with the philosophic project of subjective understanding or *verstehen*. At the same time, hermeneutics is often identified with a form of *textual* interpretation concerned mainly with the methodical analysis of different forms of texts. Is hermeneutics a philosophy, a set of methodological protocols, or a broad spirit informing qualitative inquiry? Prasad's (2002) discussion of a "weak" and "strong" sense of hermeneutics may be useful in addressing this question. According to Prasad (2002), hermeneutics may be understood as being employed in a weak sense when researchers use it to denote the interpretive and phenomenological dimensions of qualitative inquiry. When used in a "strong" sense, hermeneutics refers more precisely to research that actively engages in the interpretation of texts, and that is informed by the epistemological insights of hermeneutic philosophy. Working in the hermeneutic tradition implies the use of hermeneutics in its strong rather than its weak sense.

Hermeneutics is far from being a single, invariant, and easily comprehensible tradition. It has come into being through the brilliant philosophic insights of leading European thinkers, notably Hans-Georg Gadamer, Martin Heidegger, Jurgen Habermas, and Paul Ricoeur. Not surprisingly, it is also therefore filled with intense and vibrant debates about the nature of texts and the possibilities of interpretation, both of which have a distinct bearing on the actual practice of textual interpretation. Given the wide range of philosophic influences on hermeneutics, there is no single approach to its actual practice (Arnold & Fischer, 1994). Critical hermeneutics, for instance, relies closely on the ideas of Habermas (1990), whereas phenomenological hermeneutics is more strongly wedded to the insights of Gadamer (1960). Despite its considerable variations, the hermeneutic tradition represents certain key ideas and practices for its adherents. We will discuss both of these commonalities and variations, and how they are employed in the actual hermeneutic interpretation of texts.

The term *hermeneutics* has its linguistic roots in the Greek word, *hermeneutikos,* meaning the process of explaining and clarifying with the intent of making the obscure more obvious (Bauman, 1978). This task of clarification was of considerable importance to ancient Greek culture where even the priest at the Delphi oracle was referred to as *Hermeneios* (Kets de Vries & Miller, 1987). *Hermes* was also the name of the duplicitous messenger of the Greek gods, whose duty it was to both transmit and translate divine messages (Palmer, 1969). In the course of carrying out his duties, *Hermes* is as much credited with artfully misrepresenting original messages as with delivering them in their original form. In its very roots, therefore, hermeneutics recognizes the tricky nature of interpretation—as constituted of multiple and conflicting rather than of simple, uniform meanings.

Given its goal of clarifying the obscure, it is not surprising that hermeneutics gradually developed into a scholarly tradition within philology (the correction and translation of ancient classics), within theology—explaining "difficult" passages in the Bible—and within jurisprudence—providing authoritative interpretations of legal canons and texts (Mautner, 1996). Early on, therefore, hermeneutics established itself as a tradition keenly interested in working with *texts* of all kinds. It attained tremendous prominence in seventeenth-century Germany during the Reformation when it was joined by leading Protestant scholars who were engaged in reinterpreting the Bible in ways that supported their opposition to the Catholic Church. Two centuries later, hermeneutics once again drew the attention of German thinkers of the Romantic Movement who were involved in examining the authorial purposes behind the creation of any text.

Hermeneutics' textual preoccupations eventually led to its importation into literary theory while its focus on ancient writings made it of interest to history. With the growing interest in qualitative and other "naturalistic" forms of inquiry, hermeneutics began to exert a strong influence on the social sciences. To date, this influence tends to be more in the weak than in the strong hermeneutic sense. Yet, some of the work produced in the strong hermeneutic tradition offers extraordinary insights within applied fields such as management and consumer research (Aredal, 1986; Arnold & Fischer, 1994; Francis, 1994). If anything, the hermeneutic tradition is an underexploited one that holds immense possibilities for researchers interested in the complexities of management and organizations.

The Philosophy of Hermeneutics

The philosophy of hermeneutics is fundamentally concerned with matters of text and interpretation. What is a text? How can it be best understood? What constitutes authentic textual interpretation? These and many other questions have been seriously taken up by hermeneuticians over the last three hundred years. Most of these philosophical discussions have immensely problematized the nature of texts and the practice of textual interpretation. An early departure from conventional notions of texts can be found in the work of Friedrich Schleiermacher. Prior to his discussions, the actual practice of hermeneutics concerned itself solely with so-called difficult passages in any text, assuming that an understanding of the rest of the text would occur as a matter of course. Schleiermacher contested this assumption, arguing that all texts are such complex products of an author's personal history, social location, and specific world-view that it is *misunderstanding* that is more likely to occur as a matter of course in the process of interpretation (Palmer, 1969). Schleiermacher's argument is crucial because he alerted scholars to the complexity inherent in all portions of any text despite its deceptive appearance of transparency.

For Schleiermacher, hermeneutics needed to focus mainly on avoiding such misunderstandings in its attempt to capture the "authentic" message or spirit of a text. Schleiermacher and his German contemporaries, notably Friedrich Ast, were concerned that texts from a completely different epoch (i.e., biblical times or Antiquity) presented enormous barriers to understanding for scholars in their own times. Consequently, their main objective was to turn hermeneutics into a systematic science of interpretation that could make such an understanding possible (Palmer, 1969). For this to happen, the interpreter needed to enter both the linguistic world and the psychological mindset of the text's author. Classical hermeneutics, therefore, was all about establishing a connection or affinity between a text's interpreter and its original author(s) through linguistic and psychological appreciations. In essence, it put the interpreter into the role of cultural broker, mediating between different nations, ages, and mindsets (Bauman, 1978).

The importance of entering the lifeworld of a text's author was both reinforced and expanded by Wilhelm Dilthey (1976) for whom texts of any kind were always infused with local symbolic meanings. In Dilthey's view, many forms of lived social and cultural experience are expressed in objects or texts that we often seek to understand long after their original creation. For this to happen, we need to reconstruct the meaningful experiences that went into the text or object's formation. This reconstruction is possible only by going beyond an author's mindset to an exploration of her or his culture, including relevant histories, social customs, and political and economic institutions (Dilthey, 1976). Dilthey's contributions to hermeneutics are twofold. First is his assertion that a text is not merely the product of its authors, but also of the authors' broader cultural milieu. Full and meaningful textual analyses, therefore, necessarily call for an understanding of the wider culture in which the text was originally produced. Second is his expanded idea of the text itself from a formal piece of writing to any enduring cultural object such as a painting or pottery.

With Heidegger (1962) and Gadamer (1960), the hermeneutic debates take a somewhat different turn, moving away from questions about the nature of texts and authors' intentions to understanding the relationship between texts and their interpreters. Heidegger and Gadamer thus introduce a higher level of philosophic reflection that is less concerned with method itself and more concerned with the possibilities for understanding that stem from an interpreter's own consciousness and position in society (Howard, 1982). Both thinkers basically focus on how the act of interpretation takes place. For Heidegger, interpretation occurs within the totality of our involvements in our everyday lifeworlds and is grounded in what he calls the *forestructures of understanding.* In other words, we approach any text with certain presuppositions, ideologies, and existing familiarities with other texts, all of which shape our eventual interpretations with the text itself.

Heidegger's emphasis on prior understanding as the very basis of interpretation is elaborated by Hans-Georg Gadamer (1960) in *Truth and Method*—his seminal treatise on hermeneutics. Gadamer is equally concerned with what an interpreter brings to his or her understanding of a text. His primary philosophic contribution is with respect to his notion of "prejudice." According to Gadamer, our prejudices are unavoidable preconditions for our interpretations. However, it is important to note that for Gadamer, the term *prejudice* is not entirely pejorative. On the contrary, he makes a distinction between "productive prejudices" that enhance our understanding, and unproductive ones that hinder our understanding. The hermeneutical goal for Gadamer is somehow to suspend the nonproductive form of prejudice while strengthening the productive. It must be emphasized here that Gadamer's call for a suspension of unproductive prejudices bears no resemblance to the positivist endorsement of researcher "objectivity" since he consistently attests to the value of some prejudices over others and to the impossibility of a prejudice-free interpretation. In essence, Gadamer seeks to refine hermeneutics by making interpreters aware of their own tendencies to force a text's meaning into a framework of personal beliefs, categories, and constructs (Prasad, 2002). At a philosophic level, his goal is to bring the interpreter as close as possible to the traditions in which the text was written or to achieve what he calls a "fusion of horizons" with the text (Gadamer, 1960).

Both Gadamer and Heidegger compel a stronger philosophic reflection of the very act of hermeneutic interpretation. More recent thinkers, notably

Jurgen Habermas and Paul Ricoeur, have taken hermeneutics in a more critical direction—forcing considerations of ethics, justice, and morality in the interpretation of texts. These newer hermeneutic directions, commonly referred to as *critical hermeneutics,* are concerned primarily with uncovering the relations of power and domination that go into the very formation of a text. Let us consider Habermas's view of interpretation. For him, all texts are products of traditions embodying wider social relations of power and domination (Habermas, 1990). Texts themselves, however, tend to mask these power asymmetries and relations of domination. It is the task of hermeneutics to go beyond these *appearances of the text* to elicit an understanding of what lies behind them. In Habermas's work this is referred to as the process of *Ideologiekritik,* or a critique of the text's ideologies.

Ricoeur (1971; 1991) offers a more nuanced, yet critical, vision of the project of textual interpretation. Ricoeur (1971) primarily distinguishes between a *hermeneutics of faith* and a *hermeneutics of suspicion,* arguing that *both* are necessary for a comprehensive and meaningful understanding of any text. A hermeneutics of faith aims at carefully ascertaining a text's manifest meaning in order to gain insight into it and eventually become aware of its hidden meanings (Aredal, 1986; Ricoeur, 1991). A hermeneutics of suspicion, on the other hand, does not regard texts as innocent artifacts but as reflections of class interests and power conflicts demanding a more subversive and skeptical approach (Mautner, 1996). Ricoeur's critical hermeneutics simultaneously calls for both a generous interpretation (based on faith) and a critical one (based on suspicion) in approaching any text.

Central Concepts in the Hermeneutic Tradition

Notwithstanding the many philosophic differences found within the hermeneutic tradition, working within it demands a knowledge and application of certain key concepts discussed below. All of them instill a strong awareness of issues relating to the nature of texts, the possibilities for textual understanding, and the relationship between texts and their interpreters.

The Hermeneutic Circle

No undertaking in hermeneutics is possible without understanding and using the hermeneutic circle, one of the foundational pillars of the tradition. The idea of the hermeneutic circle is central to classical hermeneutics and is integral to establishing the linkage between a text and its wider context. In brief, the concept of the hermeneutic circle is one of an iterative spiral of understanding (Arnold & Fischer, 1994) which asserts that "the part" (i.e., the text or elements of the text) can only be understood from "the whole" (i.e., the cultural context), while "the whole," in turn, can only be understood from its "parts" (Prasad, 2002). The hermeneutic circle holds considerable intuitive appeal especially with regard to the analysis of literary texts. After all, a comprehension of words and sentences is enhanced by a grasp of the literary genre in which they are composed, while an understanding of the larger genre itself is predicated on an understanding of its minute elements or parts. The two are, however, at a meaningful level, inseparable.

In the social sciences, the hermeneutic circle has some important implications. Let us take any organizational "text" such as a set of corporate policy statements. The hermeneutic circle suggests that the meaning of these texts does not reside solely in the words and sentences of the policy statements. A researcher would have to closely examine the wider organizational background (structure, culture, interpersonal relations, etc.) to understand (a) why specific policies have been initiated, (b) which organizational actors have been most influential in its creation, (c) what local interests it may serve, and so on. At the same time, a close analysis of the policy documents themselves, especially their rhetorical elements, can tell us interesting things about what is important to members of the organization. Thus, an examination of the context sheds light on the text itself, whereas an examination of the text, in its turn, can illuminate our understanding of its context. Together, they result in a broader and more meaningful understanding of diverse organizational phenomena. In theory, the application of the hermeneutic circle involves an endless set of movements between text and context. In practice, a researcher can impose closure on this process when some kind of meaningful understanding has been reached.

It should be obvious by now that working with texts in the hermeneutic tradition does not bear any similarity to textual methods such as content analyses, which are explicitly formulated from positivist orientations. Content analysis assumes that the substance of textual understanding can be found entirely within the text itself. The hermeneutic circle completely contests that view, holding instead that the meaning of any text can be discerned only if we look at the conditions that go into its constitution. Although hermeneutics would not necessarily be opposed to the kind of systematic counting of words and phrases typically employed by content analyses, it would not regard it as being particularly insightful unless it were further reinterpreted in the light of a deeper understanding of the text's context. In essence, the hermeneutic circle tries to get beyond *the letter* of any text's message in order to capture its *spirit,* while fully recognizing that the spirit of the text will elude us unless we have a good understanding of the letter itself (Mautner, 1996).

Layers of Text

Not only is the text not seen as the sole repository of relevant meaning, but it is also a source of multiple and frequently contradictory meanings. In the hermeneutic tradition, the text's appearance is often regarded as concealing deeper and more profound meanings. The task of the researcher is to get beyond the text's obvious meaning in order to discern its latent and hidden meanings. Thus, a crucial notion within hermeneutics is that of the *subtext,* or the text underneath the surface-text. By implication, the subtext constitutes the "real" or more important text. Subtexts themselves can vary in their form and content.

In some situations, the text is *expressive* in nature—a vehicle for the public circulation and reinforcement of private anxieties, dreams, and desires. Gabriel's (1991) study of local stories told by catering workers and navy conscripts is a case in point. Gabriel treats these stories as "texts" that tell much more than their superficial narrative. Using hermeneutics to go beyond the story recitals to capture their hidden meanings, Gabriel (1991) argues that the "real" stories are myths embodying some of the collective fantasies of the workers. By carefully examining a popular story about an employee's outburst in the presence of a catering officer, he reveals that the core meaning of the story (which explains its popular appeal) lies in the emancipatory myth of defiance that it symbolizes. The value of this kind of hermeneutic analysis lies in its ability to sharpen our awareness of the complex dimensions behind seemingly ordinary or "trivial" texts, be they stories, folklore, minutes of meetings, or corporate policy statements.

In other situations, texts can be seen as *ideological*—representing attempts to mask or conceal organizational realities to a segment of the public. When a text is ideological, its "real" meanings are carefully hidden and its appearance is either a façade or a way of persuading public opinion. This idea of the text as ideological or false in some way is central to the critical hermeneutics of Habermas which stresses the importance of delayering a text to reveal whose interests it serves and whose it does not. Getting to the subtext of corporate annual reports in the oil industry (Prasad, 2002) is an example of this kind of hermeneutic analysis. Prasad and Mir's (2002) work reveals how the U.S. petroleum industry repeatedly legitimized some of its controversial activities in its annual reports 'by crafting implicit images of itself as containing the growing influence of Organization of Petroleum Exporting Countries (OPEC), and caring about the environment.

Unearthing subtexts widens our understanding of social and organizational worlds at two levels. When texts are seen as expressive, we can identify subjugated voices trying to speak out and express their hidden dreams, desires, and fears. When texts are seen as ideological, we become more aware of the deceptions they practice. In both cases, we enter a world of subterranean meaning that is not easily glimpsed in a casual encounter with the text.

Relating to Texts

Contemporary strands of hermeneutics strongly emphasize the importance of a *relationship* between a text and its interpreters. A part of the hermeneutic method, therefore, calls for an ability to develop strong connections with the text. In this aspect, hermeneutics differs sharply from positivist (Cartesian) approaches that seek to maintain a strong separation between texts and their researchers. Thus, for hermeneutics, detachment from the text is not a scholarly goal, since detachment distances the interpreter from the text, and consequently fosters unproductive prejudices.

Developing a relationship with the text is also important given the hermeneutic view of understanding as a route to self-knowledge as well (Arnold & Fischer, 1994). In other words, the goal of textual interpretation is not merely to understand the text, but also to understand the self through the interpretive process (Ricoeur, 1981). The hermeneutic ideal for a researcher is to learn more about himself or herself in the course of textual interpretation.

Since detachment from the text is not favored in hermeneutics, the suggested approach is a *dialogue* or conversation between text and interpreter as a method of achieving both textual and self-understanding (Gadamer, 1960). In Gadamer's view, the hermeneutic conversation between an interpreter and a text is a dialogue in which the interpreter puts questions to the text, and the text in return questions the interpreter (Prasad, 2002). The term *dialogue* here is obviously used in a metaphorical sense and conveys notions of "listening" to texts and allowing them to "speak" to us even though this is not possible in a literal sense (Francis, 1994). In this process, the interpreter is able to reach some awareness of her or his presuppositions and can reinterpret the text with a new set of more meaningful questions. Like the hermeneutic circle, the dialogue with the text is (theoretically) an endless iterative process done until some satisfactory level of understanding is achieved.

Questions of Author Intentionality

A series of intense debates following Gadamer's (1960) discussion of hermeneutics has complicated the question of author intentionality in a text's creation. Put simply, the early hermeneutic interest in entering an author's mindset in order to elicit the authenticity of a text's message has been supplanted by a skepticism toward establishing an author's intention in writing a text. This position is arrived at through an awareness that any text is not solely the product of an individual author's personal intentions and desires, but is the outcome of multiple sociocultural and political forces reflecting broader institutional relationships and ideologies more than individual authors' mindsets. The text, therefore, frequently assumes a life of its own, carrying messages that are not necessarily coincident with its author's intentions (Arnold & Fischer, 1994).

This position does not entirely ignore the author's voice as much as it alerts the interpreter to multiple influences on any author's creation of the text. For instance, take the corporate annual reports produced by writers working in an organization's public relations or communications department. In this case, it is quite easy to see that the actual author's voices and intentions are likely to be expressed less strongly than a whole host of messages coming from powerful organizational stakeholders. A hermeneutic reading of these texts would therefore focus on drawing out the organizational elite's concerns and the governing corporate ideology as guiding influences in the text's creation. In essence, questioning the notion of author intentionality forces the act of textual interpretation to focus on (a) wider cultural influences on the text and (b) messages that may not necessarily have been *intended* by the text's immediate authors.

Research in the Hermeneutic Tradition

Working in the hermeneutic tradition takes one into the social world of texts—holding multiple and complex interpretive possibilities. Unlike many other scholarly research traditions such as symbolic interactionism and ethnography, hermeneutics is centrally concerned with texts, over and above human action and conversation. Whereas early hermeneuticians mainly examined sacred and legal texts, post-Gadamerian hermeneutics has tended to regard texts in a broader light to include any piece of writing or any cultural artifact that has a more *permanent* character than ongoing speech and action. Hodder (1993) regards any instance of "mute evidence" as text—that is, things that have endured physically and that can be separated across space and time from their authors or producers. Texts, therefore, are distinguishable from speech and action because they can be witnessed and/or studied even when their original creators are no longer present.

Any written records and documents typically fell within the purview of conventional hermeneutics, but the list of what can legitimately be considered as "text" has steadily expanded to include genres such as film, technology, and literature. Contemporary social scientists working within the hermeneutic tradition have studied a wide range of phenomena as texts. These include electronic mail (Lee, 1994), financial statements (Francis, 1994), minutes of meetings, agendas and official letters (Aredal, 1986), magazine articles and full-page advertisements (Hirschman, 1990), local organizational stories (Gabriel, 1991), corporate image advertisements (Phillips & Brown, 1993), and corporate annual reports (Prasad & Mir, 2002). Many other organizational and social phenomena are obvious candidates for textual analyses. Policy statements, newspaper stories, laws and court decisions, official investigative reports, intraorganizational memos, web pages, office furniture, managerial clothing, and innumerable other documents and artifacts that are rich in meaning are prospective targets of hermeneutic study.

When working in the hermeneutic tradition, it is important to distinguish between notions of text as *text* and text as *metaphor.* Although all the phenomena discussed above constitute texts in their own right, it is also possible to employ text as a metaphor for the understanding of conversation, interaction, and events. A ballet performance, a marketing presentation, or a corporate board meeting can all be treated as if they were texts (metaphorically) and analyzed according to hermeneutic principles. For the most part, hermeneutics is concerned with actual texts. But whether it is used to study texts or is used as a metaphorical process, it is capable of offering enormous insights into the less obvious dimensions of work, culture, and society.

Much of course depends on the craftsmanship of the research project itself. Sometimes a study claiming to be hermeneutic is little more than an attempt to use broad interpretive frameworks to understand social phenomena (e.g., Lee, 1994). Crafting a hermeneutic research project obviously calls for more than a mere adherence to social constructionist ideas. However, it is also probably obvious by now that the hermeneutic tradition does not offer a precise set of formulas and protocols for the interpretation of texts. Each hermeneutic endeavor follows a relatively unique path of analysis depending upon the nature of the text being studied and its context. Yet, a "good" hermeneutic study would need to pay attention to the context of any text, focus on its latent messages, and show an awareness of the complicated issues of author intentionality. For all this to take place, it is imperative that the researcher develop a close relationship with the text. This can be done only by becoming intensely familiar with the text's contours and nuances, and simultaneously examining relevant features of its context.

Even though hermeneutic protocols may not be available, we can gain considerable understanding of working in this tradition by looking at exemplary studies conducted within it. Let us start by looking at the hermeneutic studies of advertisements by Hirschman (1990) and Phillips and Brown (1993). Both studies use advertising texts as vehicles for understanding broader social relations. Hirschman examines a number of full-page advertisements in several

American glamour magazines with a view to understanding messages about consumption and identity conveyed by them. She further situates the central themes emerging from the advertisements in the broader ideological climate of affluence, arguing that celebrity in America is substantially achieved through conspicuous consumption (Hirschman, 1990).

Phillips and Brown's (1993) study looks at three corporate image advertisements issued by Syncrude Canada in *Time* magazine and the *Alberta Report*. Through a careful juxtaposition of the advertisements' messages with Syncrude's recent vision statements, the researchers show how the advertisements systematically constitute Syncrude's identity as a responsible corporation committed to Canadian public interests of the future and why this particular identity is important to the organization. In the first study, the advertisements are a starting point for understanding how consumption patterns are driven by an ideology of affluence. In the second study, the analysis of the advertisements alerts us to a corporation's legitimation strategies to obtain governmental backing and public support. Both studies enhance our understanding not only of the texts themselves, but of broader social patterns, ideologies, and organizational predicaments.

The search for subtexts beneath the manifest text is a more central objective in many hermeneutic projects such the studies conducted by Aredal (1986) and Gabriel (1991). Aredal looks at minutes of meetings of a Swedish interorganizational committee, examining the inconsistencies and contradictions present in the text as a way of getting to the hidden meaning in the meeting. He also uses recollections of the meetings by various committee members to provide a social context within which the text (i.e., the minutes) can be analyzed. His final conclusion is that broader cultural pressures toward standardization of all practices forced the committee members to take decisions favoring unanimity and mediocrity, and avoiding options that would deviate from current standardized routines. Gabriel's (1991) work employs text in a more metaphorical sense to look at stories or organizational folklore repeatedly recited by navy conscripts and catering workers. His search for subtexts unearths the basic mythic structures (the epic, the comic, and the tragic) underlying everyday workplace stories. Shorn of all idiosyncratic narrative details, these stories are also shown to carry specific mythical messages either celebrating the agency of workers, mourning their victimization, or condemning the arbitrariness of management. In both the meetings and the storytelling practices, hermeneutics is helpful in getting to the kernel of events and activities by understanding the relationship between the obvious features of a text and the driving forces behind them.

Prasad and Mir's (2002) study of CEO letters to shareholders in the U.S. petroleum industry is another piece that illustrates the engagement of the hermeneutical circle and the search for the subtext. The researchers' examination of sixty-four letters to shareholders published in the annual reports of the U.S. "oil majors" lays bare the symbolic management of the companies' own complicated and controversial relationship with the OPEC governments. Conducting their analysis against the background of the growing unpopularity of the oil companies at home and the lengthy history of *orientalism,* the authors weave back and forth between text and context, showing how the letters manipulated specific cultural images of the Arab countries to deflect attention away from the companies' own problems of domestic legitimacy.

The focus on text in the hermeneutic tradition can make things both easy and difficult for researchers. Texts, for the most part, are relatively easy to access unless they are confidential in nature. Unlike the subjects of interview and observation projects, they are more under the direct control of the researcher and are not likely to be troubled by a specific research focus. In brief, texts need far less sensitive handling than interview subjects. Texts also do not change with moods or in different situations, and they are therefore appealing in the constancy they present to the researcher. However, the task of hermeneutic interpretation is obviously far from easy, calling simultaneously for a sympathetic feeling toward the text and an incessant interrogation of it. Hermeneutics is in many ways close to different forms of literary critique where the text is subjected to a powerful but sympathetic scrutiny by its interpreters. Hermeneutics also relies considerably on the researcher's *imagination* for a creative interpretation of the text. In this it calls for skills that are more typical of the humanities than the social sciences. In the final analysis, however, hermeneutics is invaluable in its capacity to go beyond the appearance of everyday life to capture its deeper meanings. It also serves as a useful critical methodology for understanding how communication patterns both expose and conceal specific dynamics.

Figure 3.1   **Highlights of the Hermeneutic Tradition**

Philosophic influences: Philology, theology, jurisprudence

Major figures: Friedrich Schleiermacher, Wilhelm Dilthey, Hans-Georg Gadamer, Martin Heidegger, Jurgen Habermas, Paul Ricoeur

Central concepts
- The Hermeneutic Circle
- Layered nature of texts
- Intricate relationship between a text and its interpreters
- Author intentionality

Key practices
- Constant movement between a text and its context
- Key differences from content analysis in its focus on a text's spirit
- Acquiring an intimacy with the text
- Pursuing a dialogue with the text

Exemplary research
- "Procrustes: A Modern Management Pattern Found in a Classical Myth" (Aredal, 1986)
- "Analyzing Communication in and Around Organizations" (Phillips & Brown, 1993)
- "Digging Deep for Meaning" (Prasad & Mir, 2002)

4

Dramaturgy and Dramatism

Social Life as Theater and Stage

The idea that our lives are fundamentally *dramatic* is a notion central to Western philosophy and literature. The stage, the play, the theater, and the drama are enduring cultural legacies of Greek civilization, informing our understanding of life in all its complexities. To the ancient Greeks, the term *drama* indicated a performance involving the acting out of a plot. The contemporary use of the term is somewhat more comprehensive, also referring to a set of events having the unity and progression of a play that typically leads to some kind of a climax, be it a disaster or *catastrophe* (tragedy) or a *consummation* in the form of lovers coming together (romantic comedy) or former injustices being avenged.

Although the dramatic tradition has constantly remained at the heart of Western art, philosophy, and literature, it has more recently also taken hold of the social sciences—as a way of looking at diverse social phenomena, including communities, neighborhoods, governments, work, and organizations. Sociology, communication, and organization studies have all embraced different components of "the drama" to make sense of intricate social situations. Research in the dramatic tradition takes different forms but broadly tends to coalesce around either *dramaturgy* or *dramatism.* Although both of these traditions share an adherence to the idea of the stage or drama as central principles of social life, they also exhibit some striking differences that can be found in the specific focus of their inquiry and their interpretations of social reality. Dramaturgy tends to be dominated by a more micro-sociological approach that primarily draws inspiration from the work of Erving Goffman, whereas dramatism is more strongly rooted in the humanities and influenced by the philosophy of Kenneth Burke. Both traditions will be explored in this chapter.

Philosophic Antecedents of Dramaturgy

Erving Goffman is unquestionably the single most inspiring figure in the social science dramaturgical tradition. Given the influences of George Herbert Mead and Georg Simmel on his thinking, it is not surprising that dramaturgy is frequently regarded as an extension of symbolic interactionism. Like symbolic interactionism, dramaturgy is also concerned with developing a micro-level analysis of social interaction, and tends to avoid systemic and structural explanations of social reality (Baert, 1998). However, dramaturgy's exclusive reliance on the metaphor of theater and its overwhelming concern with social appearances give it its own distinctive identity.

Mead's (1934) notion of the "theater of the mind" is the starting point of his influence on dramaturgy. In attempting to understand the social construction of the self, Mead suggests that the human mind itself is a theater in which a number of internal dramas are always taking place. Within this theater of the mind, every individual functions as a *playwright,* providing her or himself with scripts that guide social behavior throughout one's life. In the course of scripting one's life, the self as playwright also assigns characteristics and motivations to either him or herself and to others (Lyman & Scott, 1975). At the same time, individuals function as *directors,* rehearsing their actions in the public performances of everyday life in the imagination. Sometimes these imaginative dramas get to be actually enacted in the "real" world, but more often than not, they are never played out. Rehearsals of social roles might include preparing for an interview or a public presentation, or rehearsing one's behavior for a date, a meeting, or a situation involving a possible conflict. Eventually, the individual becomes an *actor* performing in social scenes that may or may not go according to scripted rehearsals. And finally, the individual is also the *audience* of his or her performance—either approving and applauding it or being sharply critical of it (Lyman & Scott, 1975).

Mead's ideas about the theater of the mind obviously entail two levels of analysis. The first is that of internal dramas played out entirely in the imagination. The second is that of public dramas, acted out in the theater of social life. Public dramas are much more complex situations because they constitute the terrain in which the individual playwright, actor, and director come face-to-face with other performers who have also come with scripted and rehearsed roles, and who are simultaneously audiences for one's own performance. According to Lyman and Scott's (1975) interpretation of Mead, multiple actors eventually begin to compete for the appropriation of different social scenes. In this process, they quickly realize that as individuals they have less than perfect control over the theater of social life, and therefore need to resort to constantly rescripting and re-rehearsing many of their social roles—an idea most evocatively expressed by Samuel Beckett in his play, *Waiting for Godot.*

For Georg Simmel, these human inclinations toward the staging of everyday performances are accentuated under conditions of modernity where the increased anonymity of social life creates a stronger need for the endless shaping of public opinion about oneself. The theatrical quality of social life has also long fascinated symbolic anthropologists who recognize that formal community rituals are practiced performances communicating social hierarchies and renewing collective values (Cohen, 1981). However, most of this research is based on a tacit assumption that the performative dimensions of social interaction are present only in formal ceremonial situations (Mangham & Overington, 1987). It has been the task of Erving Goffman, the well-known micro-sociologist, to extend Mead's ideas about the theater of the imagination into virtually every aspect of social life. Goffman's work, therefore, is of unparalleled importance to researchers interested in this oeuvre, and contains concepts that are central to the dramaturgical tradition.

Erving Goffman and Dramaturgy

Erving Goffman revolutionized much of American sociology in the 1960s by treating Mead's ideas about social theater with utmost seriousness in the mundane realms of everyday life. Unlike Mead's emphasis on the theater of the mind, Goffman has always been far more interested in public social performances where actors come face-to-face with other actors, and compete for the audience's approval and attention. For Goffman, our sense of identity is drawn from both our *self-image* and our *public image.* The two do not enjoy an ontological separation from one another but are in fact, mutually reinforcing. As a sociologist, Goffman has always been more drawn to the maintenance of public images since this takes place within a social context.

According to Goffman, we are constantly presenting selected aspects of our personalities while enacting social roles in what he calls "encounters" (Goffman, 1961). These encounters are face-to-face interactions in which individuals constantly monitor public performances of themselves. Each encounter, therefore, involves a "presentation of self" (Goffman, 1959) from which there is no escape. In effect, each encounter involves the staging of one's public persona, though some roles may be so well learned that their actual performance requires very little conscious effort or extensive rehearsal on the part of individual actors. Although Goffman's dramaturgy does imply the existence of some kind of internal script, these scripts are primarily self-determined by individuals with a view to maximizing their positive impact on specific audiences (Baert, 1998).

The centrality of audiences in Goffman's thinking leads to his critical differentiation between the *frontstage* and *backstage* of social life. The frontstage represents the social domain in which public presentations of the self take place (Goffman, 1963a), and is something like a *masquerade* for which individuals outfit themselves with a persona or "front" that they feel might be best suited for the occasion. One's "authentic" self, on the other hand, is more likely to be found in the backstage of social life. The backstage is also a place where we hide a self that, if revealed, might prove to be awkward, embarrassing, or even suspect.

Goffman's concept of the frontstage assumes a strong attempt by individuals to define and influence social situations. In his view, frontstage performances rely substantially on two dimensions: the setting and the personal front (Goffman, 1963a). The setting refers to the physical elements of the social scene against which the public performance is taking place, and includes the décor, choice, and arrangement of furniture. Goffman believes that individuals frequently orchestrate their own public performances by tinkering with the scene. The prominent display of degrees and credentials, the choice of a certain type of artwork in one's home and office, and the like, are all attempts to engineer the background of the frontstage. Typically, far more effort goes into presenting the personal front—that is, one's appearance, demeanor, and social status. According to Goffman, we often choose to communicate a certain personality style be it aloof, approachable, trustworthy, and so on, by adopting specific behaviors and mannerisms including a frosty tone of voice, a warm smile, or a hearty handshake. Goffman's term for these dramaturgical efforts is *face-work,* and it is a central part of his thinking.

Goffman's notion of the backstage is also an important concept within the dramaturgical tradition. The backstage is a realm of authenticity, a place where people are most likely to be "themselves." Second, the backstage is where rehearsals for the frontstage take place—where individuals consciously (and with the help of people they trust) prepare themselves for their public performances while simultaneously distancing themselves from these. Salespersons, for instance, may practice their sales pitches in the backstage, which is also a venue for the expression of complaints against difficult clients and customers. The backstage, in other words, is the more hidden and private world that nevertheless exerts considerable influence on the public world of the frontstage.

Once in the frontstage, individuals/actors not only do their face-work to the best of their ability, but also play a role in either encouraging or undermining others' performances. This face-work can be accomplished in a multitude of ways. One might exemplify one's own social standing by casual references to personal status symbols; one could lower another individual's standing by dismissively labeling them as "troublemakers," "rate-busters," or "granolas"; one might also enhance another person's public image by markedly indicating respect. The list of possible face-work strategies is obviously endless, and each situation is likely to demand a unique configuration of them. However, certain patterns of face-work used to enhance or discredit self and others are likely to recur in specific cultures. Any understanding of such patterns is of immense insight into our overall grasp of societal sense making and practice. For Goffman, this process of "managing impressions" is a key feature of human life and is deserving of sustained scholarly interest.

Goffman is equally interested in the process whereby identities are "spoiled" through the deployment of labels that denigrate or *stigmatize* certain individuals. A *stigma* refers to perceptions of attributes that are deeply discrediting and that reduce "a whole and usual person to a tainted, discounted one" (Goffman 1963b, 3). Terms such as "scab," "faggot," and "geek" can instantly conjure up negative images that become persistently attached to the individuals who have been thus labeled. Escaping from such social stigmas is not at all easy and requires a whole set of carefully thought-out impression management strategies that counter the effect of such labels in the first place (Goffman, 1963b).

Goffman's dramaturgy is appealing because it goes beyond the surface interactions of everyday life in order to uncover the hidden dynamics behind work, home, professional, and community performances. It is therefore one of the few scholarly traditions that systematically explores the complex but enduring relationship between *self-presentation, trust,* and *social tact* (Baert, 1998), looking at how individuals figure out their own roles in social situations and assess audience responses to them, while simultaneously preparing public performances that would have a desired effect on these audiences.

Despite its considerable appeal, Goffman's dramaturgy is not without its critics. A common complaint is that he universalizes human tendencies that may well be uniquely Western and modernist in their location, notably the high emphasis he places on calculation and manipulation by human beings. For Lyman and Scott (1975, 107), Goffman unfortunately leaves us with a feeling that "a brooding and suspicious sense of inauthenticity is the basic condition of performative human existence." Other limitations in Goffman's thinking can also be found. His excessive focus on the *competence* of human performances ignores the vast segments of human life in which individuals seem *unable* or *unwilling* to learn their cues and to carry out a flawless social performance at work, home, or in one's community. His conceptual framework, however, leaves ample room for explorations in the inaptitude of social actors in diverse situations.

Working in the Dramaturgical Tradition

Working in the dramaturgical tradition requires a fundamental acceptance of the theatricality of social life. Dramaturgy is rooted in a suspicion of the prevailing social order and a desire to *unmask* it with a view to uncovering hidden agendas, conflicts, and identity interests. For dramaturgists, elements of theater are present in virtually every aspect of social life whether it is the organization of work, the socialization of professionals, or the public celebration of an event. The metaphor of the theater guiding this tradition suggests that concealment is an ongoing condition of social life and that the task of research is to get beyond these concealments to reveal the complex dynamics they often mask. The tradition's strong emphasis on the frontstage and backstage of social life also ensures that researchers pay attention to both public performances and behind-the-scene activities.

Gaining access to the backstages of social dramas is not always easy for obvious reasons of confidentiality and privacy. Some researchers in the dramaturgical tradition, therefore, restrict themselves to the analysis of frontstages, treating them as performances—following script lines, assessing the quality of the "acting," and judging the effect of the "play" on intended audiences. Sutton and Callahan's (1987) study of firms filing for protection under Chapter 11 of the Federal Bankruptcy Code, for example, examines the damage the stigma of bankruptcy does to organizational reputations and the subsequent attempts by these firms to manage their adverse public images. The study focuses entirely on the frontstage arena, first assessing the impact of bankruptcy on relevant audiences (e.g., suppliers, customers, stockholders, and journalists), and then examining the impression management strategies used by these firms in trying to escape the social stigma of bankruptcy.

The goal of dramaturgy, however, is primarily to *enliven* our understanding of social interactions by bringing characters and their motives to life. This goal is accomplished by revealing their identity concerns and showing how they take care of these concerns by crafting personal performances in the public sphere. These elements of the dramaturgical tradition are completely missing in Sutton and Callahan's (1987) study, which offers little beyond a dry and self-evident discussion of firm strategies of image management. This is unfortunate, leaving readers unable to obtain the full flavor of dramaturgical complexity that is at the heart of this tradition.

Dramaturgical research comes closer to reaching its full potential when conscious attention is directed to the front- and backstage divide that is so strongly emphasized by Goffman. Van Maanen and Kunda's analysis (1989) of work in DisneyWorld provides a vivid portrait of an organization directly inspired by the theater metaphor. Their study is an excellent example of going behind the scenes to witness employees "rehearsing" for their work roles, making sure that their "costumes" are in order, and keeping up with the managerially dictated scripts that outline the public performance of their duties.

An equally strong focus on frontstage and backstage helps Westley and Vredenburg (1996) analyze the changing theatricality of contemporary zoo management. In particular, they are able to show how complex changes in the front- and backstage arenas of zoos influence managerial strategies and internal organizational conflicts. A few years ago, a zoo's frontstage was simply its display of animals in cages; its backstage was the domain in which they were fed, cleaned, and taken care of. With altered social expectations, a zoo's frontstage has increasingly become the place where wider goals of conservation and wildlife appreciation are addressed. In their study of a Canadian zoo, Westley and Vredenburg describe the frontstage as the domain in which the myth of animals in their "natural habitat" was promoted in ways that simultaneously masked the reality (backstage) of animal captivity. As Westley and Vredenburg (1996) go on to show, these strategies of frontstage management triggered a number of internal tensions and were sometimes so convincing that organizational members themselves grew confused about the divide between the zoo's performance and reality.

How can we examine the frontstage and backstage of social life in ways that are most compatible with the dramaturgical tradition? In their study of social movements, Benford and Hunt (1992) offer some useful overall guidelines for conducting dramaturgical research. In general, they recommend that researchers pay close attention to some of the common techniques used to influence an audience's reception of public performances, notably the techniques of scripting, staging, and performing.

Scripting is central to our understanding of public performances. It is a mistake to think of scripts as sets of rigid social rules that limit the range of individual performances. Rather, scripts are "interactionally emergent guides for collective consciousness and action" (Benford & Hunt, 1992, 38) that provide behavioral cues and guidelines for actors, but are flexible enough to allow for personal improvisations. Scripts are often developed and worked upon in the backstages of social life where roles are created for antagonists, protagonists, and supporting cast members. In their analysis of social movements, Benford and Hunt (1992) show how adversaries were often cast as capitalist pigs or warmongers, while the broader public was given the role of innocent and undeserving victim. What makes scripts so interesting is their variation based on structural factors (e.g., cultural and institutional contexts) and personal ones (e.g., leader visions and interpretations). Scripts are important because they supply a range of *dramatis personae* and provide broad dialogic directions in the form of specific vocabularies and phrases deemed appropriate to the situation. Although scripts may be the product of more conscious reflection in the case of social movements, implicit scripts can be found in virtually any social situation be it the planning of office parties, the design of professional training programs, or the agenda of meetings.

Staging refers to individual and group efforts at appropriating, managing, and directing materials and cast members with a view to impressing their audience(s). Although actors in social movements may deliberately engage in staging, it can be found in many other domains of social and organized life as well. Staging is a form of cognitive and emotional rehearsal during which important symbols are gathered and manipulated, and actors prepared for their eventual role-playing. Some organizations like DisneyWorld formally designate staging areas where employees or cast members learn their roles in training sessions. Staging often involves orchestrating organizational performances that are consistent with the favored script. Disney employees, for instance, are carefully costumed to represent the clean and wholesome side of America, which is at the core of the Disney script (Van Maanen & Kunda, 1989). Similarly, peace movement organizers closely monitor their use of symbols and icons, rejecting leftist symbols such as clenched fists that directly contradict the central themes of their own scripts (Benford & Hunt, 1992).

Finally, no dramaturgical study is meaningful without a careful analysis of the actual *performances* that take place. Working in this tradition calls for examining how well actors play their chosen roles, how different actors compete for the audience's attention, and how some actors may be forced to improvise in the face of unforeseen circumstances. This entire analysis can be conducted at both the individual and/or collective levels. That is, we bring both personal and group (collective) scripts to different situations. Sometimes the two are consistent with each other, but often individual scripts and performances can take precedence over collective ones, resulting in confused and contradictory performances. By paying attention to the scripts, rehearsals, and performances of everyday social life, dramaturgy destroys their *innocence* and forces an awareness of the hidden dynamics behind the seemingly smooth fabric of the social world.

An interesting variation within the dramaturgical tradition can be found in the substantial body of work on *emotional labor.* In her classic study of flight attendants and bill collectors, Arlie Hochschild (1983) develops the concept of emotional labor by building on Goffman's discussion of face-work. For Goffman, individuals engage in face-work in order to present their best possible public personas. By implication, Goffman's face-work involves the exercise of conscious choice in the selection of preferred faces to be presented in the public domain. Hochschild (1983) extends his ideas by highlighting ways in which certain forms of face-work are tacit requirements of specific jobs and occupations. Flight attendants are required to greet passengers with "sincere" smiles, bill collectors and criminal investigators are required to exhibit stern and unyielding demeanors (Hochschild, 1983; Rafaeli & Sutton, 1991), and women managers are expected to control and mask most of their emotions (Swan, 1994). Hochschild's major contribution lies in her understanding of such emotional displays and controls as a form of emotional *work* that constitutes a central part of many unwritten job descriptions.

Overall, the scholarship on emotional work gives the dramaturgical tradition a somewhat critical edge, illuminating the painful disconnects confronting people who experience a gap between their authentic emotional states and their scripted emotional duties. Recent work within this genre also evaluates the place of gender, ethnic, racial, regional, and other identities in mediating the production of emotional labor. The role of gender in particular is strongly recognized as key to the emotional roles we are all required to play. Women are invariably expected to display so-called feminine emotions (warmth and caring) in feminized occupations such as nursing and social work. Women are also expected to control and withhold such emotional displays in more masculinized occupations such as management and medicine (Seron & Ferris, 1995; Swan, 1994). In her study of self-employed Canadian women, Mirchandani (2003) adds a further identity layer to this phenomenon showing how emotional work expectations are often racialized as well. The effect of this kind of dramaturgical work can make traditional sociological variables such as age, gender, and race come alive by connecting them with the actual emotional lives of individuals who constitute them (Mangham & Overington, 1987).

Working in the dramaturgical tradition is not very difficult. One needs to identify a social situation that is underwritten by a potentially interesting frontstage–backstage dynamic, and then study it by paying attention to all components of a social performance. In general, close observation is invaluable especially in understanding the backstage dimensions of social life. It is not easy to grasp the complex nuances of social rehearsals, scripting, and staging without being closely involved in all these processes. Although interviews can be useful in understanding actors' and audiences' interpretations of both front- and backstage activities, they are unlikely to offer the full flavor of the rehearsal that one can obtain through observation. Interviews may be more useful in gauging the effect of any performance on its intended audiences.

Kenneth Burke and the Philosophy of Dramatism

The tradition of dramatism (sometimes referred to as rhetorical analysis) owes much to the ideas of Kenneth Burke (1969a; 1969b) whose complex conceptualization of the intrinsically dramatic quality of human existence provides the fulcrum around which much of it has developed. Burke's dramatism differs from Goffman's dramaturgy in very distinct ways. Life is more akin to *drama* than to *theater,* implying less of a concern with the calculated production of social performances and more of an emphasis on the dramatic meanings held by these performances for different individuals. Burke's vision is succinctly summarized by Perinbanyagam (1982, 261) who proposes that "when one talks of the drama of social life one is not engaging in a simple-minded comparison of human relations to what is going on in a theater, but saying something about act, communication and meaning as the fundamental medium of human existence since the evolutionary emergence of symbolicity." For Burke, drama is like life, and life is simultaneously like drama (Mangham & Overington, 1987), each being inspired by and imitating the other. Our lives gain meaning out of the everyday dramas that we and other people enact. Although some human dramas may well be orchestrated for public consumption, most of them are enacted for personal satisfaction and fulfillment.

Burke's ideas are built on the assumptions that the process of living gains meaning through the interpretation of one's own and others' actions and that these interpretations (which are fundamentally dramatic in nature) are constantly being communicated through language and action. In Burke's eyes, therefore, dramatism is a genre best suited to exploring the relationship between language, action, and communication in social life (Czarniawska, 1997). When Burke (1969a) suggests that drama is the symbolic process through which we interpret and enact our social worlds, he is implying that in order to understand our own and others' lives, we cast them into a *dramatic form* (with a plot, script, and principal characters). Furthermore, our dramatic presentations and analyses take place at different levels. While we make sense of individual action within the drama of their personal lives, we also see these lives as being played out within the wider drama of social and cultural history (Czarniawska, 1997).

Given the ubiquity of drama in our everyday lives, it makes sense to Burke that we also make it a part of our intellectual attempts at understanding the social worlds we inhabit. Dramatism, therefore, becomes "a method of analysis which asserts the *reality* of symbolic action as the defining activity of the human, and uses drama, not analogically, but as a formal model with which to explore both action and explanations for action" (Mangham & Overington, 1987, 71). At this point, it is probably important to underscore the key assumption in the Burkean tradition—that drama is not a "make-believe" or "unreal" part of human existence. Rather, our personal and cultural dramas are absolutely vital for a meaningful existence. For dramatists, the notion of drama also tends to be deeper than that of theater, though elements of theater are very much part of the idea of drama itself. Whereas the concept of theater is rooted in assumptions of rehearsed action and audience manipulation, that of drama refers more to the *play of life*—as something that can be noble and inspiring, or sordid, comic, and absurd.

Central Concepts in the Dramatistic Tradition

At the heart of the dramatistic tradition is the idea that individuals construct and establish their identities through a continuous process of *dramatic narration* to both themselves and others. Put differently, we are always coming up with explanations and stories that account for our own and others' actions. These stories or personal dramas help us make sense of our own actions, and simultaneously convey a sense of who we are to the wider social milieu. In this process, we engage in the formation of our own identities. Unlike many dramaturgists, dramatists view these personal accounts as being equally important to oneself as to the audience for whom they are being performed. Following from this assumption, Burke (1969a) suggests that all social action (both micro and macro) can be understood by examining what he calls *motives.*

Vocabularies of Motive

Within the Burkean tradition, motives are conceptualized as interpretations of situations that are convincing to both self and others. These motives, moreover, are not completely idiosyncratic but tend to be mediated by (a) the broader sociocultural milieu, and (b) specific interests that are pervasive at the moment of the dramatistic account. Often, several clusters of motives come together to make a convincing story or drama of good and evil, star-crossed lovers, triumph and adversity, and so on. Burke refers to these clusters of interpretations as *vocabularies of motive,* and they constitute a crucial element in the dramatistic tradition. The objective of dramatism is fundamentally to unearth these dramas in any social situation with a view to revealing the pattern of motives and interests behind them. In essence, therefore, dramatism "addresses the empirical questions of how persons explain their actions to themselves and others, what the cultural and social structrual influences on these interpretations might be, and what effect connotational links among the explanatory (motivational) terms might have on these explanations, and hence on action itself" (Overington, 1977, 133).

The Pentad

Uncovering the various vocabularies of motive that underpin the dramas of everyday is accomplished through Burke's (1969a; 1969b) *rhetorical analysis*—a technique that relies substantially on the concept of the pentad. The pentad refers to the five dramatic elements that are always present in any social event or personal narrative. Identifying all these pentadic elements and their relationship to each other is at the heart of dramatistic or rhetorical inquiry.

The following five elements constitute the pentad. The first is the *act* itself—that is, the event, incident, or phenomenon that is of interest to the dramatist. The act might refer to an organizational catastrophe or spectacular event (e.g., the NASA space shuttle disaster), a more mundane work activity (e.g., a monthly departmental meeting), or any commonplace occurrence (e.g., training sessions, the process of market research). The second element is the *scene,* which refers to both the immediate and wider context in which the act takes place. Scenes can include organizational boardrooms and offices, or the mass media or popular culture. The *agents* or principal and secondary actors (cast of characters) constitute the third element of the pentad. *Agency* (the fourth element) refers to the actions of the agents in the situation being analyzed. The fifth and final element is *purpose*—the intentions and desires (both shared and conflicting) influencing various actors in their agency. For Burke, a fundamental identification and grasp of these five elements is the starting point of any dramatistic or rhetorical analysis.

Ratios

It would be a mistake to think of the five pentadic elements as being standalone phenomena that require individual detailed descriptions. Central to Burke's thinking is the relationship or *ratio* between all of these elements. The scene or stage, for instance, may influence actors in their selection of a particular kind of agency. A scene that is commonly regarded as being one of organizational reform or organizational change is likely to elicit a particular caliber of actions and to attract certain actors to the center of the play itself. So, here we have a case of the scene influencing actors and agency. Alternatively, prominent actors such as institutional leaders or public figures can trigger a reenactment of activities or a restaging of regular organizational scenes. In this case the ratio between purpose, scene, and agency would be much stronger.

It is probably obvious by now that dramatism shares with hermeneutics a deep concern for the *wholeness* of any situation, though its own focus is more on the performative aspects of social phenomena. Within the dramatistic tradition, an identification of all pentadic elements and their relationship to each other enables this holistic appreciation. Unlike content analysis, which is more concerned with the *systematic* rigor of analysis, dramatism stresses the *systemic* nature of understanding (Kendall, 1993). In other words, the numerical frequency of words or phrases is of less importance. What is more important is their location and *connection* to other parts of the pentadic whole. This kind of analysis is intended to reveal the nature of the play that is being performed.

The range of plots in social performances is obviously rather vast. Plays can be based on plots such as "the new kid in town" (in evidence with newly appointed organizational leaders), or two incompatible individuals coming together in a romantic consummation of their relationship (as in the case of mergers and acquisitions). What dramatism attempts is the uncovering of plots with a view to facilitating a better understanding of complex and often seemingly contradictory actions.

Fantasy-Theme Analysis

Burke's ideas about rhetorical visions have been creatively extended to understand the dramas of public and community life (over and above personal and small group dramas) by Ernest Borman (1982; 1983) and the Minnesota Group of Communications. Borman builds on Burke's starting premise that dramas are present whenever people congregate under any circumstances, but that the essential dramas of the situation come to life or are exploited only through rhetoric (Jackson, 2001). Moreover, Borman's interest is not so much in individual players as in larger social entities—governments, communities, social movements, world bodies, and nations as key actors of public dramas.

The cornerstone of Borman's (1982) work resides in his notion of fantasy and fantasy-themes. At some point, he maintains, individual fantasies come to be shared in certain groups and begin to take concrete shape as a fantasy-theme. A fantasy-theme is "a dramatizing message in which characters enact an incident or a series of incidents other than the here-and-now of the people involved in the communication episode" (Jackson, 2001, 48). In effect, fantasy-themes are dramatic social messages bringing together individuals who subscribe to the same dreams and desires, and are often designated by evocative labels such as the American Dream, the melting pot, the Aryan Nation, the War on Poverty, and so on.

Eventually, these fantasies (which originate in individual and small group desires) trickle down to the wider society where they can be found in media reports, political speeches, popular literature, policy documents, and any other form of *public communication.* As the fantasies spread and begin to attract different groups in society, new *rhetorical communities* unified by common and powerful *rhetorical visions* are formed. These rhetorical visions are extremely significant, for they "provide a comprehensive interpretation of the meaning of symbols, the motives of actors and actresses and the emotional evocations attached to actions" (Koester, 1983, 166). In essence, these rhetorical visions are composite dramas that draw a number of adherents and large audiences to participate in a shared symbolic reality that is constructed out of certain central fantasy-themes. With the help of rhetorical analysis, the dramatist can identify the central fantasies present in any social event or phenomenon (Borman, 1982; 1983). Once this is done, we can better understand both the relevance and choice of certain actions for actors who are following a script that is determined by a particular fantasy-theme. Fantasy-theme analysis, therefore, helps understand how seemingly irrational commitments (e.g., white supremacy, flower power, doomed organizational projects) are perfectly rational to some individuals because of the fantasy underwriting them. Simultaneously, they also make us aware that seemingly rational and "sensible" occurrences (e.g., types of fiscal policy) can also be rooted in common fantasies about the free market and survival of the fittest.

Working in the Dramatistic Tradition

Dramatism is an approach to understanding the meaning of social life by subjecting the dramatic narratives that people produce to close scrutiny. Dramatism is a tradition dedicated to *unmasking* (a) any social situation to find the dramas that govern it, and (b) the desires, motives, and fantasies that undergird these dramas themselves. Czarniawska (1997, 34) sees dramatism not only as a moral activity (in its unmasking efforts) but also as "a sense-making operation" that helps us appreciate the world we inhabit and create.

In part, dramatism stands apart from other interpretive approaches (notably symbolic interactionism and hermenuetics) because of its strong emphasis on the role of interests (motives) that shape the contours of a plot or storyline. Unlike recent developments in hermeneutics that are skeptical of both the possibility and value of grasping actors/authors' intentionality, dramatism is fundamentally geared to capturing the interests (purposes) or vocabularies of motive that reside in the dreams and fantasies that eventually mediate the enactment of personal and public dramas.

An example of this kind of dramatistic demystification can be found in Kendall's (1993) study of rhetorical strategies employed by U.S. firms in the CEO lectures to shareholders, otherwise known as the "boiler plates." Kendall looked at the boiler plates of the Dow Jones listed companies over a specific period of time and found that the core drama being enacted was that of the heroic (good) corporation pitted against the villainous and evil U.S. government. Not only were all positive events linked with the heroism and moral probity of the corporations, but any mishaps such as financial losses and price hikes were portrayed as being outside the corporations' control. With the help of dramatism, her study reveals the kind of corporate explanations and rationales that are systematically used to justify unfortunate events and positive experiences.

At its best, dramatistic research not only unearths social dramas, but also gets to the tensions and contradiction inherent in them. With the help of fantasy-theme analysis, Koester (1983) engages in an incisive analysis of popular self-help books that offer advice to women managers on achieving success in their careers. In Koester's dramatistic study, the central protagonist is the "innocent" but eager female manager who is unaware of the organizational game and its rules, but is still prepared to learn them and thereby master her role as a manager. The central fantasy at work here is that an awareness of rules and a willingness to abide by them is the straightest path to success in one's career. In addition to identifying this fantasy-theme, Koester's work is really interesting because she also discusses how this fantasy-theme runs into problems when it encounters gender. On the one hand, women are counseled to adopt "masculine" characteristics such as candor, risk-taking, and high self-esteem. On the other hand, the same books caution that any appearance of unfemininity is to be avoided at all costs. Other contradictions are present as well. Though cautioning against the loss of femininity, the books simultaneously advise women against conforming to existing female stereotypes. In sum, the books advocate a dramatic performance in which the female manager retains her femininity but is not stereotypically female, and adopts conventional "male" traits without overly resembling men. As Koester (1983, 169) concludes, "the woman who participates in this view of organizational life receives contradictory messages concerning her femaleness. Her gender is clearly a liability for which she can compensate and adjust, but can never escape." Her study is remarkable because it does more than describe the fantasy-themes behind popular visions of successful managerial performances. It also reveals the deeply contradictory nature and ultimate hopelessness of the desired performances themselves.

Both Kendall (1993) and Koester (1983) examine *texts* (boiler plates and self-help books) to uncover the core dramatic narratives that are being communicated. Neither of them looks at the effect of these rhetorical visions on targeted and untargeted audiences. Dramatistic research that takes into account the actors, the performances, and the audiences comes even closer to achieving the tradition's full potential. Such studies are not only able to assess the success of a particular performance, but are also able to examine unsuccessful ones where actors may hold differing opinions about the nature of a play and may engage in diverse interpretations. Problems can also "occur in the performance itself, with some actors improvising in the style of the English pantomime and others in the spirit of a Greek tragedy. Some actors may refuse to play their roles properly. The audience may be in a charitable mood and support the troupe anyway, or they may boo and demand that the leading characters be replaced" (Czarniawska, 1997, 38).

Czarniawska's (1997) own study of financial reform in a major Swedish city is an excellent illustration of extracting dramatic plots out of seemingly mundane administrative situations. Her study uncovers the uncertainty and ambivalence that engulfed actors who were following what they believed to be approved plots. Some actors (e.g., local councils) believed that they were participating in a new kind of rational economistic drama only to find, midway through the performance, that the government was still expecting them to primarily display solidarity with itself and local community interests, or in effect, to continue to take part in the older Swedish communal drama. Her point is that the resulting chaos and confusion was not so much a product of administrative incompetence as much as a failure to assess and meet certain dramatic expectations. Although Czarniawska's study focuses explicitly on municipal reforms, her findings can easily be helpful in understanding innumerable cases of organizational reform. Mainly, what are often viewed as instances of administrative or governmental incompetence are more likely to be misunderstandings about desired performances, and difficulties about learning new roles that have little to do with existing established scripts.

Dramatism can also be helpful in understanding the potency of popular cultural movements such as managerial fashions and workplace reforms (Jackson, 1996; 2001). For one thing, a serious dramatist is never dismissive or contemptuous of appeals to popular sentiment. In his studies of different management gurus, Jackson uses dramatism to understand what drives management gurus and what gives their messages so much seductive and fashionable appeal. A part of his analysis focuses on Hammer and Champy—the gurus of the 1990s reengineering movement that was the fashionable impulse behind much of the downsizing and layoffs that took place in North American companies during this period. Jackson (1996) also tries to understand the appeal that reengineering held for middle managers, which somewhat ironically, were the group most likely to lose their jobs when reengineering was actually implemented. Jackson shows how management gurus like Hammer and Champy appeal directly to current dramas in middle managers' lives by playing on their anxieties regarding the economic stability of their organizations, and urging them to play central and heroic roles (as active participants in the reengineering movement) instead of passively waiting for the day of the inevitable layoff.

What Jackson helps us grasp is that the management guru is first and foremost a rhetorical performer who captures the manager's attention and then persuades her or him that reengineering is the most appropriate course of action. Second, the guru in this case is also an organizational playwright who offers a script for organizational reform and renewal. As performers and playwrights, management gurus rarely rely on rationality and logic, but depend on the dramatic power of their narratives to attract managerial attention and stir organizational action.

In sum, therefore, dramatism is an approach that helps the researcher get in touch with the inner reality of any situation by tapping into the core narratives that are meaningful to multiple participants. Dramatism can be applied to virtually any act of communication be it written, conversational, visual, or interactive. Although the tradition is far from being formulaic, it offers a relatively simple framework (i.e., the pentad, ratios, etc.) as an analytic starting point. The creative essence of dramatism, however, lies in the interpretations and narration of the plot unearthed by the researcher. Like hermeneutics, dramatism is also fundamentally rooted in a humanities paradigm where expressiveness and interpretation give the research its ultimate flair. It is hard to produce a dramatistic research account in keeping with the more conventional social science criteria for the simple reason that it does *not* belong to the positivistic scientific tradition. This may be one reason we find few studies in this tradition in the field of management and organization studies. However, when given full reign, a dramatistic study can be more insightful than conventional research on the same topic.

Figure 4.1 **Highlights of the Dramaturgic Tradition**

Philosophic influences: George Herbert Mead, Georg Simmel

Major figures: Erving Goffman, Ian Mangham

Central concepts
- The presentation of self
- Frontstage and backstage
- Stigmas
- The management of impressions

Key practices
- Unmasking public events and interactions
- Establishing connections between public and private realms
- Unearthing scripts and judging performance effects on audiences

Exemplary research
- *Behavior in Public Places* (Goffman, 1963a)
- *The Managed Heart* (Hochschild, 1983)

Figure 4.2 **Highlights of the Dramatistic Tradition**

Philosophic influences: Literary theory

Major figures: Kenneth Burke, Ernest Borman

Central concepts
- Vocabularies of motive
- The pentad
- Ratios
- Fantasy themes

Key practices
- Unearthing the plots that are central to any social event
- Connecting elements of the pentad to each other and the larger dramatic context

Exemplary research
- *Narrating the Organization* (Czarniawska, 1997)
- "The Machiavellan Princess" (Koester, 1983)
- *Management Gurus and Management Fashions* (Jackson, 2001)

5

Ethnomethodology

The Accomplishment of Ordinary Lives

In the 1960s, American sociology received what can only be described as an intellectual shockwave from within, in the form of the now famous "breaching" experiments conducted by maverick California sociologist, Harold Garfinkel. Garfinkel asked his students to engage in and report on a series of personal experiments in which they repeatedly bargained over the price of fixed-price items in shopping centers, played the roles of guests or lodgers in their own homes (where they would politely inquire about mealtimes and ask for directions to the bathroom), and constantly cheated at simple games like knots and crosses. At the time, Garfinkel's sociological experiments were often ridiculed or dismissed as prankish and immature attempts at thumbing his nose at mainstream social science in a bid to gain academic attention for himself. Such criticisms missed the main point of his experiments, which were fundamentally about *dramatically rupturing* or "breaching" the everyday taken-for-granted world in order to have a better understanding of peoples' responses to these breached situations. It has been Garfinkel's (1967) contention all along that the *methods* that people use to come to grips with mundane and ruptured realities should constitute the essence of sociological inquiry. Ethnomethodology—the term he used to designate his intellectual project— almost literally refers to the *methods* and *procedures* used by ordinary people to make sense of and act upon their everyday lives (Baert, 1998).

Despite its many early detractors and several allegations linking it to the California drug cults of the 1960s, ethnomethodology has, over the years, acquired many adherents in sociology and related disciplines, notably education, communication studies, and organization and management science. We can now safely state that ethnomethodology has come to stay and that Harold Garfinkel has emerged as a provocative and seminal thinker whose ideas have seriously challenged and disturbed many central tenets within social science. Researchers such as Harvey Sacks, Egon Bitner, David Silverman, Deirdre Boden, and Aaron Cicourel have turned ethnomethodology into a respectable (though still somewhat fringe) tradition focused on the close examination of taken-for-granted everyday activities. In the last fifteen to twenty years, ethnomethodology has even been used by scholars of management and organization to study ritual organizational processes and routine managerial tasks such as hiring, recruitment, and appraisal.

The Theory and Philosophy of Ethnomethodology

Garfinkel's (1967) central concern has always been with what he calls "the problem of order." That is, our most commonplace and seemingly mundane social activities have a strikingly systematic and organized character (Filmer, 1972). Although we are rarely explicitly aware of the highly organized nature of our social lives, we tacitly participate in this organization and seem to have a solid battery of skills that enable us to do so. Garfinkel's main focus is on the knowledgeable ways in which social actors (consciously or otherwise) recognize, produce, and reproduce these organized social situations (Heritage, 1984). His work is probably easier to follow with the help of some concrete examples.

Garfinkel first became fascinated with ordinary individuals' knowledge-ability about complex social situations while listening to tapes of jury deliberations at the Chicago Law School in the 1940s. What amazed Garfinkel was how untrained jurors seemed to be remarkably cognizant of how to go about being a juror and doing jury work. In other words, multiple social actors came together and effortlessly performed jury work with no previous training or familiarity with it. As Garfinkel (1967) asserts, the same phenomenon is present in virtually all walks of social life be it science, law, management, policework, or politics. We come to all these situations with a body of *tacit* and *practical knowledge* (Baert, 1998), which we put into use, thereby enacting a multitude of social structures such as justice, hierarchy, and delinquency. Basically, Garfinkel rejects the idea of social structures or rules as constituting a set of external facts independent of human consciousness. On the contrary, these "facts" and social structures come to life only through individual members' interpretive work (Holstein & Gubrium, 1993). It is therefore of utmost importance to examine how actors produce and organize the actual circumstances of everyday life.

Garfinkel's thinking shows the influence, on the one hand, of Edmund Husserl's and Alfred Schutz's phenomenology, and on the other, that of his mentor—Talcott Parsons and his preoccupation with social order. At the same time, ethnomethodology is also said to have "found its inspiration in Heidegger's idea that understanding is the business of life and Wittgenstein's ideas on language" (May, 1996, 97). In essence, therefore, we can describe ethnomethodology as combining a phenomenological sensibility with a concern for the social practices of reality production (Holstein & Gubrium, 1993). Schutz's phenomenological influences can also be found in

Garfinkel's interest in the lived experiences of individuals and the typifications (social categories) they use as they transform their lived experiences into a world of "signed objects" such as justice, professionalism, leadership, and love. The Parsonian influence on his thinking is to be found in his insistence that understanding the emergence of these "signed objects" should constitute the cornerstone of any sociological endeavor" (Collins, 1985).

For Garfinkel (1967), the complex process of everyday social life does not happen automatically despite a common human tendency to think so. Neither is it available in the form of scripts and rules that are then internalized by most individuals. Instead, he argues that everyday commonplace and routine activities are "accomplished" through the competent use of a variety of skills, procedures, and assumptions by different individuals (Hassard, 1990). Knowing how to greet strangers in hallways, how to give instructions to one's subordinates, how to interject important comments at meetings, and how to convey admiration for a member of the opposite sex are some of the mundane competencies that we bring to the *accomplishment* of everyday life. This idea of accomplishment is absolutely vital to the entire enterprise of ethnomethodology because it diverts our attention away from reified notions of rules and structure that dominate much of sociological inquiry, and pushes us toward an examination of the skills and tacit knowledge possessed by people in routine situations. For Garfinkel (1967; 1974), social structures are *produced* on a daily and ongoing basis by a multitude of competent individuals. The central question asked within the ethnomethodological tradition is how social actors come to know, and know in common, what they are doing and the circumstances in which they are conducting their activities (Heritage, 1984). Ethnomethodology, therefore is best conceptualized as a "study of members' knowledge of his ordinary affairs, of his own organized enterprises where that knowledge is treated by us as part of the same setting that also makes it orderable" (Garfinkel, 1974, 11).

Ethnomethdology's insistence on understanding the skillful accomplishment of social reality has clearly influenced the scholarly development of the tradition. It implies an unwavering commitment to studying the *routines* of daily life in which ordinary people draw upon an intricate network of interpretive procedures, assumptions, and expectations out of which they make sense and act upon their immediate surroundings (Baert, 1998). Dressing for work, scheduling departmental meetings, attracting a waiter's attention, and countless other unremarkable activities are seen as highly remarkable for what they reveal about the production of social order. One reason for Garfinkel's fascination with the "breaching" techniques stems from his conviction that when commonplace circumstances are unexpectedly ruptured, the assumptions and competencies of individuals who routinely hold them together are vividly exposed.

Second, the focus on skillful accomplishment calls for a minute, fine-grained, almost microscopic examination of routine activities in which even the pauses and sighs of individual actors are treated as significant pieces of empirical data. Ethnomethodology's systematic scrutiny of the tiny details of everyday living has gained it the reputation of being a *radically empiricist* tradition. That is, it is extremely empiricist in its close documentation and analysis of everyday life. And it is radical in (a) the extent to which it pushes its analysis of raw empirical details and (b) in its unequivocal rejection of formal sociological theory as being irrelevant to an understanding of ordinary life. Ethnomethodology's total reliance on everyday sense making and practical methods as the sole source of valid data is regarded as being both deviant and radical by conventional sociologists whose own absorption with abstract models and measuring devices is seriously undermined by this tradition (Boden, 1990a). In fact, to Boden, ethnomethodology's so-called radicalism is partly derived from its overall tendency to see everyday life as being far closer to chaos and disorder than most of us are willing to admit. In this aspect, ethnomethodology may well be regarded as Chaos Theory's counterpart in the social sciences (Boden, 1990a).

Central Concepts in Ethnomethodology

As discussed in the preceding section, ethnomethodology attempts an analysis of the *methods* people use (both individually and collectively) to make sense of and *manufacture* their immediate social conditions. Garfinkel and many of his colleagues have developed a somewhat complicated vocabulary for expressing some of the ideas that are central to the ethnomethodological tradition. Although some regard this vocabulary as being unnecessarily cumbersome, an appreciation of the terms commonly used in the ethnomethodological tradition is helpful for acquiring a better grasp of the overall genre and the research done within it.

The Precariousness of Reality

Garfinkel's outright rejection of social structure and his conviction that society is produced on an ongoing basis leads to a view of social reality as being completely dependent on the moves and talk of individual actors. This in turn implies that social reality is far from being fixed and immutable, being highly *fragile* instead. Garfinkel repeatedly demonstrates the precariousness of social reality, especially in his breaching experiments in which the calculated subversion of social expectations disrupts the routines of daily life. At the same time, Garfinkel also emphasizes that individuals systematically take considerable trouble to *repair* these ruptured social situations and restore the comfort of social order. Garfinkel further concludes that human beings are fundamentally cognizant of the precariousness of social life, even though they usually refuse to acknowledge this even to themselves. Any event that exposes this flimsiness is likely to prove disquieting as it also reveals the extreme arbitrariness of social conditions. People therefore move urgently to restore the appearance of order and the comfort of routines in order to avoid coming face-to-face with the unsettling chaos behind social structures. Ethnomethodology thus rests on an interesting but paradoxical assumption—that while social reality is flimsy and precarious, it ironically derives its strength from the very same flimsiness.

Accounts and Accounting

The ethnomethodological tradition is deeply committed to understanding the everyday sense making done by individuals in multiple social situations. However, its focus is not merely on peoples' beliefs, mindsets, or schemas, but in the *practical* and *situated* ways in which they are employed in the construction and forging of social reality (May, 1996). Ethnomethodology is thus more interested in the ways in which interpretive schemas are put into practice, and are either accepted, altered, or rejected in a multitude of social situations. Ethnomethodologists assert that our social order is constructed out of the seemingly disparate range of daily activities through a process referred to as *accounting* (Filmer, 1972). The concept of accounting is integral to this tradition and is not to be confused with the profession of the same name. Accounts are stories people tell or reports that they make describing, analyzing, and critiquing different events and situations (Ritzer, 1983). Accounts are more than retrospective sense-making devices. They are the social mechanisms out of which our entire social fabric is woven. As one provides an account of or discusses one's daily activities as a manager or a mother, one is also building a sense of what it means to practice management or motherhood. As we talk about our daily work of running meetings, evaluating subordinates, and meeting suppliers to our friends and families, we are also creating and establishing a reality of managerial work. To the extent to which our listeners accept our accounts, they are also contributing to the production of management as a social reality. Often our partners in a conversation can offer modified or alternate accounts, in which case the reality of managerial work emerges out of some kind of tacit negotiations between all participants in this conversation. In analyzing any situation (medical welfare, social work, strategic planning, etc.) therefore, ethnomethodologists look at how accounts are offered and whether (and how) they are accepted, modified, or rejected by others (Ritzer, 1983).

Indexicality

Ethnomethodology's focus on the *process* of manufacturing reality results in a strong emphasis on understanding immediate and local contexts. The term used to denote this concern is *indexicality*. The philosophic roots behind the term can be traced to Charles Sanders Peirce who used it to refer to expressions whose reference depends on the circumstances of their utterance (Mautner, 1996). Words and phrases such as "here," "you," "over there," and "come on" derive their meaning from the immediate situation in which they are uttered and from the relationship of actors who speak them to one another. Ethnomethodologists take this indexicality very seriously, as is reflected in the close attention they pay to all kinds of local *communicative contexts*. Not only do they examine language and vocabulary, but they also scrutinize pauses, sighs, and sounds like "hmm," "uh," and "oh." They do this in the belief that "people draw upon the context or situation to attribute meaning to practices, but the latter also enable people to create or sustain their sense of context" (Baert, 1998, 86). Ethnomethodology shares with many other interpretive traditions (notably hermeneutics and dramatism) a strong feeling for context. But unlike hermeneutics, which focuses substantially on cultural and historical contexts, ethnomethodology is more concerned with *immediate, interactive* contexts in which actions and conversations are taking place.

Working in the Ethnomethodological Tradition

Research in this tradition broadly tends to follow a *linguistic* or *situational* direction (Hassard, 1990). In either case, the research is strongly characterized by detailed and painstaking examinations of either speech or actions. Although ethnomethodology is sometimes used as a surrogate term for ethnography, especially to indicate forms of extensive fieldwork, the two traditions are substantially different from each other. The watchwords in ethnomethodological fieldwork are *close examination* rather than *lengthy involvement* in the field. Unlike ethnographers (discussed in the following chapter), ethnomethodologists are not committed to long periods of researcher immersion as a key principle of commendable fieldwork. They do, however, require that all situations and conversations be subjected to relentlessly close and careful scrutiny. Ethnomethodologists are likely to claim that one can infer more about an organization from detailed analyses of a few conversations and meetings than from extensive attempts to holistically capture its culture, structure, and so on. However, the level of analysis in all of these cases is expected to pay scrupulous attention to detail.

Linguistic Ethnomethodology

Linguistic ethnomethodology, often also referred to as *conversation analysis,* focuses primarily on language use in social situations (Boden, 1990b) and on *how* conversations are structured in everyday circumstances (Cicourel, 1974; Hassard, 1990). A central feature of linguistic ethnomethodology is its view of language as a dynamic process rather than as a static state. As a result, researchers in this tradition are less interested in texts as standalone artifacts and more interested in the ways in which language is employed in everyday situations—in meetings, casual conversations, interviews, expert consultations, and so on. The main interest in linguistic ethnomethodology is to examine "naturally occurring" language in order to (a) expose how its everyday use constitutes and sustains the social order, and (b) to demonstrate the connection between language use and immediate context (indexicality) that gives it specific local meaning and relevance.

Given linguistic ethnomethodology's emphasis on "naturally occurring" language, researchers in this tradition are somewhat averse to using interviews as a reliable source of data. Many qualitative traditions use interviews extensively as ways of entering different subjective lifeworlds. Ethnomethodology's complex understanding of language, however, makes this option somewhat problematic. After all, ethnomethodologists do not regard language as representing reality as much as producing and building it. Interviews are therefore valuable only as *accounts*—as sense-making narratives used to justify actions and grasp social situations. If treated as accounts, interviews can be reliable sources of data. But in no case would ethnomethodologists accept interview statements as corresponding or capturing any form of social reality.

Linguistic ethnomethodologists examine any form of routine speech or conversation in a multitude of institutional and organizational situations. Silverman and Jones (1973) look at recruitment interviews, Westley (1990) studies what she calls "strategic conversations" between supervisors and subordinates, and Morris and Coursey (1989) examine managerial sense making of employee accounts. A brief description of these studies can better illustrate the different nuances within the linguistic ethnomethodological tradition.

Silverman and Jones's (1973) much cited study examines the process of staff selection and hiring in a large British organization. They look closely at the language used in hiring interviews (taped) and at the language used to justify certain staff selections in conversations following the interviews (also taped). The goal of the study in the researchers' own words is "to understand the practical reasoning used by applicants and selectors to bring off what they count as comprehensible interviews and to justify after the fact, certain outcomes" (Silverman & Jones, 1973). Silverman and Jones come up with some interesting conclusions: they argue that these interviews are far from being rational and logical organizational processes. On the contrary, they appear to be socially interactive situations in which selectors work hard at fitting applicants into categories such as "acceptable" or "abrasive." Even more remarkable, these categories themselves are not clearly defined but lend themselves to multiple and flexible interpretations. In other words, behavior that is labeled as "acceptable" in one candidate may be seen as "unacceptable" in another depending on a number of background factors such as educational pedigrees and social class. Furthermore, the study shows selectors spending considerable energy justifying (to themselves and to others) their final selections in ways that reaffirm their own expert authority and judgment. Organizational hiring therefore also turns into a process in which authoritative accounts are produced in order to legitimate selectors' expertise and professionalism.

Westley's (1990) study also draws on elements of the ethnomethodological tradition to understand feelings of exclusion from strategic decision making experienced by middle managers. Westley begins by pointing out that discussions about strategic initiatives or "strategic conversations" are domains in which middle managers experience inclusion or exclusion. She then explores this phenomenon by subjecting three relatively in-depth interviews with middle managers in a large multidivisional manufacturing firm to close examination. Although Westley (1990, 342) claims that these interviews are retrospective *accounts* of superior–subordinate interactions around strategic issues, her subsequent analysis nevertheless treats these interviews as authentic representations of middle managerial experiences. Nowhere does she try to approach the interview itself as a conversation/account between researcher and middle manager in which the latter discursively constitutes his or her identity within the field of strategic decision making. Although her study starts by positioning itself in the micro-interactionist ethnomethodological tradition, it quickly turns into a more conventional qualitative description of specific feelings and experiences. Her study, therefore, fails to capture the ethnomethodological spirit even while using its concepts and vocabulary.

Ethnomethodological notions about understanding reality construction through managers' "accounts" are more strongly pushed by Morris and Coursey (1989) in their study of managerial interpretations of employee accounts. Morris and Coursey focus primarily on how middle managers and their subordinates negotiate attributions about employees' conduct in what they term problematic situations. Problematic events arise when common expectations for actions in any given event are not met by the actual conduct of participants (Morris & Coursey, 1989, 189). In such situations, individuals whose actions have fallen short of expectations are likely to provide accounts offering explanations for their less than satisfactory performance. Morris and Coursey explore how middle managers in municipal offices and in the retail business evaluate these accounts, and they offer their own accounts justifying their judgments. Their study indicates that positive evaluations of accounts had less to do with the facts of the case and much more to do with employees' character images and the plausibility of the accounts themselves. Overall, they offer a closer glimpse into the moral and practical reasoning adopted by middle managers as they confront the problem of evaluating employee accounts justifying unacceptable conduct.

Situational Ethnomethodology

Situational ethnomethodologists document the ways in which individuals construct their immediate social worlds by a tacit reliance on frameworks of rules and expectations (Hassard, 1990; May, 1996; Zimmerman, 1969). What situational ethnomethodology attempts is an understanding of how structures or "signed objects" such as profession, science, and bureaucracy are produced and sustained in ordinary situations. In essence, their argument is that all social categories (such as organization or hierarchy) have no ontological existence of their own (Bittner, 1965), nor are they entirely the product of peoples' conceptual imaginations. Rather, they are produced or *accomplished* out of the daily social interactions of individuals who routinely manufacture these categories in and through language, ideas, and action. Much of Garfinkel's (1967) own early work belongs to this genre and is perhaps best illustrated by his study of Agnes. Agnes was a man who underwent a sex change operation to become a woman. Garfinkel's interest was in understanding how Agnes figured out the sociocultural requirements of being a woman. What Garfinkel's work amply illustrates is how gender itself is something that is accomplished on a day-to-day basis. Most of us have actually "learned" how to be like men or women without being aware of this learning process. As a result, our tendency is to treat gender-related characteristics as natural biologically determined behaviors. We are usually completely unaware that our male or female personas are products of skills acquired right from childhood. Someone like Agnes, on the other hand, who had to almost consciously learn how to behave like a woman, provides a rare opportunity for appreciating the socially acquired dimensions of gender.

The situational ethnomethodological tradition is filled with classic studies illustrating how our complex and taken-for-granted worlds are put together at local mundane levels. Many of these studies take place in organizational and institutional settings such as welfare agencies (Zimmerman, 1969), research laboratories (Lynch & Woolgar, 1990), hospitals (West, 1984), classrooms

(Mehan, 1979), and business enterprises (Boden, 1990b; Boje, 1991). Basically, all of these studies are interested in revealing *how* reified social categories are produced by "ordinary" people on a daily and ongoing basis. As ethnomethodologists are fond of observing, we "do" or perform our organizational and social structures such as gender, hierarchy, science, and higher education. Golding's (1991) discussion of managerial control as an everyday accomplishment is an interesting case in point. Golding argues that managerial control is not easily translatable from the abstract official chain of command into the practice of everyday regulation. To be effectively constituted, control demands the *skillful performances* of managers who have to systematically reinforce authority without making it overly visible or oppressive. Based on his empirical work in an industrial manufacturing company, Golding (1991) asserts that control is instituted through the "artful practice" of managerial rituals involving secrecy and the instantiation of distinctiveness. Together, these rituals instill informal but impermeable boundaries that further facilitate routine managerial control.

Interesting as Golding's thesis is, his actual field study fails to live up to the kind of close examination of events demanded by ethnomethodology. Much more strongly located within the ethnomethdological tradition is Boje's (1991) insightful study of storytelling as an organizational performative process. Boje makes an important distinction between organizational stories as *texts* and organizational stories as *events in process,* focusing on the latter. His central focus is less on the structure or even content of the story (i.e., the text) and more on the processes whereby it comes to be narrated in everyday circumstances. The study looks at a number of storytelling episodes in an organization. The objective is to grasp their meaning as it unfolds through the process of storytelling within a variety of local contexts. Boje (1991) looked at storytelling processes in a large office-supply firm, recording them on both tape and video. His analysis of these tapes is meticulous, done on a line-by-line basis, with close attention paid to the core narrative contained within the story as well as to the ways in which storytellers and listeners put these stories together. As Boje powerfully demonstrates, the organizational story is not something that has a core existence of its own, but is given life in the day-to-day telling and retelling of it in ordinary situations. Stories, moreover, often do not have a finite form, nor are they narrated with a beginning, middle, and conclusion. Storytellers offer accounts that are taken up by listeners who fill in the blanks and even modify them. By focusing on the storytelling process rather than on the story itself, Boje also shows how organization members tell stories to predict, empower, and even fashion change. In many ways, his work is an exemplary study within the ethnomethodological tradition in its design, focus, and eventual analysis.

Contributions and Limitations of Ethnomethodology

In many academic circles, ethnomethodology stands out as a bold but deviant and almost cult-like tradition offering amusing but less-than-serious anecdotes about social life. However, as Boden (1990a) persuasively argues, it would be a grave mistake to dismiss ethnomethodology along these lines. Many of ethnomethodology's mischievous and provocative stances (e.g., the breaching experiments), its inclination to examine deviant situations, and its tendency to subject mundane events to extraordinarily meticulous examination, are all done with the epistemological goal of *undermining* the seeming "naturalness" of the social order. In short, ethnomethodology's main intellectual contribution lies precisely in its relentless capacity to continually expose the constructed nature of the social world.

Why is this a profound contribution to social science? Because, at its best, ethnomethodology facilitates a serious questioning of various institutional pillars such as science, profession, law, and justice. Let us take Garfinkel's (1967) or Lynch and Woolgar's (1990) work on the production of "scientific fact" in research laboratories. Their work illustrates how the actual practice of scientific method does not follow formal principles and procedures, but emerges out of local negotiations among scientists about ways to present certain phenomena. In a similar fashion, Dingwall's (1976) work shows how the notion of professionalism is built and sustained in government welfare offices, while Cicourel (1968) does much the same with the concept of juvenile delinquency. In all of these studies, pervasive and powerful social institutions—science, profession, and delinquency—are stripped of any essentialist characteristics and revealed as the products of ordinary human imagination and interaction. This prevents us from regarding scientific facts, professionalism, and the like as a given and immutable condition of social existence.

More than perhaps any other postpositivist tradition, ethnomethodology treats individual actors and their actions with utmost seriousness, privileging them way over notions of preexisting structure. "Social structure, for ethnomethodologists, does not work behind the backs of actors, but is instantiated and constituted through their actions" (Boden, 1990a, 189). Furthermore, actors in this tradition are never seen as cultural dopes mindlessly following social scripts, but as *knowledgeable agents* capable of reflective action on a day-to-day basis. Therefore, for many social scientists, one of ethnomethodology's greatest strengths lies in its respectful stance toward ordinary people who are uniformly regarded as skilled in the art of everyday living.

Paradoxically, ethnomethodology's most visible strength—its emphasis on human agency—can also be its major weakness. In their overriding drive to figure out local rationalities of action, ethnomethodologists are often guilty of neglecting other key elements of social life, notably emotion, identity, and the ways in which specific institutional rationalities are more potent than others. Like dramaturgists, ethnomethodologists are excessively preoccupied with conscious action and are too easily convinced of actors' skills in accomplishing social reality. In reading work in this tradition, one is often struck by the absence of feeling and emotion in actors' lives. Ethnomethodologists have also never satisfactorily addressed the questions of *why* some actors routinely fail to pull off accomplished performances and whether these failures might have something to do with social locations such as class, gender, and race.

Not surprisingly perhaps, ethnomethodology has been targeted for harsh criticism by the more critical traditions for neglecting the power of ideology in everyday sense making and for adopting a relativistic position that borders on a kind of "new conservatism" (Chua, 1979). At the same time, elements of ethnomethodological thinking, particularly its interrogation of the naturalness of institutional life, have been appropriated by radical feminists like Dorothy Smith (May, 1996) in exploring the relationship between women as "expert practitioners" of social life and the ideological barriers they repeatedly encounter. For all their apparent differences, ethnomethodology has something to contribute to the more critical traditions (such as Marxism and Feminism), especially its emphasis on the routine accomplishment of social order that can easily be seen as the source of hegemonic social reproduction (Chua, 1977). More recently, ethnomethodology's joint emphasis on individual agency and everyday language has made it more appealing to genres such as poststructuralism and discourse analysis.

For all its intellectual appeal, ethnomethodology is not an easy tradition to work in. In addition to mastering its somewhat cumbersome vocabulary, it demands a closeness in empirical analysis that is far from being facile. Too often, researchers who are attracted by its unusual stance and provocativeness fail to live up to its unstinting standards of data collection and analysis. Some conventional journals in fields such as management are also unfamiliar with its style and demand a conventional presentation format that is at odds with the fundamental ethnomethodological project. However, when ethnomethodology is done well, it offers a daring, though fleeting, glimpse of social order in all its fragility.

Figure 5.1   **Highlights of the Ethnomethodological Tradition**

Philosophic influences: Alfred Schutz, Martin Heidegger, Talcott Parsons

Major figures: Harold Garfinkel, Egon Bitner, Aaron Cicourel, Deirdre Boden, Candace West, Hugh Mehan, David Silverman

Central concepts
- Reality as an ongoing social accomplishment
- The precariousness of reality
- Accounts and accounting
- Indexicality
- Radical empiricism

Key practices
- Focusing on the routines rather than the structures of everyday life
- Importance of immediate rather than historical contexts
- Usefulness of interviews as accounts

Exemplary research
- *The Business of Talk* (Boden, 1990b)
- "The Storytelling Organization" (Boje, 1991)
- "Agnes" (Garfinkel, 1967)
- "Getting In" (Silverman & Jones, 1973)

6

Ethnography

Cultural Understandings of Natives

In qualitative research, few terms have the same broad-based currency as eth-nography. Commonly used to indicate intensive fieldwork and high levels of researcher involvement with subjects, ethnography is, above all, very much part of the anthropological discipline within which it developed as a way to understand "natives" in their own cultures. Thus, although ethnography has been shaped by many of the same phenomenological and social construction-ist philosophical tenets that influenced other interpretive traditions, its roots in cultural anthropology give it a distinctive character and outlook. Whereas symbolic interactionism, dramaturgy, and ethnomethodology mainly devel-oped within sociology, and hermeneutics and dramatism evolved within lit-erary theory, ethnography (until the late 1950s) was unquestionably the "trademark of cultural anthropology" (Schwartzman, 1993, 1), after which it steadily trickled down into a number of social science disciplines, includ-ing sociology, education, social work, nursing, and management. Given its intimate connections with anthropology, ethnography in recent years has been strongly impacted by intellectual debates within the field that have redefined it in interesting and unexpected ways. This also explains why even though ethnography is widely regarded as being part of the interpre-tive traditions, many of the more current developments discussed in this chapter begin to anticipate key concepts from the critical, poststructural, and postcolonial traditions that dominate contemporary discussions within cultural anthropology.

More than any of the other traditions discussed so far, ethnography tends to be most forcefully equated with methods and methodologies calling for some form of in-depth fieldwork employing participant observation as a pri-mary component of the research project. From this perspective, ethnography is conceptualized predominantly as a mode of data collection involving the development of close connections with subjects and situations being studied (Prasad, 1997). Although ethnographic methods most certainly do imply all of these elements, working in the ethnographic tradition also calls for a more complex set of commitments and understandings (Wolcott, 1995) that are very much part of its complicated anthropological legacy. As James Clifford

(1988, 13) rightly observes, "ethnography, a hybrid activity . . . appears as writing, as collecting, as modernist collage, as imperial power, as subversive critique."

Within cultural anthropology, one often finds that the terms *ethnography* and *ethnology* are used interchangeably. In general, however, ethnology refers to the body of knowledge covering socioeconomic systems and cultural heritage in premodern and less "advanced" societies, whereas ethnography denotes the actual practice of descriptive fieldwork that yields ethnological insights. Etymologically, the word itself indicates the practice of *writing* (graphy) about cultures/races (ethno), typically "other" native cultures (Vidich & Lyman, 1994). In fact, within the ethnographic tradition, this element of writing or telling the story of one's fieldwork is of utmost importance. In addition, unlike many other branches of qualitative research in which extensive fieldwork is undertaken solely to amass vast amounts of data, fieldwork in the ethnographic tradition is intended to produce an understanding of natives or inhabitants of a particular culture. This fixation on *culture,* which is the hallmark of ethnography and anthropology, results in the emergence of a complex and (more recently) highly contested tradition.

Ethnography's Anthropological Legacy

Ethnography has been developed, polished, and perfected within anthropology from which it has since been exported to many other empirically oriented disciplines (Prasad, 1997). Anthropology itself, however, is a diverse and complex discipline comprising multiple intellectual traditions. It would be a mistake to see ethnography as representing the entire field of anthropology. Many anthropological traditions such as primatology (the study of primate behavior) and evolutionary anthropology (with its close ties to archaeology) have little or no interest in ethnography. It is only cultural or symbolic anthropology with its focus on internal shared meanings that has directly spawned the ethnographic tradition with which it is now inextricably linked.

Two intertwined influences—one philosophic, the other material—are key to understanding the development of the ethnographic tradition. First, at a material level, cultural anthropology as a respectable academic discipline grew out of the European curiosity about "strange" cultures encountered in the first stage of colonial explorations in the "new" world (Asad, 1973). At this point, European governments and explorers relied on detailed diaries and logs maintained by travelers, missionaries, traders, adventurers, and early colonial administrators (Asad, 1973; Vidich & Lyman, 1994). These early precursors of ethnographic research provided elaborate descriptive accounts of native customs and practices for European consumption, albeit from a more amateur viewpoint. In time, the interest in *systematically* documenting the cultural patterns of "primitive," mainly non-Western societies consolidated on account of two major historical events. The first was the rapid growth of colonialism, and the second was the ever-expanding North American frontier.

Colonialism and the frontier movement triggered an urgent need to understand the colonial subjects and Indian nations who were both targeted for subjugation, exploitation, and/or conquest. Colonial governing bodies needed to have a cultural grasp of the "natives" under their jurisdiction and frequently sponsored lengthy field expeditions that would provide this understanding. Eventually these efforts were institutionalized into various learned ethnological societies in Britain and the United States, and as the *Institut d'Ethnologie* in France. Most of these societies grew into powerful organizations that collaborated with governments and anthropology departments in universities in the sponsorship of ethnographic field projects in Asia, Africa, and the Pacific Islands.

In North America, the westward expansion resulted in continuous frictions with the native Indians who proved far from being amenable to conquest or assimilation. Frontier administrators and the U.S. government were therefore perpetually on the lookout for "authentic" and informative accounts about different native cultures that would be useful in their pacification attempts. In the nineteenth century, two major institutions—the Bureau of Indian Affairs and the Smithsonian Institute—were early sponsors of ethnographic fieldwork conducted by qualified anthropologists among the Zuni, the Winnebago, the Hopi, and many others (Axtell, 1981). By the turn of the twentieth century, such projects involving the study of native cultures and the accumulation of native art were also supported by the Bureau of American Ethnology, the Rockefeller Foundation, the Peabody Museum, and a host of philanthropic organizations in the Southwest.

Over the years, the documentation of non-Western cultures grew into a professional academic field that produced a number of anthropologists who often succeeded in capturing popular and scholarly imaginations with their ethnographic adventures in different cultures. Legendary anthropologists such as Bronislaw Malinowski, Franz Boas, Marcel Griaule, Claude Levi-Strauss, and Margaret Mead all built astoundingly successful academic careers out of their ethnographic exploits in a diverse array of non-Western cultures. A common thread running through many of their projects was the desire to understand culture from the *native point of view* rather than from an entirely detached outsider position. Thus, the broad philosophic influences over these ethnographic efforts were definitely phenomenological and hermeneutic—that is, placing considerable emphasis on local interpretations of cultural practices and shared internal meanings.

In short, the development of scholarly ethnography was most vividly distinguished by an *emic* rather than an *etic* orientation, being committed to a discernment of culture from an endogenic rather than an exogenic standpoint (Prasad, 1997). Yet, right from its inception, the ethnographic tradition has been troubled by an interesting tension between its subjective tendencies and its quest for legitimacy as an objective and disinterested science. As Prasad and Prasad (2002) have already observed, professional ethnography has always demanded an intimate closeness to and distance from the natives being studied. Since native cultures were so clearly marked by their otherness and difference, the ethnographer needed to immerse him or herself in them to obtain any kind of meaningful understanding. But since native cultures were simultaneously regarded as data for scientific study and their artifacts were seen as potential collectibles, it was equally imperative to study them with detachment and objectivity. To some extent, ethnographers resolved this tension by developing close and intimate relationships with native cultures, but masking this closeness by adopting a dispassionate voice when writing about them (Prasad & Prasad, 2002; Tedlock, 1991). Despite these contradictions, the ethnographic tradition grew into an established one by the middle of the twentieth century, gaining a number of followers in diverse fields of scholarly inquiry.

Central Concepts in Classical Ethnography

The ethnographic tradition has gone down some interesting paths in recent years, yet it is still possible to identify a core component within it that can be thought of as classical ethnography. Although classical ethnography developed within cultural anthropology, it has increasingly been appropriated and used by researchers in diverse social science disciplines such as the sociology of work, organization studies, information systems research, public administration, and consumer research. The main distinction between ethnography in anthropology and ethnography elsewhere lies in its choice of subjects. Whereas anthropologists have conventionally looked at "strange" and "exotic" cultures, ethnographers in other walks of life are interested in *familiar* cultures in everyday work, community, and institutional settings. Beginning in the 1950s, Roy's (1960) fieldwork in a manufacturing plant and Whyte's (1955) study of an inner-city neighborhood exemplified the possibilities of extending ethnography to all avenues of contemporary society. Since then, the ethnographic tradition has dominated much of qualitative work, and ethnography has become the most popular label of choice to designate intensive and lengthy field projects.

Despite its immense popularity (or perhaps because of it), the term *ethnography* is sometimes used in a loose and superficial manner to denote little more than lengthy periods of field observation. Classical ethnography, however, is the product of generations of anthropologists who took the idea of cultural penetration very seriously. Nobody expresses the central concepts of classical ethnography as evocatively as Clifford Geertz whose masterly discussion in *The Interpretation of Cultures* (1973) gives one a succinct but powerful understanding of it. Since the scope of this chapter prevents a detailed exploration of the many cultural anthropologists from Malinowski to Mary Douglas who molded the ethnographic tradition, we will be looking primarily at Geertz's writings on this practice.

Webs of Significance

The phenomenological influence, with its emphasis on *meaning* as the central principle of human living, is the fulcrum around which Geertz's ideas are fashioned. Our day-to-day lives are replete with layers upon layers of meaning, woven together in complex symbolic systems—what Geertz terms *webs of significance*. All human action is suspended in webs of significance that can be apprehended only by grasping the specific *local interpretations* engaged in by the natives themselves. If we examine a wedding in contemporary Western society, we find that the wedding rituals (the dress, the music, the wedding march, cutting the cake, etc.) are fraught with symbolic cues for the people participating in them. Even at their most secular moments, stripped of all religious significance, wedding rituals still convey multiple symbolic messages even if they are more about consumption, status, and community than about spirituality or kinship. The point here is that different symbolics attach themselves to any kind of cultural routine be it strategic planning, lunching in the organizational cafeteria, municipal reform movements, or the annual office Christmas party.

The Cultural Context

Like ethnomethodology, the ethnographic tradition is also "about the everyday experience of a society or organization, the everyday things that people get up to in the course of their everyday lives" (Bate, 1997, 1164). And like the former tradition, ethnography is also deeply committed to understanding the context in which these everyday occurrences take place. However, unlike ethnomethodology, ethnography pays undivided attention to the broader *cultural* (rather than immediate situational) *context* within which events and social interactions unfold. Whereas the cultural context for traditional anthropology might have been an island in Bali or a Navajo reservation, for contemporary ethnographers it is more likely to be a shopping mall, a hospital, a professional law firm, an advertising agency, or a police station.

In a nutshell, Geertz's argument is that local interpretations themselves can be followed only by grasping the wider cultural sense making that is at work. Our day-to-day interpretations are embedded in broad cultural and subcultural codes that mediate even our most mundane experiences. This strong emphasis on culture makes an examination of *collective* and *public* interactions essential for obtaining the native point of view. In fact, Geertz is quite unambiguous on this point. As he observes, culture is not to be found within individuals' minds, but in the public spheres of social life. Ethnography, therefore, is intent on understanding cultural practices such as rituals, ceremonies, legends, myths, and taboos that pervade everyday social action and interaction.

Although cultural trappings of this kind are easily noticeable in "foreign" and more remote societies, it is much more difficult to arrive at a cultural understanding of one's own context. Yet ethnography in effect demands that one turns the anthropological lens inward (Rabinow, 1977), looking at one's own culture as if it were indeed strange, unfamiliar, and even exotic. To orient one's analysis in an ethnographic vein, Wolcott (1995, 95) suggests slipping the adjective "cultural" into one's thinking and writing. Using terms such as *cultural barriers, cultural setting,* and *cultural habits* will maintain one's commitment to cultural interpretation. Kunda's (1992) examination of presentation rituals in a U.S. high-tech firm exemplifies an understanding of organizations as cultural entities. Kunda shows how different presentation rituals in the company spoke to the collective interest and conveyed a sense of intimacy with the audience, who in turn actively reaffirmed the ritual frame. Similarly, Barley's (1988) study of the implementation of a CT scanner pays attention to the ritual processes that accompanied it. In both studies, organizations and technologies are presented as cultural systems and artifacts embedded in myths, ceremonies, and superstitions.

Thick Description

For Geertz (1973), *thick description* is what good ethnographers do as they go about producing an insightful narrative of their fieldwork for their readers. Like the term *ethnography* itself, *thick description* is also somewhat overused, often denoting little more than a compulsive attention to detail in any field setting. Geertz's own discussion of thick description is much more complex and compelling, calling for an incorporation of the symbolic intertextuality present in any social situation into the observation, analysis, and writing of an ethnography. Thick descriptions are possible only when ethnographers attend to the multiple and frequently contradictory levels of local meanings in the field. In essence, thick description implies that researchers do not take actions and speech entirely at their face value. Geertz, in fact, highlights the difficulties confronting ethnographers who try to make sense of social events from the observation of ordinary actions. The illustration he uses is that of the wink. How can we, asks Geertz, discern from simple observation the difference between an eyelid twitch (involuntary physical movement) and a wink (voluntary conspiratorial act)? Furthermore, the wink itself could have multiple connotative layers for local actors in specific contexts. After all, as Geertz continues, an individual might be parodying a wink by an acquaintance, in which case his own wink becomes a burlesque rather than a conspiratorial act. Geertz's overall point is quite simple. Detailed observation of actions alone may not always yield a meaningful understanding of a situation. It is only by wading through multiple complex layers of local interpretations and sorting out what he calls the "structures of signification" that one can arrive at a more comprehensive and insightful cultural portrait. This is what is entailed by thick description, which in part is "like trying to read a manuscript—foreign, faded, full of ellipses, incoherencies, suspicious emendations and tendentious commentaries, but written not in conventionalized graphs of sound but in transient examples of shaped behavior" (Geertz, 1973, 43).

For thick description to happen, ethnographers must resist the temptation to provide somewhat simplistic and unitary cultural accounts that focus on shared meanings at the expense of the pluralism and contradictions inherent in any social milieu. As Young (1989, 188) asserts, this "pre-occupation with the existence of shared values in organizations is not only naïve, but masks the extent to which apparently collective sentiments and values may also express divisions among organizational groups." Thick description demands that the researcher unravel different clusters of meaning and interest while simultaneously tracing their interconnections with each other. Young's (1989) own study of subcultures in a machinist shop (to be discussed later in this chapter) is an excellent illustration of thick description in an organizational setting.

Deep Cultural Familiarity

Given its origins as a genre in which outsiders entered unfamiliar and "foreign" cultures with the intent of arriving at native understandings, ethnography (probably more than any other tradition) has always stressed the importance of getting close to the natives being studied. Ethnographers are expected to (a) develop a strong familiarity with the culture being studied and (b) convey this experiential familiarity in their writing. Bate (1997) refers to this as its "being there" quality, and it is certainly an integral element of classical ethnography.

In the early anthropological traditions, ethnographers spent extended periods of time in foreign lands immersing themselves in local traditions, learning the language and the cultural practices of the natives. Contemporary ethnographers are required to exhibit the same levels of cultural familiarity in which they display a comfort with the jargon, terminology, and habits of communities being studied. Golden-Biddle and Locke (1993) point out that ethnographies are often evaluated favorably when they convey a sense of authenticity to their readers. Accomplished ethnographers achieve this by inserting phrases and comments made by their subjects in the final text. Van Maanen's (1973) well-known study on the socialization of policemen is remarkable for the way in which he helps his readers enter the world of rookie cops by reporting their language at various points of his text.

Given the commitment to provide "authentic" accounts of native ways of life, the ethnographic tradition has always favored the method of participant observation over all others. Authenticity is also acquired by cultivating close informal relationships with the natives (referred to as informants), who help in interpreting local events and practices.

The Narrative Dimension

Producing an ethnography is as much about writing as it is about data collection and analysis (Frake, 1983; Golden-Biddle & Locke, 1993; Rosen, 1991), and certainly the craft of writing has always been a central part of the classical ethnographic tradition. High-caliber ethnographies are convincing and readable narratives that offer a plausible account (Geertz, 1973; Prasad, 1997) of a specific culture. This is achieved mainly by paying attention to important details, by conveying an easy familiarity with the natives, and by making room for multiple local interpretations in a coherent and articulate fashion (Van Maanen, 1987). Strong ethnographic texts in the classical tradition typically have a strong storyline, show evidence of the researcher's own involvement in the field, convey a sense of historical-cultural context, and weave a coherent story of disparate events within the field.

It is also important to keep in mind that ethnography is more about generating insights than predictions (Geertz, 1973) and that the "truth-value" of a text is more important than its "fact-value" (Bate, 1997). Far too often, novice ethnographers put too much effort into documenting each and every (uninteresting?) act, speech, and incident into the final ethnographic text in an attempt to provide some mythical "whole" picture for their readers. It is far more important to weave an insightful and nuanced story out of diverse events that will be both interesting and useful to readers in parallel or even in different situations. As Rosen (1991) points out, ethnographers study "foreign" cultures in order ultimately to enhance an understanding of their own cultures. Kunda's (1992) incisive discussion of corporate rituals as part of hegemonic organizational control systems, for instance, helps us appreciate how symbolic power is likely to be exercised in other workplaces as well. In essence, a strong ethnography helps us "see" things about our own local subcultures that might otherwise be easily missed.

Maverick Ethnographic Traditions

While classical ethnography has systematically occupied the center stage of symbolic anthropology, other more experimental traditions have simultaneously developed at the margins of the discipline. The more prominent of these traditions involve either deliberately attempting to submerge one's identity in the culture being studied (turning native), or explicitly acknowledging and inserting one's identity as the ethnographer into the final text (confessional ethnography).

Gone-Native Ethnography

A reaction against the studied professionalism and scholarly distance required by classical ethnography prompted an interest in *turning native*, that is, taking cultural immersion in the field to something of an extreme (Tedlock, 1991). Going native in ethnography represents a romantic attempt to capture the authenticity of the native experience. It requires considerably more than extended periods of time spent in native cultures and implies that ethnographers "become" one of the natives in order to experience at the most genuine level possible the everyday dimensions of a culture (Vidich & Lyman, 1994). Some noteworthy examples of gone-native ethnography include Frank Hamilton Cushing's celebrated work with the Zuni, during which he even became a Zuni shaman and war priest (Evans, 1999; Vidich & Lyman, 1994). More contemporary ethnographers who turned native include Lisa Dalby (1983) who "became" a geisha in Japan and Hunter Thompson (1994) who joined the infamous Hells Angels in order to conduct a study of their culture. In the field of work and organizations, William Thompson's (1983) personal experiences as a meatpacker in a factory are used as a basis for his ethnography of the meat industry. An even more current study is Barbara Ehrenreich's (2001) penetration into the lower echelons of working-class America where she turns herself into a domestic servant working for Merry Maids and an associate in Wal-Mart.

Ethnographic Memoir

By turning native, the ethnographer attempts to submerge her or his existing identity and to acquire a native one. An almost opposite trend is one in which the ethnographer consciously recognizes his or her problematic role in the entire research project and makes this consciousness a part of the final document. In essence, an autobiographical, almost confessional element enters into the crafting of the ethnographic texts, with researchers portraying themselves as active "human" participants, frequently blundering through the data collection process (Prasad & Prasad, 2001). These "ethnographic memoirs" (Tedlock, 1991) convey a sense of researcher vulnerability and are strongly reminiscent of the literary genre of autobiography. "In the ethnographic memoir, an author takes us back to a corner of his or her own life in the field that was unusually vivid, full of affect, or framed by unique events" (Tedlock, 1991, 77). An early forerunner of contemporary ethnographic memoirs is Gladys Reichard's (1934) engaging story of field experiences among Navajo weavers in which she provides intimate glimpses into her own feelings and reactions to Navajo culture. Almost thirty years later, Gerald Berreman's (1962) intricate account of an ethnographic sojourn in a Himalayan village achieved the same effects. Other recent writings in this tradition include the works of Paul Rabinow (1977) and Nigel Barley (1983). Rabinow's piece is a highly reflective autobiographical description of an ethnography in Morocco, whereas Barley's is a delightful story of ethnographic misadventure with Barley emerging as a sadly incompetent but likeable novice in Africa.

Ethnographic memoirs, sometimes also categorized as *confessional tales* (Van Maanen, 1988), pose interesting challenges to the classical ethnographic tradition. They reinsert the ethnographer directly into the text, giving him or her a constant and visible presence that is missing in more conventional accounts. Memoirs like those of Nigel Barley's (1983) also depict ethnographers as incompetent intruders, helpless outsiders, or likeable dupes struggling to find their footing in foreign cultures (Czarniawska, 1998). Their open admissions of ethnographic inadequacy reduce the ethnographer's infallibility by demystifying her or his expertise. The confessional tone also disrupts the habitual smooth presentation of ethnographic texts, highlighting their constructed and capricious character.

Working in the Ethnographic Tradition

Even outside anthropology, ethnography tends to draw a number of followers who are attracted by its spirit of prolonged romantic adventure in both "foreign" and local territories. In fact, there is no dearth of self-styled ethnographies in diverse fields ranging from marketing and consumer research to the sociology of work and organizations. Ethnographers working outside anthropology, however, are faced with a completely different set of predicaments caused by the focus on their "own" cultural contexts. In short, studying more familiar "tribes," be they schoolteachers, managers, or consumers, poses its own set of problems. First of all, many dimensions of an organization or institution may not be accessible to ethnographic scrutiny. As many ethnographers quickly find out, the more powerful and privileged natives are adept at shielding themselves from the ethnographic gaze. Observing managers and corporate elites implies studying a significantly powerful group who can also exert considerable influence over the conduct and presentation of an ethnography (Rosen, 1991). Managerial and organizational elites can also curtail ethnographers by imposing stringent confidentiality requirements and by preventing access to certain terrains such as corporate boardrooms, workplace safety records, and sexual harassment grievances on the grounds that such measures are necessary for an organization's well being.

Despite these obstacles, really skilled ethnographers can creatively combine accounts from trustworthy inside sources with documentary material and personal observations to come up with an understanding of the workings of institutional inner circles. Very few studies do this as well as Aboulafia and Kilduff's (1988) cultural analysis of the silver market crisis of 1980 where they are able to show how key market actors strategically manipulated price movements. Relying on Aboulafia's (1996) field observations of the Wall Street bond markets, his extensive interviews with bond traders, and innumerable media reports, they depict a situation of intense struggle between Wall Street insiders, outside players, and the government. Other ethnographers get around the problem of elusive elites by observing them in public gatherings. Rosen's (1988) study of the annual Christmas party at an advertising agency is an exemplary piece in which exercises in hegemonic cultural control by senior managers are portrayed without direct access into their private worlds.

In fields such as management and organization studies, some ethnographers have been rebuked for treating native standpoints too casually and for engaging with the more superficial aspects of a culture. The sheer popularity of organizational and business culture as a concept may well be responsible for its trivialization, a tendency deplored by commentators like Barry Turner. In Turner's (1986) view, many ethnographers who claim to paint cultural portraits of organizations and society are little more than "pop-culture magicians" offering simplistic and superficial interpretations of native ways of life. Turner urges ethnographers to be "honest grapplers" who, following in the footsteps of the classic ethnographic heroes, make serious attempts to immerse themselves in a culture and grasp the native point of view.

In brief, critiques of contemporary ethnographic studies seem to maintain that genuine cultural immersion is singularly lacking in many studies. In part, the sheer proximity of local cultures is to blame for this deficiency. Anthropologists in the classic ethnographic tradition were forced to travel to distant and unfamiliar lands where they remained for months (or even years), becoming acculturated in the society. Today, a few fleeting visits are held to be sufficient to qualify a study as ethnographic. Bate (1997) strongly deplores this turn from "thick description" to "quick description" resulting in far shallower cultural accounts. As he stringently comments, these days, "prolonged contact with the field" means a series of flying visits rather than a long-term stay (jet plane ethnography). Organizational anthropologists rarely take a toothbrush with them these days. "A journey into the organizational bush is often little more than a safe and closely chaperoned form of anthropological tourism" (Bate, 1997, 1150).

In sum, both Bate and Turner lament the loss of textured richness associated with the classical ethnographic tradition. Although many of their concerns are justified, it must be pointed out that several contemporary ethnographies do manage to live up to these demanding standards. Kunda's (1992) study of cultural control in a high-tech firm stands out as a remarkable piece of data collection, analysis, and presentation. Kunda first developed contacts in the organization through MIT (where he was a doctoral student) and then negotiated formal access as an observer in the corporation. From the beginning, he held extensive conversational style interviews with various organizational actors and paid regular visits to the workplace, attending all public events such as talks, seminars, group meetings, and training sessions. With the help of local contacts (many of whom he cultivated in the course of the interviews), Kunda also managed to be present at staff meetings, design sessions, and review meetings. He constantly moved between the roles of academic observer, confidant, and expert consultant throughout his fieldwork. His study comes close to meeting the ideals of classical ethnography in the degree of cultural familiarity he was able to develop and in his nuanced appreciation of the local symbolic context.

While on the subject of ethnographic depth, we should also note that the established format of journal publication in many fields comes close to virtually discouraging the pursuit of cultural immersion with its emphasis on formulaic presentation and brevity. Ethnographies carrying a strong flavor of "being there" are usually found in books like Kunda's (1992) and Jackall's (1988) study of managerial ethics where both authors are able to lay out the rich details of their field experiences. Nevertheless, it is still possible for journal articles to offer a satisfying ethnographic *slice* (if not a fuller ethnographic *picture*) of a particular situation. A nice example is Gregory's (1983) study of Silicon Valley cultures in high-tech firms producing integrated circuits in California. Gregory's "inside" understanding of the various groups in the field results in an interesting depiction of "occupational communities" (e.g., marketers and engineers) whose cultural influence is far stronger than the organizations that individuals work in. Gregory also gives us these cultural glimpses not as a detached outsider, but from the perspectives of the natives themselves.

Another ethnography that is remarkable for its appreciation of *multiple* rather than uniform cultural strands is Young's (1989) study of a raincoat factory. Focusing on certain company rituals that appeared to symbolize workforce solidarity, Young goes beneath the façade to unearth divisions between different work groups and their manifestation in the minute structuring of these rituals themselves. In the field of consumer research, Sherry's (1990) sustained observation of a mid-western flea market is also exemplary in its rich representation of the sounds, smells, and intensity found in such venues. Sherry's study also offers some insights into the social relevance of flea markets as domains that restore a more authentic sense of the market into the sterile world of modern consumption.

Studying one's own cultures also confronts ethnographers with the problem of examining places inhabited by people very much like ourselves (Rosen, 1991). When ethnographers share many elements of a culture with the natives under observation, they may find it hard to notice the more taken-for-granted aspects of the culture itself. As Alvesson (1993) points out, organizational ethnographers often take central features of contemporary organizations completely for granted, failing to see them as unique and historically produced cultural practices. This "cultural blindness" as he calls it, is reflected in the failure of organizational ethnographers to note that "the pre-occupation with 'managing,' 'organizing,' and making things as 'efficient' as possible is a key feature of Western culture and of business organizations in particular" (Alvesson, 1993, 47). Unlike anthropologists who are starkly confronted with a culture's otherness, organizational ethnographers have to worry about "staying at home and claiming sufficient bravado to transform that which is culturally familiar into a subject upon which to interpret understandings" (Rosen, 1991, 14).

Cultural blindness can be minimized by consciously approaching familiar cultures as if they were foreign—by imagining one's self to be a visitor confronted with the "strange" practices of people in businesses, schools, the media, or government. One study employing this kind of cultural lens to maximum advantage is Aboulafia's (1996) ethnography of the Wall Street bond markets in which he treats bond traders as a unique *tribe* engaged in the "deep play" (Geertz, 1973, 433) of bond trading in much the same way as the protagonists of a Balinese cockfight. Aboulafia's skillful employment of the cultural lens helps us see the world of bond traders quite differently from the all-too-familiar one of rational economic exchange. Instead, he shows us bond markets that are intense symbolic domains where traders fight over status even more than over money, and where rational interests intersect with intuition and risk orientations to produce what we commonly think of as market behavior.

Debates and New Directions in the Ethnographic Tradition

Over the last twenty-five to thirty years, the classical ethnographic tradition in anthropology has come under serious and sustained assault as the discipline itself has had to reexamine and reshape itself in order to be of relevance in its dramatically altered circumstances. To fully grasp the tumultuous times engulfing cultural anthropology, one must remember that ethnography in particular developed to meet the needs of frontier and colonial expansions that called for in-depth accounts of native cultures. With the closing of the frontier and the demise of colonization, several important changes have taken place. First, "natives" from "primitive" and "exotic" cultures who were the erstwhile passive subjects of classical ethnography have become much more active in interrogating the ways in which they have been represented in ethnographic texts and demanding a voice in them. Former subjects have also appropriated the roles of legitimate storytellers about their own cultures.

At the same time, a series of compelling intellectual movements sometimes falling under the rubric of the narrative turn have forced us to see ethnography itself as yet another language game, an integral part of the Western narrative genre that has emerged out of a sustained neoimperial gaze directed toward "savage" and "exotic" natives. One of the most influential texts on this issue is Clifford and Marcus's (1986) collection of essays that described ethnographies as literary productions telling readers more about the author(s) than about the native cultures that constitute the text's subject matter. Increasingly, debates about ethnography in anthropology are less about the old subject/object divide or the degree of required familiarity, and more about questions of *rhetoric* and *representation* in the text (Atkinson & Hammersley, 1994; Clifford & Marcus, 1986).

In sum, these debates stem from a recognition of the not-so-innocent character of ethnography (Van Maanen, 1995), which has made its practitioners somewhat self-conscious, embarrassed, and ironic about their own roles in interpreting and representing native cultures. "If anything, the moral ambiguity and political complicity associated with ethnography has grown even more obvious and problematic in the shrinking and increasingly inter-connected postcolonial world" (Van Maanen, 1995, 8).

Within anthropology, the sheer intensity of these debates has definitely left its mark on the practice of ethnography. Ethnographic memoirs, which were formerly regarded as maverick experiments conducted at the margins of the discipline, have grown more popular and have taken over the scholarly imagination. Even in organizational studies, ethnographers feel increasingly obliged to make note of their own presence in the study even if this is more likely to find its way into an appendix rather than into the body of the text (e.g., Kunda, 1992).

Another offshoot of these debates is the rise of a more contemporary ethnographic tradition that Tedlock (1991) characterizes as *narrative ethnography*. Like ethnographic memoirs, narrative ethnographies are derived from the understanding that ethnographies are "fictions"[1]—produced not only by the authors who script them but indirectly by institutional structures such as conventions of scholarly writing, and deeply sedimented boundaries between researchers and subjects, theory and data, and so on (Clifford, 1988; Crapanzano, 1977). The objective of narrative ethnography is simultaneously to resist these influences and to communicate an awareness of them in the crafting of the ethnography itself.

One could say that narrative ethnography is fundamentally committed to portraying the processual nature of the research endeavor, showing how the final ethnographic text emerges out of negotiations between researcher, academic institutions, and multiple native subjects "within shifting fields of power and meaning" (Kondo, 1990, 8). The ethnographer tries to make this clear by focusing not only on him or herself as a human person in the research project but on the specific nature of the ethnographic encounter itself. Dorinne Kondo's (1990) work in a Japanese confectionery factory is a vivid example of a study that illuminates the ethnographic process through multiple vignettes of interactions between the researcher and the natives. Kondo is also able to show how diverse conceptual categories (such as race and gender) and institutional structures (such as academic training and broader political agendas) all constituted the "matrices of power" within which her own study was conducted and written. Like others working in this genre, Kondo subverts many of these constraints even as she weaves an awareness of them into her ethnography.

Many of these debates and questions have yet to trickle down into fields such as management/organization studies and consumer research where classical ethnography has barely acquired some kind of grudging legitimacy. This is truly unfortunate because many of these trends confront scholars with epistemological questions of enormous relevance to fields enmeshed in the context of increased globalization and multiculturalism. Consumer research, advertising, human resource management, information systems management, strategic planning and so on are all activities that can no longer be studied as if the world (and organizations) were simple uncomplicated places inhabited by homogeneous natives who can be best understood by outside experts. It is indeed high time that ethnographers looked to their traditional home discipline to see what might be learned from the intellectual struggles that are taking place there.

Note

1. The term *fiction* here is not to be equated with falsehood, but underscores the constructed and creative nature of ethnographic texts.

Figure 6.1   **Highlights of the Ethnographic Tradition**

Philosophic influences: Phenomenology, hermeneutics, symbolic anthropology, feminism, poststructuralism, postcolonialism

Major figures: Bronislaw Malinowski, Franz Boas, Frank Hamilton Cushing, Marcel Griaule, Margaret Mead, Mary Douglas, Claude Levi-Strauss, Clifford Geertz, James Clifford

Central concepts
• Local meanings
• Webs of significance
• Native points of view
• Cultural contexts
• Thick description
• Turning native
• Confessionals

Key practices
• Prolonged contact with the field
• Avoiding cultural blindness
• Multiplicity of cultural voices
• Writing persuasively
• Recognizing institutional constraints on one's writing

Exemplary research
• *Making Markets* (Aboulafia, 1996)
• *Crafting Selves* (Kondo, 1990)
• *Engineering Culture* (Kunda, 1992)
• "A Sociocultural Analysis of a Midwestern Flea Market" (Sherry, 1990)
• "On the Naming of the Rose" (Young, 1989)

II

Traditions of Deep Structure

From the end of the nineteenth and well into the twentieth century, a number of thinkers in France, the United States, and Eastern Europe began to coalesce around the conviction that knowledge of all social phenomena could be best advanced by studying their deep structural underpinnings. Variously referred to as structuralism, semiotics, or semiology, the common thread running through these theories was the notion that the appearances of social reality on their own tell us very little. For a true understanding of social forms, we need to discern their underlying deep structures. The term *structure* is obviously of enormous importance to this tradition. In essence, structure refers to the ways in which elements (parts) of any system (whole) formally relate to each other. It was also commonly held that these structural arrangements ultimately govern the behavior of actors or elements in any system. To comprehend action, therefore, one had to become closely acquainted with these deep structures.

All traditions steeped in the concept of deep structure are deeply indebted to the linguistic philosophy of Ferdinand de Saussure (1966). Saussure's ideas quickly entered diverse fields, including linguistics, psychology, anthropology, and more recently, even computer science. Many celebrated intellectual figures such as Charles Sanders Peirce, Jean Piaget, Claude Levi-Strauss, Noam Chomsky, Roland Barthes, Tzvetan Todorov, and Umberto Eco were all closely associated with some form or other of structuralism.

In many ways, the structuralist traditions make a decisive break with the interpretive tradition. Their focus on deep structure implies a strong non-, even antihumanist orientation in which individual interpretations are of little importance in comparison with the formal but less visible structural arrangements that make them possible. As Best and Kellner (1991, 19) accurately observe, any kind of structural analysis aims at "objectivity, coherence, rigor and truth" because its single-minded quest for preexisting deep structures is completely uninterested in capturing subjective evaluations. Since it accords so little importance to the individual actor, who is little more than a "speaking object" (Lemert, 1979) reflecting structural codes and rules, structuralism has also been criticized as dehumanizing.

For all its alleged shortcomings, structuralism's contributions to the social sciences are hard to ignore. Various forms of structuralism employ formal modes of analysis derived from Saussurian linguistics that view social reality as constructed largely by language and language forms (i.e., deep structures). Language, therefore, is absolutely fundamental to the structuralist tradition and is seen as playing a major *constitutive* role. In other words, language is the raw material out of which our social fabric is fashioned (Manning & Cullum-Swann, 1994). Such a vision of language results in a profound capacity to go beyond individual experiences and accounts to the fundamental linguistic frameworks that make such experiences even possible (Mautner, 1996).

Over the years, various traditions of deep structure have extended Saussure's theories of language to different forms of verbal and nonverbal communication, notably speech, writing, architectural design, music, fashion, cultural rituals, and so on. Figure PII.1 presents an overview of different structuralist traditions. An early prominent derivative of Saussure's linguistic philosophy was the structural phonology of the Prague School developed by Roman Jacobson and Nicolai Troubetzkoy, who worked on dissolving languages into their most elementary units or *morphemes* and then looked for distinctive patterns or *phonemes*. The Prague phonologists (who were eventually to have a strong influence on Noam Chomsky) shifted the study of language from observable patterns of meaning to the level of deep structure (Rossi, 1974). Other noteworthy structuralist traditions included the work of Russian formalists such as Griemas (1966) and Vladmir Propp. Propp's (1968) quasi-algebraic examination of a Russian folktale is now held to be a classic example of structuralism. Propp examined hundreds of Russian folktales, not with the intention of discussing the details of each one, but with the goal of uncovering the core skeletal framework or "morphology" behind all of them.

This idea that a basic morphology is capable of explaining forms of social behavior also developed in anthropology, mainly under the direction of Claude Levi-Strauss (1963) whose treatment of marriage and kinship systems as language forms had a far-reaching influence on the field. Basically, Levi-Strauss held that various sets of cultural phenomena have a core *hidden structure* (that is relatively fixed), which dictates and limits all possibilities of human action within its sphere (Turner, 1983). Once we have discovered these underlying structures or organizing principles, the everyday working of the cultural system becomes more comprehensible. A number of anthropologists have engaged in this kind of deep structural analysis in order to grasp the inner workings of their own and other cultures (e.g., Foster, 1974; Sapir & Hoijer, 1967). Foster's structuralist examination of American culture, for instance, proposes upward linear mobility as the dominant principle around which the entire culture organizes and expresses itself. Based on an analysis

Figure PII.1 **Traditions of Deep Structure**

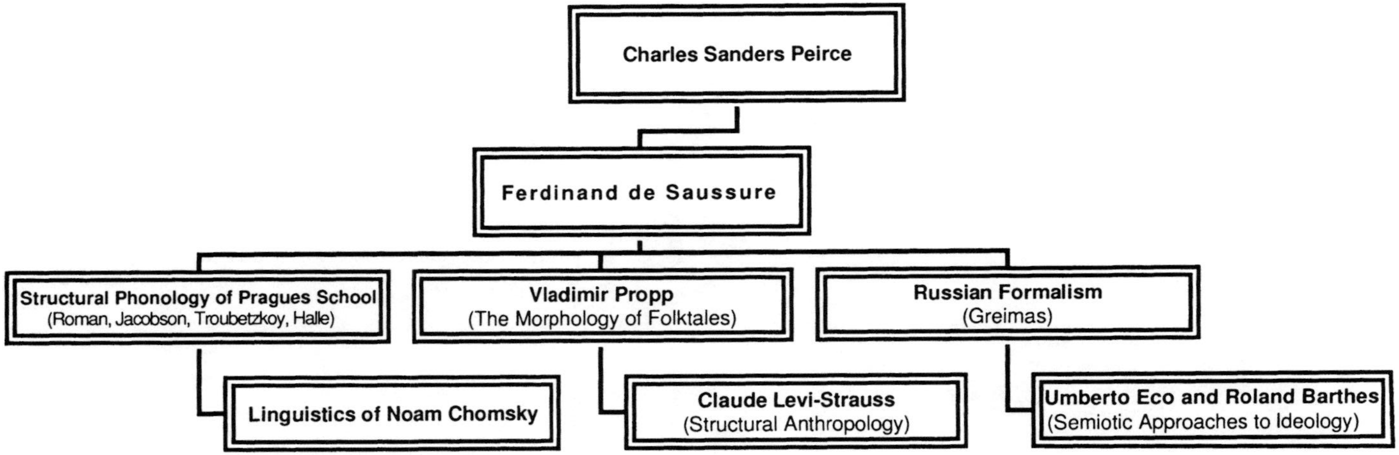

of language, urban design, and everyday rituals, Foster (1974, 336) concludes that "our skyscrapers, jet planes and spaceships all attest to the fact that the preferred line is up. We move 'up' in our profession or 'go to the top' of the class or organization. It seems no accident that we are 'up' from the ape since this is construed as progress nor that history moves 'down' to the present if no particular progress is implied. . . . As 'up' is good so 'down' is bad. To be 'down' is to be 'out.' 'Low' character contrasts with 'high' moral worth." Although this kind of structural analysis of our societies is not easy, such techniques have increasingly found their way into studies of work and organizations (Fiol, 1989; Manning, 1989), consumer research (Mick, 1986), and communication (Broms & Gahmberg, 1983).

By now, it should be obvious that structuralism is solely interested in unearthing the core abstract principles behind social forms and gives very little weight to subjective experiences and interpretations. It also does not believe that individuals have much autonomy in sociocultural situations, given that their actions are severely circumscribed by underlying deep structures. These stances are strikingly different from those held by the interpretive traditions. Although some critics condemn structuralism for its reductionism, its antihumanism, and its excessive scienticism, its adherents hold that its main strength lies precisely in its ability to bypass the fine details of everyday life and to concentrate on fundamental societal frameworks and principles. Structuralism has always had a somewhat limited following in the social sciences, but its significance has grown tremendously over the last fifty years as it began to powerfully influence the development of postmodernism and poststructuralism. Appreciating these two traditions requires an understanding of the original structuralist ideas. In this section, we will be looking at semiotics and its application in diverse empirical studies.

7

Semiotics and Structuralism

The Grammar of Social Reality

Contemporary semiotics (or semiology) and various genres of structuralism all emerged out of the linguistic philosophy of Ferdinand de Saussure in Europe and Charles Sanders Peirce in the United States. Although Saussure is often given almost full credit for the genesis of the semiotic tradition, Peirce was expressing similar ideas at approximately the same time. The term *semiotics* itself can be traced to the Middle Ages when it referred to the observation of medical symptoms or *signs* of illness. It entered the discourse of philosophy and the social sciences when the English political scientist, John Locke, began using it to designate the study of signs employed by the human mind for the purpose of social communication (Rossi, 1983). Since then, semiotics has tended to be characterized as the *science of signs.*

In practice, semiotics is best conceptualized as a formal mode of analysis used to identify the central rules that determine how signs convey meanings in any social system (Eco, 1976). It is important to appreciate that semiotics is indeed completely focused on these basic rule structures or grammars. For semioticians, any language is held together and given coherence by its *grammar,* which also controls the expression and interpretation of meaning. In other words, grammatical rules govern the ways in which words are organized into sentences (Fiol, 1989) and consequently influence the meanings that will eventually be communicated. Understanding the "true" meaning of any language is therefore not really possible without knowledge of its grammar. Many branches of semiotics and structuralism extend this linguistic model to social reality, arguing that similar rule structures or grammars dictate the expression of meaning in any communicative system, be it art, mathematics, social conventions, or even highway signs (Fiol, 1989; Manning & Cullum-Swan, 1994). It is this extension of semiotics that has interested researchers in the social sciences.

The Philosophy of Semiotics

Ferdinand de Saussure's ideas are absolutely vital to the semiotic and structuralist traditions. Often depicted as the father of modern linguistics, Saussure made his major intellectual contribution in the strong linkages he discovered between language and social behavior (Culler, 1976). The son of an eminent naturalist, Saussure was born in Geneva in 1857 and began studying early Indo-European languages at the University of Leipzig and at Berlin. In Germany, he was part of a scholarly group known as the *Junggrammatiker,* or the Neo-Grammarians, who were all interested in the formal properties of language rather than in everyday speech patterns. He then taught for a while in Paris, but eventually returned home as professor of Sanskrit and Indo-European languages at the University of Geneva. While teaching at Geneva, he developed the linguistic theories that were to eventually become so influential. Saussure wrote very little in his own lifetime, but always kept detailed and meticulous notes. After his death, his students compiled these notes into the now famous book—the *Course in General Linguistics* (1966).

Saussure's entire philosophic project was motivated by his curiosity about the intimate relationship between language and human sense making. He begins by asking an extraordinarily fundamental question—what is human language? And he answered by suggesting that any language is a *system of signs* (Culler, 1976). A sign is something that stands for or represents something else. The sign is the basic unit of any language and is itself composed of two elements: a *signifier* (word or sound pattern) and a *signified* (concept or thing). In Saussure's thinking, the signifier and the signified are inseparable at the level of meaning. The *word* dog, for instance, is a signifier, whereas the actual canine animal it refers to is the signified. Together they form the sign—dog. Saussure further asserts (and this is his radical break with earlier linguistic philosophies) that the relationship between the signifier and the signified is completely arbitrary. That is, with the exception of a few unusual cases, the signifier could be replaced by any other word and still convey the same meaning if accepted by the linguistic community. For example, the word "dog" could as easily be substituted by "grot," "trub," or "vulk" and still refer to the same animal, which is why we have *chien* in French, *Hund* in German, and so on, all referring to the same phenomenon. Saussure's main point here is that the signifier's dog, *chien,* or *hund* have no "natural" or intrinsic connections to the animal they are referring to. Rather, they are arbitrary signs that have emerged out of a particular language system. From this perspective, language can no longer be regarded as a mirror of social reality. On the contrary, it provides the actual schemas and conceptual frames then used to organize one's experience of reality.

Furthermore, these signs themselves are organized very differently in each language system. Each language is comprised of a particular arrangement of a collective system of signs that generates a fundamental framework for organizing all human experiences through the basic linguistic categories it provides. Hence, in order to understand human experience, one has no choice but to examine the basic language structures that make them possible (Culler, 1976; Harris, 1987). Each language, moreover, is a unique system of signs driven by different *inner logics* and organizing principles. In English, for instance, flowing bodies of water are referred to by signifiers distinguishing between their size (e.g., river, stream, and brook), whereas in French the words *riviere* and *fleuve* differentiate between those bodies of water that flow to the sea and those that do not. Other logics can be found in different languages. Some languages distinguish between the degrees of whiteness of snow, while others do so between textures of snow (i.e., wet, powdery, etc.); some languages like English use adjectives that indicate food tastes to describe personality types (e.g., sweet, sour, bitter, and so on), while others have no such concepts. As Culler (1976, 24) emphasizes, Saussure's point here is that "not only can a language arbitrarily choose its signifiers; it can divide up a spectrum of conceptual possibilities in any way it likes." How these different linguistic organizing principles operate is the fundamental focus of Saussure's semiology.

Central Concepts in Semiotics and Structuralism

Saussure's interest in signs is not confined to individual signs but extends to entire *complexes* or *systems* of signs (Harris, 1987). Given that any individual sign is meaningless outside its relationship to other signs within a specific sign structure, this emphasis on whole systems of signs is a key part of the structuralist tradition (Lechte, 1994). Although Saussure himself was solely interested in languages as primary sign systems, his ideas have been steadily applied to a multitude of other communicative systems ranging from clothing (Holman, 1980) and corporate annual reports (Fiol, 1989) to retail sales transactions (Pentland, 1995) and tourism marketing (Uzzell, 1984). The core ideas in Saussure's thinking, however, are very much in evidence in many of these studies.

Langue and Parole

Saussure made an important distinction between *langue* (the formal rule structures of language) and *parole* (everyday speech). *Langue* refers to the basic grammars and principles that hold a sign system together and is relatively fixed. *Langue* is present outside individual experience and exists by virtue of some sort of metaphorical contract entered into by members of a linguistic community (Rossi, 1976). Speech or *parole* refers to individual appropriations of these linguistic structures in everyday communication and is far more idiosyncratic and flexible.

Saussure (1966) argues that the only thing worth examining from a semiotic perspective is *langue,* precisely because it represents the *social dimension* of communication as opposed to *parole,* which represents individual speech acts. *Langue* is also more important than *parole* because it provides the structural framework within which different speech options are possible. Understanding *langue* can therefore provide us with a more accurate understanding of the inner logics of any language. In actual practice, this translates into a strong focus on the *grammatical rules* and other formal properties of a language as sources of the wider culture's organizational schemas. Saussure's own interest was only in languages, but contemporary semioticians extend these notions in analyzing different communication systems (e.g., advertisements and managerial policies) for their underwritten codes and grammars.

A Synchronic Perspective on Language

One of Saussure's crucial, if less easily comprehensible, notions relates to his *synchronic* position on language. This asserts that any language needs to be studied at a particular moment in time *without* reference to past influences on it (Culler, 1976). Here again he breaks with the more commonly held view that privileges the historical development of any language. Saussure (1966) therefore shifts us away from pursuing the historical evolution of a language (diachronic perspective) to examining its present configuration (synchronic perspective). In fact, semiotics is quite distinctive in its sole absorption with present-day linguistic structures and its dismissal of past influences on them (Lechte, 1994).

Saussure (1966) uses the metaphor of the chess game to illustrate the importance of a synchronic over a diachronic approach. As he argues, for anyone who unexpectedly walks into a chess game, a history of the moves is not likely to prove very informative. What is crucial is the present configuration of the pieces. A diachronic or historical approach might in fact be distracting, providing interesting but irrelevant and even misleading information. A synchronic view, on the other hand, is preferable because it provides a clearer picture of the game being currently played. In different branches of semiotics, this focus on the inner logics underlying present social arrangements is seen to be of utmost importance and semioticians are reluctant to trace the genesis of present practices.

The Relational Principle

The semiotics of both Saussure and Peirce sees language as a system—that is, a set of intricate networks of different signs. Individually, the signs have no significance outside the confines of their linguistic structures (Lechte, 1994). In sum, they acquire meaning and value only in terms of their relationships with other signs in the same system. The term or the sign, "management" for instance, acquires meaning only through its similarities and differences with other signs such as worker, employer, or supervisor in the same linguistic system. For semioticians, therefore, there is obviously little point in analyzing single signs. What are of interest are the relationships between different signs in a particular event, situation, or convention.

Saussure further asserts that there are two broad kinds of inter-sign relationships in any language or system of signs. One is *paradigmatic* and the other is *syntagmatic*. Paradigmatic relationships are oppositional in nature (Culler, 1976; Mick, 1986). In other words, they refer to those relationships in which signs acquire meanings precisely because they are NOT other signs. For example, we understand what love means only because we know it is not hate, what night is because it is not day, what work is because it is not idleness, and what technology is because it is not nature. Paradigmatic relationships essentially derive their meanings from oppositions and contrasts between signs in a set (Mick, 1986; Thayer, 1982). Syntagmatic relationships, on the other hand, refer to *associative* relationships (of degree and space) between different signs (Fiol, 1989). In any system, several signs combine in particular sequences—words in a sentence, garments in a clothing ensemble, or items in a balance sheet. These are all syntagmatic relations that define all manner of combinatory possibilities. The point to remember here is that some signs do not belong within particular syntagmatic relationships. Curtains cannot meaningfully be included as part of any clothing ensemble; reference to office gossip has no place in any balance sheet, and so on. Each sign system has its own set of diverse syntagmatic relationships that include some signs but exclude others.

Within the semiotic system, every language and sign system is seen as simultaneously being constituted of *both* paradigmatic and syntagmatic relationships. It is only through understanding both of them that we can grasp the underlying structure and inner logic of any system.

Denotative and Connotative Meanings

Not only is the semiotic tradition deeply interested in the meanings conveyed by signs in a communicative system, it also differentiates between two types of possible meanings. The first and simpler level is *denotative* and takes place when a sign refers to little more than a specific signified object or image. In this case, the sign "dog" would refer to a canine animal, the sign "red rose" to a flower, and "manager" to someone in charge of the administration or supervision of work. However, semioticians also recognize that the same signs can also carry a more complex level of *connotative* meaning (Thayer, 1982). This refers to a system of secondary and less obvious meanings that are also associated with the signified in given sign systems. Thus in contemporary Western contexts, the sign "dog" can also mean fidelity, a red rose is also a symbol of romantic affection, and a manager can also be seen as a tool of capitalist enterprise. Both denotative and connotative meanings have to be taken into account in any semiotic analysis.

Types of Sign Systems

Semioticians often distinguish between different types of sign systems varying in degrees of unity and complexity. "Sign systems can be loosely or tightly connected or articulated, and the relations within them can be various: homological, analogical, even metaphoric" (Manning & Cullum-Swan, 1994). First, there are systems consisting primarily of *explicit codes* where the relationship between signifier and signified is relatively straightforward and direct (Culler, 1976). An extreme example of an explicit code system is the Morse code where a particular combination of dots and dashes stands for one thing only. Languages in use such as French, English, Japanese, or Braille are also constituted mostly of explicit codes, even though some of them can carry complex connotative meanings.

Second, we all have systems full of *expressive codes* where the meanings conveyed by most of the signs are highly ambiguous and difficult to establish with complete certainty (Culler, 1976). Art and literature are sign systems filled with expressive codes that are rich in meaning and complicated in their symbolic content. One reason for this is that many forms of aesthetic work are systematically engaged in questioning and parodying common explicit codes, thereby making the task of studying them that much more difficult.

Finally, several ritualistic dimensions of social life that we do not immediately recognize as communicative systems are indeed so. These *codified social practices* combine syntagmatic and paradigmatic sign patterns to convey diverse symbolic messages. Office meetings, performance appraisal sessions, real estate sales, cocktail parties, and so on, are all codified social practices pervaded by rituals, etiquette, and social conventions that reflect an underlying structural logic that can be decoded with the help of semiotics analysis.

Working in the Semiotic Tradition

Saussure's insights into the self-defining nature of linguistic structures has led to the development of a scholarly tradition that looks increasingly inward at its own communicative rules instead of outward at some so-called objective world (Mick, 1986). Semioticians share a common conviction that our experience of reality is actually *precoded* for us at birth by the linguistic system in which we live (Thayer, 1982). As linguistic anthropologist, Edmund Sapir (1949, 162), holds, "human beings do not live in the objective world of social activity as ordinarily understood but are very much at the mercy of the particular language which has become the medium of expression for their society. . . . the 'real world' is to a large extent built up on the language habits of the group." Here semioticians share the interpretivist belief that "reality" has no independent meaning outside human perceptions of it. However, unlike interpretivists, the semiotic tradition regards the source of meaning as being in the codes and structures of a society rather than in individual interpretations.

This uniquely semiotic view of language and linguistic structures has steadily been extended to various social fields, which are also treated as "texts" that are decipherable through a set of institutionally generated codes or interpretive frames (Manning & Cullum-Swan, 1994). Within this tradition, virtually any social phenomenon can be seen as a cultural text—bureaucratic structures, patterns of Christmas shopping, occupational subcultures, career dressing, and automobile advertisements can all become worthy candidates for semiotic analysis.

One of the more prominent applied semiotic traditions has grown under the direction of Levi-Strauss and Sapir into what is commonly referred to as structuralist anthropology. Structuralist anthropology is based on a somewhat provocative thesis—that various sets of cultural phenomena have a *hidden structure* and that these structures are members of a limited class of formal possibilities (Turner, 1983). Levi-Strauss (1963; 1966) has systematically discussed the ways in which a myth can tell us a great deal about the culture in which it is narrated when subjected to semiotic analysis. For him, myths are ultimately interesting not because of the details and nuances of their narrative but because their hidden structure or morphology is indicative of wider and more powerful cultural tendencies. A personal example may be useful in understanding this concept.

In the last three academic institutions I worked at, a popular story (myth) that was constantly told and retold described a former time when the department had been a happy and contented place. The professors were all interested in their work without being overly ambitious, and a strong sense of camaraderie was present in the department. This somewhat idyllic state of affairs was profoundly disturbed by the arrival of a newcomer who was hired mainly because of his remarkable academic accomplishments. In all three stories, the newcomer made vigorous attempts to change the existing departmental culture, made outrageous and unreasonable demands of his colleagues, violated a number of local conventions, and, in general, made life miserable for the entire department. Although the department was initially traumatized, its members quickly rallied together to teach the presumptuous outsider a lesson. With the help of a number of artful strategies, the outsider in all three stories was eventually either dismissed or forced to leave, after which the department once again returned to its earlier contented state. From a semiotic perspective, what is interesting here is that regardless of differences in narrative detail (e.g., personality traits, cast of characters, misdemeanors of the interloper) and cultural context (the stories were told in universities in three different countries), the basic *grammar* or *langue* of the myth is virtually identical. All three stories are myths of "Trouble in Paradise," for they are all about situations of collegial contentment disturbed by an accomplished outsider. They are all also redemptive in exactly the same way, for they tell of local native resourcefulness used for vanquishing a skilled outsider. They all also contain the same cautionary message, which is beware of the foreigner (outsider) who may be highly personable and qualified. These myths therefore offer insights into the anxieties and desires of the cultures that develop them.

Not only stories and myths but also entire classes of cultural practices can be approached semiotically. Barley's (1983) detailed examination of a funeral home provides fascinating insights into the underlying code structures present in the occupational culture of funeral work. Barley treats funeral work as a cultural text and extracts the basic structures that regulate its enactment out of observation and interviews with funeral directors and their apprentices. Ultimately, Barley's (1983) study helps us grasp the driving forces behind the performance of funeral work. As he shows, the real goals in funeral work are achieving a sense of "naturalness" and familiarity for the mourning family. The code of naturalness influences the ways in which bodies are prepared to resemble some idealized vision of peaceful sleep while the code of familiarity dictates the choice of furnishings and the creation of an ambience meant to resemble that of a "normal" home. Barley's work underscores the value of semiotic analysis for occupational cultures because it goes beyond the study of superficial rituals to the skeleton or basic codes of any culture. "Such codes . . . represent tightly formulated rules for producing actions and interpretations deemed appropriate by members of the culture. Possessing such a set of interpretive rules should enable the cultural researcher to predict not only how members will interpret other aspects of their work world, but also how they will frame the mundane problems they encounter in their world of work" (Barley, 1983, 410).

Other researchers looking at complex organizations in the semiotic tradition also ask questions about the deep-seated ordering principles that facilitate the expression of everyday workplace customs and rituals (Fiol, 1989; Turner, 1983). One such study is Broms and Gahmberg's (1983) work on long-range strategic plans. To them, organizations are storehouses of mythologies in need of semiotic decoding. These mythologies typically manifest themselves in various forms of organizational "autocommunication"—that is, messages that are directed primarily at oneself and one's own culture rather than at external constituents. In essence, treating various organizational texts as forms of autocommunication implies searching for the organizational unconscious, which is similar to the *langue* or deep structure of conventional semiotics. Broms and Gahmberg (1983) study long-range strategic plans as auto-communicative texts expressing a CEO's or a company's unconscious state. "Instead of having become a recipe for action, it [the long-range strategic plan] has been made into a code that transports everyone's mind into a mythical plane of what should be, what ought to be or what would be good for the company or the organization" (Broms & Gahmberg, 1983, 489). Overall, their study suggests that strategic plans are far from being the rational documents they are supposed to be, but are mythic texts representing organizational desires, carving out various desirable roles and inculcating hope and belief in the organization as a collective.

Given the semiotic tradition's roots in linguistic philosophy, written texts of all kinds are popular subjects of analysis. Fiol (1989), for example, examines corporate annual reports of the chemical industry to establish the relationship between a company's construction of its internal and external boundaries and its tendency to engage in joint ventures. In yet another study seeking to identify the rules governing the attribution of meaning to organizational power and leadership, Fiol (1991) traces the effect of social grammars and codes on executives' own self-conceptualizations. Moving away from a conventional understanding of leaders' "having" or "acquiring" power, Fiol (1991) asks a far more difficult and fundamental question—how is power recognizable in organizations? She addresses this question through a semiotic analysis of the autobiographies of two celebrated captains of American industry, Henry Ford and Lee Iacocca.

Fiol (1991) tries to identify patterns in the use of words constructing the meaning of power in both texts. Clusters of words representing recurring themes are the primary units of her semiotic study. Using semiotic ideas about paradigmatic relationships, Fiol illustrates how both leaders create distinctions between choice and the absence of choice on the one hand, and the ability to act versus the inability to do so on the other as the core oppositional concepts around which they weave narratives of their own leadership. Ford builds up an image of his leadership around the independence of both choice and action, while Iacocca does so around action within the parameters of limited choice. Fiol's study is insightful mainly because it shows us how organizational participants combine core oppositional concepts about power into a single system of meaning within which organizational leadership can be recognized and enacted.

Recent Trends and Developments in Structuralism

The semiotic and structuralist traditions provide a rigorous and precise program for decoding various texts whether they are literary, aesthetic, or social. A part of semiotics' appeal has always lain in its capacity to pare away "superfluous" details and go straight to the anatomy of a sign system. Conventional semiotics, however, has come under fire on two counts. The first is that it adopts a *closed* conceptualization of sign systems, which is neither useful nor accurate, and the second is that it completely ignores the *value-laden* character of linguistic and cultural codes themselves. More recent developments in semiotics and structuralism, especially the writings of Umberto Eco (1984) and Roland Barthes (1953; 1972), are attempts to address some of these criticisms. Eco is best known for making semiotic analysis more fluid and open, whereas Barthes reworks semiotics in order to expose the cultural ideologies that are at the heart of any communicative system. Barthes's (1972) work is also noteworthy because it is one of the earliest attempts at linking structuralist thinking to social critique and is therefore a forerunner of many intellectual developments in poststructuralism.

Eco (1976) renders semiotics less inflexible by redefining signs and codes as "cultural units" that derive their meanings out of their cultural contexts. Eco also argues that the reader or interpreter of any cultural text has considerably more autonomy than is normally granted by conventional semiotics. In taking these positions, Eco also allows for the possibility of renewal and revitalization within any sign system. His primary contribution remains his understanding that any sign system is essentially open and dynamic rather than closed and static. Eco's attempt to open up the sign system is described by Lechte (1994) as moving semiotics from the paradigm of the *dictionary* to that of the *encyclopedia*. The earlier dictionary orientation of semiotics attempted to fix the meanings of signs and was constrained by its static view. The encyclopedic approach sees the rules governing the interpretation of meaning as a far more fluid process that is open to inside and outside influences: "the encyclopedia would correspond to a network without a center, to a labyrinth from which there is no exit, or to an infinite, influential model that is open to new elements" (Lechte, 1994, 130).

Barthes (1953; 1972) takes up Levi-Strauss's interest in myth and gives it a different flavor. In his celebrated work, *Mythologies* (1972), Barthes subjects everyday images and messages of advertising and popular culture to a highly reflective scrutiny. His departure from Levi-Strauss can be found in the contrasts that he highlights between myth and ideology. For Barthes (1953; 1972), ideological messages are important because they *hide* or conceal certain aspects of social reality. Myths on the other hand, hide nothing. They are important for what they actually say—for the flagrant messages that are so commonsensical that they appear completely natural and therefore easily become part of the taken-for-granted world. As he succinctly asserts, "myth has the task of giving historical intention a natural justification and making contingency appear eternal" (Barthes, 1972, 142). Barthes therefore likens myths to "scandals occurring in the full light of day." The task of semiotics here is to unmask the *codes of the natural* in any myth and to show that the most plausible actions and narratives are artificial constructions serving special interests. While maintaining the semiotic interest in deep structure, Barthes simultaneously examines this structure itself to see how it works to support some segments of society and to disenfranchise others. In his discussion of the mythological role of wine in French culture, he exposes the close connection between wine production and capital and colonial interests, especially in Algeria where the exploitation of peasants is carried on in the name of producing a fine and sophisticated cultural good.

The influence of Barthes's structuralism can be found in a number of studies looking at advertisements and promotional material (e.g., Williamson, 1978). Uzzell's (1984) analysis of tourism marketing is an interesting illustration. His study examines the construction of a *holiday mythology* in Western society as a liberating, constraint-free annual escape that is achieved through the simultaneous reinforcement of sexual, racial, and national stereotypes in different kinds of promotional material. Based on a semiotic decoding of photographs and text in tourist brochures, Uzzell (1984) illustrates how the entire holiday mythology is made up in part by images of male tourists playing active and powerful roles (e.g., playing energetic sports, or lifting up women) and images of female tourists playing more passive roles (e.g., sunbathing on beaches, being gazed at by other men). Uzzell's point here is that the myth of the holiday is substantially built on the codes of men as "having" (i.e., *having* power) and women as "being" (i.e., merely being present for male consumption). Furthermore, these hierarchical gender relations are not really *hidden* in the photographs and tourist brochures. Rather they are in our faces, very much like the "scandals occurring in the full light of day" referred to by Barthes. The key issue is that we cannot really even see these codes easily because they also appear to represent the "natural" way of things. Through semiotics, we can become aware of our own cultural blindspots when it comes to interpreting the mythologies of our own cultures whether they are about holidays, corporate performance, or public policy.

Does semiotics and structuralism have a more enduring place in contemporary organization and management studies? Its original appeal lay in part in its belief that there is a hidden structural reality that can somehow be captured and exposed through systematic analysis. Semiotics has always offered a certain ontological comfort that is missing in the hermeneutic world of interpretivist research. However, as semiotics becomes increasingly appropriated by poststructuralism, it no longer offers the comfort of some kind of finitude in one's analysis. Although semiotics and structuralism will always hold an important place because of their enormous influence on poststructuralism and postmodernism, it may cease to be quite so appealing in its own right to contemporary researchers.

Figure 7.1   **Highlights of the Semiotic and Structuralist Traditions**

Philosophic influences: Linguistic philosophy

Major figures: Ferdinand de Saussure, Charles Sanders Peirce, Vladimir Propp, Claude Levi-Strauss, Umberto Eco, Roland Barthes

Central concepts
- Sign systems
- Signifier and signified
- Langue and parole
- Synchronic approaches
- Paradigmatic and syntagmatic relationships
- Explicit and expressive codes
- Codified social practices
- Myth

Key practices
- Bypassing interpretive details in favor of the underlying grammar
- Denying individual subjects autonomy
- Treating language as offering interpretive frames

Exemplary research
- *Mythologies* (Barthes, 1972)
- "Semiotics and the Study of Occupations and Organizational Cultures" (Barley, 1983)
- "Communication to Self in Organizations and Cultures" (Broms & Gahmberg, 1983)
- "Seeing the Empty Spaces" (Fiol, 1991)

III

The Critical Traditions

The critical traditions are best characterized as a set of intellectual positions that examine social arrangements through the lenses of power, domination, and conflict. Although they share with interpretivists a belief that our worlds are indeed socially constructed, they also hold that these constructions themselves are mediated by power relations and conflicting interests in any given society (Collins, 1990; Prasad & Caproni, 1997). Thus, although they are convinced of the socially constructed nature of all reality, they are far more *skeptical* than interpretivists with respect to the role of interests governing individual and collective action.

Several semantic clarifications may be useful at this point. First, the critical traditions should not be confused with *critical thinking,* which is little more than a straightforward pedagogic movement intended to instill systematic reflection within the wider framework of liberal humanism (Prasad & Caproni, 1987). Although the critical traditions are equally committed to systematic reflection, this reflection is practiced within a theoretical framework of power, conflict, and interests. Second, the critical traditions go far beyond some kind of narrow faultfinding or *criticisms* of existing social formations (Alvesson & Deetz, 2000). Rather, they are committed to ongoing critiques of prevalent assumptions and social practices with the wider intent of changing the overall system.

In short, the critical traditions are simultaneously committed to both critique and change. One without the other is not considered very meaningful. The critical traditions thus break quite definitively with the stances of scientific detachment and semineutrality adopted by many other intellectual positions. In this respect, they are much more aligned with the broader tradition of the *intelligentsia,* which regards academic research and scholarship as a process of critical engagement with the broader social milieu or *praxis.*

In their emphasis on critique and change, all of the critical traditions are deeply indebted to the spirit and philosophy of Karl Marx whose pronouncement in *The Theses on Feuerbach* (1988, 123) that "philosophers have only *interpreted* the world in various ways, the point is to *change* it" [emphasis in original text] set the stage for a radically different agenda and orientation within much of Western scholarship. There is little doubt that the figure of Marx towers like an intellectual giant over the entire landscape of the critical traditions. Although some recent work within critical organization studies has been noticeably evasive about acknowledging Marx's pivotal role, his ideas about history, conflict, and emancipation are central to the development of the tradition. Many prominent thinkers in this tradition have understandably taken issue with some of Marx's more outlandish ideas as well as with his sexist, racist, and imperialist assumptions, yet the sheer magnitude of his intellectual influence on the critical traditions simply cannot be dismissed. Whether scholars wholeheartedly embrace Marx or quarrel with his ideas, he remains the main intellectual reference point for the entire critical tradition.

Marx's influence over the critical tradition is indeed very strong, but it is far from being uniform in its nature or intensity. Marx's ideas have been adapted, appropriated, and transformed in different and sometimes even unrecognizable ways. Thus, even while Marx remains the central thinker in this tradition, it is still one that is constituted of many diverse subtraditions. (See Figure PIII.1 for an overview of the different critical traditions.) These include more conventional forms of Marxism that claim to be "true" to his original writings (e.g., Carchedi, 1977; Miliband, 1969), variants of what is commonly known as Western or cultural Marxism (Gramsci, 1971; Lukacs, 1971), critical theory that developed out of the Frankfurt School (Adorno, 1951; Habermas, 1970; Horkheimer, 1947), structural Marxism (Althusser & Balibar, 1971; Poulantzas, 1975), radical feminism (hooks, 1989; Smith, 1987), cultural studies (Hall, 1982; Williams, 1980), and more recent developments in structuration theory (Bourdieu, 1990; Giddens, 1979).

For all their variation, the critical traditions remain united in their focus on the oppression and exploitation of different groups whether they are women, workers, the poor, or specific ethnic minorities. At the heart of the critical tradition are deep concerns with both material and symbolic domination and a concomitant interest in *emancipating* oppressed groups from this domination. Not surprisingly perhaps, many of the critical traditions are therefore primarily oriented toward critiquing the established social order, the nexus of ruling elites, and the conglomeration of interests that come together in any social setting. Given these emancipatory visions, most of the critical traditions are also sympathetic to somewhat radical reforms that are geared toward fundamental changes rather than toward piecemeal solutions. However, the nature of this radicalism is also quite diverse, with materialists being more likely to endorse the complete overhaul of existing structures, and adherents of the Frankfurt School being more in favor of gradual ideological changes.

The different critical traditions have exerted considerable influences over

Figure PIII.1   **The Critical Traditions**

Karl Marx and Engels

Orthodox Marxism

Historical Materialism
Labor Process Theory

Russian Communism
Lenin
Plekhanov

Anarchism
(Anti-Structure)
Peter Kropotkin

Structural Marxism
Althusser

Structuration Theory
Anthony Giddens
Pierre Bourdieu

The Frankfurt School
Adorno, Horkheimer
Marcuse, Benjamin
Habermas

Cultural Marxism
Lukacs
Gramsci

Cultural Studies
Raymond Williams
Stuart Hall

Radical Feminism

many social science disciplines, notably sociology, anthropology, and political economics. Ideas and concepts from these traditions have taken somewhat longer to enter management and organization studies. Since the 1970s, however, a steady stream of critical ideas has trickled into this field, with scholars from different critical subtraditions subjecting organizational actions and managerial practices to intense analysis. Studies in the critical tradition have (among other things) examined the role of accounting in labor relations (Cooper & Essex, 1977; Oaks & Covaleski, 1994), the patriarchal underpinnings of consumption (Bristor & Fischer, 1993), the hegemony of organizational culture (Deetz, 1992; Willmott, 1993), and the ideological dimensions of organizational symbolism (Alvesson, 1990; Everett, 2002).

Organization and management research in the critical traditions has, over the years, become so pervasive that a number of institutional arrangements such as regular conferences and academic journals supporting these ideas have emerged. These institutions have ensured that the critical traditions are here to stay. The Critical Management Studies Conference (CMS) held every two years in England, the annual critical preconference at the Academy of Management Meetings, and journals like *Critical Perspectives in Accounting* and *Accounting, Organizations and Society* all explicitly facilitate the conduct of critical scholarship and provide institutionalized forums for their expression.[1] The next few chapters will explore four distinct subtraditions within the wider critical tradition. They are historical materialism, critical theory, feminism, and structuration theory.

Note

1. Some of the institutions mentioned here use the term *critical* in a far more diluted manner than its use in this text. Conference organizers often use "critical" in an extended and flexible manner to even include any form of qualitative work in an effort to be more inclusive. However, given the purpose of this book, much can be gained from understanding the term *critical* as a product of a specific and reputed intellectual tradition.

8

Historical Materialism

Class, Conflict, and Domination

Historical materialism is a tradition that developed out of Karl Marx's analysis of history and capitalism, and his *dialectical method.* In describing this tradition, historical materialism is the preferred term to Marxism because Marxism has too many unfortunate connotations with a dogmatic orthodoxy and with the more dysfunctional aspects of Soviet-style communism. Historical materialism is a noteworthy tradition not only because of its contribution to our grasp of power relations in society, but also because of its obvious as well as its less visible influences over all the critical traditions and over segments of poststructuralism and postcolonialism.

Of all the traditions discussed this far, historical materialism is by far the most macro in its scope and ambition. Historical materialists focus on social stratifications, ideological formations, conflicts between classes, and structural power dynamics (Collins, 1990). In general, historical materialism is also less averse to using quantitative techniques and collecting statistical data, provided that both are done in keeping with the overall goals of the historical materialist project. From its inception in the prolific writings of Karl Marx, historical materialism has always been remarkably interdisciplinary, drawing freely on history, economics, political science, and sociology. It is therefore not surprising that this tradition has flourished both close to the center and at the margins of all these disciplines, and some others as well.

Historical materialism entered management and organization studies through organizational sociology by way of C. Wright Mills's (1956) incisive work, *The Power Elite,* which initiated an interest in organizational control, and through economics where Baran and Sweezy's (1966) classic text, *Monopoly Capital,* stimulated an interest in managerial dynamics within the firm under monopolistic and oligopolistic conditions. In the next thirty to forty years, materialist analyses could be found in studies of accounting practices (Oaks & Covaleski, 1994; Tinker & Niemark, 1987), business history (Rowlinson & Hassard, 1993), shopfloor relations (Burawoy, 1979), and corporate governance (Kaufman, Zacharias, & Karson 1995). In the more recent past, while historical materialism's popularity has been eclipsed by that of critical theory and genres of postmodernism in critical management circles, it is still pursued by a number of scholars interested in aspects of coercive and ideological control in organizations.

The Philosophy of Karl Marx

Karl Marx was not only one of nineteenth-century Europe's most prominent and controversial thinkers, but he was also one of its most prolific. Marx's writings on various aspects of economics, society, and philosophy are incredibly detailed and voluminous, and include fairly significant shifts in thinking. To distill his enormous literary outpourings into a few pages is obviously no easy task and is one that cannot possibly do his scholarship full justice. Such a task is further complicated by disagreements among Marxian scholars themselves as to the importance of some writings over others. Although many continue to regard *Capital* (1977) as his seminal work, several others also attest to the importance of *The Economic and Philosophic Manuscripts* (1964), *The German Ideology* (with Engels 1932), *The Eighteenth Brumaire of Louis Bonaparte* (1963), and *Die Grundrisse* (1973), to name a few.

Furthermore, over the last few decades, some scholars have also argued that a useful distinction can be made between the writings of the young Marx of *The German Ideology* (which are more ideational in nature) and the later Marx of *Capital* (which are more materialist in nature). This so-called *epistemological break* in Marx's writings becomes the point around which Burrell and Morgan (1979) developed their radical humanist and radical structuralist paradigms. It is my position that this view somewhat needlessly bifurcates Marx's thinking, creates a distinction that is not necessarily very meaningful, and obscures the enormous overlaps between his earlier and later writings. In any case, when it comes to understanding historical materialism as a tradition, it is important to consider *both* periods of his writings as he is believed to have laid the foundations of his materialist ideas while collaborating with Engels on *The German Ideology* (Bottomore, 1983).

In this regard, Marx is quite the opposite of a thinker like Ferdinand de Saussure whose entire scholarly contributions can be found in a single written piece of work. Marx's own writings are so extensive, so complex, and spread over so many years that they lend themselves to multiple (sometimes conflicting) interpretations. In many ways, however, the sheer complexity of his work keeps many of his ideas alive even while some of them lose their appeal.

Before getting into the intricacies of Marxian philosophy, it is important to recognize Marx as a quintessential product of progressive nineteenth-century European society. Literary, musical, and philosophical circles of the day were permeated by two genres that vied with each other for public attention: *realism* and *romanticism*. As a movement, realism deviated quite sharply from classicism by directly confronting the more troubling and tangible issues of the day such as poverty, violence, adultery, and social decay. Writers like Flaubert, Dickens, Hugo, and Zola dwelt on the tragic and often "messy" realities of social life and used their realist orientations to critique a number of European cultural and social institutions. The romanticism of Goethe, Schiller, and Frederic Chopin, on the other hand, focused on the expressiveness and imaginative capacities of human beings and celebrated the power of human will and autonomy.

Marx's genius and the source of his tremendous appeal lay in his ability to fuse the realist and romantic genres into his own thinking. His writings clearly bear the stamp of the Romantic tradition. It can be found in his liberationary zeal, in his faith in the power of oppressed groups to overcome social obstacles, and in his endorsement of subjective forces. Yet, Marx's romantic impulses are always grounded in a materialist analysis of human conditions— in poverty, employment relations, working conditions, and physical toil. It is also important to remember that Marx is not the first thinker to take such a strong interest in social justice and the redistribution of wealth. He wrote at a time when various genres of socialist thinking were in their ascendancy. Utopian socialists like Robert Owen, Claude-Henri Saint Simon, and Charles Fourier had already established a strong following and were a definite influence on Marx's thinking. Marx, however, has always been much more than yet another socialist philosopher. What he did was to neatly weave a number of popular socialist conceptions into a broad comprehensive framework of historical materialism, which were simultaneously a historical explanation of social conditions and a programmatic vision for an emancipated future.

We have already discussed the interdisciplinary nature of Marx's writings, which makes the task of classifying him along conventional lines an impossible one. Marx is indeed simultaneously a philosopher, an economist, a political scientist, a sociologist, a commentator of cultural affairs, and so on. Yet, unlike most social philosophers of his time, Marx is unique in the enormous emphasis he places on the *economic dimensions* of human life. For Marx, the economic structure of any society, or what he refers to as *the base,* conditions all other social arrangements including the law, the family, and the nature of political governance (Marx, 1977).

The economic base of any society can take different forms such as feudalism, capitalism, and socialism, and generates different *modes of production* (Goldman & Van Houten, 1977) or ways of transforming the world of nature for the purpose of human consumption. The cultivation of crops, the weaving of garments at home, and the factory manufacture of light bulbs would be examples of different modes of production within different economic bases. In Marx's (1977) thinking, the economic base plays a pivotal role in structuring an entire spectrum of social arrangements and relationships through the modes of production. Feudalism, for instance, gives rise to the extended family and obligatory relationships between the feudal lord and his serfs. Capitalism, on the other hand, is responsible for the emergence of the modern nuclear family and initiates a contractual relationship between owners, managers, and workers. The base is also believed to mediate all forms of cultural consciousness and practice, including literature, art, music, and the theater. In the language of historical materialism, these varied social arrangements and cultural practices are collectively referred to as *the superstructure* (Carchedi, 1983; Goldman & Van Houten, 1977).

The articulation of this close and complicated relationship between the base and the superstructure is at the heart of historical materialism and distinguishes it from all other traditions of social inquiry. Marx's principal contribution here can be found in the strong connection he made between material economic conditions and all other institutions in society. In essence, what he proposed was that any set of economic relations with its corresponding modes of production is responsible for structuring all other social formations (superstructures) including the state, culture, family, and religion. This implies that any significant change in the economic foundations of a society will inevitably trigger a set of transformations in its superstructure (Bottomore, 1983; Carchedi, 1983). From this perspective, the base is almost like the skeletal frame of a society, with the superstructure representing the flesh and the countenance.

Needless to say, this close, almost causal, relationship between the base and the superstructure has been severely critiqued for its excessive *economic determinism.* But defenders of historical materialism argue that Marx himself was cognizant of the dangers of an overly reductionist interpretation, which is why he systematically characterized this relationship as being historical and uneven and not something that moved in some exact and rhythmic tandem (Bottomore, 1983). Engels also sought to defend the base–superstructure relationship by making it clear that economic determinism was believed to occur only in the absolute final instance. His famous 1890 letter to Joseph Bloch is illuminating in this regard, for he clearly states that:

> According to the materialist conception of history, the *ultimately* determining element in history is the production and reproduction of real life. More than this neither Marx nor I have ever asserted. Hence, if somebody twists this into saying that the economic element is the *only* determining one, he transforms that proposition into a meaningless, abstract, senseless phrase. The economic situation is the base, but the various elements of the superstructure. . . . also exercise their influence upon the course of historical struggles and in many cases preponderate in determining their form.

Taking a leaf out of Engels's book, many scholars in this tradition choose to see the base–superstructure relationship as being closer to the chicken–egg relationship. To establish which exactly came first is not only an empirical impossibility, but also a somewhat pointless theoretical exercise. Regardless of these arguments about the *precise* strength of economic conditions in historical materialism, what is indisputable is that they are believed to play a prominent role in human life. Of equal importance in this tradition is the need to understand the *relationship* between different sectors of society, be they the workplace, ceremonial rituals, artistic, or political. This emphasis on grasping the *totality* of any situation is the other major distinguishing feature of historical materialism. The term used to describe this systemic approach to social arrangements in their total contexts is the *dialectical method* (Benson, 1983). The ambitious scope of dialectics is best captured by Carchedi's (1983, 352) description of it when he observes that "dialectics as a method of inquiry must be able to unify in an organic and coherent whole, the study of the whole and of the parts, of the essence or structure and of its carriers, of the internal logic, and of its concrete past and present configurations."

The dialectical method thus involves a comprehensive systems-type analysis that is also tied to the Hegelian notion of the inevitability of history. Under the influence of both Hegel and Darwin, Marx regarded historical analysis as a way of establishing how some economic epochs (e.g., feudalism, pre-capitalism) would give way to others, culminating in the ultimate grand historical moment—the communist state born out of a universal workers' revolution. This thesis, commonly referred to as the materialist conception of history, is among the more dubious elements of Marx's scholarship and often seriously compromises his more thoughtful analyses. However, if one can take these utopian visions of communist society less seriously, his approach to history can be particularly insightful in understanding multiple aspects of work, organizations, and social interactions. Ultimately, one of the tradition's greatest strengths lies in its uncompromising *empiricism*—that is, its methodological commitment to rigorous and concrete historical research and its close attention to patterns of everyday material existence.

Central Concepts in Historical Materialism

The development of the historical materialist tradition, first by Marx and Engels, and later by a number of prominent social scientists such as Gramsci (1971), Baran and Sweezy (1966), Braverman (1974), Dahrendorf (1959), Edwards (1979), Burawoy (1979), and others under diverse labels including Neo-Marxism, labor process theory, and conflict sociology has resulted in an immense body of scholarship that is less a single, unified philosophical argument and more a set of empirical theses committed to certain fundamental notions about human nature, socioeconomic life, conflict, and domination. This section examines some of these central concepts in some detail.

Surplus Value and Exploitation

At the heart of the historical materialist tradition is the conviction that exploitation is part and parcel of industrial capitalism and modern economic relations. To appreciate the primary role of exploitation in the system, one is required to have a basic grasp of Marx's theory of surplus value. For Marx (1977), *all* productive activity is made possible only through labor power. Since workers have nothing but their own labor power, they are forced to sell this to a capitalist in return for a wage. Their labor power, then, makes the *creation of value* possible either in the form of agricultural goods, factory products, or human services. The problem, however, is that most of the material benefit deriving from this value creation goes to the capitalist rather than to the worker in the form of profit. For Marx, therefore, profit is really another term for the surplus value (unpaid wages) created by labor power and appropriated by capitalists. It is important to recognize that Marx is not arguing that workers tend to be paid *unfair wages,* but rather that on account of the fundamentally asymmetric nature of employment relations under capitalism, workers' labor power can never be fully compensated.

A significant segment of the historical material tradition is therefore geared toward assessing in intricate detail the creation of surplus values in the actual production process (also referred to as the labor process), and its appropriation by capitalists. Innumerable studies document the emergence of worker exploitation and resistance in diverse economic locations including traditional manufacturing (Stone, 1974), financial service organizations (Knights & Willmott, 1990), and the production of corporate annual reports (Tinker & Niemark, 1987). The interest here is in using *exploitation* as a key explanatory variable in understanding the dynamics of workplace relationships.

Class and Class Struggle

Historical materialism and the writings of Karl Marx and Friedrich Engels are most often credited with the singular responsibility for developing the concepts of class and class struggle. The idea of class is built around notions of group identification and intergroup conflict, but is simultaneously grounded in a strong *economic* foundation. Classes emerge out of the common experiences of working and engaging in specific economic activities, and are defined by a crucial kind of *social relationship* that weaves together the material, ideological, and political threads of any society (Engels, 1945; Marx, 1977). Thus, we have a proletariat or a working class, a peasantry, a professional middle class also referred to as the *bourgeois,* a financial or capitalist class, a lower middle class or *petit bourgeois* comprising tradespeople, artisans and shopkeepers, and so on. Each class is united by strong material interests, and ultimately these internal economic bonds mediate an entire array of sociocultural behaviors ranging from educational and electoral preferences (Bowles & Gintis, 1976) to deeply ingrained cultural beliefs (Baritz, 1990) and consumer habits (Campbell, 1987).

Classes give rise to a highly stratified and materially unequal society in which some classes dominate others, and some subvert and resist domination and seek to overcome oppressive class dynamics. Class conflict and struggle, therefore, is an endemic and inevitable aspect of social life, and is simultaneously often the principal avenue to fundamental change (Dahrendorf, 1959). As Marx and Engels (1948, 9) observe in *The Communist Manifesto,* "the history of all hitherto existing society is the history of class struggles." Within contemporary historical materialism, class struggle is more like a conceptual *lens* that is useful in comprehending complex social processes over the spread of time.

In the historical materialist tradition, class struggles allude to much more than violent revolutionary activity or worker militancy. Class struggles are seen as taking place on a daily basis (both openly and covertly) over a multitude of material and symbolic resources. They can be found in the drafting of public policy, media representation of news events, the introduction of new work-related technologies, and in the attempts to arrive at worker–management collective agreements. Primarily, class analysis helps us grasp how economic interests shape specific group (or class) world-views and behavior (Goldman & Van Houten, 1977), and mediate interclass relationships. As Collins (1990) points out, class analysis minus the baggage of revolutionary politics can be an extraordinarily powerful perspective for understanding the motives and decisions of groups such as business leaders, financial investors, blue-collar workers and professional groups such as architects, accountants, and managers. What class analysis does is to make sure that researchers squarely confront the role of economic interests in defining social life.

Alienation

Although Marx tends to be most commonly identified as a theorist of class relations and revolutionary struggle, one of his more enduring contributions is to be found in his analysis of alienation in industrial society. And while Marx the economist is at his best when discussing questions of surplus value, it is Marx the humanist who finds full expression in elaborating on the problem of alienation. Marx's ideas on alienation are most strongly associated with the period of his earlier writings and are most thoroughly developed in *The Economic and Philosophic Manuscripts of 1844* (Marx, 1964). His central position on alienation follows mainly from his fundamental assumptions about the intrinsically creative inclinations of human beings, exemplified in *homo faber*—man the creator or producer.

The notion of *homo faber* is vital to any discussion of alienation in historical materialism. According to Marx, work is an act of *creative praxis* and a quintessential human attribute (Gorman, 1982) that is primarily realized within the labor process itself. Thus, to Marx, work itself is far more than mere economic activity and is really the principal source of human identity, dignity, and inspiration (Prasad & Prasad, 1993). As Marx sees it, the problem is that the experience of work and life under capitalist modes of production tends to be quite far from any kind of creative praxis and closer to extreme forms of alienation.

In Marx's view, conditions of work under capitalism (characterized by an extreme division of labor and an assembly line mode of production) are responsible for removing all *control* over work from labor and for minimizing workers' involvement in work itself. As a result, workers are *estranged* from the products of their own labor, stripped of all pride in their work, and ultimately left in a condition of total alienation. When workers play no meaningful role in the design and fabrication of the products of their own labor, their own labor power has little more than economic value. The overall consequence is alienation—individuals experiencing their own work and abilities as *commodities* to be bought and sold on the wage market (Marx, 1964).

This destruction of craftwork and the *commodification* of work itself are deeply institutionalized in capitalist society and are eventually extended to many other aspects of social life, as *exchange value* becomes the supreme touchstone of human experience. In Marx's own words, this tendency is responsible for a societywide alienation that he describes as the "fetishism of commodities." The fetishism of commodities refers to that characteristic of capitalism whereby workers lose sight of the fact that any commodity derives its value from their labor, believing instead that this value results from inherent properties of the commodity itself and/or independent workings of the market (Prasad & Prasad, 1993). As a result, commodities and markets come to be viewed as objective realities independent of human control and capable of dictating the actions and choices of human beings.

Historical materialists increasingly hold that the commodification of experience has encroached into virtually every avenue of social life, turning phenomena such as Christmas, romance, adoption, and health care into commodities with price tags attached to each of them. To scholars working in this tradition, such a wholescale commodification of society is first and foremost ethically untenable, and second, will be likely to play a key role in the eventual demise of capitalism.

Contradiction

The concept of contradiction is central to the historical materialist tradition. Broadly, contradictions refer to dissonances, inconsistencies, and disjunctures within a system that are eventually capable of undermining it. According to Benson (1983, 333), "contradictions are then confrontations between opposing or incompatible ways of arranging social life" and are always located in the structure of a system rather than in the actions of individuals. Sometimes, the structural properties of a system (e.g., capitalist relations of production) can themselves generate other structures such as workers' movements and labor unions that are capable of overthrowing the system from within (Bottomore, 1983). In the tradition of historical materialism, this would be a classic case of a contradiction.

Many other contradictions can be found in contemporary societies. On the one hand, for instance, the logic of capitalism requires efforts to substitute labor (especially skilled labor) with technology in order to reduce costs and to increase control over the labor process. However, when large pools of unemployed and underemployed workers are created by such capitalist practices, overall consumption—the lifeblood of capitalism—is likely to decline. Herein lies one of the major paradoxes or contradictions of capitalism, whereby efforts to enhance profits are likely to have the opposite effects as wage levels climb down and unemployment rises. Giddens's (1979, 141) definition of contradiction captures its essence when he suggests that it is "an *opposition* or *disjunction of structural properties* of social systems, where those whose principles operate in *terms of each other* but at the same time *contravene one another*" (emphasis in original). Contradictions play a pivotal role in historical materialist doctrine, for they are believed to provide the main starting point for radical change. Since contradictions lay bare the inner (and more unpalatable) sides of society, they can also engender serious discontent among members of society and instill among them a drive for fundamental change.

Ideology

The notion of ideology was relatively familiar to nineteenth-century Europe (mainly through the influence of Hegel), but the writings of Marx give it a unique prominence, so much so that Larrain (1979, 34) insists that "with

Marx, the concept of ideology came of age." Unlike some of the other key concepts of historical materialism discussed so far (notably class and contradiction), one does not find a systematic theory of ideology in Marx's writings as much as a cluster of brilliant insights about it. It is important, however, to distinguish the Marxian notion of *ideology* from its usage in everyday language as a cluster of values or beliefs, or a common *Weltanschaaung* or worldview. Marx actually tends to use the term ideology in a distinctly *negative* or pejorative sense—equating it with the *systematic distortions* that have their origins in material conditions and that occur widely in society (Larrain, 1983). Moreover, to Marx, ideologies should not be confused with illusions or cognitive errors that can be dispelled by scientific scrutiny alone. Ideologies are far more tenacious because they are rooted in the real circumstances of everyday life. The notion of corporate careers provides an interesting illustration of an ideology rooted in material conditions. To a historical materialist, the ideology of corporate careers is produced by the managerial and capitalist classes in order to motivate the largely underpaid and alienated working masses. While the lure of corporate advancement might instill habits of hard work and an ethic of corporate loyalty, it is ideological because it systematically conceals the real chances individuals have of "making it" in the corporate world. It is also ideological because it obscures the real dynamics of corporate advancement, which are more dependent on immediate alliances and networks than on hard work and commitment.

It is also important to recognize that in Marx's view, *all* ideas are *not* ideological. Ideology explicitly refers only to those illusory ideas that powerfully screen social contradictions, and in doing so, further the material interests of the dominant elite groups in society. Again, we need to keep in mind that all ideas produced by elites are also not necessarily ideological. They turn into ideologies only when they systematically negate, deny, or conceal social contradictions while simultaneously advancing elite interests. Another contemporary example of an ideology that might make the notion clearer is that of the free market. According to historical materialists, the so-called laws of the free market skillfully obscure the ways in which economic behavior is often manipulated by powerful groups in society. At the same time, a faith in the market is imperative for a network of institutions and actors, including Wall Street, academic economists in major universities, and the International Monetary Fund (IMF) in order for them to secure their own collective interests. Furthermore, not all elites are necessarily consciously using ideologies to further their own interests. Even when they genuinely believe in the value of corporate advancement and the workings of the market, their ideas remain ideological because of their power to distort reality and further their own interests.

Within the historical materialist tradition, Marx is not the only theorist to seriously engage with the concept of ideology. The remarkable twentieth-century Italian thinker, Antonio Gramsci (1971), developed the notion of *ideological hegemony* in referring to those widespread world-views that are promoted by ruling social groups and that eventually become part and parcel of the "common sense" of society. Ideologies for Gramsci are relatively widespread and are hegemonic in the sense that they are so taken for granted that they become virtually impossible to challenge or critique (Prasad & Prasad, 1993). This stance is responsible for his celebrated, if somewhat provocative, statement that "common sense is the enemy" of all humankind. For Gramsci therefore, it is the *pervasive* influence of certain ideas combined with their *unquestionable legitimacy* that turns them into ideologies. His notions of ideology as part of the natural order of things have been extended by some members of the Frankfurt School (discussed in the next chapter).

Working in the Historical Materialist Tradition

Historical materialism's commitment to exploitation, class analysis, and uncovering the more somber side of capitalism results in a research focus that puts organizations, work, firm decision making, and business activity squarely at the forefront of all scholarly inquiry. At the same time, historical materialism should not be conceived of as a narrow and restricted tradition. Given the sheer range of Marx's own writings (not to mention that of his many followers), working in the historical materialist tradition can mean the possibility of taking more than one path. Within the wider framework of materialism, it is entirely possible to concentrate on either micro (e.g., local workplaces) or macro (e.g., transformations in the labor pool) phenomena, to take an interest in the more objective structures (e.g., business elite networks) or the more subjective moments (e.g., ideological influences) of capitalism, or to adopt a completely historical perspective on changing social conditions. Regardless of these options, the unifying threads in the historical materialist tradition can be found in the convictions about class struggle, exploitation, and the value of the dialectic method.

Two broad strands of historical materialism can be identified within the social sciences. The first can be designated as the *sociology of work* tradition and follows broadly from the work of Harry Braverman (1974) and the *labor process* theorists (Edwards, 1979; Marglin, 1974). The second is probably best characterized as the *conflict tradition* (Collins, 1990) and has developed out of the work of Ralf Dahrendorf (1959), Alvin Gouldner (1954), and the overall intellectual project designed to forge elements of Marxian thinking with the more critical writings of Max Weber. At the risk of some oversimplification, we can assert that the first tradition is more concerned with the emergence of exploitation at the *point of production,* whereas the second is more engaged with analyzing the *structures of capitalism* and its accompanying conflicts.

Labor Process Theory and the Sociology of Work

A fundamental premise drawn from Marx's writings revolves around the *conflictual* relationships between management and labor and the *contested* nature of the workplace itself. The way in which these dynamics get played out is one of the central preoccupations of labor process theorists. Although Braverman (1974) is usually credited with revitalizing this discussion, a number of scholars in the 1970s and 1980s, including Edwards (1979) and Marglin (1974), had also highlighted the *unequal* nature of these workplace contests, arguing that the rise of oligarchic firms heavily equipped the owners and managers of capital with the tools and techniques needed for strengthening workplace controls and cheapening labor. Braverman's (1974) own crucial concern was with what he termed the *degradation* of labor—a condition he believed was fostered by the steady deskilling of craftwork through laborsaving technologies and a pernicious sexual division of labor. Marglin (1974), Edwards (1979), and others also theorized about the growing loss of labor power in late twentieth-century capitalism and the increased encroachment of managerial control in both manufacturing and service organizations. In short, this theoretical orientation (which was eventually characterized as labor process theory) was basically concerned with control and resistance at the point of production (Jaros, 2000).

The decades that followed witnessed an outpouring of field studies that were undoubtedly inspired by this brand of theorizing. Broadly, these studies examined the actual micro-processes whereby managerial controls were implemented and then either accepted or resisted by workers. Although the favored method of data collection in this tradition is some form of observation (Barker, 1993; Buraowy, 1979; Martin, 1988), the use of in-depth interviews (Ezzamel & Willmott, 1998), some combination of both (Collinson, 1988; Gottfried, 1994), and the use of archival data (Stone, 1974; Tinker & Niemark, 1987) are also considered appropriate. What is most important is that the researcher gets behind organizational and workplace facades and identifies the real issues of control and exploitation that are at stake. A brief overview of some of the fieldwork in this tradition may be of use at this point.

Any discussion of fieldwork in the labor process tradition of historical materialism must necessarily include mention of Burawoy's (1979) participant observation of shopfloor lives in the engine division of a large Chicago-based multinational corporation. Burawoy spent extended periods of time in the factory as a participant observer, learning the work routines, doing some of the work itself, and becoming part of the wider shopfloor community. Burawoy's fundamental research question was very much driven by his historical materialist orientation. His intention was to ascertain how and why workers gave their *spontaneous consent* to the managerial regime of shopfloor relations and what implications this had for the workers themselves.

Based on close observation of himself and his fellow workers, Burawoy comes up with a complex answer to his original research question. He argues that the key to understanding the question of workers' consent is to be found in the phenomenon of "making out"—shopfloor activities that are similar to "games" that operators played with machines, with themselves, and with each other. These "games" had as their objective the accomplishment of specific production targets that earned workers a financial incentive. Burawoy shows in considerable detail how "making out" was in fact the central shopfloor activity around which the local culture developed. Eventually, the culture of making out obscured the more exploitative dimensions of shopfloor relations and generated consent to the social relations of production.

Burawoy's style of intensive local-level fieldwork conducted within a distinctly materialist framework has grown into a strong tradition attracting researchers who are interested in making connections between peoples' material circumstances and their workplace lives. Thompson's (1983) participant observation of a meatpacking plant is also concerned with workers' capacity to endure demeaning work and dead-end jobs. Thompson (1983) shows how workers enter into high-consumption patterns using their ability to purchase expensive items (because of relatively high wages) to maintain a sense of personal pride and dignity that are otherwise stripped away from them on a daily basis at work. Thompson also shows how this draws workers into a consumption trap, which in turn ensures their need for continuous employment at the meat factory. The factory, then, simultaneously becomes the source of alienation and personal pride, and is therefore impossible to escape.

In more recent years, labor process fieldwork has become increasingly preoccupied with worker *subjectivities* and issues of *identity*. Arguing that early labor process theorists presented an incomplete picture of subjectivity and an overly romanticized view of craftwork (Collinson, 1992), contemporary researchers have been trying to insert an awareness of identity into the existing materialist framework of class, exploitation, and contradiction. This emphasis on subjectivity and identity has brought *gender* closer to the forefront, making researchers more conscious of the gendered nature of labor process dynamics (Gottfried, 1994) and the role of gender ideologies (i.e., masculinity) in mediating workplace relations (Collinson, 1992).

Collinson's (1988; 1992) lengthy fieldwork was conducted in an English heavy-vehicle manufacturing company that had recently been taken over by an American firm. Collinson relied mainly on in-depth interviews with sixty-four workers in the plant. Most of the respondents were interviewed twice, and some were interviewed several times. The first round of interviews was relatively open-ended, and respondents were encouraged to talk about things they considered to be important at work. Collinson then used a series of re-peat interviews to develop a stronger research focus on workplace culture issues. His simultaneous informal observation of the plant provided him with a context against which the interviews were analyzed and interpreted. To de-velop an awareness of the context, he entered into group discussions on the shopfloor, in the canteen, and in the bus en route to work.

Collinson's study shows a class-consciousness and sensitivity to the ideologi-cal forces shaping worker subjectivities that are requirements of a well-crafted materialist project. By highlighting the contradictory and ambiguous nature of workers' identities and relationships, Collinson (1988; 1992) is able to explain the reproduction of vicious circles of elite control. While "making out" emerged as the central operating principle in Burawoy's shopfloor, *masculinity* turns out to be the dominant moment in Collinson's vehicle factory. As he vividly shows, work-ers frequently engaged in an aggressive form of humor that was simultaneously an expression of masculine identity and resistance to the tight managerial con-trols at work. Overall, his study helps us see the links between informal practices at work and individual subject positions, notably class and gender.

Many of the studies discussed here (Burawoy, 1979; Collinson, 1988; Thompson, 1983) draw substantially on the conventions of the ethnographic tradition—for instance, the cultivation of closeness to subjects, the researcher's own immersion in the workplace, and the insistent focus on local cultural practices. Yet, these more materialistic ethnographies pay significantly more attention to the *totality* of the situation, interpreting local cultural practices and subjective experiences within the context of class relations, ideological formations, and capitalist control. The research questions are typically de-signed to ascertain how managerial control techniques are continually ex-tended (Barker, 1993), how and why workers acquiesce to these controls (Burawoy, 1979; Collinson, 1992), and how they resist them (Martin, 1988; Gottfried, 1994). With the microdynamics of control and resistance taking center stage, some degree of personal observation (participant or otherwise) does appear to be crucial to this tradition. When researchers rely only on interviews (e.g., Ezzamel & Willmott, 1998), the richness of their narratives tends to be definitely compromised, and they are unable to make the kind of contextualized linkages between accounts (interviews) and everyday lifeworlds that are possible in a more traditional materialist ethnography.

All of these studies are concerned mainly with the subjective moments (Burawoy, 1979) of the labor process. Put differently, they are very much part of the phenomenological domain of historical materialism in their focus on alienation, ideology, and the local lifeworlds of oppressed groups. There is, however, a more objectivist subgenre in the labor process tradition itself that concentrates on analyzing the formal institutional and structural relations of capitalism from a more historical perspective. Strongly influenced by research orientations from economic history and political science, studies in this tradition examine archival records and a range of different documents. Katherine Stone's (1974) historical study of the development of labor market structures in the U.S. steel industry from 1890 to 1920 is an outstanding example of research in this tradition.

Stone's study is entirely archival. Her diverse information sources include official company histories, newspaper stories, autobiographies, government reports, collective agreements, vocational manuals, professional yearbooks, and scholarly articles on the steel industry. Employing a theoretical framework of class struggle and conflict, Stone's examination of diverse documents reveals how the American steel industry turned skilled contract workers into semiskilled wage employees, and how this in turn enabled them to introduce labor-saving technologies and to accommodate steel workers to new manufacturing conditions. In direct contrast to conventional accounts that treat industrial changes as part of "automatic" and predetermined technological innovations, Stone demonstrates how the managers of the steel companies actively prepared for and used the Homestead strike to break the power and autonomy wielded by skilled steelworkers over their immediate work processes. She is also able to show how many of the more commonplace employment structures that we routinely encounter today (e.g., job ladders, and employee stock plans) were introduced after the Homestead strike as techniques of accommodation to gain employee consent to the new and more unfavorable work conditions. In its own way, Stone's piece is a model of historical materialist work. Her theoretical framework is clearly drawn from Marxian ideas, but her actual empirical work is careful and methodical, and all of her claims are well supported by documentary evidence. True to the spirit of the materialist tradition, her work is both *historical* and meticulously *empiricist* in its use and collection of information.

Both the objective and subjective elements of historical materialism are evocatively captured in Bertaux and Bertaux-Wiame's (1981) elegant study of the survival of artisanal bakeries in contemporary industrial France. Their study is indeed an exemplar in this tradition, combining an extraordinary grasp of the subjective lifeworlds of artisanal bakers with an appreciation for the wider terrain of socioeconomic institutions. Bertaux and Bartaux-Wiame's

(1981) research was intended to ascertain how and why French artisanal bakeries had been able to withstand the onslaught of competition from the large industrial bakeries. They found the answer to this seemingly economistic and functionalist question in complex configurations of cultural mentalities, social traditions, and everyday material practices that comprise the bakers' lifeworlds. Their research was crafted out of a blend of *life-history methodology* and *archival* sources. Their principal sources of information were the life stories of approximately one hundred people engaged in artisanal baking in Paris and its suburbs, an industrial town in northern France, and a province in the Pyrennes.

Although the interviews were fairly open, they were nevertheless targeted toward the material side of the respondents' life trajectories. Questions dealt with class and family backgrounds, career opportunities, number of hours worked, and so on. According to the researchers, (1981), these life stories gave them a sense of the actual working conditions and baking practices, and were used to develop an image of the structure of the social relations of baking. As they put it, "We kept our attention focused not on the technique of observation itself (the interview guide) but beyond, on this level of social relations that we were trying to perceive and elucidate. And this meant actually that we never separated the moment of data collection from the moment of data analysis" (Bertaux & Bertaux-Wiame, 1981, 178).

Using central materialist concepts such as class struggle, ideology, and contradiction, the researchers arrived at an intriguing explanation, arguing that the family relations undergirding the artisanal bakery were at the core of its survival. In particular, they focused on the baker's wife as a key player in the enterprise's success. A second element of the artisanal bakery's success was also found in the class militancy (directed against the large industrial conglomerates) that found expression in the bakers' ethos of grinding hard work. Bertaux and Bertaux-Wiame's study is impressive on several counts. It takes the materialist stance on totality very seriously, painting a broad picture of bakers' work, lives, and social milieus. It also moves dialectically between the micro-practices at the bakeries themselves and wider social conditions, weaving a narrative that simultaneously incorporates the concepts of class, class struggle, material practices, and ideologies without losing sight of the bakers' humanity and dignity.

The Conflict Tradition

Labor process theory's emphasis on exploitation at the point of production inevitably inclines it toward a micro-level focus. A more macro-structural approach is favored by the conflict tradition, which looks at key actors, elite control strategies, societal coalitions, and institutional processes from a materialist standpoint of conflict, interests, and domination. Also referred to as *macro-historical sociology* (Collins, 1990), the conflict tradition begins with a view of society comprising groups (or classes) with conflicting interests, which compete over a multitude of material and symbolic resources. The main interest in this tradition lies in establishing how certain groups take control over key resources and preserve dominant positions in society (Baritz, 1964; Gouldner, 1954; Mills, 1956).

Although many of the researchers working in this tradition are influenced by key concepts within historical materialism, many of them have also borrowed heavily from the more critical writings of Max Weber (1968), notably his deep concerns over the *social consequences of capitalism.* Weber shared Marx's distrust of capitalism without his commitment to revolutionary struggle and the creation of the socialist world order. Thus, "the essence of the radical Weberians' position consists of a trenchant criticism of capitalism but without any associated commitment to its transcendence by another form of social organization" (Burrell & Morgan, 1979, 350). Furthermore, while conventional materialism focuses on domination and exploitation within the production processes of capitalism, Weber (1968) explores social domination within the *administrative* realms of capitalist society and proposes the "iron cage" as a metaphor for understanding the alienation caused by the structural instrumental rationality of contemporary bureaucratic organizations.

Weber and Marx's suspicion of institutional authority becomes the basis for many foundational texts in the conflict tradition. Some of these include C. Wright Mills's *The Power Elite* (1956), Loren Baritz's *The Servants of Power* (1974), Ralf Dahrendorf's *Class Conflict in Industrial Society* (1959), and Michael Mann's *The Sources of Social Power* (1986). To most of these writers, conflict groups in society are jointly generated by a scarcity of resources and the presence of authority structures (e.g., bureaucratic hierarchies). Different groups then resort to a number of measures (coercive, persuasive, etc.) to take possession over material resources and the sources of authority. To those working in the conflict tradition, it is precisely these measures that are of interest. Not surprisingly, the phenomena that are then subject to empirical study include social networks, social conflict, and the dynamics of institutionalization. Research questions in this tradition are likely to be about what interests motivate groups to form coalitions; how systems of elite networks exercise control over organizations and key institutions; how institutional practices are interpreted in keeping with specific interests; and how multiple interest groups come into conflict with each other in a number of public arenas.

Public and private organizations are extremely important objects of study in the conflict tradition. Organizations are simultaneously seen as key agents engaging in a range of interest-laden decisions, and contexts in which the dynamics of conflict are played out. Researchers look at a wide range of organizational phenomena, including the formation of business elite networks (Useem, 1979), accounting and public policy (Neu, 1992), the creation of interlocking directorates (Mizruchi & Stearns, 1988), the emergence of powerful managerial ideologies (Scott, 1992), and the history of corporate governance (Kaufman, Zacharias, & Karson, 1995; O'Connor, 2001).

A common feature of these studies is their strong dependence on archival sources and their tendency to take the historical element very seriously. Some of the studies focus on urgent contemporary questions, whereas others examine historical trends and patterns. A strong example of contemporary research is found in Neu's (1992) study of a new stock issue process in Ontario, Canada. Arguing that neither security legislation nor its interpretation by key institutional players is completely interest-free, Neu subjects a new stock issued by the Ontario exchange and its subsequent failure to close scrutiny. The study identifies different actors and their material interests, and traces the differential consequences of the stock's failure for multiple societal groups. Relying mainly on newspaper reports of the stock issue and failure, Neu (1992) first establishes the nonexistence of neutrality with respect to drafting the security legislation. He then demonstrates how influential actors (such as investment firms) proceed to "read" or interpret this regulatory text in a manner that is strongly consistent with their own interests. Ultimately, Neu's work unravels the nexus of interests that operate behind the apparently "free" forces of the market, and shows how the actions of intermediary institutions tend to privilege the interests of owner-managers over those of individual and small-time investors.

Other studies in this tradition emphasize the historical dimensions of organizational events and personalities, contextualizing them in the wider terrain of social relations and conflicts. Both Scott's (1992) remarkable examination of Chester Barnard's "classic" text, *The Functions of the Executive,* and O'Connor's (2001) discussion of Ordway Tead's writings on the necessity of democracy in industrial administration are exemplars in the historical materialist tradition. Both writers provide a historical understanding of the cultural context in which Barnard and Tead developed their ideas, and both of them also unearth the diverse interests and ideologies that played a prominent part in shaping these texts.

Scott (1992) sees Barnard's work as a reflection of specific class interests in the United States. He argues that the early twentieth century witnessed the rise of a new class—that is, a professional and managerial one that acquired a great deal of economic power but was still lacking in the legitimacy and moral authority that could justify its power. As Scott ably demonstrates, Chester

Barnard was fully cognizant of this issue and wrote a book that could become the moral voice of management. Based on a careful review of documents, Scott also identifies the institutional networks (e.g., the Harvard Circle) that simultaneously influenced Barnard's writing and were responsible for its enormous success.

In a similar fashion, O'Connor (2001) contextualizes Ordway Tead's work in the discourse of industrial democracy that was pervasive in America in the early part of the twentieth century. O'Connor's painstaking research reveals that Tead's writings were in many ways a response to the all-important questions of the day on the role of labor unions, especially in the aftermath of violent and bloody labor–management conflicts such as the International Workers of the World (IWW) strikes and the Ludlow massacre. O'Connor makes a convincing case that Tead's writings are best understood as an intervention in the ongoing debate about employee representation and collective bargaining.

In both Scott's (1992) and O'Connor's (2001) work, the texts that are central to the study are brought to life by an understanding of the events, ideologies, and conflicts of the period. They are models of the historical materialist tradition in their emphasis on the broader totality of social relations, in their consciousness of class interests and struggles, and in their unwavering attention to the material details of the period.

The conflict tradition has also yielded extensive historical works that examine different aspects of organizations and their complicated relationships with state and society. Two well-crafted pieces of work in this genre are Martin Sklar's (1988) *The Corporate Reconstruction of American Capitalism, 1890–1916,* and Kaufman, Zacharias, and Karson's (1995) *Managers vs. Owners.* Both studies engage in historical examinations of the business corporation's uneasy relationship with sacrosanct American ideals, including individual liberty, private property, and federalism, and work entirely with documentary sources. Kaufman et al. (1995) examine relevant court cases, corporate charters, law review journals, legal commentaries, public speeches, and academic writings over a period of one hundred and fifty years in order to trace (a) the social contest over the legal *identity* of the U.S. corporation, (b) the debates over corporate responsibility and accountability, (c) the restructuration of corporate governance, and (d) the institutionalization of management as a profession by the 1960s and the rise of managerial solidarity by the 1980s.

This particular subtradition of historical materialism differs quite sharply from the ethnographic research styles that are typically associated with qualitative work. The scope of the research is often quite ambitious, and the approach longitudinal and rigorously empirical in its search for recorded "facts" and documentary evidence. In sum, such work is predominantly influenced by the historical method. In fields like management and organization studies, such studies provide a much-needed macro-perspective for the micro-level studies that pervade it. Their value also lies in their ability to examine macro-structural features such as ideology, corporate governance, and group interests across clusters of organizations and over extended periods of time while still working with qualitative rather than statistical information.

Critiques and Debates in the Historical Materialist Tradition

Working in the historical materialist tradition poses a number of challenges. To begin with, the tradition itself is a demanding one, requiring mastery over many complex ideas and a willingness to engage in meticulous and rigorous empirical research. In addition, scholars in this tradition often have to *defend* their work against charges of orthodoxy, intellectual partisanship, and a blind adherence to Marxist doctrine. Is this a fair critique of the historical materialist tradition? And how can researchers doing historical materialist work respond to these critics?

Several issues are involved here. First, it must be remembered that historical materialism is not the only Western intellectual tradition to be firmly committed to basic assumptions about human nature, social interaction, and reality. Dramaturgists, ethnomethodologists, and semioticians (to name only a few) all hold unique ontological and epistemological positions that they do not easily relinquish no less than do historical materialists.[1] Historical materialism may also have come in for more of its fair share of attack following the development of a rigid Marxist orthodoxy in some social science disciplines in the second half of the twentieth century. However, as we have been at pains to point out, much of the *academic* tradition of historical materialism eschews party-line affiliations and selectively (rather than blindly) employs many Marxian concepts to enhance our understanding of conflict and domination in society. Seen in this context, historical materialists are no more dogmatic than many of their academic counterparts, including ethnomethodologists (who are firmly committed to indexicality) and semioticians (who firmly adhere to a grammatical understanding of social reality).

A second criticism concerns its alleged *defunct* nature. Especially after the collapse of the Soviet Union, many critics argue that historical materialism is completely outdated and is therefore of little use in understanding contemporary social arrangements. This critique is somewhat misplaced. As long as there are groups and classes in society, the materialist tradition is a source of multiple insights into the changing faces of domination. One could as easily argue that the demise of state-sponsored communism relieves historical materialism of any obligation to a narrow form of political ideology and allows it to engage more freely with its examination of power, conflict, and interests.

A third critique of historical materialism charges it with being a kind of conspiracy theory—one that interprets all actions and events as elements of a wider elite strategy toward securing total societal control. Again, this criticism somewhat overstates the case. Materialists do indeed subscribe to an interest-driven view of society. And many scholars in this tradition can see little else but interests and elite domination. Many others, however, recognize that interests themselves are complex, ambiguous, and unpredictable, and are mediated by other forces such as ideologies and cultural locations (e.g., Burawoy, 1979; Collinson, 1992; Martin, 1988). Even studies that portray encroaching managerial controls as relentless and inexorable (e.g., Barker, 1993; Stone, 1974) do so on the basis of recorded evidence and close observation, and do not simply pull these arguments out of thin air.

All of the critiques discussed so far are *external* critiques; that is, they emanate from outside the critical traditions. However, researchers also need to be aware of a number of *internal* debates and criticisms as well. These debates take place both within the materialist tradition as well as within the wider terrain of critical traditions. One long-standing issue has been the relative autonomy and importance accorded to the economic base over other elements of society. Somewhat ironically, materialists have been charged with being overly *materialistic* in the primacy they give to economic factors. This criticism can only be answered on a case-by-case basis. Some writings (e.g., Braverman himself) place a pronounced emphasis on wages, job insecurity, physical working conditions, tangible control systems, and other material aspects of work, organizations, and society. Many others, however, are noticeably more nuanced (Bertaux & Bertaux-Wiame, 1981; Collinson, 1992; Scott, 1992) in their explorations of how class struggles and exercises in domination intersect with cultural locations, identity formations, and personal affiliations. It would therefore be more accurate to say that an overly economistic form of reductionism is one of the *possible dangers* (rather than an absolute certainty) of working in the historical materialist tradition.

Different facets of historical materialism have also been periodically taken to task for their lack of sensitivity to gender issues—for what Wilson (1996) describes as their overwhelming *gender blindness* and for their continuing complicity in the *suppression* of gender issues in their research (Linstead, 2000).[2] Historical materialism also does not escape charges of Eurocentrism (Gandhi, 1998) and a tendency to overlook race (hooks, 1989) in its fixed commitment to frameworks of class. In other words, critics often hold that materialism's preoccupation with class is responsible for its failure to recognize other varieties of social struggles—especially those that are mediated by diverse social identities (e.g., race, ethnicity, etc.) and different historical experiences (e.g., slavery and colonialism).

Some critical researchers have also grown uneasy with historical materialism's tendency to privilege the *consciousness* of actors, especially manifest in its assumption that all actions that are not the product of rational calculation must be the result of ideological manipulation (Prasad & Prasad, 2001; Wray-Bliss, 2002). The problem here is with materialism's firm commitment to the *rational subject* and its concomitant inability to see forces that are neither purposively rational nor necessarily ideological. This line of critique is more in keeping with a discursive orientation and has spawned inquiry that is closer to poststructural and feminist traditions.

Notwithstanding its many critics, historical materialism has left an impressive legacy of scholarship dealing with different aspects of work, organizations, and institutional practices. Its historical awareness, its acknowledgment of interests and networks of power, and its faithful pursuit of empirical material all make it an insightful and exciting tradition to be working in. It is truly unfortunate that its roots in the writings of Marx are sometimes held against it, giving it a reputation (that is not entirely deserved) of extreme dogmatism and orthodoxy. In management and organization studies, its value lies precisely in the determination of its adherents to pursue goals of empowerment and human liberation while never deluding themselves about the more unsavory dynamics of control and exploitation.

Notes

1. The strong denunciation of historical materialism found in many academic circles is partly a result of the geopolitical conditions that prevailed right up to the end of the Cold War. Given its closeness to Marxian ideas, historical materialism came to be seen by some as an endorsement of Soviet-style social arrangements. As discussed earlier in the chapter, this was often not the case at all. However, this perception probably accounted for the tradition's greater academic marginalization in the United States (which was the Soviet Union's leading adversary) than in many other Western countries such as Great Britain, Israel, and Italy.

2. For an excellent internal critique of materialism's gender bias, see Wray-Bliss's (2002) close examination of this issue in the British labor process tradition. Wray-Bliss argues that even when gender is openly acknowledged as an important element of social relations, the actual representation of women research subjects continues to be deeply problematic.

Figure 8.1   **Highlights of the Historical Materialist Tradition**

Philosophic influences: Marxism, neo-Marxism, labor process theory

Major figures: Karl Marx, Friedrich Engels, Max Weber, Antonio Gramsci, Harry Braverman, Alvin Gouldner, Ralf Dahrendorf

Central concepts
- The dialectical method
- Base and superstructure
- Class and class analysis
- Alienation
- Contradiction

Key practices
- Employing a historical lens
- Placing all action in the context of class struggles and exploitation
- Close attention to material empirical conditions
- Tracing connections between structural and ideological elements

Exemplary rsearch
- "Artisanal Bakery in France" (Bertaux & Bertaux-Wiame, 1981)
- *Managing the Shopfloor* (Collinson, 1992)
- *Managers vs. Owners* (Kaufman, Zacharias, & Karson, 1995)
- "Back on the Way to Empowerment" (O'Connor, 2001)
- *Chester I. Barnard and the Guardians of the Managerial State* (Scott, 1992)

9

Critical Theory

Hegemony, Knowledge Production, and Communicative Action

Critical theory is the extraordinary intellectual product of despair and disappointment—despair over the frightening ascendancy of European fascism and Nazism; and disappointment with the excesses of Stalinist socialism and the cultural emptiness of prosperous high-consumption societies like the United States. Critical theory's institutional roots can be traced to the founding of the Institute of Social Research in Frankfurt (more popularly known as the Frankfurt School) in 1923 (Wiggershaus, 1994). The highly reputed original members of the Frankfurt School, notably Max Horkheimer, Theodore Adorno, Erich Fromm, and Herbert Marcuse (among others), were primary architects in the development of a systematic critique of social conditions, with the wider goal of *envisioning* and *implementing* a better (i.e., a more just, meaningful, and worthwhile) world (Kincheloe & Mclaren, 1994; Steffy & Grimes, 1986). With the demise of the Institute, their ideas were given a fresh lease of life by German philosopher Jurgen Habermas who invigorated many of the Frankfurt School's major theoretical contributions by giving them a new foundation in communication theory (Murray & Ozanne, 1991).

Before grappling with the intricacies of this tradition, we should observe that the term *critical theory* can be used in a broad as well as in a more specific sense. When used broadly, critical theory refers to a wide range of diverse but interrelated traditions that are united by an interest in *cultural critique*. The Frankfurt School, variants of neo-Marxism, postmodernism, radical feminism, and cultural studies, are frequently subsumed under this label. In this chapter, however, we will be using critical theory in a far more specific way—to refer to the tradition of social inquiry that has been primarily inspired by the work of the Frankfurt School and Jurgen Habermas.

Like many of the other critical traditions discussed in this book, critical theory is committed to the core emancipatory project of Marxian philosophy. At the same time, members of the Frankfurt School and their adherents have also been engaged in recovering many of Marx's more useful ideas from what they believe to be the poverty of excessive economic reductionism (Jay, 1973;

Murray & Ozanne, 1991). The critical theory tradition, therefore, emerges out of a *revision* of Marx's critique of capitalism and his theory of worker revolution with the intent of making it more relevant for an analysis of contemporary social and political conditions (Bronner & Kellner, 1989). It is important to note that the Frankfurt School did not ever speak with a single unified voice. Nor did any of its theorists claim to have developed a systematic approach to cultural criticism. In fact, the term *critical theory* itself was coined only in 1937 after the Institute and its members had been relocated to Columbia University in New York City (Bronner & Kellner, 1989).

In the Institute's early years, its members appeared most interested in theorizing the nature of aesthetics and the far-reaching effects of the culture industry. As Germany was hit by crisis after crisis (e.g., failed governments, social upheavals, galloping inflation, waves of anti-Semitism, Nazi ascendancy), the Institute and its (mostly Jewish) members were forced to flee the country and relocate themselves in New York. There, under conditions of exile, they began writing about the roots of fascism and the multiple socializing influences of key institutions (school and family) in facilitating the widespread acceptance of irrational and demanding forms of social and political authority (Adorno, 1969).

Once in America, many of the critical theorists experienced a severe sense of cultural alienation and revulsion toward the meaninglessness and over rationalization of a materially prosperous and modern society. Adorno, Fromm, Horkheimer, and Marcuse were also equally disturbed by what they perceived to be the *mindlessness* of American culture and the ease with which public opinion and behavior could be manipulated without the use of force and violence. Much of their work, therefore, was developed with the intent of engaging in *cultural critiques* that would raise fundamental concerns about the dysfunctional consequences of modernity (Adorno & Horkheimer, 1972; Horkheimer, 1947) and the loss of meaning in contemporary industrial societies (Fromm, 1955; Marcuse, 1964). Their collective efforts also represented attempts to unravel the interest-based nature of all knowledge and stressed the importance of creating an emancipatory knowledge that would be explicitly aimed at confronting and undermining social injustices. After World War II, most of the original Frankfurt School members returned to Germany, reopened the Institute, and continued working along these lines. Only Herbert Marcuse stayed on in the United States where he eventually became one of the more prominent intellectual heroes of the 1960s counterculture movements (Wiggershaus, 1994). Even the eventual death of the original critical theorists did not extinguish the tradition of cultural critique that they had so carefully nourished. Habermas (1972; 1976) has energetically continued the tradition by further developing critiques of rationality and expert knowledge systems. His work has exerted considerable influence on different academic fields ranging from public administration and sociology to political science and communication studies.

In sum, the critical theory tradition has held onto Marx's central vision of emancipation while moving away from a preoccupation with the economic base of society and structural arrangements. Instead, critical theorists have been far more concerned with ideology and compliance, themes stressed strongly in Marx's earlier writings. Indeed, it makes sense to assert that critical theory replaces historical materialism's emphasis on the *coercive* and directly *exploitative* facets of capitalism with its *ideological* and *hegemonic* ones. The distinction between coercion and hegemony is important for our purposes. Coercion refers to the direct use of force, intimidation, and pressure (including economic pressure) to ensure compliance, while hegemony (in this tradition) refers to the processes whereby individuals become willing accomplices in their own subjugation. This overwhelming concern with hegemony has resulted in a strong focus on understanding *cultural processes* over and beyond economic ones.

Through the work of Fromm (1955) and Marcuse (1964; 1966), critical theory also brought Freud and *psychoanalysis* into the domain of cultural critique. One could, in fact, easily argue that critical theory's affinity for psychoanalytic insights is one of its more distinctive features (Bronner & Kellner, 1989; Murray & Ozanne, 1991). Denial, regression, fantasy, and narcissism at the cultural level are among some of the psychological states examined by critical theorists in their efforts to comprehend widespread alienation and ideological manipulation. Another important break with historical materialism can be seen in critical theory's vision of revolutionary agents in contemporary societies. Critical theorists are less convinced of the revolutionary potential of the proletarian working class and more likely to see this potential in students, intellectuals, marginalized groups (e.g., African Americans), and peoples of the Third World.

Critical theory's rise to popularity in the West owes much to the *zeitgeist* of the 1960s and 1970s. Many of Marcuse's (1964), Fromm's (1955), and Horkheimer's (1947) ideas resonated strongly with the spirit of cultural rebellion and political disenchantment that was sweeping through much of Europe and North America. Books like Charles Reich's (1972) *The Greening of America,* Ivan Illich's (1973) *Tools for Conviviality,* and Theodore Roszak's (1969) *The Making of a Counter Culture* were bestsellers that popularized many central themes that had been expounded by critical theorists—notably the limits of science and technology, the dangers of excessive professionalism and bureaucracy, the patriarchal and racist tendencies of capitalist institutions, and our collective inability to lead ecologically and existentially meaningful lives under conditions of modernity and economic prosperity.

Critical theory's presence in the public mindset has been rivaled by its growing influence in different academic fields. In education, critical theory has left a lasting and powerful legacy through Paolo Friere's (1970) classic denunciation of modern education as a system that has created a population of passive individuals capable only of *receiving* knowledge in his much celebrated work, *The Pedagogy of the Oppressed*. In North America, Henri Grioux (1983) keeps alive the critical traditions in his conceptualization of schools as sites of resistance and democratic possibilities. Critical theory's distinct presence can also be felt in sociology (Burris, 1989), public administration (Denhardt, 1981), consumer research (Murray & Ozanne, 1991), communication studies (Deetz, 1992), accounting (Power, 1996), and organization studies (Alvesson, 1987; Steffy & Grimes, 1986). In all of these fields, critical theorists have pursued thoughtful and sustained critiques of organizations, institutional arrangements, social habits, and professional mindsets. They have also systematically rejected a value-neutral position, and they conduct research that aims openly at meeting the goals of human liberation and social justice.

The Philosophy of Critical Theory

Many of the Frankfurt School's more enduring contributions were born out of a series of philosophic dialogues with the work of prominent European thinkers, notably Kant, Hegel, Weber, Marx, and Freud. It could easily be argued that critical theory synthesized the ideas of key phenomenologists and made them a more central part of the Marxian emancipatory project. What the Frankfurt School really did was to privilege the more *subjective* elements of Marx's writings at the expense (some might argue) of his more materialist concerns. The early critical theorists were also strongly drawn to Hungarian philosopher and revisionist Marxist Georg Lukacs whose classic work, *History and Class Consciousness* (1923), served as a major source of inspiration for their discussions of totality and ideology-critique.

If there is one single concept that is emblematic of the critical theory tradition, it would be that of *ideology-critique*—the incessant and systematic critique of ideological forces in every aspect of social life (Held, 1980). To both Habermas and members of the Frankfurt School, our acceptance of many of the more undesirable and even authoritarian features of capitalism, socialism, and fascism can be explained only by the power of ideology. Within the critical theory tradition, ideology refers to all systematically distorted accounts of reality (Habermas, 1972) that both *conceal* and *legitimate* social asymmetries and injustices. Critical theory aims at piercing these ideological veils in all walks of life—in government, public policy, law, science, education, managerial practices, media, entertainment, and even the family itself. Its ultimate goal is an enhanced public awareness of the sources of domination and a subversion of ideological forces that will jointly initiate fundamental changes in consciousness and power (Held, 1980).

In ideology-critique, critical theory has found a powerful analytic lens that can be turned relentlessly on virtually every aspect of contemporary culture and society. The founding members of the Frankfurt School, Habermas, and innumerable more recent adherents have subjected such varied domains as science and technical expertise, mass communication, knowledge production, sexuality, and alienation to ideology-critique. This section briefly discusses some of the substantive areas covered by critical theory.

The Analysis of the Culture Industry

The growing influence of the mass media over the cultural spheres of society has always been a central concern of critical theorists. In their classic work, *Dialectic of Enlightenment,* Adorno and Horkheimer (1972) express their anxiety over the increased encroachment of mass communication (e.g., radio, television, newspapers) into individual consciousness. In this and other writings, they call not only for an understanding of the working of the media, but also for a grasp of the media's control over segments of cultural consumption—especially music, drama, film, and art. At the heart of Adorno and Horkheimer's critique is a deep concern about the effects of the entertainment industry, and especially its capacity to manipulate culture equally well under conditions of authoritarianism (e.g., Nazi Germany) and free enterprise (e.g., the United States).

Although such critical analyses of the mass media are entirely commonplace today, much of this work is deeply indebted to the ideas generated by the Frankfurt School, which was nothing less than a pioneer in this field. Indeed, the critical theory tradition is largely responsible for building a philosophic framework that combines a theory of ideology with a theory of aesthetic, which can be fruitfully applied to study vehicles of mass communication (Held, 1980). Adorno's (1991) work in particular alerts us to the consequences of the commodification of art in contemporary society. Adorno believes that authentic art, or what he terms, *autonomous art,* is always fundamentally subversive because it negates reified consciousness and offers unexpected alternative possibilities. The culture industry, however, dilutes both of these functions by distancing art from its context and putting it on display solely for *commercial purposes* (Adorno, 1991). Elements of pride and rebelliousness that are integral components of many traditional folksongs, for example, disappear when the songs are performed in an "artificial" setting for audiences who pay mainly for the *pleasure* of hearing them. Similarly, original messages of irony and dissent can be lost when the Impressionist paintings of Claude Monet are exhibited in the Louvre, and when countless reproductions are sold to tourists in museum shops and trendy art galleries. Adorno's (1991) critique is substantially focused on the logic of commercial entertainment, which inevitably produces passive and uncritical consumers (rather than participants) of culture. At the heart of his critiques lies a deep sense of loss over the spontaneity and authenticity of art forms that occurs when *commodification* takes place.

These expositions on the culture industry have exerted a strong influence on the field of communication and media studies where writers from Vance Packard (1957) to Todd Gitlin (1983) have subjected the daily work of the media to ideology-critique. These influences have been particularly strong in critical studies of consumption and advertising in contemporary societies (Ewen, 1976; Jhally, 1987).

Value-Laden Science and Knowledge Production

One of the more striking characteristics of the critical theory tradition is its *axiological* approach to knowledge creation in the social sciences. To begin with, critical theorists do not treat knowledge as *neutral information.* Nor do they believe that it is possible to separate knowledge from individual and wider societal interests (Craib, 1992; Murray & Ozanne, 1991). In short, critical theorists accept the idea that all knowledge creation (i.e., economics, psychology, management theory) is mediated by power relations that are socially and historically constituted (Kincheloe & McLaren, 1994). Based on these assumptions, critical theory also insists that researchers need to be conscious of the values and interests underpinning their own scholarship, and further, that they should commit their own work to the cause of confronting the many injustices and oppressive practices that pervade contemporary societies. "Whereas traditional researchers cling to the guard rail of neutrality, critical researchers frequently announce their partisanship in the struggle for a better world" (Kincheloe & McLaren, 1994, 140).

It is this approach to formal knowledge that is appropriately labeled as *critical*—in that it refuses to take knowledge claims at their face value; relentlessly interrogates all bodies of knowledge to unearth the interests shaping them; and is committed to creating knowledge that is explicitly intended for emancipatory purposes. Many variants of the critical theory tradition also pay close attention to the *processes* whereby knowledge itself is created, asserting that the most useful and liberating forms of knowledge are those that are produced out of *dialogues* between multiple social constituencies. By contrast, knowledge that is imposed upon a passive population by scientists, academics, and other so-called experts cannot have the same local relevance. This emphasis on conversation and engagement is responsible for the development of a social science methodology most commonly referred to as *participatory research* (Freire, 1970), which takes very seriously the involvement of research "subjects" in all phases of social inquiry—research design, information gathering, and implementation.

Critical theory's skepticism about expertise is also reflected in Habermas's (1972) concerns about the heightened professionalization of many forms of knowledge today. In particular, he seriously questions our increased tendency to define everyday practical problems (e.g., environmental degradation, unemployment, racial discrimination) as *sociotechnical* malfunctions that can be solved only by qualified and credentialed experts. According to Habermas, this highjacking of routine problem solving by technical experts has some serious and undemocratic ramifications for society.

This is because expert knowledge often *mystifies* problems and their possible resolutions by codifying them into scientific and mathematical models, and by translating them into the complex languages of biology, economics, and so on. Unemployment is a good example of this tendency—whereby a problem resolution that could benefit from the input of local communities is taken over by experts (mainly economists and policy analysts) and is reformulated in a highly technical and scientific language that is not easily accessible to the very people who are most affected by it. To Habermas, this kind of expert knowledge is frequently responsible for what he calls *distorted communication*—the prevention of free and equal forms of dialogue and information exchange. Here again, the role of the critical theorist is to question the communicative value of expert knowledge and to replace it (whenever possible) with participative forms of knowledge creation and problem solving.

The Social Psychology of Domination

A major goal of the Frankfurt School was an understanding of the vulnerability of Western democracies to totalitarian and authoritarian influences.[1] Over the years, critical theorists have also incorporated psychological factors into their explanations of this phenomenon. They believed that the problem had its roots in the increasing and pervasive alienation found across much of Western society, stemming in substantial part from the oppressive conditions of industrial work (Fromm, 1955). Although alienation among blue-collar workers is caused mainly by unemployment and a growing sense of worthlessness, it is a far more complex phenomenon among white-collar workers and professionals such as administrators, salespeople, bureaucrats, and middle managers (Baritz, 1990; Marcuse, 1964). Contrary to popular belief, office work does not require much by way of technical skills and expertise. What it does call for are personality skills—an ability to please bosses and customers, to be flexible, and to network with colleagues and superiors (Baritz, 1990), all of which are (in the long run) demeaning to the self, especially the masculine one.

In many contemporary industrialized societies, this powerlessness at work is further compounded by a loss of control and authority over the family where children have a greater voice on many issues and are less reliant on their parents as sources of influence. Furthermore, the state and corporations have been steadily appropriating many traditional parental functions relating to the schooling, health, and recreation of children (Lasch, 1977). The result is a deeply *emasculated* male population that is bereft of legitimate authority in two major spheres—home and work. It is this group that then becomes most vulnerable to the charismatic appeal of chauvinistic movements whose authoritarian structures restore a sense of stability, and whose messages of hatred compensate for feelings of low self-worth.[2]

Central Concepts in Critical Theory

As highlighted earlier, the critical theory tradition is best understood as an amalgamation of diverse ideas and theories that are all oriented toward cultural critique—of modernity, science, technology, mass culture, and sexuality. Prominent individual thinkers associated with this tradition commented on different aspects of contemporary society. Adorno, for instance, was most concerned with the relationship between the culture industries and the formation of aesthetic judgment; Horkheimer wrote extensively on the perils of modernity; Fromm and Marcuse developed elaborate theories of alienation combining the insights of Marx and Freud; and Habermas has been most preoccupied with the social processes of reaching democratic consensus. All major thinkers in this tradition also shared a belief in the need for *scholarly praxis* and the constant need for ideology-critique. Beyond this, they were mostly interested in pursuing their own preferred lines of inquiry rather than contributing to some formal common body of work. In this process, they have left us a legacy of several incisive concepts that sometimes overlap with one another.

Instrumental Reason

Adorno and Horkeimer's (1972) concept of *instrumental reason* is among the more evocative and radical contributions of critical theory. Instrumental reason is a particular logic of thought and way of seeing the world that is actually born out of the philosophy of the *Enlightenment* and has come to gradually dominate all modes of social interactions and relationships (Craib, 1992). Instrumental reason arose out of the Enlightenment's tendency to *objectify* and *instrumentalize* all natural phenomena as part of the much-vaunted "scientific" attitude that regards all elements of the natural world as raw material to be worked upon for the attainment of individual human ends (Adorno & Horkheimer, 1972). From this position, a tree, for instance, would be *primarily* regarded as a source of timber or some other utilitarian purpose rather than being seen as a thing of beauty or a part of divine nature.

For Adorno and Horkheimer (1972), the main problem with instrumental reason is its spillover into innumerable spheres of social life where people and social relationships are also approached in a similarly instrumental fashion. This theme has also been developed by Fromm (1955) in his discussion of alienation. For Fromm, people lose much of their sense of self-worth because they are valued more for their material accomplishments—such as job, social position, salary, and career mobility—than for their integrity, sense of humor, emotional warmth, and so on. Instrumental reason is thus rooted in a fundamentally *calculative* stance that becomes incapable of envisioning a world outside strictly utilitarian principles.

Instrumental reason has much in common with the Marxian concept of commodity fetishism but identifies the sources of this condition in the philosophy of the Enlightenment rather than in capitalist modes of production. As such, critical theory turns into a more radical critique of *modernity* that it regards as being responsible for different forms of totalitarianism (e.g., fascism and Soviet-style communism), the excesses of late twentieth-century capitalism, and even colossal inhuman acts such as the Holocaust (Bauman, 1989).

According to critical theorists, instrumental reason also instigates a view of knowledge as being concerned mainly with narrow problem solving and functionality. This mindset is also referred to as *technocratic consciousness* (Alvesson, 1987) and regards knowledge as little more than a *means* to an end as opposed to knowledge itself as a way of life. A further critique of instrumental reason is that it converts entire fields and disciplines such as philosophy, linguistics, and mathematics into little more than handmaidens or "underlaborers" of directly applied disciplines such as computer science (Craib, 1992). In short, instrumental reason produces a cultural view of formal knowledge as being (a) detached from everyday human existence and (b) intended to *control* nature, people, and social arrangements.

Critical theorists have also deplored the way in which instrumental reason has shaped our collective beliefs about science as a completely *value-neutral* activity that should not in any way be contaminated by wider social beliefs. It is this spirit of instrumental reason that encourages economists to build models advocating specific levels of unemployment that are based on economic principles, and are completely blind to the poverty and suffering caused by them. In this case (as in many others as well), instrumental reason instigates the conceptualization of the economy as an *abstraction* instead of something that is part of the reality of lived subjective experience.

One-Dimensional Culture

Although the term *one-dimensional man* is rightly equated with Marcuse's (1964) stirring exposition on alienation in modern societies, Marcuse's ideas on the destruction of alternative modes of thoughts and being by industrial capitalism resonate with some of Adorno and Horkheimer's (1972) discussions as well. Marcuse's dystopian analysis describes a world in which technology and instrumental rationality integrates and absorbs all forces of opposition to such an extent that the possibility of subjective clashes between (a) individuals and society and (b) between classes vanishes, while the reality of exploitation and injustice actually intensifies (Bronner & Kellner, 1989). Marcuse's (1964) central argument is that industrial capitalism with its accompanying philosophy of positivism is responsible for the transformation of the natural world into a *technical world* where technology reigns supreme and increasingly subjugates the subjective world of emotions and lived reality to its technical concerns. What was formerly a two-dimensional world of subject and object is increasingly being turned into a one-dimensional one where only the object prevails. As Marcuse (1989, 122) himself argues:

> Man can no longer exist in two dimensions; he has become a one-dimensional man. There is now one dimension of reality which is, in the strictest sense of the word, a reality without substance, or rather a reality in which substance is represented by its *technical form* which becomes its content, its essence. Every signification, every proposition is validated only within the framework of the behavior of men and things—a one-dimensional context of efficient, theoretical and practical operations. [emphasis added]

It is this one-dimensionality of society that is profoundly ideological and badly in need of sustained critique. One-dimensionality is also fostered by the extraordinary levels of *standardization* found everywhere. Adorno (1991) added an interesting psychological twist here by identifying the frightening levels of insecurity created by capitalism (through heightened economic mobility, the breakup of the extended family, and so on). Standardization in virtually all walks of life—home appliances, primary education, soap operas, health care, banking, and insurance—is capitalism's response to this anxiety.

Standardization restores a false sense of security by emphasizing the familiar and removing the unexpected. Standardized products, however, often provide an illusion of individuality by giving the impression that individuals have freedom and choice in consumption, when in reality most products, services, and life experiences have become uniform and regulated.

For Marcuse and other critical theorists, the one-dimensionality of contemporary cultures is clearly substantively propelled by the ubiquitousness of consumption, which turns people and experiences into commodities. Marcuse's (1964; 1966) discussion of contemporary sexuality also illustrates the pervasiveness of this consumerist impulse. In the consumer-oriented cultures of late capitalism, the pursuit of pleasure is not only more acceptable, it is something we are all actively encouraged to engage in and spend money on. Sex (as a pleasurable activity) becomes more permissive and is brought out more into the open. As Marcuse (1964) observes, books and films grow more openly *erotic*, and sex gradually replaces religion as the "opium of the masses." Marcuse's astuteness lies in his observation that contemporary sexual promiscuity and adventuring should be understood as neither liberationary nor sinful, but as yet another element of the commodification impulse. In such a climate, sexual partners are encouraged to value sexual technique, gratification, and pleasure over and above loyalty and commitment. Sexual partners become more and more *interchangeable,* marriages lose their semipermanent character, and peoples' overall commitment to relationships, family, and home declines to be replaced by an endless search for sexual excitement. When this happens, peoples' allegiance to work and career also increases. This new sexuality, according to Marcuse, is extremely convenient for industrial employers who can demand greater time and effort at work, and is therefore in keeping with the one-dimensional logic of late capitalism.

Communicative Action

The theory of communicative action has been developed by Habermas (1984) in an effort to escape from the philosophy of consciousness and to ground critical theory in an analysis of language use (May, 1996). Although Habermas has been as concerned as other major critical theorists with the problems of technocratic consciousness and what he calls the increasing "colonization of the life-world," his more recent project has been the development of a theory of *communicative action* that is linguistically based and that is intended to overcome some of the bleakness of earlier critical theorists.

The theory of communicative action emerges out of Habermas's (1984) proposition that to be human is to communicate, and, further, that embedded in communication is the ideal of *genuine consensus*. Habermas arrived at this thesis by arguing that societies themselves are created out of and maintained by the *coordinated activities* of its members (May, 1996). This coordination, moreover, is the product of *communication,* which at specific points needs to be geared toward agreement, understanding, and consensus if society is to be accomplished in any form at all. Consensus is thus certainly a cornerstone in Habermas's theory of human communication and society.

To be effective and ethical, this consensus has to be arrived at under conditions of *rationality* and *equality.* Indeed, Habermas consistently emphasizes the importance of rationally driven consensus in all social processes. It is imperative that social agreements be arrived at rationally, discursively, and completely free of coercion and manipulation. When this takes place, we have what Habermas terms an *ideal speech community*—something that is absolutely indispensable to a functioning civilized society (Habermas, 1984).

In an ideal speech situation, all individuals have an equal right to enter the discussion, and there are no hidden motives or self-deceptions that might affect the process or outcome of these discussions (Baert, 1998). In theory, an ideal speech situation ensures authentic representation, freedom of voice, and the rational evaluation of options. Habermas strongly advocates striving for an ideal speech community in every possible communicative situation involving speech, writing, conversation, interviews, and so forth. Organizational meetings, performance appraisal interviews, counseling sessions, and business–government roundtables (to name a few) are all situations of ongoing communicative action. These ideas therefore bring critical theory quite directly into the realm of work and organizations.

Systematically Distorted Communication

Central to Habermas's (1984) concept of the ideal speech community are conditions of undistorted communication. As Habermas himself notes, most social situations are, unfortunately, more likely to be characterized by *distorted* communication. Distorted communication takes place whenever authentic and meaningful conversations are precluded and whenever any of the conditions of the ideal speech community are violated (Deetz, 1992). However, it is important to note that Habermas is most concerned with *systematically* distorted communication rather than with any form of distorted communication. Many distortions in communication can occur because of confusion among some individuals about the meaning of a message, or because messages are poorly crafted and do not represent the author's ideas accurately. Such distortions are more idiosyncratic than systematic—stemming from the peculiarities of individuals and their mutual interactions.

Deetz (1992, 187) describes systematically distorted communication as "an ongoing process within particular systems as they strategically (though latently) work to reproduce, rather than produce, themselves. . . . In this form they translate all back to their own conceptual relations, thus precluding alternative discourses or conflicts with contrary institutional interpretive schemes." It is important to appreciate that systematically distorted communication is not something that is merely deceptive or illusory, but is inscribed in the materiality of social and institutional practice (Kincheloe & McLaren, 1994) and is always mediated by power relations.

Systematically distorted communication is typically sustained by processes of discursive closure (Deetz, 1992). Discursive closure is a way of shutting down opposing views, thwarting public explorations of controversy, and inhibiting genuine dialogue without giving the appearance of doing so. Closure is also made possible by privileging certain discourses over others and marginalizing some discourses (Alvesson & Deetz, 2000). Dismissing varieties of qualitative research as merely *anecdotal* is an example of discursive closure whereby all debates and discussions are shut down because of a single sweeping indictment. Deetz (1992) expands on some of the more common strategies of discursive closure. These include disqualification, naturalization, topical avoidance, and pacification. These strategies often aid in the manufacture of consent to various social arrangements by constituencies who may not always act in their own best interests.

Discursive closure can take place in any communicative act—including board meetings, public announcements, focus group meetings, workshops, and employee counseling sessions. The exclusion of serious alternative views in the discourse of environmental management is a good example of systematically distorted communication. The discursive domain of environmental management is dominated by managerialist and corporatist voices that systematically exclude alternative opinions by constituting them as radical, naïve, ideologically partisan, or conflict oriented (Prasad & Elmes, 2005). The point here, however, is that this discursive exclusion is accomplished by subtle moves to delegitimize alternative positions rather than by crude forms of visible coercion. Discursive closure becomes a powerful way of distorting communication in multiple private and public realms, and is therefore an important target of critical social inquiry.

Working in the Critical Theory Tradition

Critical theory has claimed a great deal of attention in management and organization studies and related fields, but this interest is largely at the conceptual rather than at the empirical level. The huge outpouring of work on critical theory is oriented mainly toward introducing its central concepts (Kincheloe

& McLaren, 1994; Steffy & Grimes, 1986), discussing its methodological pillars (Forester, 1983; 1992), and highlighting its applicability for the study of management, accounting, information systems, and consumer research (Alvesson & Deetz, 2000; Lyytinen, 1992; Morgan, 1992; Murray & Ozanne, 1991; Power & Laughlin, 1992). In addition, several essays take critical theory as a philosophic starting point to comment on contemporary managerial and organizational practices (Deetz, 1992; Prasad & Prasad, 1993; Willmott, 1984) without actually engaging in what might be conventionally regarded as systematic fieldwork.[3] When researchers do engage in fieldwork, they tend to be influenced mostly by the latter-day critical theory of Habermas (i.e., the theory of communicative action) and are less interested in the social psychology of domination proposed by the early Frankfurt School. One could therefore agree with Alvesson and Deetz (2000) that the critical theory tradition is somewhat underexploited in management and organization studies.

In essence, working in the critical theory tradition requires combining a phenomenological stance with a commitment to social critique and praxis. Critical theory is as much invested in exploring subjective lifeworlds as any interpretive tradition, but brings a critical edge and an ethical tone to its analysis. It is possible, therefore, to blend specific interpretive traditions with critical theory, resulting in synergistic and vibrant hybrid traditions such as critical ethnography (Kunda, 1992; Rosen & Astley, 1988) and critical hermeneutics (Prasad & Mir, 2002). Some commentators like Comstock (1982) argue that working in the critical theory tradition requires following a five-step process that guides the design, implementation, and analysis of the research project.

The first step is *interpretive*—calling for an endogenic understanding of different stakeholders' lifeworlds in whatever situation is being studied. Critical theory also stresses the importance of dialogue (between researcher and subjects) in arriving at this interpretive understanding of individuals and groups in (preferably) their natural settings. The second step calls for an understanding of the relevant *sociocultural structures* and processes that may mediate and constrain peoples' subjective understandings.[4] The third step combines input from the first two steps into a single analysis that juxtaposes social actors' subjective interpretations with existing sociocultural structures. This is the moment of *ideology-critique* where the researcher actively looks for inconsistencies, contradictions, distortions, and asymmetries.

Although most research in the critical theory tradition stops short at this step, Comstock (1982) insists that critical researchers embark on two further steps. The fourth step is the *awareness* or participative step when the researcher shares his or her scholarly interpretations with different actors in an effort to provide them with a narrative that may be potentially empowering in developing alternative practices and social arrangements. The last step is that of *praxis* when the researcher helps actors develop a critically grounded program of action designed to change many of their own immediate conditions with a view to ensuring social justice (Comstock, 1982).

Other commentators such as Alvesson and Deetz (2000) have also insisted that working in the critical theory tradition calls for a high level of *language sensitivity.* This refers to an acknowledgment (in the research process) of the complexity and ambiguity of language, and recognition of language use as *action* needing to be understood in its local context rather than as a carrier of abstract information to be evaluated against some so-called factual reality.

Research in the critical theory tradition tends to follow one of two paths—engaging with texts and archival material, or studying ongoing situations and events. Critical researchers following the first path are usually inspired by Habermas and Ricoeur and are most closely aligned with the tradition of critical hermeneutics. Those electing to observe ongoing events are best described as critical ethnographers. These individuals broadly follow the contours of classical ethnography but bring a distinctly critical edge in their conceptualizations of the research problem and in their formulation of research questions. Both critical hermeneuticians and critical ethnographers are substantially influenced by critical theory, which they artfully blend with specific interpretive traditions.[5] In this chapter we will be focusing more on critical ethnography since critical hermeneutics has already been covered in considerable depth in Chapter 3.

Ethnography in the critical theory tradition is deeply concerned with the colonization of our lifeworlds. This refers to the takeover by corporations and the state of our consciousness at work, at play, in the home, in neighborhoods, health care, the news media and the like, and their transformations into objectified one-dimensional realities. Critical ethnographers subject different elements of our lifeworlds to careful scrutiny with the help of ideology-critique. They examine phenomena such as the absence of ethics in managerial decision making (Jackall, 1988), corporate ceremonial events (Rosen, 1988; Rosen & Astley, 1988), and a communication skills training program (Elmes & Costello, 1992), with a view to unearthing the systematically distorted communication patterns that pervade them.

Perhaps the critical ethnography *par excellence* is Robert Jackall's (1988) *Moral Mazes*—an intensive exploration of the routine world in which American managers make decisions with ethical consequences. Based on a number of case studies in corporations and interviews with managers, Jackall examines the "moral rules-in-use" that managers construct to guide their behavior at work. In accordance with the critical theory tradition, Jackall's (1988) inquiry begins with an interpretive agenda: to arrive at an understanding of managers' subjective lifeworlds that he finds to be of a nexus of career aspirations, circles of affiliation, hierarchical anxieties, and a zest for efficient action. In addition, as he notes (p. 56), it is "a world geared towards pragmatic accomplishments [that] places a great premium on the appearance of buoyant optimism."

In crafting a piece of work along critical lines, Jackall scrupulously examines the social structures (Comstock, 1982) of managerial work, which he argues creates an intricate chain of commitments throughout most organizations, which in turn engender a culture of intense fealty to one's immediate boss or supervisor. With the help of innumerable incidents from his fieldwork, Jackall then shows us how these patterns of fealty mediate everyday managerial decision making even in areas where individual reflection would be desirable. By juxtaposing the subjective lifeworlds of managers with the social structures of management, Jackall reveals *how* bureaucracy shapes moral consciousness at work. Jackall's critique of managerial decision making does not blame or fault individual managers for their indifference to matters of ethics, but focuses instead on *systemic* cultural elements such as the ethos of managerialism and the ideology of instrumentalism that shape the lifeworlds and identities of American managers. As he also points out, "the manager, alert to expediency learns to appraise all situations and all other people as he comes to see himself—as an object, a commodity, something to be scrutinized, rearranged, tinkered with, packaged, advertised and sold"(Jackall, 1988, 119).

Like ethnographers, critical theorists have a tremendous appreciation for the extraordinary *richness* of ordinary life and action. As Forester (1992, 47) notes, "what passes for 'ordinary work' in professional bureaucratic settings is a thickly layered texture of political struggles concerning power and authority, cultural negotiations over identities and social constructions of the 'problems at hand.'" These researchers are ethnographic in their empirical and phenomenological sensibilities and critical in their focus on relations of power, hegemonies, and their adverse consequences. In sum, this tradition of scholarly inquiry, which Forester (1992) characterizes as "fieldwork in a Habermasian way," is very much concerned with the ideological elements of culture in various institutional settings.

Two field studies that exemplify the spirit of this tradition will be discussed here. The first is a study of a communication skills workshop by Elmes and Costello (1992), and the second is a study of a corporate Christmas party by Rosen and Astley (1988). Both studies reveal the hidden distortions that pervade organizational dynamics, and use simple bureaucratic interactions as windows through which complex ideological forces and power relations can be viewed. Elmes and Costello (1992) focus on the *mystification* of power in a skills workshop, whereas Rosen and Astley (1988) dwell on the *obfuscation* of power dynamics in a ceremonial event. Both mystification and obfuscation are central to the notion of systematically distorted communication. Elmes and Costello define mystification as the art of manipulating others' experiences without being perceived as doing so. To Rosen and Astley, obfuscation occurs when any single principle of social organization such as efficiency or the profit principle is perceived as a concrete reality and begins to overshadow all subjective experiences.

Elmes and Costello (1992) studied ABC, a small but successful management training organization, operating all over the United States and serving a number of Fortune 500 firms. Both researchers were participant observers of a four-day management communication skills seminar and followed their observation with informal interviews of workshop participants, trainers, and owners of the company. In addition, one of the researchers had also been employed as a trainer in the organization, leading to a wider contextual understanding of the firm itself. In approaching the communication skills training seminar, Elmes and Costello conceptualized it as a *social drama*—a concept developed by Victor Turner (1969) to refer to ceremonies and events that partially suspend or unfreeze normal structural relationships and engineer a new "consensus" that is congruent with the dominant ideology. Elmes and Costello posit that ABC's ultimate goal was one of *converting* participants to a "skills" paradigm of interpersonal communication. The workshop itself can then be seen as a social drama engineered for that purpose.

Their study details some of the ways in which this conversion process is accomplished. They show how the company produces an impressive aura in the first place through a number of symbolic acts of communication. These include strategic placement of the founder's book on effective communication in the foyer, use of state-of-the-art communication technologies in the training sessions, and orchestration of a ritual ceremony on the last day of the workshop that included champagne in crystal glasses. The creation of such an aura was key to building the company's credibility in the eyes of the participants/customers and made the job of conversion that much easier. Elmes and Costello also discuss a number of other strategies used to facilitate conversion. One of the more noteworthy strategies was the elicitation of public testimonials throughout the workshop. Public testimonials were solicited by trainers in the form of input and feedback from the participants about the workshop itself. This was always done publicly and placed considerable pressure on the participants to come up with positive responses. This was one way in which a consensus about the value of skills communication was created.

Michael Rosen (Rosen, 1988; Rosen & Astley, 1988) conducted a critical ethnography (lasting approximately ten months) of an advertising agency. In that time, he was first assigned to a specific organizational member and later rotated throughout the agency through different departmental and hierarchical levels. He became very much a part of the organization, attending business meetings, following phone conversations, playing on the agency's intramural softball team, and lunching regularly with various members of the organization (Rosen, 1988). In the pieces discussed here, the focus is on the annual Christmas party as a ceremonial and ritual event that masks powerful mechanisms of social control. Like Elmes and Costello, Rosen and Astley also use the concept of the *social drama* as a conceptual scheme. The social drama is a state in which there is at least a partial suspension of normal structural relationships. Relying on Turner (1969), Rosen and Astley argue that the social drama creates a space for new interpretations and reinterpretations of social reality, and is therefore often used to engineer a favorable consensus about the forms of domination.

Every aspect of the party is scrutinized for its symbolic communication—the clothes worn by the employees (dressy) versus those worn by the bosses (casual); the physical layout of the setting; the kinds of social interaction taking place; the public joking directed against management; the dancing in which employees participate; and the skits mocking the culture of the agency. By analyzing each of these elements, Rosen and Astley (1988) show how the party itself is constituted (by management) as a *ludic space* in which people eat, drink, dance, and laugh together in order to maintain a sense of *community* within the organization. However, as they also assert, the seeming freedom and informality masks and even reproduces the bureaucratic status quo. The jokes (ethnic and sexual) against top management are tolerated only because they are of a fleeting and temporary nature, the differences in dress recall those in hierarchy (albeit in an inverted fashion), and the exclusion of employees' spouses from the event reaffirms the premise that work at the agency constitutes a major part of the employees' lives and that everybody's friends are to be found at work. In essence, the party confirms the legitimacy of the bureaucratic ethos even while celebrating freedom and appearing (in the skits and jokes) to mock the absurdities of the organization's demands. As Rosen (1988, 478) emphasizes, "In order for the Christmas party to be operationally efficacious, it is not necessary that come Monday morning the members of Shoenman & Associates [the agency] behave differently from the previous Thursday or Friday, or week or month before. Indeed it is important that they remain the same, reproducing the order that is Shoenman & Associates in the face of change."

It should be clear by now that crafting research in the critical theory tradition requires skepticism about the *innocence* of social and institutional practices, however innocuous and commonplace they might seem. Managerial networks, office parties, and training workshops are all regarded as potential sites of hegemony wherein ruling groups engineer the consent of the ruled without seeming to do so. The list of phenomena of interest to critical theorists is therefore virtually unlimited. Considering this, not that many researchers have closely studied managerial, organizational, and related phenomena. Power (1992) has suggested that critical theory be used for studying the socialization of accountants, and some have heeded his call. Deetz (1992) and Denhardt (1981) have written extensive commentaries on the domination of public and private organizations in all of our lives. A remarkably insightful study on the encroachment of instrumental standardization into our social worlds can be found in George Ritzer's (1996) treatise on the spread of the fast-food assembly-line mentality into health care, education, banking, and so on.

Another area that is ripe for critical theoretic analyses is marketing and consumer research (Alvesson, 1994; Murray & Ozanne, 1991). Given Adorno and Horkheimer's original interest in mass culture, and Habermas's focus on language and communicative action, advertising and consumption become obvious contenders for critical inquiry. Such work is to be found in a number of disciplines including history, communication, and cultural studies. A classic in this genre is Stuart Ewen's (1976) *Captains of Consciousness,* a sweeping historical study of the American advertising industry and its successful takeover of public sensibility by appeals to emotional insecurity and patriotism. Ewen's work (though it has few followers in consumer research) remains a model of historical sociology with a distinctly cultural rather than economic emphasis.

Debates and New Directions in Critical Theory

As is true of any tradition that commands such a strong following, critical theory is not without its detractors. In general, there seem to be two sources of critique: (a) from those who are largely antagonistic to the broader critical traditions and (b) from those who are somewhat sympathetic to its fundamental aims. Most of the first group follow the usual positivist route, complaining that the nature of the research is too anecdotal, that it is not possible to make reliable generalizations, and that the researchers are overly biased in terms of their overt values (Donaldson, 1985). In addition, some forms of critical theory are singled out for being notoriously unscientific, given their insistence on praxis and the participation of research subjects in the project itself.

It is hard to respond in good faith to many of these critiques partly because they often seem ill informed about the epistemological basis of critical theory and partly because they seem bent on holding critical theory to positivist standards that have no meaning in this tradition. However, the question of bias may well be worth a brief discussion. Critical theory's starting point is an acknowledgment of the *absence of neutrality* in all forms of knowledge production. Given this consideration, critical theorists also openly acknowledge their own ethical positions and value preferences. This does not mean that a diligent critical theorist will recklessly vilify individuals in elite organizational positions or that they berate business corporations for very little rhyme or reason. All it does mean is that they will approach them with a high degree of suspicion. It is also important to appreciate that this suspicion itself does not come out of nowhere but is grounded in a highly sophisticated theoretical discourse about modernity and its discontents. For a critique of this to be really valid, it needs to grapple with the core of critical theory's epistemology.

A more puzzling criticism is directed by Feldman (2000) who charges critical theory with promoting a pernicious form of modernistic individualism that severs all connections to past traditions in the name of individual empowerment. Feldman's criticism is somewhat misplaced because it appears to be based on an extremely *narrow* and *literal* interpretation of critical theory. Feldman's objections stem from his conviction that critical theory privileges individual rationality and autonomy at the expense of legacies in the form of social traditions. It is not easy to follow how Feldman actually reaches this position. Although Habermas has indeed been justifiably faulted for his valorization of modernity (and hence the rational subject), critical theorists like Adorno, Benjamin, and Marcuse are best known for their disenchantment with modernity and for their neo-Weberian anxieties about the *over-rationalization* of society. Furthermore, Feldman (2000) equates the notion of ideology-critique with a complete rejection of the past and all of its moral traditions. Again, he is under a misapprehension here. Critical theory does not call for a complete overhaul of the past but only for a rejection of those cultural practices/traditions that are hegemonic in nature. Critical theory is also guided by the principles of democracy and justice in the instigation of social change. Though often endorsing a *revision* of history, critical theory does not advocate a complete rejection of it.

Some criticisms are directed from other postpositivist traditions such as poststructuralism, which is critical of Habermas's over-reliance on the autonomous rational subject as yet another extension of the Marxian attachment to consciousness. In other words, critical theory is accused of privileging the rational conscious subject without realizing that such a subject position itself is a product of modernity and the Enlightenment and therefore in need of ideology-critique (Alvesson & Deetz, 2000). Within organization studies, some of these debates have surfaced in the discussions on routine workplace resistance where critical theorists like Jermier (1988) and Clegg (1994) are faulted for acknowledging the presence of resistance only when there is some clear evidence of conscious will (Prasad & Prasad, 2001). The problem with this position is that it neglects and even dismisses nonconscious and noncalculated oppositional actions as irrational or products of false consciousness rather than resistance.

Critical theory has also been attacked for its failure to differentiate adequately *between* the experiences of oppressed groups such as men and women, people of different ethnicities, straight versus gays, and so on. In short, when critical theorists consider dominated groups, they rarely take the trouble to figure out some of the rifts and tensions within these groups, themselves, and their relationships to the broader patterns of hegemony. To feminists, therefore, critical theory's major deficit is its neglect of *patriarchy* as a specific form of domination (Weedon, 1997), resulting in a pervasive form of gender blindness.

Under the influence of deconstruction and worldwide decolonization movements, critical theory has also been accused of perpetuating a distinctly *Eurocentric* form of theorizing that (a) places Europe and European theory at the center of all its intellectual efforts, and (b) is unable to distinguish between Western forms of domination over non-Western peoples and forms of domination experienced in the West itself (Poster, 1989). It must be acknowledged that many leading critical theorists have been consistently bound by a Eurocentric perspective. Habermas, for one, holds firmly to the idea that the completion of the European Enlightenment project is the basis of the ideal speech community. Much of Adorno's work on culture has always been openly contemptuous of non-European genres of art and music, notably jazz, which he concluded had a "regressive effect" on its listeners (Alleyne, 1999). Critical theory is thus increasingly placed in a position of having to respond to many of these critiques.

The critical theory tradition's response has been mixed. Habermas himself has continued to vigorously defend his theory of communicative action, insisting that if public conversations were only structured rationally and openly, a synthesis of reason and society would be accomplished and human emancipation would be ensured (McCarthy, 1978). Others, who are deeply influenced by many of critical theory's central tenets, have chosen to follow a more activist-participatory path originally proposed by Paulo Freire (1970). These researchers are less inclined to dwell on the theoretical intricacies of critical theory and are also less inclined to focus on problems of the industrial West. Instead, they direct their attention to issues of relevance to the Third World and the more marginalized segments of Western society (Escobar, 1995; Fals-Borda & Rahman, 1991). Still others have blended many of critical theory's central concepts with theories of popular and working-class culture and with postcolonialism to form a vibrant hybrid tradition known as cultural studies (Hall, 1990; Williams, 1980). Given these trends, it is possible that a "pure" form of critical theory may well be on the wane as the tradition becomes absorbed into newer intellectual movements.

Whatever fate awaits critical theory, and for all its shortcomings, to many scholars the tradition remains "the best of what is left of the left" (Poster, 1989, 3), holding on to the subjective and idealist visions of Marxism without abandoning its commitment to history and totality. In management studies, critical theorists have done much to problematize the commonplace elements of work and society by uncovering the ubiquity of hegemony in multiple cultural fields (e.g., Alvesson, 1987; Rosen, 1988; Willmott, 1993). In sum then, critical theory "sustains an effort to theorize the present as a moment between the past and the future, thus holding up a historicizing mirror to society, one that compels a recognition of the transitory and fallible nature of society, one that insists that what is can be disassembled and improved considerably. . . . Critical theory springs from the assumption that we live amid a world of pain, that much can be done to alleviate that pain, and that theory has a crucial role to play in that process" (Poster, 1989, 3).

Notes

1. Although the original interest of Frankfurt School members was explicitly directed toward explaining the appeal of Nazism and fascism in Europe, it is easy to see how many of their concerns are equally useful for understanding the success of chauvinistic and authoritarian movements in current Western societies—for example, the Fundamentalist Christian right and white separatist movements.

2. It is somewhat regrettable that this interesting dimension of critical theory has not been seriously pursued by researchers who study work and organizations in this tradition. This whole domain of cultural psychology (which is such an integral part of the critical theory tradition) has been largely bypassed by many prominent organization researchers (e.g., Mats Alvesson and Hugh Willmott) who confine themselves to the milder versions of ideology-critique proposed by Habermas.

3. This is in no way intended to discount the contributions of these writings, but merely to point out that many scholars working in this tradition have concentrated on the philosophic aspects of critical theory and have put less effort into empirical studies within this framework.

4. This step bears considerable similarity to that of the *hermeneutic circle* discussed in detail in Chapter 3. Critical theory would, in general, call for a greater focus on the elements of power constituting wider social structures than traditional hermeneutics.

5. The tendency of critical theorists to closely intermingle with many of the interpretive traditions illustrates the near impossibility of drawing clear lines between the traditions. Critical ethnographers, for instance, simultaneously inhabit two worlds—the world of ethnography and the world of critical theory. It is therefore possible to consider them as being part of either or both traditions.

Figure 9.1   **Highlights of the Critical Theory Tradition**

Philosophic influences: Phenomenology, Marxism, psychoanalysis,
                                linguistics

Major figures: Theodor Adorno, Max Horkheimer, Walter
                                Benjamin, Erich Fromm, Herbert Marcuse,
                                Jurgen Habermas

Central concepts
- Mass culture
- Ideology-critique
- Instrumental reason
- One-dimensional culture
- Communicative action
- Ideal speech community
- Systematically distorted communication

Key practices
- Uncovering the hegemony of institutional practices
- Focusing on the symbolic dimensions of society
- Dialogue and participation of research subjects
- Acknowledgment of researchers' values

Exemplary Research
- "Mystification and Social Drama" (Elmes & Costello, 1992)
- *Captains of Consciousness* (Ewen, 1976)
- *Moral Mazes* (Jackall, 1988)
- Christmas Time and Control (Rosen & Astley, 1988)

10

Feminism

Gender as the Core Social Principle

The feminist tradition emerged largely out of a widespread concern with the *invisibility* and *exploitation* of women over the past several centuries. Women's invisibility has been a concern mainly in the public sphere—that is, in the workplace, in government, and the media where they have been denied access to a majority of positions. The exploitation of women has been a concern in both public and private realms. In the workplace, women have systematically occupied underpaid positions without much career mobility. At home, their work in caring for the family has been institutionalized as a form of unpaid wage labor, and their contributions as wives, mothers, and homemakers have gone largely unrecognized. In addition, women's bodies have been the subject of incessant exploitation—in prostitution, pornography, and segments of the entertainment industry.

Although noteworthy individual women (such as Abigail Adams or Mary Wollstonecraft) have raised the issue of women's rights in the past, the Western feminist tradition as we understand it today is primarily the offspring of ideas and social movements generated during the 1950s and 1960s. The writings of early feminists such as Simone de Beauvoir (1957) and Betty Friedan (1963), and the coming of age of the women's liberation movement constitute the foundations of the contemporary feminist tradition. It is important to appreciate the evolution of the feminist tradition as *both* an academic scholarly tradition and a sociopolitical movement, and in this respect, feminism bears a striking similarity to Marxism. Feminist scholarship implicitly presents a wide-ranging system of ideas about the world from a *woman-centered* perspective (Lengermann & Niebrugge-Brantley, 1990). Political feminism is concerned mainly with women's education, equality of opportunity, wage discrimination, abortion rights, the objectification of women's bodies, women's health, maternity rights, and so on (Weedon, 1997). It would be a mistake, however, to see feminism as occupying two separate realms. Most feminists take their political agendas very seriously and constantly try to weave them into the more scholarly forms of feminist inquiry and practice. This refusal to separate feminist politics from academic feminism is probably responsible for a widespread misconception that feminism is intrinsically militant and hostile to all things male and masculine. This is obviously far from being an accurate portrayal of feminism. The feminist tradition is sharply critical of past and continuing patterns of male dominance but is not uniformly opposed to men or maleness.

Unlike many of the other traditions discussed in this book, feminism initially came into prominence as a sociopolitical movement, which then began to exert a strong influence on academic research. The feminist tradition was first institutionalized in universities as Women's Studies departments and programs that were frequently cross-disciplinary in nature (Calas & Smircich, 1992). In a few years, feminist scholars could be found in a variety of disciplines, including literature and literary theory, history, sociology, anthropology, education, and philosophy. Feminists were engaged in rewriting histories to more accurately reflect women's participation, and they focused on understanding women's lives and concerns in areas such as the family, health, education, and work. By the late 1980s the feminist tradition began to influence management and related fields, and by the 1990s it was clearly discernible as a critical mass. Over the last fifteen years or so, there has been a sustained interest in examining multiple managerial and organizational issues from feminist standpoints. These include studies of consumer research and feminism (Bristor & Fischer, 1993), the gendered nature of organizational leadership discourses (Calas & Smircich, 1992), pregnancy in the corporate workplace (Martin, 1990), gendered work regimes in banks (Acker, 1994), and gendered subtexts found in team-based work (Benschop & Dooreward, 1998a).

More so than any other tradition covered by this book, feminism is perhaps the most varied in terms of ontological and epistemological assumptions. In fact, speaking of a single feminist tradition is somewhat misleading. We should really be referring to multiple feminist traditions that are often united by little more than an overall interest in women's lives and the role of gender in structuring different aspects of society. Some of the better-known feminist scholarly traditions include liberal feminism, women's voice/experience feminism, radical feminism, and poststructural feminism. The following section will look more carefully at some of the different intellectual strands within the broader feminist tradition.

Feminist Theory and Philosophy

Despite striking intellectual variations within the different feminist traditions, they are all united by their focus on women as the central subjects of inquiry (Lengermann & Niebrugge-Brantley, 1990). Liberal feminism is the most straightforward and least complex of all the feminist traditions, being primarily interested in improving women's legal status, ensuring equal pay levels with men, and transforming institutions into places in which women can pursue lucrative and fulfilling careers (Ferguson, 1984). We will not be discussing liberal feminism in this chapter for the simple reason that it does not depart from the ontological and epistemological positions of positivism, and is therefore not likely to be of interest to researchers working in the postpositivist traditions. Nevertheless, liberal feminism remains one of the most popular strands of the feminist tradition (both within and outside academe) and is often mistakenly believed to represent the entire spectrum of feminist thought. This section looks carefully at three other subtraditions that have been influential in the development of feminist research.

Women's Voice/Experience Feminism

Heavily influenced by Simone de Beauvoir (1957) and certain genres of social psychology, a growing body of work in the 1970s and 1980s grew out of the assumption that women's typical life experiences which in turn shape their mental processes, values, and identities, are so fundamentally different from men's that their notions of self and their relationships to their social worlds are also likely to be very different (Bernard, 1981). Many feminists argue that although most of these differences have their roots in powerful social constructions (rather than in nature or biology), they nevertheless result in completely different female subjectivities that are rarely acknowledged in different walks of life. Even more serious, men's experiences and value systems are institutionalized as normal, and women's deviations from male standards are either completely overlooked or judged as being deviant. The central goals of this particular feminist tradition are (a) to recognize and celebrate women's experientially based differences, (b) to privilege women's voices and identities, and (c) to eventually modify social arrangements in such a way as to make them more compatible with women's needs (Belenky et al., 1986; Bristor & Fischer, 1993).

Carol Gilligan's work on the importance of understanding differences in women's experiences can provide a better understanding of this subtradition. Gilligan's (1977) work is best known for its reformulation of Kohlberg's theory of moral development from a feminist perspective. In his model, Kohlberg argued that women tended to operate at a lower stage of moral development than men. When Gilligan conducted her own research on men and women, she pointed out that women adopted a mode of reasoning that took them in different (though not necessarily inferior) moral directions. More important, she claimed that moral development is substantially shaped by gendered structures of socialization that prepare men to be individualistic and independent, and women to be caring and community-oriented. According to Gilligan (1977), these socialization processes strongly mediate the ethical development of men and women along different lines, with men embracing *abstract* notions of justice and women emphasizing an ethics based on *connections* with their local communities.

Gilligan's work remains noteworthy for its attempt to puncture an established theory on the grounds that it wrongly extended the assumptions and experiences of one social identity group to all of humanity. Gilligan thus raises significant feminist questions about the extent to which the social sciences may be based exclusively on male experiences and their consequent validity for women. Gilligan's work was followed by a spate of research exploring women's psyches and the "different" worlds inhabited by women in history, culture, and contemporary institutions. Belenky et al. (1986), for instance, looked at women's tendency to develop different "ways of knowing" based on their own gendered experiences; Boulding (1976) examined the hitherto largely invisible role of women in history; and Keller (1985) considered women's experiences in the world of science.

The primary contribution of the women's voice/experience tradition lies in its refusal to accept solely male-based experiences as the foundation for explaining all social dynamics. The work of Belenky et al. (1986), Gilligan (1977), and others have rendered many male-based managerial theories of motivation, leadership, and work commitment suspect on account of their complete neglect of gender differences. Voice/experience feminism thus *relativizes* much of our accepted wisdom by highlighting the central role played by male experience in the development of knowledge. Voice feminism, however, also goes beyond relativizing contemporary social science. It often implicitly presents women's conceptual processes and ways of relating to the world as "superior" to men's. Jean Baker Miller's (1986) relational theory of social psychology illustrates this tendency. Offering an alternative developmental model based on women's experiences, Miller celebrates the preeminence of connection and mutuality over the individualism and autonomy stressed by models based on male experience. Relationality (which is seen as the more feminine mode) is then privileged for its ability to forge connections and preserve social ties within the family, the neighborhood, and the immediate workplace. Needless to say, several commentators (including feminists of a different stripe) are quite critical of this tendency to romanticize women's psyches and womanhood.

Women's voice/experience feminism is also taken to task for bringing essentialism in through the back door (Eisenstein & Jardine, 1985). In other words, although the tradition maintains that women's identities and relational styles are indeed shaped by circumstances (i.e., are socially constructed) rather than being formed by nature, they nevertheless continue to reify these characteristics as supposedly feminine and implicitly extend them to all women regardless of class, ethnicity, or national origin.

The Radical Feminist Tradition

While women's voice/experience feminism is very much the offspring of social psychology, the radical feminist tradition bears strong imprints of Marxian social theory. With gender replacing class as the central concept of importance, radical feminists adopt a materialist standpoint in pursuing questions relating to the exploitation and oppression of women. In keeping with its Marxist roots, this tradition is definitely more macro-historical in orientation and adopts a less romanticized view of women who are simultaneously regarded as both victims and reproducers of the patriarchy (Walby, 1990). To radical feminists, female exploitation is strongly imbricated in multiple *institutional structures* such as the family, industrial capitalism, bureaucracy, education, science, and the media (Ferguson, 1984).

At the heart of radical feminism lies the idea that gender is not just a social role but also a pervasive *system of stratification* (Hartsock, 1983) that emerges out of the organization of social production. Radical feminists also extend the materialist notion of social production beyond that of noneconomic goods to include the production of social life itself. This would include childbearing and child-raising activities, household maintenance, sexual and emotional work, and the creation of social status (Hartsock, 1983). Radical feminists also alert us to the hierarchical ordering of the social production system along gendered lines. As Lengermann and Niebrugge-Brantley (1990, 323) note, "Gender, like class is a social structure within a universal system of stratification based on the organization of social production and sustained by ideology."

Ideology is, therefore, another concept of significance to radical feminism. It is ideology (very much in the materialist sense) that explains not only how women are consistently locked into subordinate positions, but also why most women accept these conditions in the first place (Martin, 1988). Ideologies establish the normative and taken-for-granted dimensions of society. The formation of womanhood is thus an ideological process that can explain what Smith (1979) calls the "relations of ruling"—the set of positions in the structures that rule/manage/organize and otherwise control women (Smith, 1979; 1987). Many ideologies of contemporary womanhood, for instance, can also be very seductive even as they continue to reproduce the exploitation of women. The ideology of the Supermom (which pervades much of middle-class North America) is a good illustration of this, for it ensures that many women relentlessly pursue careers at work while simultaneously striving to be perfect mothers and homemakers. In this process of succeeding as mothers, wives, and professionals, women in contemporary Western societies take on far too many daily tasks and endure high levels of stress, frustration, and anxiety. Yet, many women continue to be paid far less than men and encounter far more obstacles to career advancement. However, the ideology of the Supermom is so powerful that most women willingly accept that they will work harder in both public and private realms even as they earn fewer material and symbolic rewards than men.

Above all, radical feminism is intent on recasting ideas about social structure while keeping gender at the center of all analyses. "The goal of feminist discourse is to articulate the relationships between women's experiences, and the forms of institutions that can encourage and legitimate them" (Ferguson, 1984, 29). Of special importance to this tradition is an understanding of the worlds of business, bureaucracy, advertising, and consumption where institutional practices routinely specify women's locations within the system while appearing to be entirely "rational" and gender-neutral in all their activities.

Radical feminists constantly emphasize that organizations are *gendered entities* that initiate gendered divisions of labor and produce symbols and images that further reinforce these divisions. Acker's (1990) discussion of job evaluation as a reflection of organizational logic is a good illustration of this viewpoint. Job evaluation is a common technique used in industrial firms to rationalize the organizational hierarchy and to set "equitable" wages. Job evaluation eventually results in a set of rules and policies that regulate various organizational activities. The logic of job evaluation assumes a congruence between responsibility, job complexity, and hierarchical position. Within organizational logic, both jobs and hierarchies are abstract categories that have no occupants, no human bodies, and no gender. Eventually, however, the abstract job will be filled by a disembodied worker, and at this point, "the closest that the disembodied worker doing the abstract job comes to a real worker is the male worker whose life centers on his full-time, life-long job, while his wife or another woman takes care of his personal needs and his children" (Acker, 1990, 149). Acker's point here is that the implicit image of the worker in job evaluation is male and that the concept of the job itself becomes implicitly gendered.

As Acker and many other feminists have been quick to note, the abstract notion of the bodyless worker plays a vital role in *obscuring* and at the same time *reproducing* underlying gender relations. Consequently, organizations are pervaded by an overall silence about gender and by the suppression of sexuality and gender conflicts (Martin, 1990). The suppression of sexuality is integral to bureaucracy and emerges out of the exclusion of women and the depersonalization of organizational spheres. Here again, we are left with the invisibility and oppression of women. The radical feminist tradition, therefore, provides a stringent critique of institutional structures as the primary source of sexual stratification and female exploitation. Radical feminism has recently been broadened by the efforts of writers like Carby (1985), bell hooks

(1984), Friedman (1998), and others to confront the processes whereby race, ethnicity, and nationality *intersect* with gender to sustain and reproduce structures that are oppressive to women. From this perspective, the oppression and subjugation of women cannot be wholly attributed to gender but to the relationship of gender with these multiple indices of otherness.

The Feminist Poststructural Tradition

Feminist poststructuralism explores the connections between language, subjectivity, social organization, and power, and their ramifications for gender dynamics in all walks of life (Weedon 1997). Inspired substantially by the work of Michael Foucault, Jacques Derrida, and other French linguistic philosophers, feminist poststructuralists (Irigiray, 1974) have placed *language* and *discourse* at the center of feminist inquiry. Furthermore, this tradition is highly skeptical about universal and transcendental truth claims, and regards all systems of knowledge production as exercises of power through which women are discursively (and disadvantagedly) positioned in society (Diamond & Quinby, 1988; Gavey, 1989). "Poststructural feminism exposes the apparently unimpeachable structures of truth and knowledge in society, and helps to debunk mythical social constructions which silence and oppress many of society's members" (Calas & Smircich, 1992, 244).

It is hard to fully appreciate this tradition's intellectual position without some elemental grasp of poststructuralism (discussed in Chapter 13) in the first place. Nevertheless, a brief sketch of feminist poststructuralism is attempted here. At the risk of some oversimplification, we can assert that feminist poststructuralism is interested in how language and other forms of representation play crucial roles in *constructing gendered subjectivities* in a range of social spheres. In particular, it borrows the notion of *discourse* from poststructuralism to understand how gendered identities and experiential interpretations come into place within matrices of power. Discourse in this tradition refers to far more than speech, writing, or conversation; it refers to "varied bodies of knowledge, regimes of ennunciation, strategies and protocols of knowledge production, [and] cultural and sub-cultural grammars of behavior" (Prasad, 2001) that govern the formation of subjectivities and mediate interpretations of the social world. To Weedon (1997), discourse is a "structuring principle" of society that constitutes and is reproduced in social institutions, modes of thought, and individual subjectivity. It is through discourse that material power is exercised and that power relations are established and perpetuated (Gavey, 1989).

Discourses are responsible for prescribing roles and expectations for different individuals and groups, and are substantially gendered. Discourses of femininity, the family, management, consumption, science, and so on chart out gendered spheres of action (Flax, 1990) and create gendered identities such as the housewife, the career woman, and the Supermom, each with its accompanying script and expectations. "Poststructural feminism draws on the notions of language, subjectivity and discourse to understand existing power relations that disadvantage women and to identify opportunities and strategies for change" (Bristor & Fischer, 1993, 522).

A major contribution of poststructural feminism can be found in its transformation of subjectivity into a fluid phenomenon that can actually be changed. This is a substantial departure from the women's voice/experience tradition, which views subjective states such as womanhood and femininity (while socially constructed) as much more immutable. It would be erroneous, however, to conclude that poststructural feminism regards this matter of changing discourses as an easy task. Although they regard powerful discourses as difficult to dislodge, they also insist that discursive change is possible and is one of the primary tasks of feminists who are engaged in making society more comfortable for women.

Feminist poststructuralists regularly *interrogate* dominant discourses by asking, for instance, why we have no notion of "career men" or "Superdads," even though we constantly refer to their female counterparts. Or they might ask why images of work and professionalism continue to be linked with men while women continue to be associated with images of home and leisure. The notion of power in this tradition is also much more *diffuse*. Power lurks everywhere rather than being concentrated only in the hands of a male elite. Power is especially found in discursive sites where single individuals are less likely to exert it. In sum, poststructural feminism is able on a case-by-case basis "to explain the working of power on behalf of specific interests and to analyze the opportunities of resistance to it. It is a theory which decenters the rational, self-present subject of humanism, seeing subjectivity and consciousness as socially produced in language, as sites of struggles and potential change. . . . It can also account for the political limitations of change at the level of subjective consciousness, stressing the importance of the material relations and practices which constitute individuals as embodied subjects." (Weedon, 1997).

Feminist poststructuralism has been criticized by radical and voice feminists for its renunciation of the humanistic female subject and its premature rejection of any form of essentialism. It has also been attacked for its excessive relativism and its stance on female experience, being dependent on social and linguistic processes rather than standing apart from them. Its defenders, however, argue that its real contribution is to be found in its theoretical basis that offers us a way of linking the subjectivities of men and women to language, power, and the material contexts of our lives. As Gavey (1989, 472) posits, feminist poststructuralism "embraces complexity and contradiction and . . . surpasses theories that offer single-cause deterministic explanations of patriarchy and gender relations."

Central Concepts in the Feminist Tradition

Even while the feminist tradition is characterized by a striking diversity, certain concepts are of shared interest to all of them. The notions of sex and gender, the patriarchy, and the sexual division of labor are of interest to all the subtraditions discussed above, even while each of them might approach them differently. In addition, the question of a feminist epistemology is of central importance to the wider tradition. The remainder of this section briefly deals with some of these concepts.

Sex and Gender

Notions of sex and gender constitute the very building blocks that have gone into the construction of the different feminist traditions. The distinctions between sex and gender, as well as their relationship to one another, are remarkably salient to scholars in this tradition. It would not be an overstatement to claim that feminism of all stripes has emerged out of a strong sense of injustice about the discrimination and subjugation of one identity group (i.e., women) on the basis of their biological characteristics (sex) and the social construction of gender.

Sex is really ascribed by biology. Sex is a determination made through the application of socially agreed upon biological criteria for classifying people as males and females (West & Zimmerman, 1987). Others understand biological sex as determined by the chromosome constellation, which then manifests itself in the sexual organs, the reproductive system, and hormonal differences (Alvesson & Due Billling, 2002). One's sex status is thus entirely determined by physical criteria that are believed to be relatively immutable.

Gender, by contrast, has more of an achieved status, for it is socially constructed through social, psychological, and cultural means. Gender refers to the *behavioral aspects* of being a man or a woman, and is produced in and through multiple dynamic social processes. In general, gender refers to "patterned, socially produced distinctions between female and male, feminine and masculine" (Acker, 1992, 250). To many feminists, moreover, gender is not a neutral process, but a hegemonic and dominating one since it aids in "the classifications that societies construct to exaggerate the differences between females and males, and to maintain sex inequality" (Reskin & Padovic, 1994, 3).

At first glance, the concept of sex might seem to be completely fixed and that of gender to be somewhat fluid. Both concepts, however, are more problematic than they seem. First, as Alvesson and Due Billing (2002) suggest, biological sex itself is socially defined and must therefore be understood as a cultural phenomenon. Second, several biological features themselves are increasingly subject to medical modifications and can no longer be regarded as completely immutable. This, in turn, further complicates our understanding of gender as well. Third, although gender is undoubtedly constructed socially, it remains surprisingly resolute and resistant to change. Differences between men and women, for instance, though socially produced, are typically regarded as fundamental and enduring, which in turn makes them so. Thus, "doing gender furnishes the intellectual scaffolding of social structure, along with a built-in mechanism for social control" (West & Zimmerman, 1987, 147).

Feminists argue that gender is maintained on an ongoing basis through a multitude of institutional and informal mechanisms. Institutional reinforcements of gender are evidenced in the physical layouts of buildings (e.g., separate bathrooms for men and women), in the widespread societal expectations that men are more suited to construction work and finance while women make excellent nurses and librarians, and in the separation of sports tournaments for men and women (Goffman, 1977). Gender is also produced in a host of informal everyday interactions—when men carry heavy objects for women, and when women are either ignored or interrupted in casual conversations (Fishman, 1978). Categories of male and female also become pointedly relevant when societies grapple with issues pertaining to resource allocation or public policy (West & Zimmerman, 1987). In such cases, women-centered projects and feminized occupations inevitably receive the short end of the stick. Gender is therefore of continuing interest to the feminist tradition because of its capacity to *essentialize* behavioral differences between men and women, usually to the disadvantage of women. Unearthing the gendered nature of social arrangements is a vital part of the feminist agenda, for it is the first step in accommodating women's interests and preferences in the wider fabric of society.

Patriarchy

The term *patriarchy* first came into prominence with the work of Engels (1902), who argued that patriarchy emerged with the rise of private property and the treatment of women as such. Our present understanding of the term, however, owes more to the radical feminist theorizing of the late 1960s and early 1970s when patriarchy was absorbed into the broader framework of the "dialectic of sex" (Firestone, 1970) within which it (rather than class) came to be regarded as the *prototype* of all female oppression.

Within radical feminism, patriarchy is identified as the structural source of women's exploitation. In brief, patriarchy refers to the *systematic domination* of women by men that is achieved, sustained, and reproduced primarily through the male control of economic, social, and cultural institutions (Ferguson, 1984; Smith, 1987). It is the *institutional* character of patriarchy that makes it at once so pervasive and difficult to dislodge. Although patriarchy is a distinct configuration of sex/gender institutional arrangements in its own right, it is also intricately intertwined with other systems of oppression such as capitalism and imperialism (Millet, 1970). The church, the state, the family, all forms of bureaucracy, and the professions are all considered to be patriarchal institutions that systematically exclude women from the centers of power and subjugate them in different ways.

Organizations and workplaces are typically regarded as quintessential patriarchies. As many feminists point out, patriarchy has a remarkably tenacious grip on organizations. Even as conventional bureaucratic organizations give way to new forms, they retain strong patriarchal elements in their morphology and in their cultures. Burris's (1989) discussion of technocracies is an illustrative commentary on this tendency even with the advent of new and supposedly liberating computer technologies. Technocratic organizations have emerged under conditions of late capitalism around high-tech workplaces and service computers reliant on computer technologies, and are changing economic opportunities and the texture of work in significantly gendered ways (Burris, 1989). Through the erosion of internal job ladders, the polarization of "expert" and "nonexpert" systems, and the spread of powerful technocratic ideologies, technocratic organizations are creating a semiskilled, relatively immobile class of female or "pink-collar" workers at the lower echelons of organizational hierarchies. Technocratic organizations are thus only the most recent in a long chain of institutional work arrangements that embody the patriarchal tradition even while they pose as "modern" and progressive organizations.

How does patriarchy work on a day-to-day basis in organizations? Under patriarchal conditions, those behavioral elements associated with men and masculinity are valued and even celebrated, whereas those deemed to be female and feminine are at best, undervalued, and at worst, even denigrated (Firestone, 1970; Mills, 1988). Patriarchal organizations thus adversely impact women in two ways. First, they essentialize certain qualities as male (e.g., mental toughness, capacity for objectivity, etc.) whether or not these are to be always found among men. And second, they erect firm but less visible barriers to women's entry into supposedly male-suitable occupations such as finance, accounting, and computer design. Above all, patriarchies confine women to the less powerful realms of organizations and prevent them (through structural and cultural means) from breaking out of them. Patriarchal organizations are also astoundingly resilient and are difficult to transform despite the numerous laws that are designed to ensure equal opportunities for men and women.

Gendered Divisions of Labor

Of fundamental interest to the overall feminist tradition is the systematic organization of work into gendered spheres across all cultures and time periods even while there is considerable variation with respect to what tasks are considered appropriate to which sex, and the degree of rigidity of sex-typing of various forms of work (Marshall, 1994). Seen as an integral element of the patriarchy, gendered divisions of labor are sources of female exploitation and mechanisms for the reproduction of patriarchal structures. Feminists hold that in order to grasp the full scale of female oppression, it is important to understand the multiplicity of gendered divisions of work. A major segment of feminist work is thus engaged in documenting the nature of these sexual divisions of labor and in estimating whose interests they serve and how they may be redrawn.

To begin with, it is important to recognize that sexual divisions of labor can be found between waged and unwaged labor, within waged labor, and within unwaged labor. Historically, the most striking gendered division of labor has been between the overwhelming employment of men in salaried/waged employment and the disproportionate number of women in unpaid work. Unpaid female labor itself can take different forms. The most visible form of unpaid female work is in the home, involving regular household maintenance and caring for the children and the elderly (Marshall, 1994). With the rise of a (predominantly male) professional and executive class engaged in running capitalist enterprises, women's unpaid work has also substantially grown to include activities intended to support the male breadwinner in the extra social aspects of his job (Kanter, 1977). Such unpaid labor typically includes entertaining executives, accompanying husbands on business or diplomatic trips, and engaging in volunteer work that is of symbolic value to a husband's career ambitions (Finch, 1983). Within agricultural and small-business sectors, women are frequently drafted into a host of unpaid activities such as packing fruit, looking after the finances, and so on (Smith, 1987).

In many instances, women's unpaid work is not engineered through direct coercion but is secured through voluntary compliance on the part of the women themselves, who work because they believe it to be their duty to husband and/or family, because of the nonavailability of other opportunities, or because they lack the qualifications and self-confidence to search for waged alternatives. For radical feminists in particular, this becomes an important domain, for it is one in which patriarchal ideology intersects with material interests to ensure the continued exploitation and confinement of women within the private sphere.

Of equal interest to the radical feminist tradition are the strong gendered divisions within waged labor itself, both in the West and between the West and the non-West. Women in the West are predominantly found in low-paying clerical, sales, and service positions. Another disturbing North American trend is the growing erosion of full-time employment for women and the rise of part-time work or "limited contract" opportunities for them (Marshall, 1994). As a result, more women are moving into remote work sectors as data entry or call center operators with poor remuneration and few or no benefits. Globalization and its accompanying dynamic of "runaway capital" further displaces many lower-level female workers in the West who are forced into different forms of casual or part-time work. At the same time, their counterparts in the Third World are being hired at low wages to work under hazardous and tyrannical conditions by a host of multinational corporations. In all these cases, patriarchal structures of work, organization, and employment legislation are seen as continuing to subordinate and exploit women through new divisions of labor.

Sexuality

As a concept, sexuality subsumes the notions of *both* sex and gender, as well as the articulation between them (Caplan, 1989). Sexuality refers to the entire configuration of sexual behaviors, feelings, and mindsets that can be found in any social situation. How we (individually and collectively) come to understand the categories of man and woman and how we express ourselves as such is a part of sexuality. People are encouraged to see themselves in terms of their sexuality, which is interpreted as the core of the self (Caplan, 1989). In sum, sexuality refers to the full range of sexually related phenomena comprising sex roles, sexual identities, sexual preference, notions of masculinity and femininity, sexual attractiveness, and sexual harassment (Hearn & Parkin, 1983). Sexuality is clearly a shifting concept. As Caplan (1989, 2) notes, "What is sexual in one context may not be so in another; an experience becomes sexual [only] by the application of socially learned meanings." Sexuality is of tremendous interest to feminists because it is a major discursive site for both the subjugation of women and women's resistance to this subjugation.

Formal institutionalized structures such as organizations and the media play key roles in the development of different sexualities because they shape the ways in which men and women view themselves and their relationships to each other (Burrell & Hearn, 1989; Ferguson, 1984). Sexuality is produced by and in organizations in multiple ways, the most obvious being through the construction and maintenance of gendered divisions of work (Acker, 1990; Marshall, 1994). Less obvious is the sexuality that is produced out of organizational symbols and images that explain, express, reinforce, and even sometimes challenge gendered roles and divisions (Acker, 1990).

Organizations produce sexuality by (somewhat paradoxically) both suppressing and reinforcing it at the same time. Ferguson (1984), Martin (1990), Acker (1990), and others have convincingly shown how the denial of sexuality occurs through (a) the initiation of "gender-neutral" logics and (b) the refusal to acknowledge the active presence of sexual dynamics among managers and employees (e.g., sexual attraction, sexual harassment, pregnancy, and so on) in the workplace. This systematic tendency toward organizational desexualization makes women either less visible or more problematic to organizations. At the same time, organizations also routinely sexualize women—in advertisements and corporate annual reports—by representing them as sources of comfort, pleasure, and desire (Benschop & Meihuzen, 2002; Mills, 1997). Mills's, (1997) study of the early years of British Airways (then BOAC) offers an interesting illustration of sexualization in an organization, with the original discourses of desexualization of female flight attendants giving way to a discourse of eroticization in which they were glamorized and depicted as objects of desire. Both discourses, those of desexualization and eroticization, worked to confine women in specific organizational roles and did not permit them access to other domains of the organization.

Working in the Feminist Tradition

The feminist traditions have succeeded in inspiring an impressive outpouring of fieldwork in diverse academic fields such as accounting, anthropology, history, communication studies, organization studies, and the sociology of work. It is worth pointing out, however, that research on gender issues per se does not necessarily imply a feminist bent. Many studies of women in management (e.g., Powell, 1988) and sex differences in organizations (e.g., Ibarra, 1992), though focusing on women and gender, have few affinities with the epistemological and ontological orientations of the different feminist traditions discussed in this chapter.

Researchers in the feminist tradition cover a great deal of ground in terms of the phenomena they examine and the methods they use. Women's efforts to enter traditional male work spaces (Fonow, 1997), gender and race dynamics in public organizations (Ostrander, 1999), the gendered subtexts of organizational leadership discourses (Calas & Smircich, 1991), the gendered abstractions of the so-called ideal worker (Tianari, Quack, & Theobald, 2002), and the aggressively masculine discourses of nuclear war experts (Cohn, 1987) are just some of the issues that form a part of feminist preoccupations. When it comes to data collection, feminists show a marked preference for participant observation (Fonow, 1997; Ostrander, 1999), and in-depth ethnographic type interviews (Cohn, 1987; Mirchandani, 2003), though discourse analyses of formal and informal texts are not entirely uncommon (Benschop & Meihuizen, 2002; Calas & Smircich, 1991). What feminists almost uniformly reject, on ontological and epistemological grounds, is a positivist scientific procedure.

Feminists infinitely prefer methods that bring them *closer* to their subjects because of their primary commitment to understanding the *subjective* lifeworlds of women—worlds that have largely been ignored or are simply unseen in the male-dominated domains of the social sciences. Feminists are therefore intensely phenomenological, with an interest in placing gender at the core of their phenomenological inquiry. Feminists are opposed to distancing themselves from their subjects on the grounds that "objectivity is not a transcendent truth-seeking principle, but derives from the particularistic experiences of dominant males in capitalist society" (Lengermann & Niebrugge-Brantley, 1990, 326). Feminists therefore assert that it is neither possible nor desirable for a researcher to separate her- or himself from the subjects of his or her research. Indeed, feminist scholars like Reinharz (1983) have even explicitly called for a "mutuality of recognition" between researchers and their subjects, and an awareness that research is jointly produced by both parties.

In practice, such a position demands, at the very least, that researchers *insert* themselves explicitly into the research text—acknowledging their own social location and coming to an awareness of the personal agendas guiding their research project. Part of crafting feminist research is therefore to *personalize* it by providing many more autobiographical details and by laying bare some of the messier realities of the research account that are usually left out of conventional research accounts. Cohn (1987), Fletcher (1999), and many others working in this tradition take considerable pains to make readers aware of who the researchers are and what kind of dilemmas they experienced in the course of their fieldwork. Furthermore, the belief that research subjects are responsible for the production of research requires a strong commitment to the *inclusion* and active engagement of research subjects in the design and interpretation of research findings. It is not uncommon for feminists to share their research notes, preliminary analyses, and first drafts of write-ups with their subjects and to invite reactions to them (Fletcher, 1999; Ostrander, 1999).

Several sections of the feminist tradition demand that researchers give *voice* to women's subjective experiences by *translating* them into texts that can eventually be shared in a broader community of women (Lengermann & Niebrugge-Brantley, 1990). Fletcher's (1999) study of women engineers in a high-tech U.S. firm is a good example of research that inserts a woman's perspective into a predominantly male world—in this case, the world of engineering.[1] Fletcher "shadowed" six female engineers on a regular basis and followed her daily observations with follow-up interviews in which the same engineers offered interpretations of the activities that she had witnessed. Based on this data, Fletcher posits that female engineers engage in what she calls "relational practice." Relational practice refers to patterns of behavior that emerge out of the private sphere (typically, the world of women) and include characteristics such as connection, interdependence, and collectivity (Fletcher, 1999). Fletcher then shows how these relational practices eventually *disappeared* in the wider male organizational culture of engineering where it was neither valued nor understood.

Feminist researchers of a somewhat radical persuasion tend to be more interested in uncovering the *gendered* nature of organizational practices and policies. The gendering of work and organizations is believed to exist at both the formal and informal levels of the organization and is elicited with the help of interviews, documents, and observation. Many of these processes are not easily visible, and the search for the hidden dimensions of gender marks much of radical feminist research. In their study of the Dutch banking sector—a sector that is distinguished by a relatively balanced workforce in terms of gender representation—Benschop and Dooreward (1998b) used interviews alongside official company data to unearth the gendered subtexts of these organizations. This, in turn, exposed the pervasiveness of power-based gender dynamics. Their subtextual analysis primarily revealed certain organizational tendencies toward employing women as "showpieces" in senior positions, tracking women with small children into less visible and less important jobs, and developing promotional criteria that implicitly favored men over women (Benschop & Dooreward, 1998b).

Researchers in the feminist traditions also make full use of documents such as company newsletters (Mills, 1997) and annual reports (Hammond & Oaks, 1992) exploring how representations of gender in texts, figures, and photographs all contribute to the gendering of organizations. As Benschop and Meihuizen (2002) argue, the cultural representations of gender in annual reports produce meanings that both constitute and reflect the *symbolic gender order* in organizations. Annual reports can also indirectly contribute to shaping an organization's culture. Benschop and Meihuizen show how annual reports systematically reinforce classic stereotypes of men as breadwinners and women as caregivers in their texts and images. These images are problematic because they endorse organizational expectations about differences between men and women's attitudes to career. The subtext of the annual reports continues to hint that women are likely to be distracted in their pursuit of careers by family responsibilities, whereas men can devote themselves singlemindedly to their jobs. Men, therefore, once again emerge in the banks' discourse as the more reliable and productive candidates for important positions (Benschop & Meihuizen, 2002).

Leidner's (1991) study of interactive service work provides an even more complex picture of the gendering of work as an everyday social process. As Leidner reveals, the gendering of work is not accomplished through some cognitive attachment of crude male or female stereotypes to specific occupations. Leidner conducted her fieldwork at McDonald's where she studied food servers—the people who deal with the public at window centers—and at Combined Insurance where she studied insurance agents. Although the food servers were predominantly women and the insurance agents were predominantly men, neither job was *prima facie* completely saturated with gender assumptions (Leidner, 1991). However, Leidner's interviews and conversations led her to conclude that the food server's jobs were routinely defined as feminine and the insurance agents' jobs as masculine. The servers' job was seen as being more suitable for women because it required that the incumbent be able to swallow her pride and tolerate considerable rudeness and discourtesy from customers—something that men supposedly would not be able to handle owing to their tendency to lose their tempers.

Paradoxically, the insurance agent's job was defined as manly even while it called for behaviors that are typically identified with feminine attributes— for example, congeniality and an eagerness to please. As Leidner (1991, 173) notes, "Even when the work is seen as expressive of feminine capacities, however, it is not seen as offering proof of female identity in quite the same way that manly work supports male identity, because adult female identity has not traditionally been regarded as something that is achieved through paid work." Leidner's work is a remarkable piece of crafts(wo)manship in the feminist tradition for its portrayal of the enormous complexity underwriting the gendering process. Gendering, as Leidner shows, is simultaneously both resolute and fluid.

The feminist tradition has historically focused mainly on the exploitation and subjugation of women at work. However, a number of feminist researchers are equally interested in exploring women's capacities to *cope* with these situations and to *resist* them as best they can. Feminist studies of resistance look at both formal collective forms of women's resistance, such as union organizing and reform (Fonow, 1997; Sugiman, 1992) and at informal attempts to subvert patriarchal structures by less obvious means (Hossfeld, 1993; Paules, 1991). Both sets of studies, however, highlight *gendered strategies of resistance* that are mediated by meta-discourses of female sexuality such as motherhood and womanhood (Costello, 1987; Prasad & Prasad, 1998).

Hossfeld's (1993) study of (mainly immigrant) women workers in Silicon Valley's high-tech manufacturing industry is an interesting piece of feminist fieldwork dealing with control and resistance. Hossfeld first examines how managerial ideologies rooted in sex, class, and race divisions were successfully used to manipulate worker compliance. Factory supervisors blatantly used countless stereotypes about immigrant women's stupidity, superstition, and hormonal tendencies to discipline, admonish, and humiliate the workers. However, Hossfeld (1993) also shows that ideological manipulation was not only a supervisory tool. Behind their seeming passivity and meekness, the women workers used these very same stereotypes to obtain informal concessions from management and to make more favorable changes in their work arrangements.

Although much of feminist research treats "women" as a somewhat monolithic and unproblematic category (e.g., Fletcher, 1999), others have urged a stronger awareness of the sheer heterogeneity along class, race, religious, and ethnic lines characterizing women. Feminist researchers have also been advocating an examination of the complex relationships *between* women from diverse social, economic, and cultural locations. Many feminist researchers have indeed responded to these calls by increasingly focusing on interactions between women from different race/class/ethnic backgrounds, and between women and other minority groups (Ostrander, 1999; Tom, 1993).

Tom's (1993) study of intraorganizational dynamics in a feminist bank is a particularly well-crafted piece examining the conflicts between different groups of women in an organization. Based on a year's ethnographic fieldwork in the bank, Tom provocatively explodes the myth of a common shared female experience. Instead, she reveals the development of the serious rifts between the bank manager and her staff on one side and the low-income women who were intended to be the beneficiaries of the bank's policies on the other. What Tom (1993) brings to this study is a willingness to treat female experience as *differentiated* rather than uniform and to understand women's relationships as potentially conflictual rather than as intrinsically collaborative and communitarian.

These intersections of race and gender are also carefully examined in Mirchandani's (2003) study of self-employed women in the Canadian Maritimes. With the help of extensive in-depth interviews, Mirchandani offers a portrait of women entrepreneurs' emotional work that is rich in its sheer diversity. Mirchandani begins by challenging most studies of women's emotional work, which she faults on two counts. First, they tend to rely entirely on racially homogeneous samples, and second, they assume that all women workers and professionals (regardless of race, religion, and ethnicity) have identical experiences as their white female counterparts. Her own study of a diverse sample of female entrepreneurs tells a completely different story. Her study indicates that different *racial locations* mediate forms of emotional work resorted to by self-employed women, especially when it comes to dealing with difficult customers. In part, these different strategies are necessary because the customers/clients themselves approach women entrepreneurs with a whole set of assumptions and prejudices about their skill levels. Thus, white female entrepreneurs were more likely to adopt detached procedural routes in dealing with difficult customers while their ethnic counterparts (especially African Canadians) worked harder in the immediate situation in persuading their clients to see things differently. In sum, Mirchandani's (2003) study offers useful insights into how race intersects with gender to function as relational sites of privilege and exclusion.

No discussion of fieldwork in the feminist tradition would be complete without some mention of feminist studies of language and discourse. Language as a site of female exploitation has always been of central importance to radical feminism, whereas language as a part of discourse continues to preoccupy poststructural feminists. An extraordinarily powerful piece looking at linguistic work worlds is Carol Cohn's (1987) study of the everyday world of defense intellectuals—the (almost entirely male) administrative and scientific experts who work at senior levels of nuclear policy. Cohn was a participant observer in a university center on defense technology and arms control where she attended lectures, conversed with defense intellectuals, and conducted in-depth interviews with them. In her analysis, Cohn extricates the gendered and sexual motifs that pervaded the discussions of nuclear war and arms buildup. Terms like *missile envy, vertical erector launchers, thrust to weight ratios,* and *deep penetration* peppered the daily discussions of nuclear arms. Cohn proposes that both the military and arms manufacturers insidiously exploit this phallic imagery with its promise of *homoerotic excitement* to promote a culture in which the prospects of nuclear arms buildup and even nuclear war is valorized as a kind of male fantasy.

At the same time, Cohn (1987) demonstrates how the language of defense intellectuals is also suffused with an aura of rational, male scientific expertise. She goes on to argue that this combination of scientific and phallic imagery produces a highly *seductive* language that offers its participants a feeling of control over, and a sense of distance from, the specter of nuclear war. As she notes (Cohn, 1987, 706), "*structurally* speaking, technocratic language removes them [defense intellectuals] from the position of victim and puts them in the position of the planner, the user, the actor. . . . the speakers of technostrategic language are positionally allowed, even forced. . . . to escape viewing nuclear war from the position of the victim, by virtue of their linguistic stance as users rather than victims of nuclear weaponry." Ultimately, Cohn's study offers us some disturbing insights into a professional world in which imminent death, danger, and destruction are obscured by a masculine language of expertise and sexual dominance.

Researchers working in the poststructural feminist tradition who share this interest in language are much more drawn to the study of organizational texts. These texts can refer to "classic" writings in organization theory (Calas & Smircich, 1991; Mumby & Putnam, 1992), popular books on managerial practice (Fondas, 1997), or corporate policies and announcements (Martin, 1990). Substantially influenced by Derrida's philosophy of deconstruction (discussed extensively in Chapter 12), feminists engage in a close reading of these texts— looking not so much for embedded meanings and images as for gendered identities and codes that appear between the constantly shifting binary oppositions that form the backbone of any text. With the help of deconstruction, these feminists problematize concepts (such as leadership or management) that emerge out of a system of dichotomies that privilege the masculine over the feminine and men over women (Mumby & Putnam, 1992). An illustrative example can be found in Calas and Smircich's (1991) examination of classic leadership texts, more specifically the writings of Chester Barnard, McGregor, Henry Mintzberg, and Peters and Waterman. Calas and Smircich do not look for the hidden messages of gender contained within the texts. Rather, they deconstruct them with a view to exposing the *cultural and rhetorical conditions* that sustain leadership as a seductive game. In a slightly different vein, Martin (1990) closely examines a corporate announcement launching a new product and shows how allusions in the text to the female product manager's recent delivery of a baby positions women employees in limiting ways and simultaneously suppresses several gender conflicts.

These feminist deconstructions differ quite noticeably from the textual analyses performed by radical feminists or critical hermeneuticians who are always searching for gendered subtexts or hidden messages in any texts. Poststructural feminists, on the other hand, are more interested in assessing how any text (spoken, written, or otherwise) is put together, and in understanding how the fundamental *structural composition* of a text dictates how gender can be articulated in the first place. In doing so, they also keep an eye very firmly on the matrices of power that are at play in the composition of a text. Feminist poststructuralists often resort to unconventional styles of research presentation—juxtaposing fragments of different texts, violating standard grammatical rules to make a point, and so on. Such stylistic deviations are philosophically compatible with the tradition's more subversive aims and are not (as commonly believed) merely a series of cute gimmicks designed to do little more than draw attention.

This brings us then to one of feminism's more controversial tendencies—that is, its refusal to follow many of the established conventions of academic writing. The tradition's emphasis on the personal, its willingness to borrow from diverse disciplinary sources, its frequently visionary and poetic tone, and its willingness to experiment with a number of textual forms can make it seem suspect and "unscientific" to those who are unfamiliar with its epistemological and ontological orientations. However, within many feminist circles, creative expression and a merging of disciplinary influences are deemed integral to crafting feminist research. As Lengermann and Niebrugge-Brantley (1990, 321) appropriately note, "Feminist accounts deliberately weave formal analytic modes with procedures that appeal to intuitive, personal, aesthetic and even revelatory modes of knowing. . . . To feminist theorists, this tone is deeply satisfying for they claim that it is necessary to bring together art and science, indeed all truth-seeking strategies, if one hopes to escape the restricted disciplinary vision which may be one instrument of domination."

Debates and New Directions in the Feminist Tradition

From its very inception in the 1960s, the feminist tradition has been the subject of much controversy and debate. Concerns about the role of feminist theory, the nature of feminist politics, the extent of feminist inclusiveness, and the development of future feminist agendas have all been cause for extensive debate and deliberation.

Feminism's unwavering commitment to social change has made it the target of much criticism that accuses it of being overly *political* and lacking in *scientific neutrality*. To many feminists, however, this accusation of politicization is not so much a vice as a virtue that derives its legitimacy from the theoretical critique of patriarchy and female subjugation. Just as praxis is required in the historical materialist tradition, so, too, feminist politics is very much theoretically driven and is an integral part of the tradition. Feminism's endorsement of "the politics of the personal" is after all its starting point for looking at women's everyday experiences as the location for resistance to the patriarchy and social transformation.

Yet, as Weedon (1997) points out, there is a noticeable tension between feminist politics and feminist theory. Some strands of feminism are even openly hostile to feminist theory, arguing that most theory is a male form of discourse rooted in narrow conceptions of rationality that invariably ignore and even dismiss women's subjective experiences. Other feminists maintain that discarding all forms of theory is more likely to be counterproductive. They advocate working even more intensely at changing both the type of knowledge produced about women and the social relations of knowledge production (Weedon, 1997). In particular, they stress the importance of embracing a *reflexivity* that increasingly interrogates the relationship between knowledge and knowledge production (Calas & Smircich, 1992). Recent developments in feminist poststructuralism come closest to doing this.

At the same time, poststructuralism's strong influence on feminism is not without its controversial elements. In general, poststructuralism is averse to essentialism of any kind, and is deeply suspicious of the use of such *fixed categories* as "woman" and "femininity." Poststructuralists question basic notions such as "man" and "woman" as fundamentally problematic, preferring to replace them with more pluralistic and fluid understandings of gender (Alvesson & Due Billing, 2002). Several sections of the feminist tradition remain distinctively uneasy with this position, arguing that such a deliberately relativistic stance might weaken feminism's social impact just at the point when women's voices are beginning to gain an audience and when feminism has acquired some measure of academic legiticmacy. Many feminists remain somewhat ambivalent about poststructuralism even as they embrace its ideas on reflexivity and its rejection of universality (Flax, 1990).

The feminist tradition also continues to wrestle with the relationship between race, religion, ethnicity, and nationality to feminist theory and research. For over twenty years, sections of Western feminism have been strenuously critiqued for their tendency to categorize women as a *singular* group on the basis of some assumed shared oppression (Mohanty, 1988), for their neglect of issues of concern to nonwhite and Third World women (Davies, 1983; Friedman, 1998), and for their astounding unself-consciousness about the effects of their own theorizing practices on marginalized women in both the West and in the Third World (Bulbeck, 1998; Mohanty, 1988). Some feminist scholars have certainly taken these critiques to heart, recognizing that "all major axes of difference—race, class, ethnicity, sexuality and religion intersect with gender in ways which proffer a multiplicity of subject positions within any discourse" (Moore, 1999, 61). The work of Calas and Smircich (1993), Holvino (1996), Hossfeld (1993), Mirchandani (2003), Tom (1993), and others demonstrates a keen sensitivity to these problematics. All too often, however, feminist research in organization and management studies continues to treat women as a relatively invariant category and gives scant attention to the complex dynamics of gender across diverse social and global locations (e.g., Benschop & Dooreward, 1998a; Fletcher, 1999). With the few exceptions mentioned above, feminist studies within organization science are yet to recognize the tremendous impact of the global economics of neo-imperialism, the continuing legacies of colonialism, and the institutional pressures to conform to Western cultural patterns on the lives of women at work, and on the structuring of gender in organizations.

The overall feminist contribution to organization and management studies is beyond question. Feminists have been responsible for breaking the silence about women in organizations, for bringing women's standpoints closer to the forefront, and for helping to develop an understanding of organizations as gendered entities. For the tradition to remain relevant, however, it must move away from examining only the cognitive and demographic aspects of sex/gender in organizations, and become more conversant with an *institutional* understanding of women and sexuality at work. In this respect, sociologists of work and researchers of public policy (e.g., Acker, 1990; Cohn, 1987; Mirchandani, 2003 Tom, 1993) have been more adventurous than their feminist colleagues in management. With a few noteworthy exceptions, feminist work in management and organization studies rarely moves out of the women's voice/experience tradition. The strong influence exerted by social and cognitive psychology on organizational behavior may well be partly responsible for this. Psychology pushes feminist researchers into endless studies of female leadership styles, women's ways of decision making, women's patterns of mentoring, and so on. The discipline's strong managerialist bias also limits feminists from looking at women in more subordinate organizational positions and from exploring relationships between women in power and women on the periphery of organizations. This psychologistic (and therefore individualistic) emphasis also prevents researchers from studying ways in which gender and sexuality are enmeshed with global configurations of power. World Bank policies, the increased flow of global capital, the dissolution of trade barriers, and so on, have implications for women and gender dynamics that just might be more profound than female managers' ability to form social networks or to work in teams. One can only hope that researchers in the feminist tradition will increasingly take up these complex issues and produce an even richer portfolio of feminist research.

Note

1. Although Fletcher (1999) styles her study as being partly poststructural, it is far more representative of the women's voice/experience tradition, with its quasi-essentialist assumptions about women's ways of working and women's values being derived from the private sphere.

Figure 10.1 **Highlights of the Feminist Tradition**

Philosophic influences: Marxism, existentialism, relational psychology, poststructuralism

Major figures: Jean Baker Miller, Carol Gilligan, Dorothy Smith, Joan Acker, Luce Irigiray, Chris Weedon

Central concepts
• Sex and gender
• Sexuality
• Masculinity and femininity
• Women's ways of knowing
• Patriarchy
• Gendered divisions of labor

Key practices
• Achieving closeness with subjects
• Personalizing the research account
• Pursuing multidisciplinarity
• Providing a space for women's voices
• Understanding the gendered nature of all social arrangements
• Interrogating the processes of knowledge production

Exemplary research
• "Reporting Gender" (Benschop & Meihuizen, 2002)
• "Voicing Seduction to Silence Leadership" (Calas & Smircich, 1991)
• "Sex and Death in the Relational World of Defense Intellectuals" (Cohn, 1987)
• "Their Logic Against Them" (Hossfeld, 1993)
• "Serving Hamburgers and Selling Insurance" (Leidner, 1991)
• "Challenging Racial Silences in Studies of Women's Emotion Work" (Mirchandani, 2003)
• "Children of Our Culture" (Tom, 1993)

11

Structuration and Praxeology

Transcending Dualisms Within
Frameworks of Power

Structuration theory refers to some of the collective writings of British soci-ologist Anthony Giddens, whereas *praxeology* refers to the work of French anthropologist Pierre Bourdieu, especially as they relate to overcoming a num-ber of conventional dualisms in Western social theory.[1] Writing quite inde-pendently and making few references to each others' work, Giddens and Bourdieu have initiated a tradition of scholarship in which the resolution of many enduring tensions (e.g., between objectivity and subjectivity) are re-solved through ideas of structuration and praxeology. From his early writ-ings, Bourdieu's (1977) goal has been the bridging between objective conditions and subjective interpretations, as well as between theory and prac-tice. Writing only a few years later, Giddens (1976; 1979) has also sought to overcome the pervasive dualisms between agency and structure, and between micro and macro levels of analysis. Over the next twenty years, both writers attained considerable intellectual prominence and began to exert a powerful influence in diverse disciplines in the social sciences, including sociology, anthropology, political science, communication studies, organization and management studies, and information systems research.

In short, structuration theory and praxeology emerged out of Bourdieu's and Giddens' personal dissatisfaction with both the structural emphasis of twentieth-century Marxisms (notably Althusser and the French structuralists) and the excessive subjectivism of phenomenology and existentialism. They have attempted to reconcile these two traditions by (a) developing notions of power that are more *relational* and *process-oriented* (Everett, 2002) and (b) recognizing the active and reflexive engagement of individual actors in all social situations (Baert, 1998; Craib, 1992). Both Giddens and Bourdieu have unquestionably been influenced by Marx. In fact, Giddens (1973) first intro-duced the notion of structuration as a way of going beyond reified notions of class in order to understand how classes operate and are experienced in prac-tice (Whittington, 1992). Bourdieu's affinity for Marx can be seen in his in-sistence that *power struggles* are endemic to social life (Inglis, 1979). For Bourdieu, however, these struggles are as much symbolic and cultural as they are economic. May (1996) is therefore correct in his observation that Bourdieu employs Marx's concern with the *reproduction* of oppressive social relations but tempers Marx's economism with Durkheim's sociology of symbolism. The same can as easily be said of Giddens as well.

Despite their common grounding in Marxian theory, Bourdieu and Giddens exhibit interesting and substantive differences in the development of their own theoretical positions. Giddens' extension of Marx is definitely more *micro-sociological,* whereas Bourdieu's is much more *anthropological.* Giddens (1976; 1979) relies considerably on Harold Garfinkel's ideas (discussed in Chapter 4) about everyday accomplishments and individual proficiency in order to establish how structures are *appropriated* and creatively interpreted by people in keeping with their own agendas and interests. His structuration theory, therefore, tends to emphasize the importance of individual *choice* and *social competence* within a broad framework of power. Bourdieu's anthropological training and his reliance on Levi-Strauss point him toward *culture* as the central dynamic in his vision of structuration (Bourdieu, 1972; 1990). In attempting to bridge the micro and the macro as well as the objective and the subjective, Giddens and Bourdieu take somewhat divergent paths—Giddens focusing on the role of individual interpretations in the reproduction of structure, and Bourdieu emphasizing cultural constraints on individual choice, competence, and action. Both theorists are considered to be *critical*—not only because they are influenced by Marx, but also because they take power seriously, and are concerned with questions of structure, its reproduction and social transformation—all of which are central to the broader critical tradition. The remainder of this chapter will closely examine the theoretical discussions of Giddens and Bourdieu and the concepts that are central to each of their writings on structuration and praxeology.

Anthony Giddens and Structuration Theory

Commentators on Giddens's work frequently characterize him as being *ambitious* (Baert, 1998; Cassell, 1993; May, 1996) in his scholarly goals and in his vast coverage of social issues. Over a period of thirty years, Giddens has (a) challenged the classical sociology of Durkheim and Marx, (b) argued the significance of social theory as a constitutive force, (c) developed a theoretical approach that overcomes the dualism between structure and agency, and (d) examined the circumstances of modernity and its impact on social relations and the formation of self-identity.

Giddens, however, is probably best known for his articulation of structuration theory, which he first systematically developed in *New Rules of Sociological Method* (Giddens, 1976)—a book that shot him into prominence as much for its bold challenge of the Durkheimian idea of stable symbolic orders as for its intriguing and fluid conceptions of social structure. Giddens's structuration theory has been described as a meta-theory whose principal goal is the connection of human action with structural explanations (Riley, 1983). Structuration theory represents a serious attempt to blend the central assumptions of the interpretive traditions with those of structuralism within a wider framework of power and domination that is more the hallmark of the critical tradition.

Not surprisingly, structuration theory carries visible traces of multiple theoretical influences. In Giddens's efforts to emphasize sedimented structures while simultaneously acknowledging that individuals have control over and knowledge of their own actions (Riley, 1983), he draws upon Marxism, ethnomethodology, Heideggerian phenomenology, autopoesis, and the linguistic philosophy of Wittgenstein (Baert, 1998; Craib, 1992). Giddens weaves these diverse philosophic threads into a coherent explanation of both the structural basis of social action and the individual constructivist basis of social structure (Giddens, 1976; 1979; 1984). To commentators like Craib (1992) and Cassells (1993), structuration theory is not really cast in the formal mold of conventional "Grand Theory" in the way that Marxism or structural functionalism is. Instead, Giddens regards his structuration theory as the means for addressing specific queries that keep reappearing in the social sciences (Cassells, 1993). Others suggest that structuration theory is more like a general guide to what we might find in our social worlds (Craib, 1992).

In essence, structuration theory is a carefully thought-out explanation of the *processes* whereby people routinely draw upon structures and use them, in either conventional or creative ways, thereby also sustaining and reproducing these structures themselves, albeit in somewhat altered forms (Giddens, 1976; 1979). For Giddens, structures are both the *preconditions* and *unintended outcomes* of peoples' agency (Baert, 1998). Individuals must necessarily draw upon social structures (e.g., language, rules, conventions) as they go about their daily work and social interactions. Even as they employ these structures in their mundane activities, they reaffirm and reproduce them. In Giddens's (1976; 1979) scheme of things, therefore, structure and agency do not enjoy any kind of ontological separation, and structures are not the fixed externalities so often envisaged by different genres of social theory.

Giddens's structuration theory is more than a mere *synthesis* of diverse sociophilosophic strands. His claim that the *reproduction* of social structure takes place through the active agency of social actors and is manifested in "the situatedness of interaction in time and space" (Giddens, 1984, 110) is the fulcrum around which his structuration theory revolves. Indeed, Giddens's ability to link different temporal levels with his ideas about the reproduction of social structure may well constitute his major contribution to social theory (Cohen 1989). According to Giddens (1979), at one end of the temporal spectrum, we have Alfred Schutz's concept of *duree*—the day-to-day experience of repetitive and routine tasks. At the opposite end of the temporal spectrum is Ferdinand Braudel's concept of *longue duree* or *institutional time*—referring to invariant structures that extend over long periods of time. In between everyday existence and institutional time is the life span of the individual—best captured by Heidegger's notion of *Sein zum Tode* or the finitude of people's existence. In developing structuration theory, Giddens (1979) links these different temporal spans, showing how action at the level of everyday existence or *duree* contributes to the reproduction of *longue duree* (Baert, 1998). In doing so, Giddens transcends not only the structure-agency divide, but also the micro–macro divide that is present in so many genres of social theory.

In developing his theory of structuration, Giddens also comes up with his own definitions of power, structure, agency, and institution. Giddens's ideas about both structure and agency are very specific and somewhat complicated, and help explain social transformation and people's abilities to withstand oppressive social structures. In his more recent writings, Giddens has attempted to grapple more directly with the empirical consequences of modernity (Giddens, 1990), using his ideas of structuration to examine the formation of self-identities and the transformation of intimacy under conditions of late modernity (Giddens, 1991; 1992).

Central Concepts in Giddens's Structuration Theory

In developing his structuration theory, Giddens' principal aim has been the breaching of the conventional divide between structure and agency, and the simultaneous generation of an explanation of social action that recognizes the importance of power and the temporal dimensions of human action. In order to accomplish this aim, Giddens is compelled to rethink the notions of structure and agency, and to come up with other concepts such as structuration and practical versus discursive consciousness. This section explores many of his more central concepts.

Structure

Giddens's understanding of social structure is noticeably more fluid and diffuse than any other consideration of it in social inquiry. Avoiding an overly deterministic view of power, Giddens (1984, 25) argues that "the structural properties of social systems are both medium and outcome of the practices they recursively organize." That is, although people necessarily have to draw upon structures as they engage in everyday actions, structures also come into being and are constantly reproduced through human action. Thus, for Giddens, structure has no independent ontological status except as it is initiated in activity or is retained cognitively by individuals in society (Whittington, 1992). At some level, Giddens's notion of structure can even be said to lack a concrete exteriority, because structure is part and parcel of an individual's existential makeup. As Giddens (1984, 25) himself notes, "Structure is not 'external' to individuals: as *memory traces* and as *instantiated* in social practice, it is in a certain sense more 'internal' than exterior to their activities" (emphasis added).

Given that structures exist only in the mindsets and actions of individuals, Giddens cannot see them as entirely monolithic or single handedly capable of determining social action. Instead, he comes up with his key concept of the *"duality of structure,"* whereby structure is seen as being simultaneously *constraining* and *enabling*. In other words, although structures can indeed restrict the range of individual actions, they can also be interpreted in unconventional ways and employed creatively to suit different circumstances. These ideas are best captured by Giddens (1984, 179) himself in his observation that "the structural properties of social systems . . . are like the walls of a room from which an individual cannot escape but inside which he or she is able to move around at whim." Language is another illustration of structure's capacity for constraint and enablement. Although any formal language limits what and how we can say things, the same language can be employed in many forms of creative expression (Craib, 1992). Giddens's notion of the duality of structure is of paramount importance to structuration theory because it allows "an adherence to an ontology of potentials whereby the opportunities for innovative social conduct are deliberately held open in opposition to the idea of the constraining regularities of systemic forces" (May, 1996, 108).

Structures in Giddens's thinking refer to entire sets of social *rules* that comprise norms, procedures and conventions, and *resources,* including both allocative and authoritative resources. Capital, technology, skill, and expertise are all resources. Giddens further identifies three types of structures that are present in all societies: (1) structures of signification, (2) structures of domination, and (3) structures of legitimation. *Structures of signification* refer to the rules, scripts, codes, and conventions that govern our interpretations of the world and our communication in it. Language is one of the most powerful structures of signification, as are social and cultural rituals that give meaning to our lives. *Structures of domination* refer to controls over resources and include economic and political institutions such as banks, governments, and commercial enterprises. Finally, *structures of legitimation* refer to normative institutions and cultural repositories of values, taboos, and moral codes of conduct. Churches, temples, regulatory bodies, and the entire judicial system are all key elements in a society's structures of legitimation.

Although Giddens uses these three classifications of social structure as a matter of analytic convenience, it should be noted that in actual social situations, these structures enjoy a great deal of overlap with one another. Churches are an excellent example. Churches are part of any structure of legitimation, being the institutional purveyors of social values and moralities. In contemporary Western societies, churches are also very much a part of the power structure or the structure of domination: they hold vast amounts of capital and control domains of knowledge through church-affiliated schools and universities. Finally, churches are also part of the symbolic order of signification since their religious and spiritual messages fundamentally structure the cognitive worlds that individuals inhabit. Notions of sin and virtue, redemption, the Protestant work ethic, duty to God, and so on, are fundamental structuring concepts that are produced by churches and other religious institutions. Many other structures in today's world similarly overlap with each other and in different structural domains.

Agency

The importance Giddens gives to individual agency is somewhat unique within the critical traditions. In essence, he takes the ethnomethodological idea of *reflexivity* very seriously, arguing that individuals are acutely aware of their actions and the conditions and consequences of these actions (Giddens, 1976; 1982). Thus, when actors draw upon rules or other structures, they rarely do so mindlessly, but in skillful and knowledgeable ways. However, lest we think of individuals as paying close and tireless attention to their own uses of structure, Giddens also incorporates Heidegger's notion of action or agency as a *continuous flow of conduct* rather than as a series of discrete acts (Baert, 1998). In doing so, Giddens decouples agency from calculative conduct and argues that individual agency derives more from people's capabilities and social competence than from conscious motives of self-interest. Thus, what Giddens (1982) terms *strategic conduct* is for him "purposive" rather than "purposeful." That is, although people are not solely guided by deliberate intentions, they are nevertheless attending (albeit in a less focused manner) to their own and others' action (Baert, 1998).

In taking such a strong line on agency, Giddens deprives social structures of some of their omnipotence and empowers individual actors even when they are operating in situations that appear to be constrained by social structures. Above all, Giddens forces us to pay attention to the *choices* available to actors in rule-bound circumstances (Giddens, 1976; 1979). The presence of choice implies that individuals can always either *interveve* or *refrain* from action. With the help of both choice and competence, Giddens sees individuals as having an innate capacity to *resist* structure (Whittington, 1992) and to *transform* society. In his later writings on modernity, Giddens visualizes the spectrum of personal choices as outstripping the power of structural constraints. The modern cultural emphasis placed on being true to oneself (Giddens, 1991), coupled with the waning of innumerable traditions (Giddens, 1990), creates conditions in which individuals exert even greater choices over crafting personal lifestyles and identities. Giddens also argues that individuals are finding it easier to break away from social ties and traditions that are not to their liking, and therefore are experiencing unprecedented *transformative capacities* in modern societies.

Structuration

The notion of structuration emerges from Giddens's arguments about the fluidity of structure and the active agency of individuals. The process of structuration represents Giddens' attempt to rescue the importance of society while still insisting that it is produced and reproduced only through human action (Craib, 1992). Structuration theory bears distinct imprints of the Marxian concept of the *dialectic of control*. For Giddens, the dialectic between structure and agency contains the seeds of social transformation and individual empowerment. All actors take part in this dialectic of control, which at the very least affords individuals the power of defiance and at best the power of social transformation.

"Structuration is the production and reproduction of social systems through the application of generative rules and resources" (Riley, 1983, 415). Structuration takes place in concrete social situations in two ways. First, it must be remembered that actors do not interpret structural properties in identical ways. Actors draw *selectively* on some dimensions of social structure while ignoring others. Actors also interpret and frame structures (for themselves and others) in unconventional and unexpected ways. As these novel and selective interpretations of structure are accepted and imitated by other actors, they eventually become sedimented as structures themselves. All manner of structural arrangements, including legal principles, organizational policies, religious doctrines, and social rituals, are open to such selective and creative interpretations.

Second, as Whittington (1992) notes, actors' own membership in multiple social organizations is another source of structuration. Managers of major corporations, for instance, also participate in organizations such as community associations, ethnic clubs, and consumer advocacy groups from which they might import into their firms diverse and even contradictory structural properties. For Whittington (1992, 697), this "does allow for the possibility of managerial agency built upon forms of authority and norms of behavior independent of strict capitalist logic." In such cases, therefore, structure does not crush or even inhibit agency but actually enables it under conditions of *complexity* and *contradiction*. In sum, therefore, structuration is the process that connects social systems and the situated activities of human beings via the reproduction and transformation of social systems in actual social practice (May, 1996).

Working in the Structurationist Tradition

Considering the recency of Giddens's work on structuration theory, one can only be amazed at the sheer number of empirical studies that have already been inspired by his writings. Researchers have looked at (among other things) the implementation of technology (Kling, 1992; Orlikowski, 2000), the political dimensions of organizational culture (Riley 1983), entrepreneurial practices (Boissevain, 1990), the computerization of the insurance market (Barrett & Walsham, 1999), and ideologies in a public relations department (Filby & Willmott, 1988) from a structurationist perspective. Working with this perspective requires primarily the steadfast maintenance of a *processual* focus over all social phenomena. What is of interest is society or culture in the process of being *enacted* or in the making. Technologies, social rituals, languages, and ideologies are all studied, as they are being produced, reproduced, appropriated, and transformed, and not as fixed structures and rigid entities.

For those working in the structurationist tradition, some familiarity with Giddens's much-cited concept—the *double hermeneutic*—is helpful. Through the idea of the double hermeneutic, Giddens stresses that any social scientist must take the trouble of decoding the world of her or his subjects, while simultaneously remaining conscious that the theoretical world of social science is also being decoded and interpreted by the same subjects in their capacity as social actors (Cassell, 1993). Giddens thus visualizes the social scientist as a highly productive and influential individual with the potential for constituting and changing society.

Working in the structurationist tradition also calls for an *iterative* orientation—that is, a willingness to move continuously between concept and data, between actors and structures, and between micro and macro domains. In this respect, structuration bears a strong resemblance to the pursuit of the hermeneutic circle (discussed in Chapter 2). Structuration theory is more sharply focused than hermeneutics, however, and as Barrett and Walsham (1999) note, it can be immensely valuable as a sensitizing device in the course of fieldwork, directing a researcher's focus toward specific individuals and interactions. Giddens's own writings underscore the incredibly complex and dynamic nature of the structuration process. His acute sense of *movement* between actors and social structures is not easily captured in actual research projects; unfortunately, many researchers working in this tradition tend to concentrate excessively on either agency or structure at the expense of the *relationship* between the two. Riley's (1983) study of the political dimensions of an organization's culture is a case in point.

Riley's study looks at two professional subsidiaries of a large parent organization with the intent of identifying the symbols used therein in creating a political culture. Her study also sought to understand the reproduction of this culture. The data for Riley's (1983) study is the language from forty interviews with different organization members. She examines an array of clichés, metaphors, phrases, and jargon used in the interviews to understand their use in the construction of a political culture in the organization. Unfortunately, Riley's subsequent data analysis and presentation bear little resemblance to Giddens' notion of structuration. She does little more than develop a classification of structures along Giddens's lines of signification, legitimation, and domination. There is no elaboration of any kind of structuration process that might have been at play, or any discussion of *how* actors worked with structural material to build some kind of political culture. The overall study is therefore somewhat frustrating as its claim to use structuration theory offers few insights into the dynamic production of an organization's political culture.

In short, working in the structurationist tradition requires a more *dialectical* and *nuanced* approach to the relationship between structure and agency. Orlikowski's (1993; 2000) studies of the adoption of technology accomplish some of this. Orlikowski's (2000) basic position that computer technologies have a *virtual existence* dependent on users' interactions with them rather than some concrete independent existence reflects the central ideas of the structuration tradition. In her study of *Notes*—a computer software product— she argues that technologies can only exist as "technologies-in-practice" that are strongly influenced by users' own understandings of their properties and functions. In her study of the adoption of *Notes* by two different companies, Orlikowski (2000) helps us understand how the technology is enacted in three ways—inertia, application, and change. Inertia and application-driven enactments typically help maintain and even strengthen the status quo, whereas change-oriented enactments are more likely to result in organizational transformations. Orlikowski's study is interesting because she provides a *spectrum of possibilities* that are present in any situation of technology-in-practice. Her focus on individual choice and competence is in keeping with the structurationist tradition.

A far more comprehensive study of the links between information technology and social transformation in the structurationist tradition is found in the empirical work of Barrett and Walsham (1999) who examine the implementation of electronic trading applications in the London insurance market. Their study looks at LIMNET—a service offered by the electronic data exchange that was designed to electronically coordinate the passing of risk placement between brokers and selected underwriters. Barrett and Walsham (1999) conducted an extensive, longitudinal study of the implementation of LIMNET using a wide variety of data sources. Although the core of their study relied on ninety-four in-depth semistructured interviews with insurance brokers and underwriters, they also used a number of primary and secondary data sources that gave them a strong sense of the history and culture of the London market. These included strategy plans, mission statements, newsletters, annual reports, and local newspaper accounts. In addition, they also observed the process of insurance risk placement in the market around the city of London, as well as brokers and underwriters working in their offices and in the trading room of Lloyds.

Barrett and Walsham show how the new technology (LIMNET) facilitated the conduct of business interactions across a number of different time–space configurations, thereby threatening the comfort of conventional face-to-face work that took place between brokers and underwriters. These face-to-face interactions were considered crucial to the decision-making process concerning the placement of acceptable risk. As the study progressed, Barrett and Walsham (1999) saw LIMNET as a "disembedding mechanism" that removed the placing activities from the localized contexts of Lloyds and opened up the possibilities of global interactions across time and space. They then proceeded to examine the impacts of this disembedding on the forging of trust, on organizational reflexivity, and on the formation of self-identities of individuals working in the market. Overall, their study works skillfully with structuration theory to examine the relationships between individuals and technology within the wider context of the London insurance market, thereby providing us with a picture of social transformation that is driven by neither individual perceptions nor technological determinism on their own.

In their structurationist study of contradictory ideologies in a public relations department, Filby and Willmott (1988) make links between individual conduct, organization structures, and structures external to the organization (in this case, occupational myths). Their study is an interesting exploration of the *symbolic mediations* between public relations specialists and their own enactment of the organization's definition of their work. The study, which was primarily conducted by one of the authors, was done in two stages. In the first stage (lasting nine months), the researcher operated as a covert participant observer in his official capacity as a trainee in the department. The second stage took place eighteen months later when the same researcher reentered the organization, this time openly as an observer. During this period, he also conducted a number of unstructured interviews with staff members who were asked to interpret some of the events and discussions that he had already observed.

In keeping with the structurationist tradition, Filby and Willmott (1988) deliberately avoided viewing the organization's culture as cohesive and homogeneous, focusing instead on the cultural fragmentation and ideological differentiation that was present at the workplace. They then identified certain professional structures as the source of some of this differentiation. They observe, for instance, that employees with a background in journalism emphasized the *informational* dimensions of their work, whereas employees without a journalistic background emphasized its *promotional* elements of the job and regarded their work in a far more glamorous light. This study is faithful to the structurationist tradition because it makes an effort to understand agency (in this case in the act of identity formation) as deriving from multiple sources, including professional communities outside the organization.

In the same study, Filby and Willmott (1988) also explore ways in which the public relations specialists employed structures such as bureaucratic conventions to safeguard their own more organic subculture. By authoring an internal informational booklet that deferred to standard bureaucratic expectations about the rationality of public relations work, the specialists in essence used structural myths to reassure the rest of the organization about the nature of their own work and to thereby protect themselves from undue bureaucratic interference. Yet, even as they used these structures to their own advantage, they were caught in a paradox of their own making. As Filby and Willmott (1988, 346) observe, "by imbuing the bureaucracy with a massive, reified power, these specialists effectively denied themselves the possibility of recognizing, let alone seizing the opportunity to confront the relations of power which locked them in their departmental closet." Observations such as this one make the study exemplary in its ability to portray the complicated structuration process, and to credit both agency and structure with a role in everyday organizational action.

Giddens's ideas have attracted a number of adherents who label their work as structurationist and who claim to be applying his concepts to their empirical work. However, the extent to which these researchers are all able to faithfully translate Giddens's ideas is open to question. Admittedly, they do not have an easy task: Giddens's structuration theory is far from simplistic and calls for an intricate balancing of micro and macro levels of analyses. Yet, researchers such as Filby and Willmott have shown us that the task is not entirely impossible. In general, as Whittington (1992) noted, Giddens's ideas on structuration have an unfortunate tendency to be selectively appropriated in a somewhat lopsided manner, with researchers stressing either his structural or agency arguments to the detriment of the other. Furthermore, the far more difficult (but central) task of examining the dynamic relationship between them receives far less attention. This can be noticed in the field of information systems where structuration theory enjoys considerable popularity. Researchers in this area are definitely slanted toward emphasizing agency as they focus on users' appropriations of information technology (structure) and neglect the mediation of social structure itself on diverse ways of appropriation.

Concentrating on social actors' interpretations does little justice to structuration theory, which is explicitly intended to transcend the dualism of structure and agency. Moreover, focusing on the individual user's interpretation can easily be done from a symbolic interactionist or even ethnomethodological standpoint. The tradition of structuration can continue to remain meaningful only if researchers take Giddens's notions of a dialectical and dynamic relation between structure and agency more seriously.

Bourdieu's Understanding of Society and Social Research

Comparisons between Bourdieu and Giddens are hard to avoid given both their interests in transcending the subjective–objective divide in the Western intellectual tradition, and their mutual concerns with reviving the reflexivity issue in social research. Even more than Giddens, Bourdieu has committed himself to a *social praxeology*—where theory and practice are developed simultaneously and constantly inform one another (Bourdieu, 1977). Bourdieu's social praxeology is also wedded to his somewhat complex vision of the social world. In developing his coherent vision of social processes, he weaves an intricate intellectual tapestry drawing on conceptual threads from Durkheim, Weber, and Marx. In essence, Bourdieu combines Marx's materialism with the idealism of Durkheim, and tempers both with Weber's ideas on the lived experience of social status (McCall, 1991). This complex amalgamation of classical sociological ideas eventually enables him to analyze the relations between lifestyles, life chances, and material resources (May, 1996).

Bourdieu thus offers us a *sociology of symbolic power* that examines the relationships between culture, social structure, and action (Swartz, 1997). While Giddens connects structure and agency through his notion of structuration, Bourdieu does much the same through the idea of *cultural struggle*. In fact, this notion is central to Bourdieu's vision of society, which he sees as an endless cultural struggle between different groups (along class, ethnic, or other lines) over different sets of resources (or capitals)—be they economic, symbolic, or cultural (Bourdieu & Wacquant, 1992). Through his emphasis on cultural struggle, Bourdieu departs from Giddens in two major ways. First, his emphasis on the *cultural* dynamics within social processes makes him less inclined to have quite as much faith in individual agency as Giddens does. And second, his insistence on the prevalence of *struggles* in social life make him more inclined to favor a conflict-based view of society than Giddens. In sum, although both writers are deeply concerned with (a) bridging structure and agency, and (b) with understanding the ability of social systems to persist and reproduce themselves, Bourdieu's approach takes him in a more macro anthropological direction that stresses the power of cultural constraints over agency (Alexander, 1995; Inglis, 1979).

Bourdieu's starting point is identical to Marx's—that power struggles are endemic to social life. Far more than Marx, however, Bourdieu's interest is in the *symbolic world,* which he defines as that which is material but not recognized as such (Harken, Mahar, & Wilkes, 1990). Aesthetic preferences, managerial styles, advertising images, and rock music, for example, are components of the symbolic world. Bourdieu (1977; 1990) first establishes the enormous significance of this symbolic world and then seeks to develop a research tradition that would study how the symbolic realm mediates everyday life and global relations of domination between classes and groups (Cronin, 1996). Understanding symbolic systems is crucial to Bourdieu's praxeology because it is symbolic systems that legitimate domination by tacitly imposing a "correct" definition of the social world. In other words, symbolic systems directly aid in the existence and reproduction of stratified and oppressive hierarchical systems by trivializing gross social injustices, and in some cases even making them seem perfectly legitimate or desirable. An example is the easy acceptance by a large number of Americans of the enormous disparities between executive and worker salaries. Certain elements of the symbolic system such as glossy magazines and television shows glorify the lives of the rich and create a cult of corporate leadership that can almost make these disparities seem glamorous. Other elements (such as economists) justify these disparities as being reflections of authentic market forces in action. Together, they create a culture that is (a) unable to recognize these disparities as a violation of the American dream, and (b) paradoxically sees these inequities as in fact a part of the same American Dream.

In broad terms, Bourdieu's symbolic system corresponds quite closely to notions of ideology and systematically distorted communication that are at the heart of the historical materialist and critical theory traditions. However, Bourdieu uses this idea quite uniquely in his attempt to explain how different social groups engage in *contests* over the symbolic space by employing different forms of capital and repositioning themselves in the broader institutional field. In developing his comprehensive (if somewhat complicated) arguments, Bourdieu reworks a number of familiar social concepts (such as capital, game, and field) and comes up with a whole set of new ones (such as doxa and habitus) as well. The result is "a political economy of practices and symbolic power that includes a theory of symbolic interests, a theory of capital, and a theory of symbolic violence and symbolic capital" (Swartz, 1997, 8). In essence, Bourdieu compels us to attend to the symbolic world while constantly considering its relation to both the *cognitive structures* of the individual and the *social structures* of society (Everett, 2002) within a broader framework of cultural struggle.

Bourdieu's primary contribution lies in his appreciation of the symbolic sphere as being no less material than the so-called material world itself. The worlds of art, music, travel and leisure, fashion, and entertainment are symbolic spheres that have substantial material impacts on our everyday lives and are themselves domains for interest-ridden conflicts over the shape of social meanings (Bourdieu, 1977). Bourdieu's main interest is to open up the black box of cultural and institutional processes as a political arena in its own right rather than to treat it as incidental or peripheral to the "real" world of material objects and exchanges (Swartz, 1997).

In scrutinizing the symbolic sphere, Bourdieu also directs our attention to the interest-laden *strategies* used by various social groups in order to maximize their material and symbolic advantages. It is also important to note his somewhat unusual conception of strategies. Bourdieu does not regard strategies as always being the products of conscious calculation. According to him, they can often be shaped by habits, traditions, customs, beliefs, folklore, and other cultural and social legacies (Bourdieu, 1977). Thus, although individual actors may well exert agency in developing social strategies, it remains an agency that is strongly mediated by past and present social structures. In short, Bourdieu rejects a rational model actor of strategic action, arguing that the kind of action he is looking at is beyond the scope of conscious manipulation. Rather, he sees both interests and strategies as being defined by an actor's position within the social hierarchy. One's location as a blue-collar worker, an artist, an accountant, or a CEO plays a vital role in determining one's choice of strategies in the symbolic sphere.

Bourdieu's social praxeology also emphasizes the need for developing a critical reflection within the practice of social science. His reflexive standpoint demands "participative objectification"—an ongoing critical revisitation into the sociohistorical and epistemological conditions that favor the emergence of particular theoretical frameworks and ways of seeing the world (Bourdieu & Wacquant, 1992). In brief, Bourdieu is arguing that for social science to be entirely meaningful, it needs to be aware of the sociology of knowledge that forms the backdrop to its own development. Along with many feminists and postmodernists, he is also emphasizing the importance of having researchers recognize the impact of their own social locations on the kind of scholarly claims that they make (Everett, 2002).

For Bourdieu, reflexivity is also important because of its usefulness in overcoming three types of common researcher biases: *social bias, field bias,* and *intellectualist bias.* Social bias arises from a researcher's identity locations, as pertaining to age, gender, nationality, ethnicity, occupation, membership in the Western hemisphere or the Third World, and so on, and influences a researcher's interpretation of any social situation. Field bias stems from the researcher's position in her or his academic field, whether he or she is a novice researcher or an experienced scholar, and determines the choice of a research focus, degree of investment, and so on. Finally, the intellectualist bias is driven by the demands of the profession and the researcher's desire to be recognized as a leading scholar, a prominent intellectual, or an expert social scientist. These professional ambitions can entice researchers into treating social phenomena as mere scholarly curiosities that are of academic interest rather than as a set of important problems requiring practical (Bourdieu & Wacquant, 1992). To overcome these biases, Bourdieu insists that researchers subject their own social locations to the same cultural analysis that they bring to the study of social interactions. This must not, however, be confused with adopting a first-person voice in presenting the research or with providing an autobiographical account in the form of ethnographic memoirs (as discussed in Chapter 5). As Everett (2002) notes, Bourdieu actually shuns such moves as being pretentious and even unduly narcissistic. What he is really looking for is the researcher's serious evaluation of his or her position in the wider context and an estimation of its influence on the research being conducted.

No discussion of Bourdieu's praxeology would be complete without some mention of his notion of *relational analysis.* This term is another name for his insistence that social life not be studied as having *substance,* but as always being *in relationships* with a multitude of phenomena. For example, a phenomenon such as executive salaries has no intrinsic meaning in itself but develops meaning only when considered in relation to worker salaries or other organizational reward systems. Thus Bourdieu emphasizes building variables into "systems of relations" that are differentially and hierarchically ordered (Bourdieu, Chamboredon, & Passeron, 1991). "It is this relational, dialogical approach than enables Bourdieu to grasp particularity (the unique) within generality (the universal), and generality within particularity" (Everett, 2002, 71).

Central Concepts in Bourdieu's Praxeology

At their very core, Bourdieu's writings are all about social practice. In outlining his theory of practice, Bourdieu (1977) focuses on the creative strategies used by social actors in carving out and maintaining their social positions and on the cultural influences over these strategies. In theorizing about these social practices, Bourdieu employs a carefully crafted vocabulary consisting of terms like *field, game, capital, symbolic violence,* and *habitus.* A rigorous understanding of these concepts is vital for those who want to work in Bourdieu's tradition of praxeology.

The Field and the Game

The field refers to the relevant context for those cultural struggles that are the focus of the researcher's attention. Fields are occupied by dominant and dominated (in varying degrees) groups who are struggling to maintain positions that are advantageous to themselves (Harken, Mahar, & Wilkes, 1990). Health care, education, museums, the bond market, and the tobacco industry are a few examples of fields in which a number of struggles are likely to be taking place. In Bourdieu's (1990) own words, fields are "networks of social relations, structured systems of social positions within which maneuvers take place over resources, stakes and access."

Bourdieu's elaboration of the field compels researchers to identify a whole set of actors and institutions that are directly and tangentially relevant for understanding specific social relationships. Indeed, *mapping* a relevant field is a central task for anyone working seriously with Bourdieu's ideas. We should also note that fields are not static or fixed entities but are always *dynamic* and *relational.* Fields are also not to be thought of as homogeneous or internally cohesive. Rather, they are marked by endless tensions and struggles over (a) the mechanisms of the field's reproduction and (b) the material and symbolic resources in it (Everett, 2002). Bourdieu's emphasis on the importance of the field gives his research a far more macro flavor, as it goes beyond understanding local practices to an appreciation of wider social forces and patterns.

Fields can also be understood as social spaces in which specific *games* are played according to very specific rules (both written and unwritten). Unlike games of sport, however, these games are deadly serious, carrying important prizes and rewards (such as career advancement) for winners and serious adverse consequences for losers (such as the loss of a job or a social position). Each field is the context for different games that are constantly being played by different groups of social contestants. Within the field of academics, for instance, the publication of scholarly articles and the competition for major research grants are central games that are engaged in by academic players. In the tobacco industry, on the other hand, important games might include lobbying efforts for favorable legislation or the launching of a public relations campaign that diffuses concerns about smoking and health. The contestants engaging in these games are rarely on an equal footing with each other, some being far better positioned than others. Some players, for instance, start out with the advantage of having been dealt certain "trump cards" in the form of specific types of economic capital. Others have a better *feel for the game* either because of their upbringing or because of other experiences linked to their social positions (Bourdieu, 1977; 1984; 1990). Much of Bourdieu's interest is in the way these games are then strategized and played by different groups in society.

Capital

Bourdieu's complex reformulation of the concept of capital is among his foremost contributions to social inquiry. With the help of Weber's discussions of social status and prestige, Bourdieu brings a far more nuanced and differentiated approach to the notion of capital (May, 1996) and extends Marx's views on capital to multiple forms of social power, be they material, social, or cultural (Swartz, 1997). Bourdieu's basic argument is that individuals and groups draw upon a variety of economic, social, and cultural resources in order to improve, maintain, or strengthen their positions in the social order. These resources constitute different forms of capital (Bourdieu, 1991).

Bourdieu distinguishes between three types of capital: economic, cultural, and social capital. *Economic capital* refers to tangible material assets such as property, investments, and oil wells. *Cultural capital* is far more nebulous and comprises *objectified* and *embodied* forms of capital (Bourdieu, 1991). Objectified forms of cultural capital would include such objects as rare books, art works, and fine wine collections, which are dependent on specific cultural spheres for defining their value and their legitimacy. Objectified forms of cultural capital can be used and appreciated only by those who possess specialized cultural abilities such as scholarly training in medieval literature or an ability to distinguish between different kinds of wine. Embodied forms of cultural capital refer to the ensemble of *cultivated dispositions* that are internalized at an early stage in life, resulting in such aesthetic preferences and schemes of appreciation that carry cultural marks of distinction (Bourdieu, 1984). Knowledge of ancient Egyptian monuments, an appreciation for Baroque music, an ability to converse fluently about Surrealism, and a personal familiarity with different gourmet foods are all embodied forms of cultural capital. "Cultural capital is the linchpin of a system of distinction in which cultural hierarchies correspond to social ones, and people's tastes are predominantly a marker for class" (Thornton, 1996, 10).

Social capital, on the other hand, refers to those personal connections that give one easy access to the corridors of power and privilege. Membership in exclusive clubs, an acquaintance with politicians and business leaders, family connections with the aristocracy, and access to influential social networks are all forms of social capital. Bourdieu (1986) also enters into discussions about other forms of capital, notably *institutional capital* and *symbolic capital.* Institutional capital (sometimes also referred to as certified capital) would typically include things like degrees from renowned universities and formal affiliations to prestigious associations. Having a degree from Harvard or Cambridge, or being a fellow of the Council on Foreign Relations are ways of garnering institutional capital. Bourdieu also frequently uses the term *symbolic capital* to refer to all forms of noneconomic capital. Thus, symbolic capital can be social, institutional, or cultural capital.

By distinguishing between different forms of capital, Bourdieu is able to move away from rigidly vertical models of social structure and to locate different social groups in a highly complex multidimensional space rather than along a rigidly calibrated social ladder (Thornton, 1996). He thereby introduces considerable flexibility into materialist models of class while still holding on to Marx's ideas of social stratification. Bourdieu's understanding of these capital-related dynamics is also driven by *particularistic* rather than universalist assumptions. In other words, although one's position in social space is indeed largely dependent on one's capital, different forms of capital are likely to be valued differently in different fields. Flexibility is also obtained through Bourdieu's (1991) notion that some forms of capital can be converted into others. Social connections (social capital), for instance, can quickly lead to advantageous career opportunities that in turn come with high salaries (economic capital) and so on. Owners of cultural capital are also able to move comfortably within circles of power and thereby develop access to economic capital. Despite his emphasis on the *convertibility* of capital, Bourdieu does admit that neither cultural nor social capital has the stability of economic capital, in part because the accumulation of cultural capital can be undermined by criticism and suspicion. Economic capital is also much easier to conserve, transmit, and calculate (Bourdieu, 1991). Still, it is possible for groups to be rich in economic capital but lacking in cultural capital (as in the case of the *nouveau riche* who are stigmatized for this lack). All told, capital use and accumulation in Bourdieu's thinking are characterized by a remarkable amount of dynamism and fluidity.

Habitus

Few terms are as consistently associated with Bourdieu as that of *habitus*—a concept that he has formulated in order to theoretically connect social space and capital with individual identity (Everett, 2002). Unfortunately, too, few terms are as consistently misused. Habitus is often taken to indicate either routinized behavior or compliance with cultural scripts, when in fact it is considerably more complex than that. The word *habitus* derives from the Greek word, *hexis,* meaning an individual's deportment, manners, and style. Habitus becomes Bourdieu's vehicle for exploring the embodiment of history in human beings (Shilling, 1993) and is best understood as those *cultural components* that are *deposited* in social actors' minds and bodies, and that are eventually responsible for these actors' selection and enactment of specific social strategies.

Habitus is the sum of one's cultural inheritances interacting with one's personal experiences, and it includes an individual's conversational style, gestures, body movements, notions of beauty and justice, and self-identity (Shilling, 1993). For Swartz (1997), habitus is a concept that captures the mutually penetrating realities of individual subjectivity and social objectivity. Bourdieu (1990, 53) himself defines habitus as "a system of durable, transposable dispositions, structured structures predisposed to function as structuring structures, that is, as principles which generate and organize practices and representations that can be objectively adapted to their outcomes, without presupposing a conscious aiming at ends or an express mastery of the oppositions necessary in order to attain them."

In brief, we can posit that habitus is present in the form of mental and corporeal schemata (Everett, 2002) that derive from the inventive capacities of individuals as well as from the sum of their acculturation experiences. One's accent, use of language, style of dress, ability to appreciate vintage cheese, familiarity with the opera, and ability to interact pleasantly with colleagues are all part of one's habitus. Although each person's habitus is obviously unique to them, it also reflects a range of culturally learned dispositions. It is this connection between individual propensities for action and the social structure that makes habitus such a key element in Bourdieu's discussion of social practice. Moreover, Bourdieu links habitus to *class positions,* arguing that habitus is a kind of grammar of actions that serves to differentiate one class from another (Calhoun, 1993).

According to Bourdieu, habitus generates both a *sense of place* for oneself as a member of a specific identity group (e.g., women, professional, blue-collar worker), and a *system of schemes* for enacting of social strategies (Calhoun, 1993; Lechte, 1991). Bourdieu is thus more cognizant than Giddens of the ways in which social structures perpetuate existing opportunity patterns, for he argues that actors' estimations of their own life chances in social space are strongly mediated by their class positions. "Habitus, then, represents a sort of deep-structuring cultural matrix that generates self-fulfilling prophecies according to different class opportunities" (Swartz, 1997, 104). Given this position, habitus must also be understood as relatively *durable*. Although one's habitus might change over time, it certainly does not do so overnight. Taking the notion of habitus seriously, therefore, does imply an acceptance of a certain degree of sociocultural determinism and the adoption of a stance against methodological individualism (Everett, 2002). At the same time, Bourdieu cautions against reading habitus as completely omnipotent. "Habitus is not the fate that some people read into it. Being the product of history, it is an *open system of dispositions* that is constantly subject to experiences" (Bourdieu & Wacquant, 1992, 133) (emphasis in original). Above all, habitus is the cornerstone of Bourdieu's attempt to build a research tradition of understanding *culture as practice* (Swartz, 1997).

Symbolic Violence

In articulating a theory of culture as practice, Bourdieu focuses substantially on the "symbolic violence" pervading contemporary complex and differentiated societies. In doing so, he is part of the long critical tradition that alerts scholars to the problem of *legitimacy* in the exercise and perpetuation of power. Bourdieu's thoughts on this issue are strikingly reminiscent of Antonio Gramsci's considerations on hegemony (see Chapter 7) and the entire neo-Marxian preoccupation with ideology. In essence, Bourdieu (1990) argues that any set of oppressive and stratified social relations needs constant justification, or else it will be threatened by too many tensions and acts of resistance against it. He also suggests that such a process of justification or legitimation is at work even though it may not be clearly visible to all of us.

It is the successful legitimation of unequal and oppressive social arrangements that constitutes symbolic violence. Symbolic violence is most potent in those societies that (according to Bourdieu) are "doxic" in nature—that is, societies that are distinguished by an absence of questions (in the public and private spheres) about the socioeconomic structure and an overpowering silence about social injustices. Symbolic violence takes place when dominated groups impose their preferred structural and cultural arrangements upon others (dominated groups) without the use of force or coercion, and are yet able to make these arrangements seem perfectly natural and even desirable (Baert, 1998; Swartz, 1997). The widespread acceptance of and even reverence for a high-priced and class-oriented system of privatized higher education in the United States is an excellent example of *doxic* (or commonsensical) acquiescence to the unequal distribution of social goods and services.

Symbolic violence is also present when the interests behind unequal social structures are "misrecognized" (Bourdieu, 1990) for neutrality or even morally driven choices. A classic illustration of this misrecognition is offered in Bourdieu and de Saint Martin's (1974) discussion of philanthropy and public education. They draw our attention to the philanthropic activities of the early robber barons and the patronage of twentieth-century capitalist families in fields such as art, music, public education, religion, and broadcasting. Although such activities have broadly been regarded as being driven by "higher" motives such as charity and benevolence, philanthropies are often strategies of symbolic violence designed to reassure the public about the excessive concentration of economic capital and to put a benign face on the power of the affluent minority. Philanthropy therefore becomes a highly effective way of controlling public consciousness and can often subvert the raising of awkward questions about wealth and injustice. Philanthropy as a form of symbolic violence is therefore far more effective than physical coercion. In order to succeed, symbolic violence also relies considerably on the tacit compliance of the dominated (whether or not they are aware of this). Everett (2002, 67) provides a succinct definition of this phenomenon when he asserts that "symbolic violence is implacably exerted through the order of things, through the logic of practice, through complicity and interior defeat, suggesting that the symbolically dominated conspire and commit isolated treasons against themselves."

Working in Bourdieu's Tradition of Praxeology

Few traditions call for as much rigor in reflexivity, theoretical coherence, and careful attention to data as Bourdieu's praxeology. Although many find his compelling insights about social practices attractive, they can also be daunted by formidable expectations regarding the collection, analysis, and presentation of data. Bourdieu's praxeology, however, remains an excellent way for researchers to bring the micro subjective world of social actors together with the macro world of objective structures. This budding tradition is particularly well suited for the study of cultural and institutional arrangements, for it offers a way of examining historical and structural forces alongside individual and group strategies of social positioning.

Unlike most other postpositivist traditions, Bourdieu espouses a praxeology that is not at all averse to the administration of large-scale surveys as ways of collecting certain kinds of "objective" information such as wage and salary levels, consumption patterns, and professional mobility. Surveys can often be of use in assessing the sheer amount of economic, institutional, and symbolic capital possessed by some groups and individuals. What praxeology is opposed to is the *measurement* of entirely subjective phenomena (such as habitus). Working in this tradition thus implies a preparedness to work with different kinds of data, including survey data, on-site observations, and archival records. Bourdieu's own empirical work reveals a highly eclectic orientation, relying on questionnaires, interviews, and document analyses.

Bourdieu's praxeology has inspired studies of diverse social phenomena, including political practices in the radical women's movements in Denmark (Walter, 1990), the internationalization of financial and legal expertise (Dezalay, 1995), the legacies of colonialism in Africa (Goke-Pariola, 1993), ethical discourses within the accounting profession (Neu Friesen & Everett, 2003), and the popular subculture of the "rave" dance clubs in Britain (Thornton, 1996). Bourdieu's (1984) own masterly study of the development of aesthetic preferences along class lines in French society offers the finest example of work in the praxeological tradition. An extensive questionnaire administered to over one thousand individuals in Paris and in Lille, a small provincial French town, forms the bulwark of Bourdieu's (1984) project. This survey collected "objective" information about individuals' educational qualifications, their income levels, class backgrounds, musical preferences, moviegoing habits, furniture purchases, and preferred styles of dress. The questionnaire was complemented with several in-depth interviews as well as other governmental surveys on income levels, leisure activities, and readership of the French press. Using all of these sources, Bourdieu eventually produced a rich narrative about the development and exercise of taste in contemporary France.

Bourdieu's study is most remarkable for his contextualization of so-called objective data (i.e., income levels, class backgrounds) in French cultural history. This results in his explanation of aesthetic preferences and taste formation that is grounded in a distinct class-based habitus, each with its own predominant logic (Bourdieu, 1984). As he carefully shows, the habitus of the French aristocracy and upper classes is largely governed by the logic of *ostentatious indulgence,* whereas that of the intellectuals is more likely to be dictated by the logic of *aristocratic aestheticism.* The middle-class habitus, on the other hand, is shaped mostly by the logic of *awkward pretension,* whereas that of the working class is governed by *antipretentious ignorance* and *conformity.* Resorting to multiple sources of data, Bourdieu (1984) paints a convincing picture showing how each of these *master dispositions* influences the practice of taste and aesthetic consumption in every sphere of French life. Even while relying so strongly on objective data, Bourdieu's final analysis is amazingly fine-grained, textured, and completely nonpositivistic. Far from attempting to prove the "facticity" of specific class relationships, Bourdieu uses objective information about societal structures alongside subjective accounts of everyday experiences and an understanding of history to develop a complex theory of taste, social locations, and the enduring power of institutions.

His work alerts us to the importance of situating all social phenomena (objective and subjective) in the wider sociocultural milieu with a special emphasis on the frameworks of stratification.

In general, Bourdieu's praxeology lends itself well to the study of different kinds of social struggles and strategies—in political movements (Walter, 1990) and in the professions (Dezalay, 1995). Walter's examination of the Redstockings, a radical women's movement that emerged in the late 1960s in Denmark, offers some interesting insights into some of the ways in which social strategies must negotiate tensions between social determinism and free will. Her study looks at some of the early attention-getting strategies that were opposed as much by feminists and socialists as they were by elements of the more mainstream patriarchal society. With the help of interviews and archival records, Walter (1990) examines the causes behind and directions of the Redstockings movement. Her main focus is on the Redstockings' public renunciation of the ideals of female attractiveness and romantic love as a way of revolting against the prevailing *doxa* (or taken-for-grantedness) of sexuality and monogamous relationships. Walter helps us understand the Redstockings not as an outlandish wing of the feminist movement, but as a group of women struggling with the existing habitus of sexuality, while striving collectively to invent a new one that would free Danish women from the emotional prison houses created by beliefs in female sexuality, romantic love, and monogamous marriage. Walter's reliance on praxeology can also be witnessed in the attention she gives to the *structural preconditions* that facilitate the Redstockings' resistance. At the same time, she also explores the appeal of these heretical discourses and their capacity to trigger hostility among different sections of Danish society. In every part of her study, the focus thus remains on the cultural struggles waged by the Redstockings and their opponents.

Dezalay's (1995) study of financial-legal firms focuses on a different kind of struggle over the symbolic space. His interest is in the pressures of internationalization that changed the contours of a professional field and opened the way for a contest over the dominant discourse on both sides of the Atlantic. Dezalay traces the response by legal, tax, and accounting firms to these global changes in their attempts to control the new symbolic space. In the new globalized arena, the major discursive struggle is between American and English business models. Although the American model tends to be dominated by the habitus of legal expertise, the English model is more likely to be dominated by the habitus of accounting expertise. At the same time, firms and their members are also engaged in positioning themselves differently by moving away from established craft and professional identities toward those of entrepreneurship.

In crafting research along praxeological lines, Dezalay (1995) also attends to the role of class, showing how these various discursive moves are accompanied by strategies that protect the financial and middle classes from uncertainty. Primarily, he points out that the rules of the new game are drawn in such a way as to privilege certified capital (in the form of degrees from prestigious business schools). The elites and the bourgeoisie then make sure that their children obtain these credentials (and hence legitimacy) in colleges that are endowed by leading business families. In the long run, this accumulation of certified capital shelters these classes from economic and political risk by securing the durability and transferability of professional expertise. It is to Dezalay's credit that he is able to sustain Bourdieu's interest in struggles over the symbolic space without forgetting the centrality of class positions in these struggles.

An exemplar in this evolving tradition of praxeology is Thornton's (1996) study of "rave" dance club subcultures in Britain. Like Bourdieu, Thornton argues that club cultures are essentially *taste cultures,* congregating on the basis of shared tastes in music, people, and dance. She treats the "rave" clubs as *ad hoc* communities with somewhat fluid boundaries that stay together for either an entire summer or for a longer period of two to three years. In order to understand these club cultures, Thornton focuses on their internal *cultural hierarchies* around what is *authentic* and therefore legitimate in popular culture. Thornton (1996) is both meticulous and thorough in her approach. She examines archival material in tracing the history of evolving authenticities of music records and recorded events since World War II. In addition, she conducts an ethnography (comprised of both interviews and observation) of club cultures and examines the complex role of the media in crystallizing "acid house" subcultures into the rave movement of the 1980s and early 1990s. Most noteworthy are her problematization of the notion of authenticity and her appreciation of the media's contradictory role in the constitution of authenticity in the clubs' identities. Thornton's (1996) tracing of this culture parallels Bourdieu's concern for the *positioning* of identities and extends his ideas into an understanding of the media's influence even in deviant popular cultures.

Oakes, Townley, and Cooper's (1998) study of cultural and historical organizations (e.g., museums, monuments) in the Canadian province of Alberta is another outstanding piece of work in this tradition. The researchers examined an entire field from a restricted field of production (Bourdieu, 1989) to a field of large-scale production, showing how the introduction of systematic business planning in multiple organizations facilitated these changes through the exercise of symbolic violence. Oakes et al. (1998) conceptualized the new business planning initiatives in the field of cultural and historic organizations as symbolically violent because their enormous influence and control over these organizations was either completely invisible to participants or completely misrecognized. Yet, as they convincingly show us, the process of business planning had significant implications for restructuring the field's capital and for reformulating of the field's identity.

The researchers consulted a variety of documentary sources at multiple provincial governmental bodies, including the Treasury, the Department of Community Development, the CFHR (Cultural Facilities and Historical Resources) Division, as well as individual historical sites and museums. Documents consulted included internal memos, business plans, planning documents, and letters. In addition, the researchers also conducted fifty-six semistructured interviews with individuals from different departments. With the help of all of these data, Oakes et al. trace the extraordinary influence of business planning on all these organizations. By initiating a new vocabulary (of results, managerial objectives), the business plans replaced a traditional set of world-views with another. Through this new language, the plans were also instrumental in reformulating the identities of the employees who went from seeing themselves as curators, researchers, and educators to entrepreneurs and risk-takers in a matter of a few months.

This study by Oakes et al. (1998) is exemplary of the praxeological tradition in its theoretical refinement, its attention to cultural and institutional contexts, its nuanced reading of private and public discourses, and its astute understanding of symbolic violence. The researchers offer us an insightful view of large-scale organizational change without ignoring its subjective features and without romanticizing the nature and effects of this change. The Oakes et al. study partly positions itself in the institutional theory tradition; in fact, no discussion of Bourdieu would be complete without acknowledging his influence over the development of new institutional theory (DiMaggio & Powell, 1983; Meyer & Rowan, 1977). In their introduction to new institutional theory, DiMaggio and Powell (1991) explicitly acknowledge their indebtedness to Bourdieu's notion of habitus in their own development of the concept of practical action. But institutional theory exhibits other parallels with Bourdieu's thinking as well, notably in their own use of the term *institutional field.* DiMaggio and Powell (1983) have defined the field as the "totality of relevant actors," a definition that comes close to Bourdieu's own understanding of it. Institutional theorists also greatly concern themselves with the dynamics of legitimation in ways that do not depart very far from Bourdieu's preoccupation with symbolic violence. Although institutionalists take a somewhat less than overtly critical view of this process, much of their formulations of organizations and institutions is very similar to Bourdieu's own thinking. Greater efforts to connect the two traditions are only likely to benefit both and to enhance our understanding of organizational and social processes.

Note

1. Whereas Giddens (1976; 1984) has explicitly referred to his own theoretical writings as *structuration theory,* Bourdieu has rarely used the term to describe his own work. In his discussions of patterns of domination, however, Bourdieu notes that they are not rigid but open to many possibilities and *structurations* (Harker, Maher, & Wilkes 1990). A growing number of commentators describe both men's work as dealing with questions of structuration.

Figure 11.1 **Highlights of the Structuration Tradition**

Philosophic influences:	Karl Marx, Martin Heidegger, Ludwig Wittgenstein, and Harold Garfinkel
Major figures:	Anthony Giddens

Central concepts
- Structure and agency
- Structuration
- The double hernmeneutic
- Structures of signification, domination, and legitimation

Key practices
- Iterations between concepts and data
- Focusing on the relationship between actors and structure
- Relating local structurations to wider institutional context

Exemplary research
- "Electronic Trading and Work Transformation" (Barrett & Walsham, 1999)
- "Ideologies and Contradictions in a Public Relations Department" (Filby & Willmott, 1988)

Figure 11.2 **Highlights of the Praxeological Tradition**

Philosophic influences: Karl Marx, Max Weber, Emile Durkheim, and Claude Levi-Strauss

Major figures: Pierre Bourdieu

Central concepts
- The field and the game
- Capital
- Habitus
- Symbolic violence

Key practices
- Mapping the field
- Adopting a relational approach
- Using reflexivity to overcome researcher bias
- Focusing on the cultural struggles between different social groups

Exemplary research
- *Distinction* (Bourdieu, 1984)
- "Business Planning as Pedagogy" (Oakes, Townley, & Cooper, 1998)
- *Club Cultures* (Thornton, 1996)

IV

Traditions of the "Post"

The second half of the twentieth century witnessed an unprecedented out-pouring of philosophic, economic, sociocultural, literary, and political dis-cussions that were carried out under a multitude of rubrics prefixed by the term *post*. Postindustrialism, postcapitalism, post-Fordism, postmodernism, poststructuralism, postcolonialism, and so on are terms that are commonly used to refer to either (a) a set of socioeconomic and cultural conditions that followed in the wake of late capitalism, or (b) intellectual positions intended to offer a radical critique of the entire fabric of modern Western thinking from both within and outside it. Our concern in this section is primarily with the latter meaning of these terminologies, and we will focus on intellectual inno-vations that are subsumed under the traditions of postmodernism, poststructuralism, and postcolonialism.

These three *post* traditions collectively constitute the single most formi-dable challenge to Western metaphysics, taking issue with virtually every major plank of the edifice of Western philosophy and science that came into being after the Enlightenment. Together, and in different ways, postmodernism, postcolonialism, and poststructuralism go to the heart of Western metaphys-ics and demolish it (Lemert, 1997; Rosenau, 1992). These traditions basically take issue with the central pillars of Enlightenment thinking and the institu-tions engendered by modernity. Industrialization, scientific rationality, the nation-state, liberal democracy, professional expertise, the pacification of nature, and so on are all severely called into question and rejected as being oppressive at a number of different levels. In many respects, therefore, the post traditions are far more *radical* than many of the critical traditions, espe-cially some genres of feminism and the critical theory of Habermas. Although some commentators (e.g., Alvesson & Deetz, 2000) see many benefits to treat-ing postmodernism and poststructuralism as newer variants of the critical tra-dition, such overly inclusive classifications frequently tend to do the post traditions insufficient justice, stressing only their commonalities with the criti-cal traditions and not taking the differences between the two traditions seri-ously enough. This, however, is in no way meant to imply that the post traditions have no deep-seated connections with the critical traditions or that they represent clean and complete breaks with generations of Western thinking. Obviously, this is far from being the case. All three traditions owe much to major Western philosophers, especially Nietzsche, Heidegger, Saussure, and Marx himself, even though they take considerable issue with both establishment Marxism and critical theory. At the same time, they have also looked beyond the European traditions to intellectual and cultural influences originating in Africa, Asia, and Latin America and to Third World resistance philosophers (such as Gandhi and Ho Chi Minh) for inspiration (Young, 2001).

Although the three traditions share the prefix *post* and a deep, abiding suspicion of the legacy of the Enlightenment, they also differ substantially in their origins, fixations, and agendas. At the risk of some oversimplification, we can assert that postmodernism tends to be preoccupied with the semiotic codes of contemporary consumer cultures (Baudrillard, 1983) and the language of science (Lyotard, 1984) while poststructuralism is far more concerned with the discursive mechanisms of social regimentation (Foucault, 1973; 1977) and the deconstructive possibilities that present themselves in any text (Derrida, 1976). Postcolonialism, on the other hand, is more interested in the cultural and institutional legacies of colonialism (Said, 1978; Spivak, 1991) and their role in the continuing attempts to subjugate entire populations on the basis of race and geography.

It is widely held that the post traditions owe much to French linguistic philosophy and are best understood as being quintessentially French in nature. Certainly, some of the more prominent figures representing postmodernism and poststructuralism emerged out of the French intellectual movements that followed in the wake of the 1960s disenchantment with both existentialism and structuralist Marxism. Jean François Lyotard, Gilles Deleuze, Felix Guattari, and Jean Baudriallard are among the better-known figures in the postmodern tradition, while Jacques Derrida and Michel Foucault are the two leading representatives of poststructuralism. However, both postmodernism and poststructuralism also have non-French and indeed non-Western antecedents and variants (cf., Bhabha, 1994; Docherty, 1993; Young, 2001). Similarly, postcolonialism (though sharing affinities with some strands of poststructuralism) has developed largely outside France in India, the United States, the United Kingdom, Turkey and the Middle East, Italy, Latin America, China, Ireland, and the Netherlands. In a relatively short period of time, all three traditions have commanded a global reach that extends across a multitude of academic, aesthetic, and professional fields ranging from literary criticism, history, political science, and geography to anthropology, communication, art history, and architecture. In the last fifteen years, all three traditions of the post have also made considerable inroads into management and organization studies, where researchers have incorporated their ideas into their own work on contemporary and historical organizational arrangements (Boje, 1995; Clegg, 1990; Cooper & Burrell, 1988; Prasad & Prasad, 2003).

Although the post traditions have elicited many articulate adherents, they have also generated huge waves of hostility both within academe and in the popular and highbrow press (PIV.1). Much of this hostility can be easily attributed to a case of misunderstanding postmodern, poststructural, and postcolonial positions. Nor is this made easier by the seemingly dense vocabulary used within these traditions. Terms such as *logocentric, bricolage, intertextuality, hyperreal,* and *simulacrum* (to name only a few) can be quite confusing to even trained philosophers and social scientists who are unfamiliar with the post traditions. To some, the constant use of this vocabulary comes across as both aggravating and pretentious. In the interest of fairness, however, one must ask scholars to suspend such judgments until they have reached a better understanding of these terms.

Much of the hostility to the post traditions is also engendered by the genuinely *subversive* nature of their agendas (Lemert, 1997). Their sustained critiques of modernity and its institutions are nothing short of being potentially dangerous to the status quo. All three traditions are fully capable of undermining the central pillars of authority and legitimacy that hold up contemporary society, with their assaults on the existence of a rational human subject, the tyranny of science and liberal values, and the oppressive nature of the nation-state. Although the next three chapters will lay out the unique features of each tradition, it might be worthwhile to first explore some of their commonalities.

The most obvious common ground among the three traditions is to be found in the prefix *post,* which they all share. The term, *post* would appear to signal some state of *aftermath*—that which follows modernity, structuralism or colonialism. In some respects, such an interpretation (though partly valid) would be incomplete. For, in addition, in all three traditions, the term *post* also refers to a *negation* of, and a *rupture* with, past traditions (Best & Kellner, 1991). In practice, postmodernism explicitly rejects modernity, postcolonialism condemns colonial practices, and poststructuralism breaks away from French structuralism (Lemert, 1997). Furthermore, in all three traditions, the *post* refers not only to rupture and repudiation, but also to the *regeneration* and *reconstellation* of new ideas and social practices (Hassan, 1987). Neither breaking away nor reconstitution, however, is a discrete event, and the term *post* therefore also implies a *dependence* on the past as well as some *continuity* with it (Best & Kellner, 1991).

For all three traditions discussed here, the central logics and dynamics of modernity remain the crucial problem. It is therefore vital to have some

Figure PIV.1 **Traditions of the "Post"**

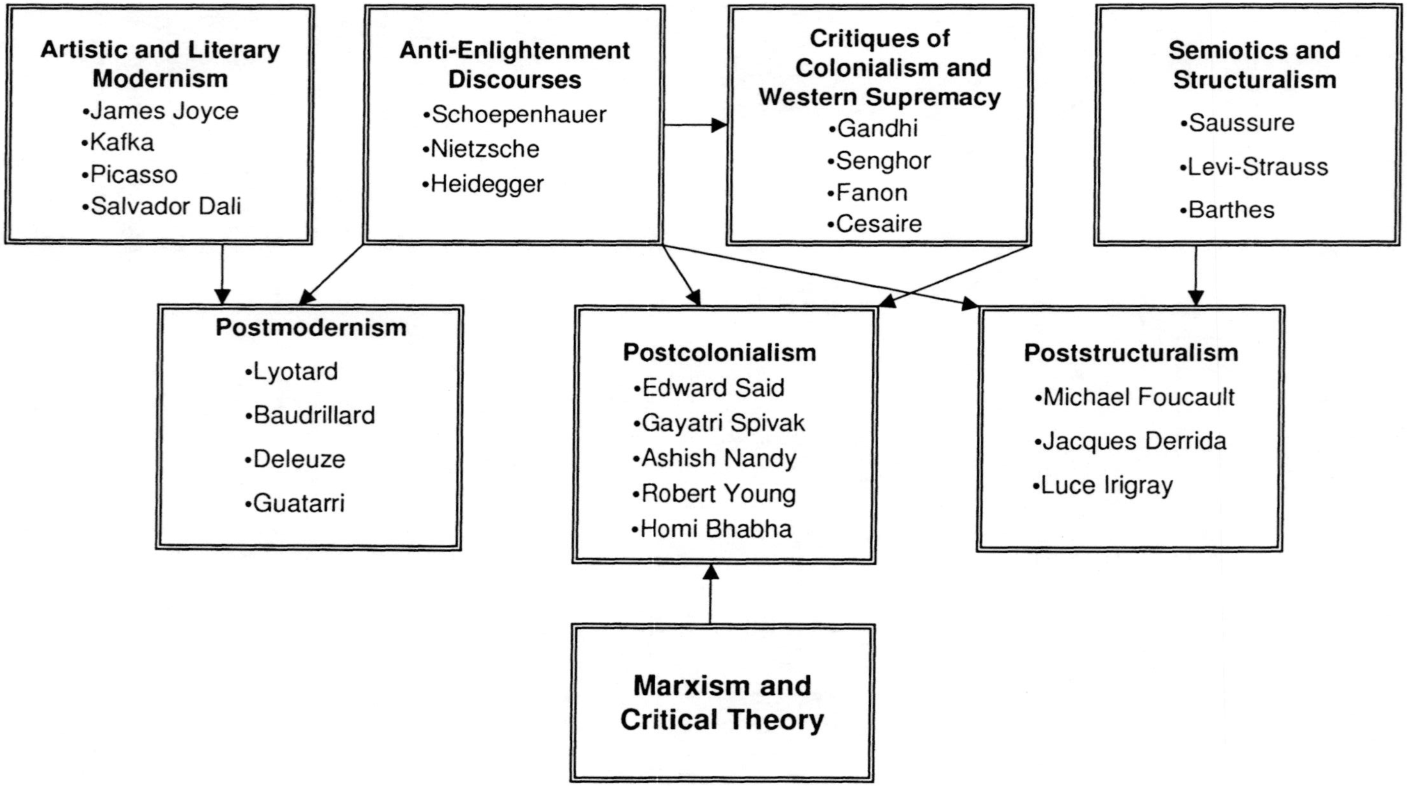

understanding of what may be meant by the term *modernity*. It is equally important to distinguish between *modernity* and *modernism* on the one hand and between postmodernity/postcolonial (as epochs or time periods) and postmodernism and postcolonialism as scholarly traditions. Both modernity and modernism are derived from the Latin root *modo* meaning either recently or current. Around the tenth century, the word *moderni* was commonly used in Italian cities to designate "men of today" (Kumar, 1995). By and large, *modernity* refers to the time period following European feudalism and the Middle Ages, whose birth largely coincides with the Renaissance (Kellner, 1990; Sarup, 1993). The ascent of modernity is also signaled by a multitude of revolutionary changes in the political (through the American and French revolutions) and socioeconomic (through the industrial revolution) spheres.

The period of modernity is also closely tied to Enlightenment thinking, with its total rejection of mystical and superstitious beliefs and its embrace of rationality and scientific procedure (Rosenau 1992). The impact of Bacon and Descartes on the formation of modernity is undeniable. Their celebration of *reason* as the distinctive hallmark of humanity has turned the entire trajectory of modernity in the direction of scientific and technical rationality and liberal humanism. Modernity is also very much about the spirit of innovation and the constant invention of new things (Berman, 1983; Kellner, 1990), and implicitly reflects the notion that past traditions (especially religious and cultural ones) offer very little that is useful or valuable. Modernity is thus intensely forward-looking and future-oriented and is often regarded as the culminating moment of human development (Kumar, 1995) or the "end of history" (Fukuyama, 1989).[1] Above all, modernity is also that period that begins to be sharply marked out by high levels of institutionalized *differentiations* in all walks of life. Modernity is the moment when health, religion, education, work, family, and the like begin to occupy separate social spaces and interact less and less with each other.

Modernity is certainly not synonymous with *modernism* (Kumar, 1995). Modernism is more of a cultural and aesthetic movement that first came into prominence in the late nineteenth century and eventually blossomed in different artistic and architectural fields in the first half of the twentieth century (Best & Kellner, 1991). In many respects, modernism is best understood as a cultural rebellion against the harsher and more alienating features of modernity—in particular against modernity's responsibility for alienation at work, within the family, and in the wider public realms of society and politics (Sarup, 1993). In the fields of art and architecture, modernity is also a reaction against classicism and the baroque tradition. Here, it celebrates simplicity and functionalism over decorative embellishment, which is rejected as a needless distraction from the execution of pure style (Connor, 1989). Modernism is also closely linked to bold experiments in style. Novelists like James Joyce and Kafka, dramatists like Strindberg and Brecht, architects like Corbusier and Walter Gropius, poets like Yeats, Ezra Pound and Mallarmé, and painters like Picasso and Salvador Dali represent different facets of the modernist movement.

Many of the stances adopted within modernism can often resemble some of the critical positions found within postmodernism. This can understandably be quite confusing. To clarify some of this ambiguity, we must first recognize that some figures within the modernist movement (e.g., James Joyce) are often regarded as precursors to postmodernism. There is therefore some significant overlap between the two traditions. Second, on closer examination, we will find that despite modernism's critiques of modernity, it does not disavow many of the fundamental premises and goals of modernity—notably individualism, freedom, progress, and liberation. As Kumar (1995, 85) aptly notes, "modernism both affirmed modernity and denied it, both continued its principles and challenged it at its very core."

A similar kind of confusion also pervades the use of terms such as *postmodernity* and *postmodernism,* and *post-colonial* (hyphenated) and *postcolonialism.* In general, one could say that postmodernity and post-colonial are *epochal* terms, referring to time periods as they relate to specific global events, whereas postmodernism and postcolonialism refer more to entire artistic, scholarly, and cultural traditions. We will briefly consider the terms *postmodernity* and *post-colonial* here since the other two terms are elaborated in much greater detail in Chapters 11 and 13, respectively.

Put simply, *postmodernity* is the period that follows modernity. Some regard it as more of an *extension* of modernity (Bell, 1973; Jameson, 1992) or even a more *intensive* variant of modernity (Best & Kellner, 1991), whereas others see it primarily as a period characterized by its *rupture* from modernity (Sarup, 1993). Neither is there complete agreement on what constitutes postmodernity or on whether it is a time period calling for rapture or regret. Critics and detractors of postmodernity (from both sides of the political spectrum) such as George Steiner (1971) or Daniel Bell (1976) see it as a nihilistic and culturally dangerous moment for Western civilization. Writers like Bell (1976) also highlight the axial role played by *knowledge* and *information* (as opposed to production) in postmodern society, a view that is shared by many other commentators as well. Jameson (1992), who offers a more Marxian critique of postmodernity, notes that it may well be regarded as a development of late capitalism. He sees it as a period marked by hyperconsumption and social decay.

Admirers of postmodernity such as Charles Jencks (1989) depict the postmodern age as being distinguished by an "information explosion" that will eventually liberate all corners of the globe from every kind of religious and economic orthodoxy. Moreover, Jencks (1989) and others (Lash, 1988) also visualize postmodernity as a time of mounting *disorder,* as old bureaucratic regimes crumble and begin to give rise to a much more de-differentiated society. This idea of *de-differentiation* or the splintering of various boundaries (between nations, work and home, different artistic genres, etc.) is repeatedly advanced as the defining moment of postmodernity (Lash, 1988). In some circles, these changing conditions of postmodernity are believed to give rise to postmodern organizations that take on network-type forms. Work in these postmodern organizations is expected to be driven by a dependence on knowledge and information, and managerial styles are expected to become much more flexible (Clegg, 1996). It is important to note here that all of those who write glowingly about postmodernity or the postmodern age are *not* necessarily postmodern in their scholarly orientations, though this may sometimes be the case (e.g., Jencks, 1989; Lyotard, 1984). More often than not, discussions about postmodernity are sharply critical of both postmodernity (as a set of social conditions following modernity) and postmodernism (as a cultural and intellectual movement). These critiques moreover, reflect both conservative (Bell, 1976; Howe, 1970) and Marxist (Callinicos, 1989; Jameson, 1992) concerns.

At its most simplistic level, *post-colonial* designates something that takes place *after* colonialism. The term appears to have been first used in literary circles, as an alternative to "Commonwealth literature"—to refer to those writings that were being produced by the natives of the erstwhile British colonies (Mishra & Hodge, 1994). Post-colonialism (hyphenated) therefore most commonly indicates a historical stage developing in the aftermath of colonialism. Post-colonial societies can include those cultures and nations *"affected by the imperial process* from the moment of colonization to the present day" (Ashcroft, Griffiths, & Tiffin, 1989, 2). If we were to adopt a broad interpretation of this definition, we would include directly colonized countries (such as India, Algeria, Mozambique, and Indonesia) as well as more indirectly colonized ones (such as China and Egypt) where different European powers marked out varying degrees of "spheres of influence."

In general, post-colonial also indicates the end of an era of colonialism. When Said (1989) depicts anthropology as a post-colonial field, he is also suggesting that Western-based ethnographers can no longer conduct their studies of "natives" with the same authority and privilege that they had in colonial times. At the same time, however, post-colonialism also carried implications of *latent colonialism* (Zantop, 1997) that still pervades many of these societies. Post-colonial societies can therefore also include those places in which the *cultural* and *institutional memory* of colonialism is still a felt presence, even though the former colonial power is no longer officially responsible for the governance of the country. And finally, we can also have post-colonial societies when certain imperial powers (e.g., the United States) exercise enormous influence over the economic and political destiny of other countries through trade policies and global institutions such as the International Monetary Fund (IMF) and the World Bank.

In conclusion, we can assert that the traditions of the *post* have all developed as reactions to and reflections of dramatically altered material and ideological conditions that have taken place over the last fifty years across the globe. The collapse of communism, the official demise of colonialism, the renewal of aggressive capitalism, the incredible speed of technological change, and the terrifying possibilities of scientific invention have all combined to create a world in which old certainties about truth, justice, and the good life no longer carry much conviction. In one way or another, postmodernism, poststructuralism, and postcolonialism are all coming to terms with the left-over hopes and disappointments of modernity. In particular, they grapple with the disenchantment over communism, the harmful excesses of fast capitalism, and the painful realization that many of the grand meta-narratives of post-Enlightenment Western civilization such as individualism, progress, and liberal humanism have not only failed to materialize into a promised empowerment, but may well have resulted in lasting damage to certain cultural and environmental resources. The next three chapters examine these three traditions in greater detail.

Note

1. Modernity remains very much a Euro-American or Western phenomenon. Not all parts of the globe are regarded as having entered the period of modernity at the same time. Entire sections of the world are still regarded as being "backward" or premodern.

12

Postmodernism

Playing with Images and the "Truth"

Postmodernism represents one of the most *radical* internal challenges to the entire Western metaphysical tradition. Postmodernism is radical in a very different way from Marxism (which is one of the main targets of its critique). Primarily, postmodernism is fiercely critical of the fundamental assumptions of the Enlightenment—notably its celebration of rationality, individualism, and progress (Bauman, 1992; Hassard, 1994). Postmodernism rejects modern assumptions of social coherence and linear causality in favor of multiplicity, plurality, fragmentation, and indeterminacy (Best & Kellner, 1991), and is equally skeptical of such "grand (modern) narratives" as Darwinism, Marxism, and the ideology of the "free market." Postmodernism cannot therefore be considered a "left" critique in the conventional sense. In its broadest sense, postmodernism refers to a cultural and intellectual movement that comprises such diverse fields as art, architecture, philosophy, literature, film studies, sociology, and literary theory. Although the focus of this chapter is on the more "intellectual" aspects of postmodernism, we must bear in mind that postmodernists would be singularly averse to this kind of compartmentalization. In fact, one of the distinguishing features of postmodernism is its self-conscious commitment to *blending* diverse fields and genres, and collapsing as many traditional disciplinary boundaries as possible (Bauman, 1992; Lash, 1988). As Connor (1989, 7) notes, "Postmodernism finds its object neither wholly in the cultural sphere nor wholly in the critical-institutional sphere, but in some tensely re-negotiated space between the two."

The term *postmodern* appears to have been first used as early as 1870 by the English painter, John Watkins Chapman, to describe a particular style of *avant garde* French painting. Around the middle of the twentieth century, the term resurfaced, first in Arnold J. Toynbee's discussion of postmodernity as a stage of Western civilization characterized by anarchy and complete relativism (Best & Kellner, 1991) and later in American sociologist C. Wright Mills's anticipation of a new postmodern period (May, 1996) that would follow the collapse of liberalism and socialism. Although none of these early definitions quite grasped the spirit of postmodernism as we now know it, they nevertheless accurately anticipated certain elements of postmodernism—notably its insistence on plurality, its sense of being beyond modernity (*avant gardism*), and its celebration of disorder and differentiation.

The close affinity between artistic and intellectual genres within the postmodern tradition makes it imperative for us to examine some of the key features of the artistic. Postmodern art, architecture, and literature are deliberately unruly, refusing to comply with a single set of artistic rules or principles such as baroque, cubism, or art nouveau. If anything, postmodernism appears to be most inspired by the artistic notion of *pastiche,* which purposely employs multiple and contrary genres in a single work of art, writing, or construction (Bauman, 1992). The Sony building in Manhattan with its flagrant combination of diverse architectural styles is often regarded as a classic example of postmodern architecture. Here and elsewhere, the main idea is that a plurality of styles and interpretations is desirable. In fact, postmodern artists, writers, and architects take pride in exploring and displaying incompatibilities in style, form, and texture (Connor, 1989; Jencks, 1984). Postmodern art also rejects the practice of *mimetic representation* as both impossible and undesirable, and is more concerned with shattering the illusions of coherence and authenticity that is at the heart of classical and modernist traditions.

Much of what is regarded as postmodern philosophy and social theory strongly echoes these artistic preoccupations. Combining these artistic notions with different strands of Continental philosophy (notably the ideas of Nietzsche, Heidegger, Saussure, and Bataille), postmodernists have initiated a hybrid tradition that is committed to the practice of plurality, undermining the metanarratives of modernity, and the fusion of multiple fields, genres, and disciplines. Lyotard's (1984) vision of postmodernity as a space for diverse language games, Baudrillard's (1983) development of a *radical semiurgy* to analyze societies as cultures of the sign, and Deleuze and Guattari's (1983) micro-analysis of the schizophrenic desires underpinning capitalism are all central texts within the postmodern tradition.

One thing that postmodernists share (with each other and with poststructuralists) is an unmitigated hostility toward grand narratives or metanarratives. *Metanarratives (grand recit)* are widely shared cultural stories or myths through which societies express themselves and attempt to realize their most fundamental aspirations (Lemert, 1997). Metanarratives are authoritative and totalizing philosophies whose central organizing principles evolve into explanatory frameworks that are then used to understand virtually every historical and social event (Childers & Hentzi, 1995). Docherty (1993) regards metanarratives as intricate *coded systems* whose abstractions necessarily overlook and even negate the specificity of innumerable local narratives. Modernity is full of metanarratives that explain action at a universal and abstract scale in accordance with a specific system of ideas. Marxism and theories of the free market are both examples of modern metanarratives that (while competing with each other) seek to explain all human action solely in accordance with their own theoretical frameworks. Marxists, for instance, interpret all social dynamics in terms of capitalist exploitation, the creation of surplus value, and Marx's own teleological view of human civilization. Free market adherents, on the other hand, understand all social problems ranging from poverty and crime to corruption and inflation as stemming from failing to follow a free market system.

Both narratives are used as analytic frameworks to understand events all over the globe regardless of historical and cultural variances. Metanarratives are ultimately rigid orthodoxies that often masquerade as "scientific" or value-neutral thought systems. It must be noted that for postmodernists, science itself is yet another modern narrative as are Progress, liberal democracy, and Social Darwinism. All metanarratives are wedded to a particular ideal state or condition (e.g., the free market, the worker's collective, a developed society, the survival of the fittest), which are then put forward as universal blueprints. Dissenting views are typically regarded as heretical and survive only at the margins of the society in which these metanarratives reign.

Ultimately, postmodernists are most troubled by the totalizing tendencies of modern metanarratives and their ruthless suppression (through coercion, ridicule, and contempt) of dissenting voices. Not only do metanarratives produce totalitarian knowledge systems, but also these systems are structurally flawed because of their systematic neglect and dismissal of contrary and oppositional ideas. For these reasons, postmodernists and poststructuralists focus on those populations that have been trampled upon or set aside by the metanarratives of modernity. Their interest is in the recovery of lost and marginal voices, especially the irrational, the forgotten, the repressed, the silenced, the dispossessed, and the accidental (Rosenau, 1992).

It should be apparent by now that postmodernism presents us with a singularly problematized approach to truth and reality. The two major modernist traditions—positivism and Marxism—hold very different ideas about truth and reality. Positivism adopts a correspondence view of truth, believing that the language of science is fully capable of capturing and representing the truth of an external reality. Marxism and critical theory are more concerned with getting beyond surface truths (i.e., false consciousness or ideology) to encounter the "real" truth. Both assume the existence of some concrete, tangible, or authentic reality that has an existence outside language and our own imaginations. Postmodernism, by contrast, focuses on *language* itself as the source of "truth" and reality. Postmodernism also takes the image world far more seriously, arguing that the world of images (e.g., television, film, the Internet) itself not only constitutes reality, but is as "real" as anything else.

Postmodernists also inject a deliberately *playful* mood into their contemplations and discussions of social phenomena. This posture of playfulness (which some academics find intensely aggravating) is a deliberate move intended to dilute the solemn authority of scientific and scholarly propositions. In art, literature, architecture, philosophy, and sociology, postmodernists employ irony and playfulness in order to reduce the earnestness of their own truth claims. Unlike Marxism or critical theory, the postmodern tradition does not offer any kind of a social blueprint for an ideal or desirable society in lieu of what is being critiqued. Postmodernism's refusal to postulate concrete alternatives combined with its provocative playfulness can sometimes create an impression of a cynical and exhausted tradition that is almost childish in its ironic destructiveness. Some critics (Kroker & Cook, 1988, 73) characterize postmodernism as "a coming home to the perfect nihilism, which has always been at work in Western consciousness, and which only now, in the fully realized technological society, reveals itself in the fateful meeting of power and the sign."

Is this a fair characterization of postmodernism? Is postmodernism just another attempt to be intellectually audacious without accomplishing substantive change? As we shall see, the answer to these questions would have to be a well-qualified yes and no. The postmodern tradition comprises a pretty mixed bag of writers, some of whom are more radical and cynical than others. Certainly, there are some key texts such as Baudrillard's *Cool Memories* that are well deserving of Best and Kellner's (1991) critique that they do little more than express a state of Euro-modern ennui, stasis, and decadence. Yet, Baudrillard's (1975) own earlier work on the mode of consumption offers startling insights into changing relationships of exchange. Lyotard, another postmodern writer who draws charges of neo-Conservatism on account of his denunciation of Habermas's theory of consensus, also raises troubling but important questions about the violence inherent in many so-called liberal democratic metanarratives. We will discuss these and other debates surrounding the postmodern tradition toward the end of this chapter.

In addition to Baudrillard (1975; 1983) and Lyotard (1984), one can locate many other figures who are very much part of the postmodern tradition. These include Ihab Hassan (1984), Deleuze and Guattari (1983), Paul de Man (1971) and Richard Rorty (1979). Given our constraints of space, this chapter will focus on the work of Lyotard and Baudrillard, who while jointly exercising considerable influence over the development of postmodernism, also focus on substantively different dimensions of social life.[1]

Lyotard and Postmodern Knowledge

If any single individual could be held responsible for popularizing the term *postmodern* within the discourse of philosophy and social theory, it would be

Jean-François Lyotard. In 1984, Lyotard published a report on the state of contemporary knowledge that had been commissioned by the government of Quebec in Canada that was titled *The Postmodern Condition: A Report on Knowledge*. In this undoubtedly seminal piece of work, Lyotard offers one of the most fundamental criticisms of the *modern scientific mindset* and then anticipates an optimistic postmodern future that would be characterized predominantly by a fragmentation and incommensurability of knowledge systems. In a single piece of work, therefore, Lyotard simultaneously pursues a strategy of radical denunciation and a highly aggressive Nietzschean philosophy of affirmation (Best & Kellner, 1991).

Lyotard's role in the budding postmodern tradition is very much that of a champion of heterogeneity, plurality, and constant innovation. His work is motivated primarily by his concerns over the standardization and overrationalization of modernity in general, and modern knowledge systems (science) in particular. Lyotard's suspicion of modernity is in many ways only the latest in a long line of Western writers including Max Weber and Nietzsche who were also deeply disenchanted with the pervasiveness of modern rationality. Lyotard, however, differs from Weber (though not entirely from Nietzsche) in (a) his argument that the central problem of modernity lies in its attachment to overarching metanarratives such as Darwinism or Marxism, and (b) in his blithe expectation that the metanarratives of modernity would be eventually supplanted by a diversity of local and contradictory narratives that would flourish under conditions of postmodernity. Lyotard is thus both a philosopher and a prophet of postmodernity.

Lyotard visualizes modernity as the period most thoroughly saturated with grand narratives. These include metanarratives of the nation-state and liberal democracy, the free market and the creation of wealth, natural evolution and Social Darwinism, the workers' revolution and the collectivist state. All of these grand narratives offer seemingly unquestionable statements about truth, beauty, and the good life—all woven together in a master template that directs action and thinking in public and private spheres. What perturbs Lyotard is that all these grand narratives are, in effect, *dangerously totalitarian* because in their own way, each of them is highly reductionist, oversimplifies the human condition, and is completely intolerant of any deviation from its central principles. For example, any political system that fails to conform to the standards of Western liberal democracy is dismissed as tribal or primitive, while any economic arrangement that does not respect the dictates of the market becomes the object of derision. This is as true of leftist narratives as it is of mainstream modern ones. Marxists, for instance, are completely wedded to their own teleological metanarrative of capitalist exploitation and worker revolution, and are extremely intolerant of any other interpretation of history or prognostication of the future. Lyotard's critique of modern metanarratives is thus decidedly impartial in its identification of orthodoxy across the entire spectrum of modern intellectual and political positions. In general, he sees something intrinsically repressive about traditional social theory and its concern for truth, universality, and totality (Kellner, 1990). It should therefore not surprise us that his ideas draw so much hostility from both conservative and critical camps.

A considerable portion of Lyotard's writing advocates the demolition of all grand narratives and their replacement by a number of little and local narratives that are of immediate relevance only to specific groups and communities. In taking up this project, Lyotard (1984) also addresses the role of science in modern societies. Ultimately, Lyotard's discussion of science (which is much indebted to Wittgenstein's idea of language games) is one of his major contributions to the development of the postmodern tradition.

Lyotard's (1984) *The Postmodern Condition* basically traces the relationship between different narrative forms and modern and postmodern knowledge systems. Lyotard identifies science as the ubiquitous mode of knowledge production in modern societies. He also makes an important distinction between *scientific* and *narrative* knowledge. Although both forms can be found within modern societies, scientific knowledge enjoys far greater prominence and legitimacy. Premodern and nonmodern societies, on the other hand, depend mainly on narrative forms of knowledge. According to Lyotard, scientific knowledge relies on abstract, denotative logical and cognitive procedures, and develops only through its ability to refute contrary evidence. Science is best understood as a *language game* (rather than as a reflection of reality) that follows its own internal rules and procedures (or grammars) such as hypothesis testing or statistical sampling and advances only through consensus from the relevant linguistic community (i.e., scientists). Narrative knowledge, on the other hand, is a completely different language game dealing in myths, fables, fantasies, and legends. Both scientific and narrative knowledge define speech, action, and belief, albeit in very different ways (Sarup, 1993). Science prides itself on its detachment and objectivity and is intensely contemptuous of narrative knowledge, which it dismisses as ignorant, barbaric, superstitious, anecdotal, and irrational. In Lyotard's view, the domination of science has resulted in the elevation of reason and an accompanying devaluation of the senses. His aim is to defend and recover narrative knowledge in the hope that this will incline our sensibilities in a more aesthetic and sensory direction (Best & Kellner, 1991).

As Lyotard examines the language game of science, he makes another remarkable observation—that somewhat ironically science itself derives much of its legitimacy from two of modernity's most powerful grand narratives.

The first of these grand narratives is a political one, born out of the ideals of the French Revolution. This is the grand narrative of *human emancipation* from slavery and serfdom into freedom and democracy. Science plays a major role in this narrative by rescuing individuals from irrationality, ignorance, and superstition. The second grand narrative legitimizing science is the sociophilosophic one of *progress* that is derived from the ideas of Hegel and Darwin, and celebrates human and cultural development. In this epic of progress, science once again takes center stage in its supposed capacity to engender societal advancement. Both progress and emancipation are overarching modern metanarratives that organize, subordinate, and account for all social phenomena in such a way that even the notions of scientific discovery and invention acquire meaning and legitimacy because they resonate with and uphold the grand narratives of liberation and progress (Connor, 1989).

Lyotard thus comes up with a fascinating paradox. Although science (by virtue of its own internal logic) is committed to denouncing narrative knowledge, at the same time it (somewhat ironically) derives its own legitimacy from two wider sociocultural narratives. Thus, for all its aversion to narrative, science finds itself dependent on narrative for its own legitimacy. Within this dependency relationship, Lyotard also identifies science's fallibility, for as the grand narratives of progress and liberation gradually lose their appeal in a changing postmodern society, the legitimacy of science itself begins to weaken. Moreover, as Lyotard predicts, under conditions of postmodernism, science fragments into a number of discrete specializations and is more concerned with following internal rules (performativity) than with uncovering universal "truths." The overall result is likely to be a "shift from the muffled majority of grand narratives to the splintering autonomy of micronarratives" (Connor, 1989, 32). We can thus see how Lyotard equates postmodern knowledge with trends in postindustrial society and ends up celebrating and affirming both of them.

Baudrillard and Postmodern Society

A sociologist by professional training, Jean Baudrillard is regarded by many as the preeminent and most controversial prophet of postmodern society. Baudrillard's sweeping discussions about modernity are tinged with a distinctly absurdist, ironic, and surrealistic hue. His main concern is with the recent dramatic transformations in society that have been triggered by an exponential surge in consumption and the increasing encroachment of information technologies and the mass media into every aspect of daily living. Baudrillard (1975; 1983; 1988) simultaneously draws a seductive yet eerily dystopian vision of postmodern society, which he alternatively describes as a "black box," "a statistical crystal ball," and an "opaque nebula" that absorbs all energy (Kellner, 1990). Although he touches on a variety of subjects, Baudrillard's primary intellectual contributions remain (a) his understanding of postmodern society as the political economy of the sign, (Connor, 1989); (b) his concept of the hyperreal society (Baudrillard, 1983); and (c) his advocacy of specific micro-political strategies of resistance (Baudrillard, 1988).

In the earliest of his more influential works, *The Mirror of Production*, Baudrillard (1975) begins to seriously reevaluate Marx's theories of utility and exchange with the help of the more linguistically oriented theories of Saussure, Marcel Mauss, and Bataille. In short, Baudrillard argues that our highly informatized societies have experienced a dramatic shift from a production mode to a consumption mode in which the central economic problems are no longer those relating to production, but are those of marketing and communicating with consumers (Poster, 1990). Within this context, Baudrillard augments Marx's understanding of two kinds of goods—those that have utility value (i.e., goods that have a direct use for consumers) and those that have exchange value (i.e., goods that have value because they can be exchanged for something else) by suggesting that postmodern societies are saturated with goods having *symbolic value* and are organized around the need to constantly market these goods. Goods that have symbolic value are desired mostly for what they *represent* rather than for what they are or what use they serve. In essence, symbolic goods are valued because they confer respect, esteem, and social standing on those who consume them. Thus, a BMW is not purchased primarily for its ability to transport its owners from one place to another, but because it is a symbol of upper middle-class success and affluence; custom-made kitchen cabinets are desired not because they offer storage space, but because they symbolize good taste, and so on. The need to incessantly promote the consumption of symbolic goods is, according to Baudrillard, the driving force behind postmodern society and has serious implications for the constitution of selfhood and experience.

As mass symbolic consumption becomes the central economic imperative and finds expression through vehicles of mass communication that increasingly encroach into people's homes and intimate spaces, Baudrillard (1983) sees postmodern society as turning increasingly "semiurgic"—a place where signs take on a life of their own and constitute a new social order structured by codes and symbols. Baudrillard's arguments about the shift from a production-oriented society to one dominated by signs and signifiers is at the heart of his understanding of postmodern society as operating under a *mode of signification* rather than under a *mode of production* (Poster, 1990). He then proceeds to highlight the striking characteristics of postmodern society (distinguishing it from the industrial period) that follow from this argument.

Although Marx was fully cognizant of the power of capital to commodify diverse aspects of life (see Chapter 8), Baudrillard (1975) further extends the Marxian theory of commodification by proposing that commodification now dominates entire realms of culture and signification, turning thoughts, language, and psychic structures into elements of the economic realm. This is what Baudrillard means when he refers to postmodern society as operating under the *political economy of the sign*—where commercial images intrusively reshape languages, thereby constituting selves, experiences, and desires.

In the frenzy to generate and sustain endless consumption, advertising begins to occupy the center stage of postmodern life, taking over our linguistic and psychic structures in that process. How does this actually take place? According to Baudrillard, television ads are an excellent example of this. In essence, TV advertisements create a new linguistic system by semiotically linking (see Chapter 6) words to objects with which they have had no traditional or ongoing relationship, thereby initiating a completely new system of signs. Baudrillard illustrates this phenomenon with his discussion of floor wax advertisements. In the advertisements, a gleaming and freshly polished floor becomes an arena for a pair of lovers to glide easily and sensuously into each other's arms. The ad therefore unmistakably links floor wax (signifier) to romance (signified) in much the same way as the word "dog" is linked to a member of the canine species and to notions of fidelity. Similar examples abound. Television commercials selling automobiles link cars to adventure, career success, and sensual pleasure; financial firms like Merrill Lynch are inextricably connected to family warmth and comfort; NIKE sneakers to youthful revolution; and so on. Baudrillard's main contribution here is his understanding of how these images structurally transform our sign systems by merging fantasies (such as romance, sensuality, and adventure) with banalities (such as floor wax and automobiles), and thereby also effect transformations in our cognitive and emotional structures (Poster, 1990).

It should be obvious by now that Baudrillard takes a far grimmer view of postmodernity than Lyotard. In particular, he remains highly critical of the oppressive reach accomplished by mass communication technologies, notably television, which incessantly talks to an audience that is unable to respond. Baudrillard also cautions of the forms of "bogus interaction" with viewers (Connor, 1989) engaged in by television shows that use strategies such as studio audiences and viewer polls. Furthermore, these new technologies of mass communication create and perpetuate a language of *empty referentials*—that is, a system of signs of consumption that only refer to each other without being meaningfully embedded in social relations (Baudrillard, 1984). For Baudrillard, therefore, postmodernity is very much a place of alienation where meaning evaporates in an endless frenzy of consumption and mass entertainment (Gane, 1991).

Baudrillard sees postmodern society as being held together by a network of media images and messages, and by powerful cybernetic steering systems. It is also a society that is strikingly marked by a proliferation of signs (Best & Kellner, 1991; Childers & Hentzi, 1995). The central role of signs and symbols in his vision of postmodern society is eventually responsible for his theory about the gradual disappearance of reality. In some respects, he shares Marshall McLuhan's view that the medium is the message. In other respects, he carries this idea even further in his discussions of *simulacra* and the *hyperreal*.

Baudrillard's central argument is that postmodern culture and society are defined by technologies of reproduction and replication—where exact copies of pictures, songs, and even experiences are made possible by multiple sophisticated technologies. With the help of powerful computer equipment, it is possible, for instance, to make innumerable copies of Van Gogh's masterpiece, *Sunflowers*, without even observing any differences between the copies and the original. Similarly, famous musical performances can be endlessly reproduced, films can be recorded and replayed, and even family picnics and weddings can be recorded on video to be enjoyed again later. In all of these cases, specific visual, auditory, and social experiences can be reproduced across time and space, enabling us to live in a world of *copies*. It is this idea of the copy being as powerful as the original that leads to Baudrillard's (1983; 1984) development of the *simulacrum*.

The term *simulacrum* was used first by Plato in referring to a false and tawdry copy, as opposed to an essence or an original idea. In Plato's writings, therefore, simulacra refer to *debased reflections* that are definitely regarded as inferior to the pure and pristine abstractions from which they are derived (Childers & Hentzi, 1995). In Baudrillard's hands, however, the notion of simulacrum receives a radically different treatment. In a postmodern world that is saturated by simulacra (which makes it hard to distinguish between copies and originals), the privileged position of the original is itself called into question (Baudrillard, 1983; 1984). As Baudrillard asserts, we live in an increasingly simulacral world surrounded by copies of artworks, photographs of family events, and recordings of rock concerts. Our dependence on so much simulacra creates and maintains a growing distance between our experiences and any kind of reality, and contributes to an overall "fading of the real" (Connor, 1989).

As Baudrillard (1983) asserts, these simulacra constantly constitute themselves by referring to other simulacra as well. Television commercials refer to characters in movies, who in turn refer to television programs, and so on, whereas news programs often report stories about their own and rival news anchors. In this process, our everyday worlds (that are enmeshed in these simulacral webs) begin to lack a depth dimension (Connor, 1989; Kellner, 1990) and lose all sense of an underlying reality, essence, or structure. This intensification of simulacra and its consequent disconnection with the material world stimulate a widespread desire for intense encounters with "reality." The result is an endless proliferation of *simulations of reality* which themselves eventually become more "real" than reality itself. When this happens, we are, in what Baudrillard calls the realm of the *hyperreal*.

Baudrillard's (1983) main point here is that under conditions of postmodernity, it becomes increasingly difficult to distinguish between the "real" and reproductions of the real (Poster, 1990). As the boundaries between images, simulacra, and reality *implode*, our sense of being grounded in some kind of reality is also seriously undermined. His notion of hyperreality, however, is not only about the blurring of the real and the unreal, but also about those situations in which the copy of the real is more fulfilling (and therefore more real) than reality itself (Gane, 1991).

In a hyperreal world, our pleasures and our identities are derived predominantly from a range of simulacra. Theme parks simulate the experiences of being on a safari or climbing a mountain; reality shows on television give people a sense of vicariously participating in personal and intimate situations; news coverage of war and adversity bring pain and suffering into millions of living rooms; and so on. The hyperreal takes over society when *images* and *models of reality* dominate our daily experiences and take the place of direct material experiences. These images and models also begin to take over our notions of morality and aesthetic. As Best and Kellner (1991, 119–120) observe, "The hyperreal for Baudrillard is a condition whereby models replace the real as exemplified in such phenomena as the ideal home in women's and lifestyle magazines, ideal sex as portrayed in sex manuals and relationship books, ideal fashion as exemplified in ads or fashion shows, ideal computer skills as set forth in computer manuals and so on. In these cases, the model becomes the determinant of the real and the boundary between the hyperreal and everyday life is erased."

Baudrillard's (1983; 1984) notion of postmodern society is thus far more dismal and paradoxical than Lyotard's notions of postmodern knowledge. Although Baudrillard also sees social meaning as being increasingly fragmented, he also talks of a *master code* that governs systems of symbolic exchange (Connor, 1989). Yet, Baudrillard's conception of power remains intriguing precisely because of its ambivalence. On the one hand, he posits that technologies of mass communication such as television have removed communication from local communities of speakers, have converted individuals into passive and dependent spectators, and have locked them into a hierarchical discourse that recognizes only commodity and sign exchange (Poster, 1990). At the same time, Baudrillard refuses to clearly identify the sources and centers of power, arguing that power, in postmodernity, tends to be diffuse, free-floating, intangible, and elusive.

Baudrillard's complicated vision of power ultimately makes him wary of conventional (or modernist) forms of resistance. For instance, although he castigates mass media as the enemy of democracy, he also cautions that taking over the media is unlikely to be of much use since the logic of symbolic exchange would continue to support viewer passivity and subjugation. Baudrillard (1984) also posits that mass media are fully capable of *neutralizing dissent* by converting political resistance into another set of empty signs and simulacra. His main concern here is with the dominant system's ability to ultimately absorb and coopt most oppositional practices. This can be witnessed when protest movements become the subject material of TV dramas, and when oppositional leaders and slogans are routinely commodified into T-shirts, mugs, and a host of other memorabilia.

In response to this oppressive system, Baudrillard advocates a new form of postmodern resistance that is profoundly *micropolitical*—that is, rooted in everyday actions and lifestyles. Baudrillard's understanding of micropolitical resistance takes different directions at different times. In his earlier work (Baudrillard, 1975, 1983), he supports a resistance based on *total rejection* (rather than confrontation) of the cultural and symbolic system. He celebrates resistance that is informally expressed through body language, sexuality, appearance, and aesthetic at the margins of society. He offers few concrete examples of what this resistance might look like, except to celebrate urban graffiti, which he sees as far more potentially empowering than organized collective resistance.

In his later writings, Baudrillard (1990) begins to endorse *ironic playfulness* as a form of resistance. He argues that postmodernity is best understood as a period when most subjectivity has evaporated into a world of signs and objects. Fighting this system of signs and objects is, in Baudrillard's view, quite pointless. One can only accept the supreme *absurdity* of the postmodern condition, surrender ironically to the world of objects, and abandon all efforts to exercise control over society. Baudrillard also begins to advocate the use of *fatal strategies* as ironic interventions. A fatal strategy is a course of action that pursues a certain logic (e.g., bureaucracy, consumption) to its absolute extreme, anticipating that this will expose the flaws and limits of the system itself and thereby open up some spaces for more fundamental change. Baudrillard's fatal strategies are individualistic, unorganized, and idiosyncratic, and are completely opposed to formal collective political action. His refusal to endorse conventional political opposition alongside his retreat into irony has drawn considerable criticism from the older critical tradition. We will examine some of these criticisms in the final section of this chapter.

Working in the Postmodern Tradition

Carrying out a postmodern agenda in social research is no simple task. We should not then be surprised that although so many postmodern ideas have attracted a following in management and organization studies, a corresponding effort has not been made to engage in postmodern research. Many organizational scholars (Clegg, 1990; Cooper and Burrell, 1988) are staunch advocates of the postmodern cause. Far fewer are prepared to conduct postmodern research. Alvesson (2002, 107) is therefore correct in his observation that "there seems to be more talk about the case for postmodern ethnography than successful examples of such work." One can easily speculate on why this might be the case. First of all, postmodernism is interested primarily in challenging centuries of received wisdom about knowledge and reality, and therefore calls for a radically different orientation toward phenomena such as data, method, and analysis. Postmodernism also eschews the scientific style in favor of artistic *pastiche*—deliberately blending multiple genres (historical, literary, psychological) in one's data collection and presentation.

In short, postmodernism calls for a radical reformulation of the nature of research and its representation. It invites scholars to become more playful and ironic, and to inject a certain degree of whimsy into their research. Not only are such things hard to do (especially if one has received one's formal training in a more conventional tradition), but they also do not have the approval of established publication outlets. Thus, anyone preparing to work seriously with postmodern ideas should be prepared to meet considerable academic resistance.

Postmodernism also prompts researchers to ask questions about cultural images and reality creation that are different from those asked in other traditions. These questions typically focus on the role of organizations in orchestrating societywide spectacles; on the media's fascination with sensational stories of triumph and tragedy; on the nature of fantasies that are created by advertising; and on the rise of hyperreal organizations such as Disney Enterprises and the Las Vegas casinos. Research that comes closest to being in the postmodern tradition includes a study by Boje (1995) and another by Preston, Wright, and Young (1996). Boje's study relies mainly on extensive archival records, whereas Preston et al. (1996) focus on the visual images found in corporate annual reports. Both studies abide by key postmodern principles such as voice and pluralism, and work with key postmodern concepts such as the constitutive role of images in society.

Boje (1995) conducted a historical exploration of Disney Enterprises as a storytelling organization. Using a postmodern perspective, he analyzed the relationship between the official (and favorable) stories and the excluded (problematic) stories about the organization. He was thus able to take us behind the myth of the joyful Magic Kingdom (which is the corporation's self-image) and show us a tyrannical organization that was actively engaged in the surveillance and suppression of employee stories. Boje (1995, 1000) conceives of the storytelling organization as "a *wandering* linguistic framework in which stories are the medium of interpretive exchange." His postmodern affinities influence his emphasis on the term, *wandering*. As an aspiring postmodern scholar, he does not see stories as stagnant and complete accounts with a clear beginning and end. Rather, he perceives his task as that of chasing down elusive stories, searching out alternative conclusions to company legends, and presenting conflicting tales about life and work in the Disney corporation. For instance, his research shows us how the official myth of Walt Disney as the sole creative genius behind Mickey Mouse (inspired by a house mouse that Walt supposedly befriended in his struggling artist days) has been staunchly contested by animators, former employees, and unauthorized biographies. Altogether, Boje is able to portray the Disney corporation as a story-producing organization that simultaneously produces stories for profit and stories about itself. There is something distinctly hyperreal about the Disney storytelling mode. At the same time, Boje also shows us how the official Disney legends are constantly undermined by series of underground stories that make the corporation much more insecure and precarious.

Boje's work is a good illustration of postmodern research because of the importance he gives to presenting a plurality of *voices*. Boje strives to create a *cacophonic* rather than a *singular* effect, where much of what is customarily regarded as *noise* is reconstructed as *voice*. These include forgotten stories, accounts by employees who left the company, and so on. Unofficial stories, threads from the grapevine, and underground legends are all surfaced and hold their own alongside the more glamorous official accounts of Walt Disney and the Magic Kingdom. At the same time, Boje (1995) also retains his own critical voice by alerting us to the dominance of some stories and the suppression of others.

Preston et al.'s (1996) study is noteworthy because it takes the postmodern preoccupation with images very seriously. The authors examine visual images in corporate annual reports with a view to exploring "ways of *seeing into* or *through* various representative and constitutive strategies employed in annual reports" (Preston, Wright, & Young, 1996, 115). The authors borrow criticism techniques from art and photographic studies (a) to decode deeply embedded social significances brought to the image by both the photograph/art

designer and by the viewing subject, and (b) to uncover the multiple contradictory and shifting meanings that are present in the visuals for all parties.

A detailed description of this study is obviously beyond the scope of this
chapter, but we can get a sense of what postmodern research looks like by
spending some time with the authors' analyses of one set of visuals found in
a Tambrands annual report. Tambrands is a sanitary products company whose
1989 annual report carries (among other images) a reproduction of Judith I—
the famous Gustav Klimt painting on the left page of the text, while the right
page carries a much smaller reproduction of a photograph by Shiela Metzner.
This photograph is of a contemporary woman bearing a distinct resemblance
to Klimt's Judith I. The same annual report is filled with copies of other famous paintings of women, always juxtaposed against much smaller photographs of contemporary women.

Preston et al. (1996) proceed to offer several interesting interpretations of
these visuals that highlight their affinities with central postmodern themes.
First of all, they argue that both visuals (i.e., the painting and the photograph)
are completely severed from their referents. In other words, the historic and
aesthetic context of the Klimt painting, and the social location of the "real"
woman in the photograph are completely missing. What we are left with is a
pair of decontextualized images that function like empty simulacra without
either depth or significant meaning. For Preston et al., therefore, these images
contribute to a condition of hyperreality in which all we have are models of a
real woman without either origins or references to specific material contexts.

Given their postmodern orientations, however, the authors also explore a
host of other plausible interpretations. One interpretation is that annual reports routinely appropriate cultural images in ways that displace their original meanings altogether and turn them into signs whose primary function is
within the wider system of symbolic exchange. It is also possible, they argue, to interpret the real woman in the photograph as somehow subordinate
to the symbolic woman in Klimt's painting, with the real mimicking the
symbolic in an effort to attain some kind of transcendent womanhood. Womanhood thus gets somehow discursively entangled with a modern masterpiece and the Tambrands products, and a new set of signs and signifiers are
thereby institutionalized.

The Preston, Wright, and Young (1996) study highlights the usefulness of
postmodernism in examining and understanding visual texts. Although some
strands of critical theory and feminism have recognized the importance of
visual images, the postmodern tradition goes further by frequently placing
visual images at the center of all social analyses and by linking them to distinctive elements of postmodernity, notably hyperreality. Postmodernism is
also relevant because it alerts us to the effects of *fantasy worlds* created by

organizations in fields such as advertising, fashion, and entertainment. In a sense, therefore, postmodernism helps us see organizations as dream merchants rather than as institutions engaged in purely rational activities.

Critiques and Debates within the Postmodern Tradition

Postmodernism tends to elicit rather strong reactions from both its supporters and detractors (Lemert, 1997). Newcomers to postmodernism are often astounded by the sheer intellectual heat generated by debates and controversies relating to this tradition. It is important to put some of these conflicting positions in perspective as we evaluate the contributions of postmodernism to different fields in social research.

At some level, the extreme hostility to postmodernism is perfectly understandable. The sheer magnitude of the challenges offered by writers such as Baudrillard, Lyotard, and Deleuze to entrenched Western ideals of science, progress, and liberal democracy can be both discomfiting and intellectually threatening. In addition, many leading postmodern protagonists couch their arguments in a somewhat audacious manner and adopt a style that is provocative and irreverent. It is not surprising then to find that both conservative and critical members of the academic establishment are often deeply aggravated by postmodern attitudes. In other words, some of the harsh reactions to postmodernism can be attributed to its playful and ironic *style*. This style, however, is not something that can be easily changed or abandoned since style itself is an integral part of the development of the postmodern tradition.

Postmodernism's lack of popularity within critical circles can be partly explained by its sustained attack on Marxism and communism, which it holds as responsible for twentieth-century atrocities and the dehumanization of society as it does capitalism. In assessing critiques of postmodernism, it therefore becomes important to understand the source and context of these discontents. It is also important to distinguish between some of the sweeping, knee-jerk, and frequently misplaced criticisms of writers like Rosenau (1992), Thompson (1993), and Alvesson (2002) and the more thoughtful and pointed criticisms of Gane (1991), May (1996), and Best and Kellner (1991). One problem of postmodernism that is identified by Gane, May, and Best and Kellner is their tendency to depict the same vision of a technologically driven postmodern world that is usually drawn by neo-conservative writers such as Peter Drucker and Daniel Bell. As Kellner (1990, 269) pointedly observes, "They take trends as constitutive facts, and developmental possibilities as finalities, and both assume that a postmodern future is already present." Much of postmodern theorizing can indeed be quite lopsided, concentrating on its fragmenting and imploding tendencies, while ignoring growing trends toward economic concentration and political dominance.

Some critiques of postmodernism within management and organization studies appear to be grounded in a somewhat imperfect understanding of the tradition (Alvesson, 2002; Thompson, 1993). For instance, in a lengthy chapter dedicated to expressing reservations about postmodern genres, Alvesson (2002) fails to differentiate between postmodernism and poststructuralism, and ends up clubbing Foucault and Derrida with Baudrillard and Lyotard. His nonspecific criticisms (stemming from this sweeping categorization of postmodernism) then suffers from a certain validity since one is not even clear whether he is directing his remarks against Derrida, Lyotard, or De Mann. Alvesson goes on to make some puzzling comments about postmodernism that indicate his own imperfect understanding of the tradition. Alvesson (2002, 28) argues, for example, that postmodernism "has little or nothing to say on its own, but relies on others to say something that the pomo can then get his teeth into." In this case, Alvesson appears to be referring to a central postmodern principle—that is, its critique of modernity and its metanarratives. Two observations are warranted here. First, the postmodern passion for critique as a dominant element of knowledge production is not unique to it. Critique is equally central to other older intellectual traditions such as hermeneutics, dramatism, and critical theory, even though the targets of these critiques may be quite different. Second, to dismiss Lyotard and Baudrillard as simply having nothing to say on their own can only suggest a lack of familiarity with their original writings. Baudrillard, in particular, has given us a new vision of contemporary society with his notions of simulacra and hyperreality, and has (in his earlier writings) made some interesting refinements to Marx's theory of exchange.

More compelling critiques of Baudrillard's work are presented by Gane (1991, 43) who faults the postmodern sociologist for developing a "nonhumanist idea of alienation" that recognizes the meaninglessness of a commodified sign system, yet fails to promote subjective resistance to it. Similarly, Best and Kellner (1991) are skeptical of Baudrillard's brand of *exhausted nihilism*, which they argue is, unlike Nietzsche's *active nihilism*, without any hope, joy, or energy. Baudrillard's nihilistic tendencies may well be responsible for his rejection of collective oppositional politics in favor of an individualistic micropolitics of resistance based on irony and playfulness. Needless to say, Baudrillard and Lyotard's advocacy of playful resistance has drawn considerable ire from critically inclined scholars who dismiss these postmodern politics as a series of empty gestures that are unlikely to yield lasting or meaningful change.

A serious problem with postmodern positions is that a number of their proponents theorize from their own Western European vantage points but voice these observations as if they were matters of universal concern. When Baudrillard anticipates the rise of a semiurgic society, and when Lyotard dwells on the advantages of pluralistic knowledge societies, they seem to be completely oblivious of the fact that global poverty, ecological degradation, and AIDS epidemics remain the central problems confronting much of the world outside the privileged contexts of North America and Western Europe. The unfortunate paradox here is that a tradition so committed to heterogeneity and pluralism ultimately ends up focusing entirely on a set of circumstances of relevance mainly to affluent Western societies.

Despite these shortcomings, the postmodern tradition has much to recommend it. For one thing, it offers us a vocabulary and perspective that is refreshingly different from both the interpretive and critical traditions. Second, it creates new and interesting synergistic effects with its emphasis on blending different genres and breaking down conventional boundaries between art, literature, and science. Finally, postmodernism has forced many of the more liberal and left academic traditions to confront their own blindspots and to at least consider the case for greater plurality and diversity.

Note

1. Given the complexity of postmodern thinking, it is more difficult than usual to separate the central concepts used from the overall philosophy. Hence, this chapter does not have a separate section detailing the central concepts. On the other hand, the concepts form part of the overall discussion of Lyotard and Baudrillard's thinking.

Figure 12.1 **Highlights of the Postmodern Tradition**

Philosophic influences: Ferdinand de Saussure, Friedrich Nietzsche, Martin Heidegger, Claude Levi-Strauss, Guy Debord

Major figures: Jean-Francois Lyotard, Jean Baudrillard, Paul de Man, Giles Deleuze, Felix Guattari, Richard Rorty, Georges Bataille

Central concepts
- Metanarratives of modernity
- Performativity
- Language games
- Mode of signification
- Symbolic value
- Simulacra
- Hyperreality
- Fatal stratgies

Key practices
- Critiquing grand narratives
- Emphasizing plurality and fragmentation
- Injecting irony and playfulness
- Research as pastiche

Exemplary research
- *The Mirror of Production* (Baudrillard, 1975)
- "Stories of the Storytelling Organization" (Boje, 1995)
- "Imag[in]ing Annual Reports" (Preston et al, 1996)

13

Poststructuralism

Discourse, Discipline, and Deconstruction

Poststructuralism's unique identity and separation from postmodernism is a matter of some dispute. Although some writers (Alvesson, 2002; Rosenau, 1992) see little point in distinguishing poststructuralism from postmodernism, others (Culler, 1982; Lemert, 1997) make strong arguments for doing so. Poststructuralism is often viewed as yet another variant of postmodernism even while it is primarily identified with the ideas of Foucault, Derrida, and Lacan rather than with those of Baudrillard or Lyotard. Poststructuralism is part of the wider *post* moment of late twentieth-century Europe and shares a number of attitudes with postmodernism, notably its suspicion of "Grand" narratives and its disenchantment with Enlightenment thinking. Nevertheless, poststructuralism has some distinctive features of its own, especially to be found in its focus on language as it relates to institutions and power.

Poststructuralism has an interesting yet complicated relationship with structuralism. Derrida, Lacan, Foucault, and other well-known poststructuralists are definitely influenced by classic structuralism (see part II) even while they make significant breaks from it. Primarily, structuralists like Saussure and Levi-Strauss use linguistics as a basic *template* for understanding social reality, and they search for underlying codes or grammars that account for the form and meaning of literary and social texts. Poststructuralists, on the other hand, are ultimately more interested in how the texts themselves *subvert* the structuralist project by resisting order and systematization (Culler, 1982). Poststructuralists therefore see texts as being far more *unruly* than structuralists, and they also reject the idea of the text as having some kind of unique essence.

Commentators such as Lemert (1997) describe poststructuralism as a form of "strategic postmodernism" that is committed to (a) reinterpreting the modern classical social theories of Freud, Husserl, and Nietzsche, and (b) employing notions of language and discourse to fundamentally alter our ideas of science, history, philosophy, and literature. Poststructuralists also tend to be less engrossed with artistic genres and usually confine themselves to literary and intellectual (rather than artistic) critique. Detractors of the broader *post* traditions usually find it harder to dismiss poststructuralism as yet another fashionable intellectual trend, or as a Western genre that is saturated with *ennui* and exhaustion. Derrida, Foucault, and their many adherents have to be credited with raising serious questions that challenge the many institutional pillars of contemporary society. Although they have gone down somewhat diverse disciplinary paths, both Derrida and Foucault have succeeded in unsettling many established notions about knowledge, Western civilization, and progress.

Derrida's orientation is definitely much more philosophical, whereas Foucault's is more historical. At first glance, Derrida's work does not seem to be all that relevant to management and organization studies. A closer examination will show that his own brand of textual analysis—popularly known as *deconstruction*—can open up new strategies for interrogating administrative and organizational texts. Foucault's *archaeological* and *genealogical* historical methods have much more obvious relevance to the field. In particular, his analysis of diverse social institutions including prisons, mental asylums, and medical clinics have inspired a host of studies that look at institutional patterns with the help of very alternative historical lenses. The remainder of this chapter will examine the central ideas of Derrida and Foucault, and will discuss the rise of a growing poststructural research tradition.

The Philosophy of Deconstruction

Jacques Derrida is inextricably linked with the theory and philosophy of deconstruction. A philosopher by training and inclination, Derrida has had a prolific academic career almost entirely devoted to undermining the Western philosophic traditions by making philosophers acutely self-conscious of the mediating role of *writing* in the communication of philosophic ideas. Though greatly interested in the ideas of Saussure and the French structuralists, Derrida transforms their concern with language into a more specific concern with writing and written language. Questions about the nature and form of writing have conventionally been addressed by literary theorists and critics, and it is only with Derrida that such questions have been seriously raised in philosophy and other disciplines. Derrida is, therefore, the central driving force in the movement to extend the literary turn into many different intellectual realms.

Derrida's writings (1976; 1981; 1988) are considered philosophical because he raises so many questions about language, thought, and identity that are central to philosophic discourse (Norris, 1987). However, in both style and presentation, his texts depart substantially from most Western philosophic conventions and indeed resemble hardly anything in philosophy. Primarily, Derrida (1976) takes philosophy to task for failing to grasp the centrality and significance of *writing* in the overall philosophic project. He points out that the commonly agreed upon tasks in philosophy are (a) commenting on the state of the world and human nature and (b) solving human dilemmas. All of these philosophic tasks, however, are accomplished only through writing. Derrida further adjures philosophers to take the relationship between language and the world, and between philosophers' own use of language and the ideas they are working with more seriously. In short, he urges us to treat philosophy as yet another species of writing (Culler, 1982; Norris, 1987), and to try and understand it as such.

For Derrida then, the problem with Western philosophy is that philosophers have always regarded their writing as nothing more than a *conduit* for expressing ideas and have failed to recognize that the ways in which these ideas are represented (i.e., the writing) are as much a part of the philosophic arguments as the ideas themselves. In other words, Derrida (1976; 1978; 1981) quite decisively tears apart the illusory boundary line between philosophic form and content, insisting that all texts (philosophic, scientific, managerial, etc.) should be subject to rigorous rhetorical analysis (Cooper, 1989). In taking this position, Derrida places the literary critic on an equal footing with the philosopher and denies philosophy its customary privileged status as the sovereign dispenser of reason (Norris, 1982).

Derrida has personally opened up several philosophic texts (e.g., the work of Hegel and Husserl) with the help of a brand of rhetorical analysis that has come to be known as *deconstruction.* Although Derrida himself is not responsible for coining this term, deconstruction does tend to be closely associated with his ideas, even while it is increasingly being used to refer to any kind of rhetorical or textual analysis that seeks to undermine different strategies of representation (Morrow, 1994). Deconstruction also remains extraordinarily controversial, drawing considerable ire from scholars of diverse intellectual and political persuasions. Deconstruction has been castigated as being nihilistic and destructive, as well as reactive and parasitical (Margolis, 1989). Others have even interpreted deconstruction as "a style of extravagant metaphorical whimsey" (Norris, 1987, 79) that leans more toward the frivolous than the serious (Sim, 1999).

Defenders of deconstruction contend that its opponents are missing its main point, which is not annihilation as much as a way of working with cultural texts in order to reconstitute them (Lemert, 1997). Neither is deconstruction to be understood as a method in the more conventional sense of the word. Culler (1982) advises us to understand deconstruction as a *philosophic strategy* that is simultaneously a rigorous *philosophic argument* and a *displacement* of prominent philosophic categories. Others like Lemert (1997) caution against interpreting deconstruction as a destructive position, seeing it instead as a sociotheoretical attitude that relies substantially on *irony* to rethink, rewrite, and reconstrue the basic features of modernism and modernity.

For all of his declarations against Western metaphysics, Derrida is still the intellectual offspring of the Marxian and critical theory traditions. Yet, Derrida is often denounced by these two traditions because he has stringently interrogated both of them and has taken some of their own ideas in radically different directions. Derrida's iconoclastic and uncompromising ideas on language and representation have earned him many adversaries in diverse fields. In addition, unlike critical theory and historical materialism, which are explicitly committed to the goals of human liberation and emancipation, deconstructionists (along with postmodernists and other poststructuralists) are openly suspicious of such romantic objectives themselves. Deconstruction, therefore, does not come with grand promises of permanent empowerment and liberation, but with more tenuous guarantees of constant destabilization and critique, laced with irony. Yet, for all its reliance on irony, it would be a mistake to regard deconstruction as some sort of frivolous exercise or to see Derrida as little more than the *enfant terrible* of Western philosophy. Deconstruction's aims and strategies are nothing short of deadly serious. "Ultimately, deconstruction is to be regarded as a very thoroughgoing form of philosophical skepticism that calls our unexamined assumptions into question, and at its best, demonstrates where there are gaps in these that render our value judgments more than a little suspect" (Sim, 1999, 332).

This still leaves us with the question, how is any of this of relevance to scholars of management and organization? The answer can be found in Derrida's (1976; 1978) discussions on the importance of writing as a social process, in his notions that speech itself is a form of writing, and in his ideas that most forms of human behavior are akin to *textual productions*. From this it follows that organizational texts—policy documents, white papers, corporate newsletters, minutes of board meetings, and so on, lend themselves to deconstruction in much the same way that philosophic and literary texts do. We need to keep in mind, however, that in deconstructing these texts, the goal is not to destroy or demolish them but to (a) explore how certain themes and notions are at the center of the text, and (b) how these themes are employed to systematically exclude or inhibit other themes and categories. In fact, deconstruction is mostly concerned with all that is routinely overlooked, trivialized, or marginalized in social texts. A deconstructive reading thus "opens up the text to renewed debate concerning the limits of the text and the relationship between explicit and hidden textual levels" (Kilduff, 1993, 15).

Central Concepts in Deconstruction

Derridean deconstruction is not content with merely exposing a text's weaknesses or contradictions. Above all, Derrida engages in such textual analyses with the intent of rewriting and repositioning textual utterances in order to unsettle established hierarchies of thought and to eventually put new language forms in its place. Thus, Derrida is very much preoccupied with the project of *reinventing* writing in ways that will not reproduce institutionalized categories of thought. As one might well imagine, this is no easy task. However, since Derrida takes this rather seriously, his own style of writing can often appear to be starkly unfamiliar at best, and incongruously bizarre at worst. In adopting a position of both critic and inventor, Derrida also uses a number of terms that can seem quite complicated to novice readers. This section discusses some of his more commonly used terms.

Logocentrism

Derrida's entire and monumental critique of Western philosophy rests on what he sees as its logocentrism. Logcentrism refers to the Western metaphysical tendency to treat written texts as complete and accurate representations of speech, and to put speech in a direct and natural relationship with meaning (Culler, 1982). Put more simply, a logocentric attitude regards a written text as being able to fix and capture meaning (Culler, 1982). Derrida calls this mental strategy logocentrism because "it centers human experience around the concept of an original 'logos' or presupposed meaning to human activities" (Cooper, 1989, 482).

Logocentrism thus refers to a form of metaphysics that understands writing as merely reflective of speech, with speech being implicitly privileged over writing. Logocentrism also privileges the primary or "superior" aspect in the set of binary oppositions that are the foundational structures of all forms of writing (Childers & Hentzi, 1995). Thus, male is privileged over female, mind over body, civilized over savage, and so on. Deconstruction aims at rupturing these logocentric tendencies in Western metaphysics by resolutely building on the assumption that all language is ineradicably marked by *instability* and *indeterminacy* (Sim, 1999) and that all textual interpretation must therefore be committed to fluidity and pluralism.

Decentering Texts

Along with other poststructuralists and postmodernists (notably Foucault and Lyotard), Derrida is strongly opposed to philosophies or thought systems of the center. Anything occupying a central or pivotal place in society is suspect on account of its logocentric tendencies as well as its ability to control and direct the terms of the discourse. Science, progress, liberal democracy, development, and the like, are all discourses of the center. The goal of deconstruction is to develop a form of intellectual politics based on the notion of *decentering*. According to Lemert (1979), decentering is a reasonably precise philosophic concept conveying Derrida's original attacks on central philosophies such as phenomenology's philosophy of consciousness. The project of decentering is committed to *destabilizing* logocentric thought systems and endlessly replacing them with a stream of ideas from the margins.

Even while advocating the decentering of pivotal texts, Derrida (1976; 1978) remains sensitive to the reality that one can never leave a language completely behind nor can one replace it with an entirely new language. Despite his vigilant mistrust of metaphysical language, he recognizes that he still needs to work *within* the linguistic structure in order to dismantle it (Norris, 1982). Derrida has therefore developed several writing strategies that are aimed at destabilizing language by using its own structures against it. This insistence on using the features of a sign system against it is one of deconstruction's distinguishing features, marking it out from other traditions of textual analyses such as semiotics and hermeneutics. In his early work, *On Grammatology*, Derrida (1976) had already begun experimenting with some resistant writing strategies. He began, for instance, placing under suspicion those words and phrases that appeal to centralized authorities and those that rely on notions of recoverable origins. He did this by deliberately crossing out words even as he uses them in order to alert us to their deeply problematic messages. This is commonly referred to as the strategy of writing *under erasure* and exemplifies deconstruction's ability to fragment a text by using the text against itself.

Writing and Difference

The notion of *différance* is Derrida's own and is arguably one of his most important contributions to contemporary linguistic and philosophic debates. Derrida's discussion of *differance* has emerged out of his single-minded concern with the problem of meaning in language. In working on this question, Derrida emphasizes both the importance of writing as a social process and the need to resist all attempts at fixing meaning in writing.

Derrida's notions of writing are among the most complicated and comprehensive treatments of it. Writing for him is to be understood as "a process whereby human beings inscribe order and organization on their environments. . . . Writing is not concerned with the meaning and content of messages, but more fundamentally with the structure and organization of representations" (Cooper, 1989, 484). In this respect, Derrida shares the structuralist interest in oppositional categories. He goes beyond structuralism, however, in emphasizing the instability of these structures and in directing his energies toward *overturning* the hierarchical nature of oppositional categories found in language.

Derrida examines the French words *différance* and *différence,* to make some interesting points. Although both words sound the same, they are spelled differently—a difference that can only be discerned in writing. The first word is drawn from the French verb, to differ, whereas the second is drawn from the verb, to defer, signifying an act of postponement. Derrida further argues that this word *différence* is then able to resist reduction because its meaning is always suspended between these two French verbs, to differ and to defer, both of which give it its textual force. Derrida's contribution lies in his ability to show us how differ shades into defer and in his argument that meaning is always deferred and is never present with some kind of finality. The notion of difference therefore also comes with a call to produce texts in which meaning is multiple, layered, and never definitely fixed.

Foucault's Archaeology and Genealogy of Knowledge

Few individuals have commanded as much influence and controversy in the late twentieth century as Michel Foucault. Foucault's work has been described as neo-structuralist (Wuthnow, 1984), neo-eclectic, and Spinozist (Clark, 1983), transcendental historicist (Habermas, 1974), and, most frequently, as poststructuralist (Gane, 1986; Poster, 1984). It makes sense to treat Foucault as a poststructuralist because of his emphasis on language and his simultaneous rejection of linguistic and structural essences. At the heart of his writings is a keen interest in understanding *relationships of power* (rather than power as an absolute) and their intersections with wider social institutions and micro-level individual practices. With this goal in mind, Foucault covers an impressive sociohistorical terrain that includes studies on madness and reason (1973), the institutionalization of medical practice (1974), the rise of pervasive, if invisible, disciplinary structures (1977a), and the history of sexuality (1979).

Not only is Foucault's empirical scope extraordinary, but he also draws on the ideas of a wide range of Western thinkers including Nietzsche, Saussure, Althusser, Bataille, and Canguilheim. His appeal, therefore, also lies in his ability to transcend structural and phenomenological approaches (Dreyfus & Rabinow, 1982) as well as Marxism and critical theory (Poster, 1984). In short, Foucault is a disruptive and innovative thinker whose writings have forced us to recognize the profoundly *regulatory* and *disciplinary* nature of our times. More than anything else, he has enabled us to understand our own social institutions as disciplinary apparatuses that achieve social control through the *constitution of subjectivity* (Best & Kellner, 1991).

Foucault's methods for arriving at this understanding are historical, and he is firm in his assertion that important questions about the meaning of human existence today can only be answered in the context of humanity's understanding of its past (Fink-Eitel, 1992). Indeed, not since Marx has any social theorist of note emphasized historical understanding to the extent that Foucault does. Yet, Foucault's approach to history is very different and quite divergent from Marxian visions of historical method. To begin with, he eschews any kind of evolutionary history that views past events as marching in a progression toward some presumed superior culminating point. Instead, he stresses *discontinuity, accident,* and *rupture* as integral elements of any historical narrative. In brief, Foucault concentrates on the complexity and randomness of past events rather than on a coherent narrative in which past events come together under some totalizing narrative such as class war, the nation-state, or the march of human progress.

Most commentators of Foucault's work agree that his historical method first passes through an *archaeological* phase and then enters a *genealogical* period. His early masterpiece, *Madness and Civilization* (1973), illustrates many features of his archaeological period. In this book, Foucault traces the discursive formation of insanity from the Middle Ages to the present, and explores its complicated relationship with reason. He argues that madness in the Middle Ages occupied a grand and tragic place, quite unlike what it does today. Although madness was deeply feared, it was also regarded as a source of truth, wisdom, and dissent (Foucault, 1973). Mad men and women roamed relatively freely across the European countryside and were regarded as awe-inspiring individuals gifted with strange and mystical powers. By the end of the medieval period, however, the disappearance of leprosy from Europe left a void that needed to be filled by another excluded group. Foucault (1973) argues that madness slowly came to occupy the place left vacant by leprosy as a feared and stigmatized condition.

Foucault's archaeological method uncovers other startling discursive features about madness and rationality as well. For instance, even while madness began replacing leprosy as a feared and excluded condition, it was still regarded as a *social* malaise. This only began to change around the nineteenth century when insanity began to be constituted as an *illness.* As Foucault concludes, this eventually resulted in the *medicalization* of madness and its take-over by medical experts and professionals such as psychiatrists and mental health workers. Thus, insanity, medicine, and internment are brought closer together in Foucault's analysis to help us understand the nexus of institutional configuration and confinement in Western societies.

The archaeological method helps Foucault identify the conditions of possibility of knowledge and the determining rules of formation of discursive rationality (Best & Kellner, 1991; Sarup, 1993). In other words, archaeology focuses on the cultural rules that made statements on madness and rationality possible at different time periods. Not once, however, does Foucault suggest that these rules of formation might be inevitable or immutable. Rather, archaeology helps him examine the historical and culturally specific conditions that led to madness first being constituted as the "other" of reason and later being locked up within mental asylums. His historical examination of madness and reason help us acknowledge the contingent and precarious nature of insanity as a concept in Western society. Indeed, this is one of the main objectives of the archaeological method—to unsettle taken-for-granted contemporary concepts and practices including the notion that madness needs to be confined within professionally administered mental institutions. By juxtaposing specific elements of the past with the present, archaeology undermines the stability of contemporary institutionalized practices and opens up the possibility of alternative institutional arrangements.

We have explored some of the themes in *Madness and Civilization* in order to give readers a tangible sense of Foucault's ideas and his use of the archaeological method. In essence, the central premise behind this method is that "the present has not always been" (Baert, 1998). The scope of this chapter prevents a similar exploration of Foucault's other writings belonging to his archaeological period. However, it is important to recognize that he continues with this method in *The Birth of the Clinic* (1975) and in *The Order of Things* (1974). In *The Birth of the Clinic* Foucault examines the shift from the premodern practice of medicine (which was more theoretical and speculative in nature) to modern empirically based medicine that is rooted in the rationality of the scientific gaze. *The Order of Things* has been described as a complex piece of work, aimed at uncovering the laws, regularities, and rules of formation of systems of thought in the social sciences of the nineteenth century (Smart, 1985). In this text, Foucault also develops the notion of *episteme,* which he describes as "the total set of relations that unite, at a given period, the discursive practices that give rise to epistemological figures, sciences, and possibly, formalized systems" (Foucault, 1974, 26).

Foucault's archaeological method derives from the word "archive," even though he understands the term in unconventional ways. Foucault uses the term *archive* to refer to the general system of the formation and transformation of statements present in a given society at a given moment in time. Entering the archive enables one to understand the rules that govern (a) the salience and expression of ideas at a particular point in time, (b) which ideas endure in cultural memory and which ideas disappear over time, and (c) the relationship between prominent ideas in the present and those in the past. Unlike critical hermeneutics or ideology-critique, the archaeological method is not in search of some deep and hidden meaning but is committed to documenting and describing *discursive conditions* and the practical field in which they operate (Smart, 1985). In this process Foucault takes the history of ideas and the sociology of knowledge in radically different directions.

With the publication of *Discipline and Punish,* Foucault is said to have entered his genealogical period. This does not mean that Foucault completely abandoned his archaeological method. Smart (1985) argues that archaeology did not completely disappear from Foucault's analysis. Others (Baert, 1998; Best & Kellner, 1991) propose that the genealogical method merely represents a widening of the scope of the archaeological method. Foucault himself acknowledges his deep debt to Nietzsche in developing the genealogical method. Nietzsche's influence is most observable in the centrality that Foucault gives to *power struggles* over the institutionalization of discursive meaning. Thus, although Foucault retains his archaeological interest in discursive formations, he begins to pay more attention to the imbrications of social institutions and power networks in the shaping and sedimentation of these discourses. Nowhere is this as brilliantly illustrated as in *Discipline and Punish.*

Foucault's central (Nietzschean) assumption is that humanity does not tend to move from a state of barbarism to one of civilized governance, but from one form of domination to another (Foucault, 1977a; 1977b). This thesis is very much at work in *Discipline and Punish* where he explores the transition in Europe from *sovereign power* to *disciplinary power.* The book opens with a detailed description of a gruesome execution ordered by a reigning monarch in eighteenth-century France. Foucault's purpose here is to vividly illustrate the horrific and frequently arbitrary nature of punishment at that time. Sovereign power (which was embodied in the king) was frequently displayed through grotesque public punishments. Such punishments filled the public with fear and awe, and were intended to discourage any kind of opposition to monarchial authority. Such punishments also had the stamp of personal authority and vengeance by monarchs who used them to maintain power and contain public opposition.

Foucault then documents Europe's transition to disciplinary power in the next eighty to one hundred years. Disciplinary power is exercised through social institutions (law courts, prisons, etc.) and is characterized by impersonality, facelessness, and compliance to a clearly articulated system of rules and procedures. Disciplinary power dispensed with spectacles of public punishment and adopted a bureaucratic system of justice that was presumably less arbitrary and more humanitarian. In describing the modern prison system, however, Foucault presents us with a chilling portrait of intimate surveillance and regulation at work. In this process, he raises serious doubts about the humanitarian and progressive nature of our courts and prisons. Foucault also extends his discussion of incarceration into other societal spheres, suggesting that much of our daily lives are embedded in systems of domination that have unobtrusively begun to discipline our minds and our bodies. Schools, law courts, welfare agencies, clinics, banks, and in fact, virtually every institution of modernity is engaged in eliciting our compliance with social control. Foucault's genius lies in his ability to pinpoint the subtlest forms of domination, especially that which is achieved through what he calls a process of *normalization*. In other words, by defining and institutionalizing the idea of "normal" action and behavior in various discursive realms (such as medicine, psychology, and education), and by increasing the scope of surveillance techniques, modern society has been able to ensure social conformity on a global scale.

The sheer range and immediacy of themes covered by Foucault in both his archaeological and genealogical periods ensures his intellectual influence over multiple academic fields, including history, sociology, legal studies, anthropology, psychology, and women's studies. His overpowering interest in institutions also makes his work relevant to management and organization studies. In fact, Foucault is best understood as a philosopher and historian of institutions who is able to connect institutional power and social control with individual decisions and everyday habits of body and mind. His genealogical method is thus capable of overcoming the micro-macro divide more successfully than most other intellectual traditions.

The appeal of Foucauldian poststructuralism to serious scholars is therefore not really surprising. First, he has been able to respond to contemporary concerns about social control by historicizing them in ways that do not *naturalize* specific events and tendencies. Like Marx, Foucault also takes the material world (rather than the world of abstractions) very seriously. Yet, he avoids the Marxian trap of coming up with neo-utopian solutions to humanity's problems. He also writes in a captivating and provocative manner, much influenced by the narrative style of Nietzsche and the ideas of excess and limitlessness proposed by Artaud and Bataille. The result is "a new sophistic rhetoric in which the denial of truth, the awareness of transgression, the shock of perversity and the proliferation of language are endlessly celebrated" (Megill, 1985, 189).

Central Concepts in Foucault's Poststructuralism

Foucault's archaeological and genealogical methods are founded on a number of sophisticated concepts that deal with questions of power, control, knowledge, and resistance, as well as their relationships to each other. This section will explore some of these concepts in detail.

The Panopticon

Foucault's enduring interest in the more unobtrusive aspects of social control is responsible for his discussion of the *panopticon* as the ultimate technology of surveillance in contemporary society (Foucault, 1977a). His interest in prisons and prison systems stems from his conviction that all modern institutional forms (including schools, factories, hospitals, offices, and barracks) mimic patterns of organized surveillance that characterize prisons (Poster, 1990). In particular, Foucault argues that they are all increasingly following the principle of the panopticon. The original panopticon was an architectural form envisioned by English utilitarian thinker, Jeremy Bentham, to solve the problems of monitoring and controlling prisons. Bentham visualized the panopticon as a highly sophisticated watchtower from which inmates of each and every cell could be observed at any time of day or night. However, the inmates themselves could never be completely sure as to when they were being observed and when they were not. This element of uncertainty would result in prisoners beginning to self-monitor and self-correct their own behavior in accordance with prison norms and expectations. This is the essence of panopticon power—that is, getting inmates involved in monitoring their own behavior by bringing them under a relentless institutional gaze (Foucault, 1977a).

Foucault's distinctive contribution lies in his ability to show us how the metaphor of panoptic power has invaded huge segments of contemporary society. As Rofel (1992, 93) observes, "The panopticon, that visionary architectural plan of Benthamite utilitarianism, was transformed by Foucault into a metonym of the modern disciplinary gaze." In essence, Foucault argues that the social text of the prison has inspired multiple social institutions in their efforts to perfect techniques of social control and surveillance (Poster, 1990). According to Foucault, the panopticon is, in many ways, the perfected apparatus of social control, relying less on brute force and coercion, and more on an impersonal, continuous functional surveillance to produce subjects who routinely assume responsibility for their own self-discipline (Foucault, 1977a).

Foucault's panopticon is at once an embodiment of incarceration, hierarchical surveillance, and regulation (Baert, 1998; Rofel, 1992). His notion of a *panopticon society* is one in which extensive and systematic recordkeeping merges with incessant surveillance to produce a *disciplinary gaze* that spans across most of society. By making individuals aware of the possibility of being monitored, a panoptic society encourages them to regulate their own conduct in keeping with desired social and institutional norms. The panopticon society is therefore a highly standardized one in which individuals participate substantially in their own discipline and control. In the last few decades, moreover, new forms of information technology have further intensified the power and reach of the panoptic society by centralizing data gathering and information sharing in institutional locations. As he himself observes (Foucault, 1977a, 24), "Our society is one not of spectacle but of surveillance; . . . the circuits of communication are the supports of an accumulation and centralization of knowledge." Some commentators (e.g., Poster, 1990) even suggest that with the rise of electronic databases and supercomputer linkages, we may well have moved into a *superpanopticon* society—a surveillance system without walls, windows, towers or guards, one, moreover, that disciplines and monitors individuals through an elaborate system involving social security cards, driving licenses, credit cards, and so on.[1]

Discourse

Few concepts are so closely associated with Foucauldian poststructuralism, or have elicited as much confusion and debate, as *discourse*. Part of the problem lies in the fact that the term *discourse* has had a long history of usage in philosophy, linguistics, social psychology, and cultural theory (Mills, 1997) where it holds very specific meanings. The term is commonly used to denote speech, conversation, text, or a body of knowledge (e.g., philosophic discourse). Foucault's own use of discourse subsumes all of these meanings and then transcends them, endowing them with an additional layer of institutional materiality as well. Foucault is sometimes seen as personally contributing to the confusion around discourse by admitting that he uses the term in a number of different ways, "treating it sometimes as the grand domain of all statements, sometimes as an individualizeable group of statements, and sometimes as a regulated practice that accounts for a certain number of statements" (Foucault, 1972, 80).

Searching for precise definitions of discourse in Foucault's own writings is something of a fool's errand. We are more likely to understand what he means by discourse by looking at how he uses the term in his own writings. First, we need to recognize that Foucault's understanding of discourse is much broader than anyone else's and crosses several intellectual and physical boundaries (Mills, 1997; Smart, 1985). Although his notion of discourse includes speech, talk, documents, and other texts, it is fundamentally also about much more than these phenomena. Primarily, Foucault is interested in how discourses (comprised of some or all these elements) come into being. That is, he is interested in the *internal rules* that govern and structure any discourse (Smart, 1985; Young, 2001). These discursive rules dictate what can be spoken about and what cannot; whose speech or writing may be considered legitimate; what sequence of arguments is to be followed in any discourse, and so on. Thus, internal rules within something like the discourse of management education, for instance, are responsible for its silence about the brutality of managerial practice (as in strikebreaking or disregarding worker safety), give legitimacy to specific management pundits such as Peter Drucker and Henry Mintzberg, and call for a rhetorical style that favors clarity and brevity over linguistic expressiveness or complexity.

Second, Foucault is far more concerned with the *effects* of any discourse than with its so-called truth-value or validity. His much quoted reference to discourses as "practices that systematically form the objects of which they speak" (Foucault, 1972, 49) reflects this interest in *discursive effects*. His interest in discursive effects directs Foucault's attention toward the *constitutive* nature of discourse and is responsible for his argument about discourses actually giving shape and form to different categories of experience and identity. For instance, the discourse of management constitutes such identity positions as manager, worker, executive, and employee, simultaneously investing them with specific meanings and expectations. In Foucault's own work, he uses discourse analysis to *denaturalize* a number of categories such as madness, criminality, and sexuality by exposing them as nothing more than the products of particular discourses.

Third, Foucault's understanding of discourse is a highly *materialist* one, a point missed by some of his less discerning critics such as Paul Thompson (1993) who charge him with limiting his discursive analyses to only language and representation. In actuality, for Foucault, discourses are formed and operate at the intersection of language and the material world. As Young (2001, 398–99) asserts, "Foucault's very radical notion of discourse is primarily directed *away* from any form of textualism, textual idealism, texts as disembodied artifacts, or intertextuality towards a concept of the *materiality of language* in every dimension" (emphasis added). Foucault's materialization is to be found in his commitment to tracing the intricacies of institutional power that plays a role in various discursive formations. Thus, he never approaches discourses as abstract or disembodied textual bodies but as active processes working in the realm of materiality and the body, in the domain of objects and specific historical practices (Young, 2001). In considering contemporary discourses of discipline and surveillance, he (Foucault, 1977a) grounds them in the material practices of prison reform and in the wider demise of monarchical authority. Foucault's brand of discourse analysis is therefore capable of offering valuable insights into a range of managerial and organizational discourses.

Power and Power/Knowledge

Alongside discourse, Foucault's unique conceptualization of power is a common thread running through his entire ouevre and reflecting Nietzsche's remarkable influence over his writing (Foucault, 1977b). Like Nietzsche, Foucault adopts a complex, processual view of power that departs radically from conventional as well as critical discussions of it. It is important to understand what Foucault saw power as *not* being in order to grasp his understanding of it. First and foremost, power for Foucault (1981) is neither a property nor a possession belonging to the state, a social group (e.g., a ruling elite), or specific institutions (e.g., banks, government bodies). As he himself (Foucault, 1981, 94) observes, "Power is not something that is acquired, seized or shared, something that one holds onto, or allows to slip away." Foucault also dismisses a coercive view of power, thereby calling into question established Marxist ideas about power struggles between the classes (Sarup, 1993).

How then does Foucault actually conceptualize power? Except for maintaining that power is a *relationship,* Foucault offers very few precise definitions of it. From his writings (Foucault, 1977a; 1981) however, we can glean that power operates through social circuits and networks and is a pervasive feature of modern society. In short, "Foucault conceptualized power neither as an institution nor a structure, but as a 'complex strategical situation,' as a 'multiplicity of force relations,' as simultaneously 'intentional' yet non-subjective" (Smart, 1985, 77). Foucault's vision of power has important implications for how it is studied. Questions such as "Who has power?" or "How much power does a particular group have?" give way to questions about how power is exercised and what kinds of social effects it produces (Townley, 1993). Studying power in the Foucauldian poststructural tradition thus involves examining the techniques, practices, and procedures through which it is exercised.

Thus, in Foucault's view there are no recognizable pockets of power residing in clearly identifiable social locations. Rather, power *circulates* throughout society, and works through countless institutions and institutionalized practices that govern our everyday lives. For instance, a number of classificatory and recordkeeping procedures followed by bureaucracies (such as credit agencies, universities, and motor vehicle agencies) are all part of the *technologies of power* that regulate much of our lives. Foucault also avoids the more macro-institutional analyses of power favored by historical materialists and conflict sociologists who are all wedded to a top-down view of power. By contrast, Foucault favors an *ascending analysis of power* (Smart, 1985; Townley, 1993) that examines (a) the practices and effects of power at a micro-level and (b) the capacity of individuals to appropriate and extend different technologies of power.

In sum, Foucault regards power as a strategy emerging out of relationships between people that are transmitted through subjects (Baert, 1998). Interestingly, he does not hold a solely *negative* view of power, even going as far as to emphasize its creative and productive side effects. He is careful to note (Foucault, 1977a, 194) that "power produces: it produces reality; it produces domains of objects and rituals of truth. The individual and the knowledge that may be gained from him belong to this production." This stance also implies that Foucault refuses to accept categories such as "the powerful" or "the powerless" at face-value, preferring to examine the circuits of power that constitute them and link them with each other and with institutions in society.

Foucault's complex understanding of power is also responsible for his discussion of *power/knowledge*—one of his more enduring contributions to the poststructural tradition. Using the concept of power/knowledge, Foucault completely overturns our conventional view of knowledge as a source of power. Instead, he develops and maintains a rigorous understanding of the coterminous and interdependent nature of power and knowledge (Sarup, 1993; Townley, 1993). In essence, Foucault is proposing that power and knowledge cannot be thought of as separate or distinct phenomena. Each one is completely dependent on the other for its existence and development.

What does Foucault mean by this? His main point is that the exercise of power is responsible for the emergence of new objects of knowledge, while, conversely, knowledge developments mediate the ways in which power is exercised. In Focuault's (1977a, 27) own words, "there are no power relations without the correlative constitution of a field of knowledge, nor any knowledge that does not presuppose or constitute at the same time, power relations." This further implies that there exists no possibility of disinterested or neutral knowledge.[2] Knowledge and power are mutually dependent and constitute one another. Put differently, a site where power is exercised is also a place where knowledge is produced (Smart, 1985). The exercise of managerial and administrative power in the late nineteenth and early twentieth centuries, for instance, triggered the formation of a field of knowledge called management science. This body of knowledge, in turn, has shaped and legitimized the exercise of managerial power. Foucault's insistence on formulating power/knowledge as a single term is quite deliberate and is intended to constantly remind the reader of the relational character of power and knowledge.

Working in the Poststructural Traditions

Over the last decade or so, poststructuralism has drawn a staunch and dedicated following of researchers while simultaneously daunting a number of others. Within the field of management and organization studies itself, Foucauldian poststructuralism appears to elicit far more interest than Derridean deconstruction. However, both traditions are increasingly leaving their imprints on the field. Scholars within the deconstructionist tradition have mainly conducted close examinations of managerial decision-making texts (Chia, 1996; Kilduff, 1993). Foucauldian analysis, on the other hand, has been used more widely—to study human resource management practices (Townley, 1993), interorganizational collaboration in project management (Clegg et al., 2002), the emergence of a discourse of employment (Jacques, 1996), the consolidation of enterprise culture (Du Gay, 1996), and new techniques of regimentation in a Chinese silk factory (Rofel, 1992).

Two research pieces that engage in deconstruction both examine popular and "classic" texts on organizational decision making. Kilduff (1993) deconstructs March and Simon's renowned work, *Organizations,* while Chia (1996) does the same with a number of managerial writings on decision making. Kilduff's deconstruction exposes the texts' inescapability from the mindset of the machine. Even while March and Simon offer their own version of the satisficing man as a more humanistic alternative to Weber's and Taylor's mechanistic models, they are still caught up in the logic of the machine. Kilduff's deconstruction illustrates how their satisficing manager continues to resemble a machine, even though it is now closer to computers than conventional factory machinery. Similarly, Chia's (1996) deconstruction of other managerial texts goes to the heart of the authors' inability to relinquish causality and the primacy of action despite their efforts to do so. Both Chia and Kilduff demonstrate the *internal fragility* of established managerial texts, a fragility that is witnessed in the text's own capacity to deconstruct itself. Their close deconstructive readings are able to subvert the authority of classical texts by interrogating the texts' own construction and internal logic. We should note here that while Chia (1996) and Kilduff (1993) have confined themselves to formal written texts, deconstruction can also be used with virtually any *social text,* be it public announcements, organizational rituals, electronic correspondence, or cultural monuments and edifices.

A great many more researchers seem interested in crafting research that is informed by Foucauldian poststructuralism. Like Marx, Foucault exhibits a historical and materialist orientation, albeit in very different ways. Researchers can choose to work with either Foucault's archaeological or genealogical approaches. But either way, they would be compelled to focus on discursive formations and their links to power/knowledge processes. An excellent example of a well-crafted study in this tradition is Jacques' (1996) cultural history of the discourse of employment in America. Foucault's influence is reflected in Jacques' interest in the emergence of certain key categories such as "the employee," "the manager," and "the professional" in the twentieth century, a development that he traces to the triumph of industrialism over federalism. Although many histories frame the period as an endless clash between capital and labor, Jacques (1996) poses a far more interesting and unusual question: How did industrial thinking *itself* become possible? He goes on to argue that shifts in social relationships and the meaning of work in the nineteenth century were what made the new thinking possible through the creation of a discourse of the employee. As Jacques skillfully shows us, the category of the employee itself was further enmeshed in a wider discourse about regular wages, job security, organizational loyalty, and worker diligence. The discourse of the employee also became the site of new bureaucratic disciplinary practices that turned the worker into a docile and acquiescent subject. Overall, Jacques is able to provide a richly textured portrayal that offers an alternative understanding of the burgeoning industrial order.

Du Gay's (1996) study of four British retail organizations is another well-crafted piece of work in the Foucauldian poststructuralist tradition. Du Gay's primary focus is on the discursive production of identities in contemporary organizations and its links to the overall political culture of the time. Du Gay's work is deeply influenced by Foucault's (1991) own discussion of *governmentality*. Foucault coined the term *governmentality* out of government and rationality, and used it to refer to those discursive activities that are involved in ordering actions, processes, and subjectivities.

With the help of interviews and observation, Du Gay (1996) studied four consumer intensive organizations in the United Kingdom: a retail division of a corporation specializing in the manufacture and marketing of cosmetic products; the clothing division of a large fashion retailing organization; a firm selling health and beauty products; and a leading vanity store chain. Du Gay's main interest was in examining the active role played by the discourse of work reform in the formulation of new images in all these firms. He further examined how these images were instrumental in bringing the government of the enterprise into alignment with political rationalities, cultural expectations, and changing social values. In addition, he also explored how these discourses mediated employees' self-images and perceptions of self-interest.

Du Gay's fieldwork led him to conclude that the wider political culture of Thatcherism in the United Kingdom was very much at play in the emergence of a new kind of *enterprise culture* in all of these organizations. This enterprise culture defined an ideal set of relationships that individuals were expected to develop with themselves and with the organizations in which they worked. Enterprise culture also fostered specific habits of action, notably risk-taking and self-reliance. He also shows how an earlier "craft" culture was replaced by a more "professional" one that was far more impersonal and risk-oriented in nature. At the same time, Du Gay does not overlook the possibility of resistance developing to enterprise culture. He discusses, for instance, how employees sometimes interpreted the discourse of enterprise culture in ways that promoted their own autonomy and self-actualization at the expense of enterprise culture itself.

A few things stand out in Du Gay's study. First, he is able to connect different societal spheres (e.g., the political and the organizational) through his exploration of enterprise culture. In this effort, he is significantly helped by Foucault's notion of discourse, which sees discourse as being simultaneously present in different levels of society. Indeed, working with this kind of poststructuralist discourse analysis enables researchers to traverse from the micro to the macro and from the global to the local and back again. Second, Du Gay takes seriously Foucault's adage that "where there is power, there is resistance." Thus, he is also able to show us that power does not always move downward, but is also present in the multiple resistant interpretations made by ordinary employees in the course of their everyday work lives.

Foucault's discussions of power/knowledge and resistance also guide Rofel's (1992) evocative study of the disciplinary effects of factory space on worker subjectivities in a Chinese silk factory. Rofel's distinctly poststructural ethnography examines the techniques of *spatial discipline* employed in this factory, and the multiple ways in which they were contested and subverted. Her insistence on historically and culturally contextualizing these struggles over factory space reflects the poststructural influences over her study. In the course of her ethnography, Rofel (1992) argues that the ostensibly *global* space of the factory system actually collides with the polysemous histories of past spatial relations in China, thereby opening up unanticipated spaces for *local* resistance.

Rofel's poststructual ethnography is remarkable not only for its fine observational details but also for its historical sensibility. Early on in her study, Rofel noted that even while the use of spatial disciplinary techniques (e.g., the position wage or the *gangwei gongzi zhi* system) was on the rise in the silk factory, workers still found ways to preserve their physical mobility at work, constantly collecting in informal groups and striking up conversations on the shopfloor. Rofel then traces the roots of these resistant behaviors in the Chinese Cultural Revolution when radical workers frequently left the factory in pursuit of Communist Party politics, and repeatedly challenged managerial authority with the help of communist doctrine. Indeed, as Rofel points out, a high level of political consciousness during this period was sometimes associated with a refusal to participate in some forms of production. In short, Chinese factory workers were more accustomed to having some control over their immediate workspaces and were not so easily subjugated by new techniques of spatial control. Her study is remarkable in part because of its refusal to accept universal explanations about factory regimentation and its ability to provide a culturally nuanced description of discipline and resistance.

Reactions to the Poststructuralist Tradition

The social sciences and the humanities have not been the same ever since Michel Foucault and Jacques Derrida burst upon the Western intellectual scene. For better or for worse, both of these thinkers and their adherents have severely questioned the conduct of philosophy and the social sciences, and have shown how the production of knowledge and the exercise of power are inextricably interlinked. Like postmodernism, poststructuralism has also initiated a tradition that calls for radically different perspectives and styles of representation. And like postmodernism, poststructuralism has also drawn a number of critiques.

Critiques of the poststructuralist tradition can originate in both left and right political camps, and can range from the arcane to the incisive. Some critiques are clearly better informed than others, and others are heated and polemical while still others are couched in more reasonable terms. Within the field of management and organization studies, some of the more forceful criticism against poststructuralism tends to originate from orthodox labor process theorists (best exemplified by Thompson, 1993) and adherents of critical theory (e.g., Alvesson, 2002). Unfortunately, both critiques appear to be based on somewhat inadequate and limited understandings of poststructuralism,[3] especially around such notions as text and discourse. A couple of examples will illustrate this tendency.

Thompson (1993), for instance, sees deconstruction as nothing more than an attempt to break down taken-for-granted textual assumptions. He further proceeds to argue (1993, 196) that "while deconstruction might help us spot inconsistencies and metaphors, it does not enable us to reveal the interests and power structures that underpin such texts." This is a patently limited, one might even say a flawed understanding, of Derrida's ideas. When dealing with such criticisms, we need to keep in mind that (a) Derrida's notion of the text is far broader than Thompson's interpretation would suggest and (b) Derrida's interest is in seeing how texts *control* social encounters rather than merely uncovering metaphors and assumptions. Similarly, Alvesson's (2002) dissatisfaction with poststructuralism can be traced to a somewhat narrow understanding of discourse as employed by Foucault. To both Alvesson (2002) and Thompson (1993), poststructuralist terms such as *text* and *discourse* (which are fraught with complicated meanings) are reduced to their common usage in ordinary language and are not carefully distinguished from related terms such as *language* and *representation*. As anyone who is familiar with just the contents of this chapter can appreciate, this is indeed far from being the case. Their limited appreciation of such complex concepts, however, can explain some of their frustrations with the poststructural tradition.

At various moments, both Alvesson and Thompson also complain about poststructuralism's supposed neglect of power and materiality. Thompson (1993) explicitly objects to Foucauldian notions of power as a relationship rather than as a possession, arguing that such a position obscures the workings of power by seeing it everywhere and nowhere at the same time. Thompson's main problem here is that he is still in pursuit of specific locations and holdings of power, quite forgetting that power is an abstraction in the first place, and not some tangible entity that can be tracked down at will. At times some of Alvesson's objections to poststructuralism are also a little vague and unconvincing. He argues, for instance (2002, 29), that it "gives social science a very restricted space" and that "it strongly discourages empirical work." Both pronouncements are rather puzzling. There is no self-evident reason to believe that poststructuralism restricts the practice of social science. Many would assert that the opposite is far more likely to be the case (Connor, 1989; Cooper, 1989; Poster, 1984). What is likely is that critics like Thompson (mis)construe Derrida's famous statement "there is nothing outside the text" to infer that he wishes to reduce all social science to literary analysis, when in actuality, he is calling for an appreciation of the entire social world as textual production. In any event, for these anti-text sentiments to gain greater credibility, one would expect writers like Thompson to philosophically engage with and refute Derrida's arguments about the importance about writing over speech—something that neither of these writers does.

It is also unclear why Alvesson postulates that poststructuralism discourages empirical work. True, both postmodernism and poststructuralism reconfigure the boundaries around what might be considered empirical research, but by and large, they tend to *extend* the scope of empirical work rather than confine it. An entire range of social phenomena, from sexual habits to mental asylums, has been brought under the purview of the poststructuralist tradition. Closer to home (as illustrated by some of the pieces discussed in the previous section), poststructuralist research engages with such diverse issues as managerial decision making, factory space and regimentation, and the effects of enterprise culture. One could even argue that Foucault's notion of discourse has a far more *material* component to it than many others found in literary criticism and the social sciences.

A more thoughtful critique of poststructuralism is offered by Poulantzas (1978) who faults Foucault in particular for overlooking the role of the modern state and its derivation out of capitalist modes of production. For Poulantzas and like-minded critics, therefore, poststructuralism suffers in part because of its failure to acknowledge the omnipresence and domination of the contemporary nation-state in all walks of life. A major fallout of this failure is the neglect by poststructuralists of geopolitical dynamics and their influence over discursive regimes in society.

A second important criticism of both Derrida and Foucault is directed against their suspicion of collective voices and organized social movements. Both Derrida and Foucault are skeptical of the ability of a single supposedly unified movement (e.g., the women's movement or a Third World Alliance) to equally speak for and represent *all* women or Third World inhabitants. To many feminists (Fraser, 1989) this poststructuralist suspicion of a collective voice is somewhat misplaced and possibly even deleterious, as it needlessly creates fissures within movements that are only now on the brink of achieving social justice for historically disadvantaged groups.

Finally, poststructuralism is also critiqued for its tendency to privilege discursive effects over individual agency (Poster, 1984). Foucault's singular emphasis on discursive formations, for instance, is sometimes interpreted as overlooking the potential of human agency. In other words, since power is overwhelmingly discursive, there is a tendency to discount individual resistance or to accord it a secondary place in poststructuralist research.

Notwithstanding these more valid critiques, the poststructural tradition has much to offer management and organization studies as well as the broader field of the social sciences. To put poststructuralism in perspective, we need to recognize that although some of its questions and concerns might seem provocative and even outlandish, many of them echo concerns that have resurfaced in a long (if somewhat alternative) tradition in dissenting philosophy in Europe. Schopenhauer, Nietzsche, Freud, and Heidegger were all responsible for raising important, if deeply troubling, questions about ourselves and our approaches to our worlds and truth. In many ways, poststructuralists continue this tradition of opening up a Pandora's box that might hold some salutary, if discomfiting, ideas about Western civilization.

Many of the questions raised within the poststructuralist tradition about the nature of power and truth, and about the importance for pluralism and disorder, are particularly important given recent shifts within the global geopolitical and economic orders, and radical developments in technology. As Lemert (1989, 17) astutely notes in his discussion of poststructuralism (which he subsumes under the label postmodernism), "Forgotten in all the postmodern anxiety is the fact that postmodernism is the currently fashionable name for a complicated series of cultural and theoretical inventions, each of which were adjustments to the realities of the world in the second half of the 20th century."

Notes

1. Foucault's notion of the panopticon is not exactly the same as the idea of "Big Brother Watching You." It is true that both concepts center on anxieties about constant surveillance in our lives. However, Foucault's panopticon is far more complex. The panopticon does not derive its power from its omnipresence, but from the fact that we do not know when we are under observation and when we are not. Second, the panopticon, unlike "big brother" is more about how individuals participate in their own self-regulation and discipline.

2. Foucault's notion of power/knowledge is quite different from the *ideological* view of knowledge adopted by Marxists and other proponents of the critical tradition, who implicitly assume that some version of ideology-free knowledge is possible and should be striven for. Foucault, on the other hand, rejects even the possibility of disinterested and value-free knowledge that is untainted by power.

3. As mentioned in the previous chapter, writers like Thompson and Alvesson unfortunately tend to use *postmodernism* as a generic label to refer to a range of theoretical positions informed by linguistic philosophy. This inability to *differentiate* between the writings of Derrida and Baudrillard, for instance, not to mention an entire spectrum of organizational researchers, results in criticisms that are neither pointed nor especially helpful.

Figure 13.1 **Highlights of the Poststructutralist Tradition**

Philosophic influences: Friedrich Nietzsche, Karl Marx, Sigmund Freud, Ferdinand de Saussure, Martin Heidegger, Louis Althusser

Major figures: Michel Foucault, Jacques Derrida, Jacques Lacan, Giles Deleuze, Felix Guatarri

Central concepts
- Logocentrism
- Decentering texts
- Writing under erasure
- Difference
- Panopticon
- Power/knowledge
- Governmentality
- Discourse

Key practices
- Undermining one's own writing
- Highlighting the margins
- Building ambivalence into one's texts
- Practicing an archaeology and genealogy of knowledge
- Being aware of discursive effects

Exemplary research
- *Organizational Analysis as Deconstructive Practice* (Chia, 1996)
- *Consumption and Identity at Work* (Du Gay, 1996)
- *Discipline and Punish* (Foucault, 1974)
- *Manufacturing the Employee* (Jacques, 1996)
- "Rethinking Modernity" (Rofel, 1992)

14

Postcolonialism

Unpacking and Resisting Imperialism

Alongside poststructuralism and postmodernism, postcolonialism also pursues the project of critiquing and resisting Western modernity. However, postcolonialism undertakes to do this while constantly emphasizing the West's relationship to its *others*—notably the peoples of its former colonies and the indigenous populations within its own geographical enclaves. As the term would indicate, postcolonialism is indeed all about the legacies of the European colonial encounter, but it is also very much about the continued presence of Western imperialism in global institutions and relationships today. The postcolonial tradition came into being as a result of both internal critiques of Western imperialism (e.g., Marx and Raymond Williams) and the numerous decolonization movements that swept across Asia, Africa, and the Middle East in the twentieth century. It is therefore a highly complex and syncretic tradition (Young, 2001) that brings diverse intellectual strands and political positions together.

Postcolonialism as we know it today is both remarkably focused and distinctly unruly. It is focused in its critique of colonialism and its continued resilience in contemporary social arrangements, and it is unruly in its eclectic use of diverse ideas and methodologies in accomplishing its goals. Although it shares many poststructural assumptions about language and representation, postcolonialism is far closer to Marxism and radical feminism in its commitment to a wider *political engagement* both within and outside the academy. Postcolonialism has emerged as a tradition to be seriously reckoned with over the last twenty years or so, beginning with Edward Said's (1978) pathbreaking and monumental work, *Orientalism*. Although Said along with many prominent early postcolonial scholars had disciplinary affiliations with departments of English literature (e.g., Bhabha, 1990; Spivak, 1987), the tradition has rapidly expanded to include scholars from anthropology (Appadurai, 1990; Clifford, 1988; Ong, 1987), history (Chakrabarty, 2000; Dirks, 2001), women's studies (Bulbeck, 1998; Mohanty, 1988), and cultural studies (Gilroy, 1987; Emberly, 1990). In the last few years, writings in the postcolonial tradition have also surfaced in business and organization studies (Cooke, 2003; Mir, Mir, & Upadhyaya, 2003; Prasad, 1997; Prasad & Prasad, 2002) as well.

The sheer diversity of voices and perspectives that constitute postcolonialism warns us against regarding it as a monolithic or unitary tradition. Postcolonialism is far more akin to feminism in the sheer *plurality* of its constituents. Indeed, it may well be more useful to think of postcolonialisms rather than a single invariant postcolonial tradition. These postcolonialisms emerged out of a growing impatience with the persistence of economic and cultural imperialism (sometimes also referred to as neocolonialism) long after political decolonization had taken place. In other words, the continuing dominance of "Western" (i.e., Europe, North America, and Australia) countries over their erstwhile colonies and over countries of the so-called Third World instigated a reexamination of the historical dynamics of colonialism and its lingering presence today. The postcolonial tradition is thus equally committed to understanding and reevaluating our colonial heritage and its current reformulations. It is also equally concerned with the economic, psychological, social, cultural, and aesthetic dimensions of colonialism in both *past* and *present* circumstances.

Postcolonialism is extraordinarily relevant to management and organization studies because it offers an alternative historical explanation for many commonplace business practices that have their origins in colonial structures (Cooke, 2003; Gopal, Willis, & Gopal, 2003). Further, postcolonialism's sustained focus on the undercurrents of neocolonialism in contemporary social contexts provides us with valuable insights into the darker side of globalization. Given the relentless march of globalization and the institutional championship of this process, the postcolonial tradition becomes particularly important in understanding some of its less visible and more unsavory facets. The next sections will trace forerunners to the postcolonial tradition and its own emergence as a serious intellectual position in both Western and non-Western academia.

The Emergence of a Postcolonial Tradition

At the risk of some simplification, one might observe that resistance to colonial rule (in the last one hundred years of European colonialism) manifested itself in two distinct, though overlapping, spheres. The more prominent form of resistance could be found in the numerous nationalist political movements that sought to overthrow different colonial powers and to replace them with local autonomous governments. A second (interlinked) form of resistance could be discerned in the various writings of colonized peoples, condemning all forms of colonial rule and expressing serious reservation about the West's (i.e., people and societies of European descent) relationship with and understanding of otherness in the context of colonialism.

It is worth noting that these two spheres were never isolated from one another. A number of individuals who were active in the freedom struggles of their day were also engaged in intellectual work that spawned widespread reflection about colonialism. Mao Tse Tung, Mahatma Gandhi, Leopold Senghor, and Che Guevara (to name only a few) were active liberation leaders who wrote and influenced contemporary thinking about the practices of colonialism. At the same time, the work of intellectuals like Fanon, Cesaire, and Cabral also shaped the imagination of freedom struggles and paved the way for the development of postcolonialism as we know it today.

Most of these early critiques of postcolonialism went far beyond condemning the coercive brutality of colonial regimes to exploring the *psychological* and *cultural* effects of colonialism. An early exposition of this nature was Cesaire's (1950) *Discourse on Colonialism,* a classic piece of writing that sought to affirm the identities of black colonized people while undertaking an incisive attack on colonialism itself. Cesaire was one of the active founders of the Negritude Movement, a cultural movement of French-speaking black intellectuals who were committed to restoring a sense of cultural pride to native Africans, who, they believed, had lost this pride in the debasing process of colonialism.

In many ways, Cesaire was deeply influenced by Marx's notions of commodification. He (Cesaire, 1950) argued that not only does colonialism oppress and exploit entire nations, but it also turns their inhabitants into *objectified commodities* in much the same way that capitalism operates with workers. As he observes, this objectification, which robs people of their dignity and humanity has always equaled "thingification." Cesaire further extended this thesis of objectification in proposing that the brutal effects of the colonial process eventually worked to decivilize and dehumanize the colonial power as well. His considerations on the brutality of colonialism led to his conceptualization of colonized societies as *morally superior* and infinitely more civilized than colonizing societies.

A more disturbing psychological critique of colonialism was offered by Franz Fanon (1961; 1967), the legendary black psychoanalyst from Martinique, who reconstituted class dynamics by shifting class conflict into the divisions between colonizer and colonized (Young, 2001). According to Fanon (1968), colonization was best understood as a *pathological* condition that eventually made all who participated in it mentally sick. Fanon subjected the psychological dynamics of colonialism to close scrutiny, focusing strongly on the desire and anxiety that pervades it. He argued that European colonizing societies were consumed by Negrophobia—a mindset that comprised both a desire for and fear of the black man's supposedly limitless sexuality. He also argued that colonialism was responsible for the widespread social construction of differences along racial lines, differences that ultimately annihilated black subjects into nothingness. For Fanon, the tragedy of the colonial situation lay in the ubiquity of racial identity, which overrode every other aspect of peoples' existence. Fanon also explained that blacks responded to these demeaning situations by imitating white behavior, a practice that meant the *negation* and virtual disappearance of black identity (Loomba, 1998).

The Tunisian revolutionary thinker, Albert Memmi, continued this focus on the *pyschological tenacity* of colonialism even after decolonization had formally taken place (Gandhi, 1998). Memmi remains one of the earliest thinkers to anticipate the strong grip that colonialism would exercise over the imaginations and cultural practices of different societies. Memmi (1967) is also notable for acknowledging the dialectical relationship between the colonizers and the colonized, and for elaborating on their mutual pathological dependency on each other. Memmi also recognized how difficult it would be to break this pattern, even in the wake of decolonization. As Gandhi (1998, 6–7) acutely observes, "Memmi's political pessimism delivers an account of postcoloniality as a historical condition marked by the visible apparatus of freedom and the concealed persistence of unfreedom."

The long-term psychological ill effects of colonialism were not the only phenomenon causing unease among progressive thinkers, worldwide. A growing concern centered around the question of *development* as well. By the 1970s, it was becoming quite clear that the world was broadly split into developed (i.e., affluent and technologically advanced) and underdeveloped societies. It was equally apparent that the developed tended to comprise those nations that had participated (directly or indirectly) in colonial rule, whereas the undeveloped (for the most part) tended to include the subjects of colonial rule. Eventually, two different critiques regarding the state of uneven development emerged. The first pointed to the legacies of colonialism that perpetuated the economic dependency of Third World nations on former colonial powers (Amin, 1974; 1977; Frank, 1969) and critiqued global institutions such as the World Bank and the International Monetary Fund (IMF) for regulating economic processes in ways that continued to place the West at a greater advantage.

The second critique was far more fundamental, and questioned the legitimacy of the development project itself. For the most part, these critics regarded development as another unfortunate manifestation of postcolonial modernity and were skeptical of its ability to create just and sustainable conditions within former colonized countries (Apffel-Marglin & Marglin, 1996; Escobar, 1995). Much of this group's critique of development is *cultural* and *epistemological,* arguing that frameworks of development were almost always predicated on Western modern assumptions of economic production and notions of the "good life," and were unwilling to accommodate alternative visions that were indigenous to the Third World and the non-West. Altogether, frustration and anger against the staying power of colonialism was being expressed on a number of diverse intellectual fronts.

It was not until Edward Said's pathbreaking work, *Orientalism,* made its appearance in 1978, however, that the postcolonial tradition began to take on a more coherent form and direction. Interestingly, although Said himself did not use the term, his commanding historical exploration of the institutionalization of colonial mentalities provoked a tremendous interest in the role of colonialism in shaping the cultural, economic, political, and aesthetic dimensions of various societies. Regarded as "a canonical event" (Gandhi, 1998, 67) and as "an inaugural text" (Prasad, 2003, 10), Said's *Orientalism* intertwined the poststructural discourse analysis of Michel Foucault with the cultural neo-Marxism of Antonio Gramsci and Raymond Williams to challenge the unquestioned authority of Western knowledge of and power over the Orient (Bayoumi & Rubin, 2000). Yet, Said's own inventive appropriation of these writers is quite distinctive and set in motion a wider interest in studying the historical and continuing encounters between the West and its others, that had their decisive origins in colonialism. Indeed there can be little doubt about Said's lasting impact or the global reach of his scholarship. As Bayoumi and Rubin (2000, 67) observe, "After *Orientalism,* scholars in the humanities and the social sciences could no longer ignore questions of difference or the politics of representation. Art history, anthropology, history, political science, sociology, philosophy and literary studies were all forced to confront its vision of culture."

In essence, Said (1978) examined the rise and consolidation of orientalism as a discursive formation in the West that was responsible for a specific understanding of Islamic culture and the Middle East (i.e., the Orient) as exotic, luxurious, depraved, and degenerate. Said further showed how such a constitution of oriental culture was the product of administrative, scholarly, and cultural institutions operating within the framework of colonialism. It is important to note that Said's discussion of orientalism does not refer to a collection of crude individual stereotypes about the Middle East but to an institutionalized way of imagining and representing it. As he himself (Said, 1978, 2) observes, "Orientalism is a style of thought based upon an ontological and epistemological distinction between the Orient and (most of the time) the Occident." Thus, to Said, the Orient is, in many ways, the cultural invention of European colonialism, whereas orientalism is a reflection of its colonial mindset—a mindset that impacted every element of the relationship between Europe and the West on one hand and the Middle East and the non-West on the other.

Said's work is so widely acclaimed, in part, because he identified respectable Western personalities (i.e., literary figures and artists) and institutions (i.e., universities and learned societies) as playing a pivotal role in the development of orientalism. His work remains postcolonial because of its ability to rupture the intellectual authority of Western scholarship by implicating it in the less savory material practices and agendas of colonialism. *Orientalism* stirred a number of researchers in the burgeoning postcolonial tradition to examine a number of institutional arrangements and cultural expressions in order to unearth the colonial and neo-imperial imprints on them, and to understand their implications for relationships between the West and the non-West today. Subject matters covered by these researchers have ranged from journalism (Spurr, 1993) and travel writing (Pratt, 1992) to psychoanalysis (Nandy, 1995) and the discourse of nationalism (Chatterjee, 1989). Increasingly, researchers have also been paying attention to managerial and business practices such as early accounting conventions (Neu, 2003), the origins of action research (Cooke, 2003), conflicts over museum exhibits (Harrison, 1997), and the West's interactions with OPEC (Prasad, 1997).

Central Concepts in the Postcolonial Tradition

At the core of the postcolonial tradition lies an understanding of colonialism as one of the most significant and omniscient social processes to have taken place over the last five centuries (Prasad, 2003). Hence, scholars from this tradition examine economic, philosophic, cultural, political, and aesthetic currents from the perspective of colonial control and domination. In much the same way that historical materialists see class as the central variable in all social analyses, and feminists take gender and patriarchy to be the defining moments in all social arrangements, postcolonialists view their subjects and all of their interactions through the prism of colonial domination and anticolonial resistance.

Postcolonialism simultaneously shares much with and differs from the postmodern and poststructuralist traditions (Hutcheon, 1989). Both postmodernism and poststructuralism are directly concerned with the *constitution of subjectivities* by liberal humanism and modernist ideals. Postcolonialists extend this concern by examining the role of imperialism in constituting the subjectivities of both colonial rulers and their subjects (Mishra & Hodge, 1994). In addition, postcolonialism has striking affinities with both historical materialism and feminism. It stresses the historical importance of colonialism as a distinctly materialist force (even while refusing to accord class and surplus value a central place in its analysis) and is close to radical and poststructural versions of feminism in its critique of dominant epistemologies and in its considerations of the intersections of race, gender, and geographical positions against matrices of power.

What primarily unites a diverse set of scholars and researchers who are postcolonial is their sustained *critique of colonialism* and their active attempts at *disengagement* from the entire colonial syndrome (Loomba, 1998). The postcolonial tradition has become one that combines historical analyses of colonialism with a theorized account of contemporary culture (Young, 2001) and includes historians, sociologists, ecologists, anthropologists, and literary theorists who are marked by an oppositional consciousness with regard to the past and continuing effects of colonialism. To Young (2001, 65), "postcolonial critique marks the moment where the political and cultural experience of the marginalized periphery developed into a more general theoretical position that could be set against Western political, intellectual and academic hegemony and its protocols of objective knowledge." The remainder of this section looks more closely at some of the central concepts within the postcolonial tradition.

The Nature and Forms of Colonialism

The postcolonial tradition understands European colonialism of the last five hundred years as being quite distinct from other types of empires and other forms of conquest. The mighty empires of the Mongols, the Egyptians, and the Aztecs (which were also mired in conquest and invasion) are regarded as differing in fundamental ways from the colonial forms of rule that had their nascence in the Europe of the latter part of the fifteenth century and were taken up (albeit in an altered form) by the United States and other "Western" powers in the second half of the twentieth century. European colonialism stands apart because of its *planetary reach* and the sheer scale of its operations (Prasad, 2003; Stam, 1995). At its zenith, a handful of European powers exerted considerable control (directly or otherwise) over approximately three-quarters of the world. Bessis (2003) argues that European colonialism actually introduced an era of *globalization,* which she sees as the appropriation of much of the world by Western Europe and the interdependence of all of its parts in the pursuit of Western domination.

Modern colonialism's encroachments into the societies that it colonized went way beyond the political arena. Colonial powers did far more than merely extract revenues from their subjects. Rather, alongside industrial capitalism, colonial rule *restructured* the economies and societies of the colonies, drawing them into a complex dependent relationship with the colonial home power. In all of these domains, European colonialism went hand in hand with industrial capitalism; the two are, at an ontological level, inseparable from one another. As Loomba (1998, 4) notes, "Colonialism was the midwife that assisted at the birth of European capitalism." In practical terms, this implied that colonialism restructured such diverse social formations as revenue collection systems, the role of the family and neighborhood, economic activities such as the nature of trade and enterprise, the meaning of the nation-state, various administrative apparatuses, an array of cultural codes and rituals, and so on.

The cultural impact of colonialism is also of particular interest to the postcolonial tradition. Not only is culture seen as a theater where various colonial politics and ideological causes were played out (Said, 1994), but innumerable cultural categories such as Europe, the Orient, the West, civilization, and savagery were formulated and given new meaning by colonial practices and institutions (Said, 1978; 1994). Dirks (1992) goes even as far as to suggest that the notion of culture itself was recast in its present form because of its indispensability to colonial governance. In his own words, (Dirks, 1992, 3), "If colonialism can be seen as a cultural formation, so also, culture is a colonial formation." Dirks' point, of course, is that culture has always been imbricated in both the means and ends of colonial conquest and domination.

In considering the dynamics of colonialism, writers in the postcolonial tradition insist that it not be regarded as a singular and monolithic process. Young (2001), for instance, makes some important distinctions between predominantly white settler colonies (e.g., Australia and Canada), colonies whose resources and natives were subject to naked exploitation (e.g., India, Kenya, and Vietnam), and maritime enclaves (e.g., islands like Guam and Diego Garcia that continue to be occupied by Western nations who use them as military or naval bases). Mishra and Hodge (1994) make a similar point when they argue that all colonial relationships between the imperial centers and their subject states are far from being identical. White settler colonies, even after undergoing the experiences of colonialism, continue to identify culturally with the erstwhile imperial home country. This, however, is obviously not the case with ex-colonies like Sri Lanka or Uganda. Then again, the nature and extent of imperial involvements differed from colony to colony. In much of Africa, colonialism was heavily tinged with an evangelical missionary flavor, while in Algeria the imperial thrust was far more cultural. Needless to say, these differences in colonial relationships produced a set of diverse effects that linger on today.

Above all, the postcolonial tradition focuses on the persistence of colonial dynamics and mindsets long after decolonization has officially taken place. Postcolonialists conclude that old colonial empires have transformed themselves (along with newer affiliates) into a clearly demarcated group that is seen as "the West" and that the West's affiliation with global institutional power has resulted in a situation wherein former colonies continue to be *economically dependent* on their erstwhile colonial masters (Stam, 1995). The Ghanian leader, Nkumrah, described this state of affairs as one of *neocolonialism*—a term that has come to imply the continuation of colonial rule by economic and other means. Neocolonialism is orchestrated in and through various world organizations such as the World Bank, the IMF, and the World Trade Organization (WTO) that enact trade and monetary policies ensuring that old global asymmetries remain in place.

All of this begs the question as to how *post* the postcolonial really is. And this is indeed a major focus of the postcolonial tradition beginning with the acknowledgment that not all colonialism has come to an end. On the contrary, postcolonialists recognize that colonial relations are perpetuated through cultural discourses, global economic policies, political coalitions, and many other institutional practices. Furthermore, innumerable social texts such as media reports, trade policies, and marketing campaigns contain elements of what Zantop (1997) refers to as *latent colonialism*. Latent colonialism refers to the presence of a colonial mentality, which is masked by seemingly neutral discourses of economics and communication. The postcolonial tradition seeks to unravel these imperialistic habits and agendas in a multitude of historical and contemporary circumstances. In essence, therefore, postcolonialism is "a dialectic concept that marks the broad historical facts of decolonization and the determined achievement of sovereignty, but also the reality of nations and peoples emerging into a new imperialistic context of economic and sometimes political domination" (Young, 2001, 57).

Eurocentrism and Western Supremacy

A unifying thread running through the postcolonial tradition is its opposition to and critique of *Eurocentrism*. At a broad level, Eurocentrism refers to the unshaken belief (shared by people of *both* European and non-European descent) that European ideas and institutions constitute the bedrock of civilization and should therefore be adopted by the rest of the world. Eurocentrism is obviously a byproduct of European colonialism and is part of the myth of European (and later, Western) supremacy that was invented to justify and legitimize colonialism (Bessis, 2001). Eurocentrism places Europe and (more recently) "the West" at the center of history, economic development, and political modernity, and judges every other culture in reference to it. Stam (1995, 98) offers a succinct definition of Eurocentrism that he sees as "the procrustean forcing of cultural heterogeneity into a single paradigmatic perspective. Eurocentrism sees Europe as the privileged source of meaning, as the world's center of gravity, as ontological 'reality' to the rest of the world's shadow."

According to postcolonialists, the problem with Eurocentrism is that European or Western ideas and practices are systematically privileged over non-European ones, to the detriment of the entire world. For example, if we look at something like health care, we find that Western medicine occupies a central and legitimate position, against which all other medical systems are judged. As a result, many ancient and *bona fide* medical systems (such as acupuncture and homeopathy) are designated as "alternative" forms of medical practice and are regarded with suspicion or dismissed as quackery by pillars of the Western medical community and the insurance industry. The same holds true for business practices where the modern Western notion of *the firm* is regarded as the desirable commercial prototype for the rest of the world.

Postcolonialists also emphasize the sheer ubiquity and pervasiveness of Eurocentrism in everyday conversations, academic disciplines, and central institutional structures. As Chakrabarty (2000) points out, even such basic concepts as state, citizenship, civil society, science, and rationality bear the distinct stamp of European culture and history. Nor have the more progressive intellectual traditions (such as Marxism and critical theory) been untainted by Eurocentrism. Bessis (2001), for instance, identifies Marx's Eurocentric inheritance in his pronouncements about Indian society having no known history and in his conviction that colonialism was an important and inevitable stage in society's inexorable march toward a utopian communist state. Not only does Eurocentrism reproduce colonial ideologies, but it also *normalizes* many hierarchies (such as the Occident and the Orient or civilized over primitive) that were generated in and through colonialism (Stam, 1995).

One of the main problems of Eurocentrism lies in its *blindness* about the flaws and limitations of Western culture, while simultaneously being unable to recognize the strengths and contributions of non-Western cultures. Thus, Eurocentrism is responsible for portraying Europe as the crucible of civilization and democracy, while at the same time glossing over horrendous events such as the Spanish Inquisition, the Holocaust, and the dropping of the atomic bomb as mere aberrations from Europe's and the West's customary civilized conduct (Bessis, 2001). Ultimately, Eurocentrism *sanitizes* Western history while simultaneously *demonizing* or *patronizing* the non-West (Stam, 1995).

Colonial Discourse

A common theme running through the entire postcolonial tradition is its focus on colonial discourse. The notion of colonial discourse owes much to the work of Edward Said (1978) who examined systematic Western representations of the Orient in multiple institutional contexts. Said, moreover, knitted the poststructural ideas of Michel Foucault with the cultural Marxism of Antonio Gramsci in developing his own ideas of colonial discourse. Drawing upon Said, we could argue that a colonial discourse refers to an entire way of seeing, thinking, and writing about colonized and/or formerly colonized people that simultaneously flourished in diverse institutional domains, including art, cinema, literature, the church, education and public administration. Loomba (1998, 54) describes colonial discourse as "a new way of thinking in which cultural, intellectual, economic and political processes are seen to work together in the formation, perpetuation and dismantling of colonialism."

Colonial discourses are characterized by certain key features. First, they are integral elements of the apparatus of colonial power, being produced by immensely respectable individuals allied with powerful colonial institutions. Highly regarded literary figures, artists, scientific experts, historians, and anthropologists (among others) have all been engaged in (re)producing specific images of colonial subjects and their cultures that eventually become some kind of "reality." Second, these innumerable cultural productions frequently inspire one another and consequently end up producing a relatively homogeneous and undisputed picture of colonized cultures. Third, these colonial discourses have instituted *structures of thinking* (Said, 1978; Young, 2001) that are hierarchical and oppositional—with the colonizers (the West) being largely constituted as the superior or vanguard culture over the colonized or the non-West (Loomba, 1998). Fourth, colonial discourses both anticipated and *legitimized* colonial governance, and continue to legitimate different forms of neocolonialism and neo-imperialism across the world. Lastly, colonial discourses are indeed *ideological* because they reproduce a "false" and fictionalized vision of the non-West, which, in essence, is little more than a figment of the colonial imagination.

Colonial discourses are thus simultaneously "real" in the sense of referring to and constituting existing cultures, and at the same time "unreal" in the sense that they deal almost endlessly with stereotypes, images, and fantasies of the other. Although *orientalism* (Said, 1978) has taken the spotlight as a prominent colonial discourse, some other powerful and enduring discourses include *primitivism* and *tropicalization*. Even while these three discourses overlap in significant ways, they each have some unique characteristics and are quite distinct from one another. In general, the discourse of primitivism pervades representations of Africa and cultures of the African Caribbean, although it can also be found in representations of African Americans and indigenous peoples living in Western societies. Orientalist discourses, on the other hand, are found in representations of Turkey, the Middle East, India, and (more recently) the Far East, whereas tropicalization dominates representations of Mexico, Latin America, and parts of the Caribbean.

The discourse of primitivism has much to do with the West's experiences in colonizing Africa and the Caribbean, and represents these cultures as overwhelmingly primitive, savage, and wild (Coombes, 1994). Accordingly, primitivism celebrates the supposedly unrestrained, spontaneous, and exuberant side of African and Caribbean cultures while simultaneously expressing fears about their uncontrolled savagery and irrational tribalism (Torgovnick, 1990). The discourse of primitivism is not a thing of the past but continues to linger in many institutional fields, notably art movements and economic development where African and Caribbean cultures are admired for their simplicity and elemental ferocity and denigrated for their "backwardness" and their inability to progress (Coombes, 1994; Torgovnick, 1990).

Orientalism, as described by Said (1978), represents the cultures of Turkey, India, and the Middle East (i.e., the Orient) and is, in his view, mainly responsible for creating the vast cultural disjuncture between the East and the West, and between the Orient and the Occident. An array of literature, art, social science, and history in late nineteenth- and twentieth-century Europe collaborated in the discursive production of an orient that was mysterious and exotic, and inhabited by cunning, degenerate, sensual, and ferocious people. Paintings by the British Orientalist School, literary works by Flaubert and Nerval, travel accounts by Lamartine, and "expert" reports by T.E. Lawrence all contributed to the idea of the Orient as a place of barbaric splendor, haunting beauty, and despotic cruelty. Images of veiled women, colorful and noisy bazaars, and closely guarded harems pervade the visual, scholarly, and literary discourses of orientalism (Richon, 1985; Said, 1978). Orientalism also substantially sexualized these cultures, investing them with a languid and concealed eroticism.

It is important to appreciate the extent to which this institutional production of the Orient reflected the European (colonial) imagination of the nineteenth and early twentieth centuries. As Said (1978, 177) astutely notes, "The orient is less a place than a *topos,* a set of references, a congeries of characteristics that seems to have its origin in a quotation or a fragment of a text, or a citation from someone's work on the orient, or some bit of previous imagining or an amalgam of all these."

The term *tropicalization* is indebted to Said's (1978) notion of orientalism and is best understood as its etymological correlative within the Latin Caribbean context (Aparicio & Chavez-Silverman, 1997). In much the same way as the discourse of orientalism ontologically distinguishes between the East and the West, tropicalization creates a discursive separation between the so-called temperate world (i.e., Northern Europe and its affiliates) and the *tropics* (Latin America, Mexico, and the Caribbean). The discourse of tropicalization is very much a part of the colonial imagination of the United States and primarily represents "tropical" cultures as luxuriant earthy paradises filled with indolent, alluring, and incompetent people (Benz, 1997).

The lethargy and incompetence of people inhabiting the tropics is a regular theme within this discourse. Neither should we believe that such a representation is accidental or entirely innocent. As Urraca (1997) argues, this discursive production of tropical backwardness and incompetence provides a perfect contrasting background for a display of North American virtue and exceptionalism. In addition, tropicalization also inscribes Latin cultures as sexually charged and erotic. Their eroticism, however, is represented somewhat differently from that of oriental cultures. Whereas oriental women are mostly depicted as sexually desirable but hidden (veiled) and pliant, tropicalization represents Latinas and women of the Caribbean as torrid, passionate, sexually eager, and available. Violence is another strong theme within this discourse, with Latin America and Mexico in particular being represented as domains of searing and ruthless violence—in the jungles of the Amazon and in the urban ghettos.

It is probably obvious to the reader that all three colonial discourses considered here are *ambivalent* rather than overtly pejorative. Indeed, all three discourses distinctly romanticize "natives" and colonial subjects by casting them as noble savages or enticing sexual figures. At the same time, these identical colonial subjects are uniformly inscribed in distinctly negative and even frightening ways—as irrational, dangerous, primitive, lazy, degenerate, and corrupt. It is suggested that in identifying and examining colonial discourses, Muecke's (1992) characterization of them as being simultaneously *anthropological, romantic,* and *racist* is very helpful. Colonial discourses uniformly anthropologize non-Western subjects by treating them as objects of scientific knowledge and expertise. They also frequently romanticize non-Western cultures while also representing them in racist terms as somehow intrinsically inferior and backward.

It is also important to remember that colonial discourses are far from belonging to the past. As many postcolonial writers argue, the discursive effects of colonialism have long outlasted formal colonial rule. Discourses of primitivism can be found in policy debates about economic development in Africa; orientalism is rampant in the Western media's coverage of the Middle East; and tropicalization is alive and well in international business textbooks and their discussions of corrupt and demotivated Latin business cultures. These are by no means the only domains in which colonial discourses operate. Orientalism, tropicalization, primitivism, and other colonial discourses can be easily located in educational material, consumer reports, policy statements, and everyday public conversations. They undoubtedly occupy vital spaces within our social and institutional lives, and consequently shape a number of our perceptions, attitudes, opinions, and interactions.

Hybridity

Theorists and scholars working in the postcolonial tradition focus on the notion of hybridity as something that grew out of the colonial encounter and something that preoccupied colonial ruling elites (Young, 1995). Also referred to as *syncretism* and *creolization* (Loomba, 1998), the term *hybridity* first and foremost signals some level of cultural intermingling and/or fusion. With its etymological roots in botany and zoology, hybridity originally referred to forms of cross breeding that yielded new species among plants and animals. Within the humanities and the social sciences, hybridity has moved closer to center stage, largely because of the work done by individuals working within the postcolonial tradition. Here, the term has legitimacy partly because it offers a progressive way of adopting an anti-purist stand on race and culture without necessarily relinquishing the importance of difference.

We should note that there is no single uniform understanding of hybridity within the postcolonial tradition. Rather, what we have is a number of debates and discussions regarding the nature and effects of hybridity. Many writers within the postcolonial tradition, however, would agree on the important role of *travel* and *global migrations* (initially triggered by colonialism) in intensifying the levels of cultural hybridity (Clifford, 1997; Hannerz, 1987) in the twentieth and early twenty-first centuries. Indeed, a number of postcolonial scholars would argue that any form of cultural blending or fusion needs to be studied against the backdrop of cultural traffic and patterns of migration. This would imply that the cultural syncretism of North American workplaces needs to be understood within the context of NAFTA, the history of U.S. immigration law, the formation of Asian and Latin diasporas, and so on.

Some writers attest that hybridity is involuntary and inevitable (Rosaldo, 1993). Others see it as a product of deliberate colonial policy (e.g., the Hispanization of South and Central America) that is, nevertheless, often quite difficult to control (Bhabha, 1992). Postcolonial discussions of hybridity tend to insist that questions of cultural fusion and assimilation are contextualized and addressed in terms of the colonial dynamics and power relations that undergird them. Friedman (1998) notes that the postcolonial tradition raises such questions about hybridity as: Is hybridity hated or embraced? How much control over the hybridization process is exerted by colonial authorities versus colonial subjects? How is hybridity actually negotiated in everyday practices? Which social and geographic groups benefit most or lose most from hybridity? Are all groups equally hybridized and in the same way? How does any hybrdization process intersect with other relevant social stratifications?

In addition, postcolonial researchers take different stands about the *politics* of hybridization. One view is markedly skeptical about the benefits of hybridization, seeing it primarily as a byproduct of the oppressive legacy of colonialism (Friedman, 1998). This view warns of situations when a dominant culture succeeds in *deculturing* and/or *assimilating* the less powerful group with which it comes into contact. The problematic outcome here is that much of the less powerful group's cultural heritage is lost or suppressed. A common situation exemplifying this is the formation of contemporary Native American cultures out of the genocidal policies and practices of the Westward frontier movement.

A second view regards hybridity as primarily *subversive,* capable of ultimately undermining any kind of colonial neo-imperial authority structures by displacing and reordering the very binaries on which the entire system rests. Within the postcolonial tradition, Homi Bhabha's (1986) work exemplifies this position. Bhabha's arguments about hybridity are extraordinarily complicated and are hard to cover in a few pages. He draws on the ideas of Fanon (1961; 1968) whom he also substantially reinterprets to claim that any colonial encounter culminates into a situation of *mimicry* wherein the colonial subjects appear to eagerly imitate and adopt colonial cultures as their own. However, Bhabha also argues that the hybridity or cultural mixing born of this mimicry is both two-sided and transgressive because of the enormous ambivalence that the process holds for both imperial authorities and colonial subjects. This ambivalence then opens up a space for irony, doubt, and confusion—all of which end up disrupting the colonial order (Bhabha, 1992).

Within this perspective, hybridity is largely positive (Appadurai, 1996; Bhabha, 1986; Silko, 1977) to the extent that it reaffirms cultural differences and consequently disrupts the prevailing neo-imperial order. Writers like Silko (1977) and Hannerz (1987) also affirm that syncretism and hybridism are far more relevant to contemporary global culture because of their constantly evolving and changing nature. Postcolonial ideas on hybridity can be used to gain some fruitful insights into multicultural organizational encounters in this age of globalization. Acquisitions and mergers, transnational corporate movements, company takeovers, and unique global organizational forms such as *maquilladoras* are all engaged in hybridization processes requiring questions of a more complex and problematic nature.

Working in the Postcolonial Tradition

Considering the relative recency of postcolonial ideas, the amount of fieldwork conducted in this tradition is nothing short of impressive. Postcolonial ideas have influenced research in literature (Brantlinger, 1988; Spurr, 1993), history (Dirks, 2001), anthropology (Clifford, 1988; Pratt, 1992), political science and international relations (Darby, 1997), and communication studies (Perera & Pugliese, 1998), among other areas. In all of these works the research is guided by a focus on colonial and neocolonial processes in past and present circumstances and by many of the concepts discussed in this chapter. Above all, research in the postcolonial tradition is strikingly interdisciplinary (even while individual researchers are affiliated with specific disciplines) since colonial relations cannot be easily contained within academic boundaries. More recently, with the intensification of globalization, postcolonialism has also begun to draw a number of researchers in management and organization studies. These scholars examine a variety of phenomena, including representations of Third World economies in the business press (Priyadarshini, 2003), national policies and aboriginal rights issues in Australian mines (Bannerjee, 2003), efforts at inducing structural transformations in museums (Harrison, 1997), the production of multicultural training videos (Jack & Lorbiecki, 2003), and the promotion of Third World tourism destinations (Echtner & Prasad, 2003).

Like other *post* traditions, postcolonial researchers also are not bound by rigid methodological preferences. They tend to use a wide variety of data sources and methods, including government documents (Neu, 2000), business press reports (Prasad, 1997; Priyadarshini, 2003), tourism brochures (Echtner & Prasad, 2003), and participant observation of organizations (Harrison, 1997). In general, these and other studies go behind the seeming normality of routine organizational processes to reveal the enduring colonial legacies that undergird them. Many of the studies are historical (Cooke, 2003; Neu, 2003), tracing the neo-imperial roots of many contemporary managerial ideas and practices. Cooke (2003), for instance, traces the roots of Kurt Lewin's action research and group dynamics models in U.S. state-sponsored efforts to restore order and stability among multiethnic groups, and in the overtly colonialist manipulations that shaped them.

Neu (2003), on the other hand, tries to understand how national and global accounting policies have systematically functioned as "softwares of colonialism." Neu uses the term *softwares of colonialism* to refer to administrative techniques such as finance and accounting practices that help realize specific colonial objectives in a manner that obscures both the partisan nature of the techniques and the devastating (sometimes genocidal) consequences for the groups targeted by these techniques (Neu, 2000; 2003). He then uses historical empirical examples from Canada and more contemporary examples from Chiapas, Mexico, and the World Bank in Ghana to illustrate this point. In effect, Neu relates prevalent accounting categories, financial inducements, and global fiscal policies to the accomplishment of neocolonial objectives. His work helps us understand how bounty payments for the scalps of dead Indians were institutionalized features of Canadian administrative policy— leading eventually to the decimation of the Micmac people (Neu, 2003). He also notes that these types of legally accepted bounty payments could be found in the United States right up to the end of the nineteenth century. In addition, he documents various other financial policies (e.g., distribution of agricultural implements) that were designed to encourage the containment of native people on the reservations. His research has identified and described similar chilling contemporary efforts at colonial control and manipulation of people in Mexico and in Ghana.

Neu's work directly focuses on administrative policies and practices. A bigger segment of postcolonial research looks at *representations* of erstwhile colonial subjects and their cultures in prominent Western discourses. An excellent example of such work is Prasad's (1997) examination of Western reactions to the rise of OPEC (Organization of Petroleum Exporting Countries) in corporate boardrooms and the business press. He focuses on two noteworthy moments in these reactions—the first is the labeling of Abdullah Tariki (a one-time Saudi minister for oil and active cofounder of OPEC) as "the red sheikh," and the second is the *Washington Post*'s dismissive characterization of OPEC as "a quarreling collection of camel sheikhdoms and banana republics." Prasad subjects both depictions to a close postcolonial analysis, showing how both are substantially influenced by a long tradition of orientalist imagery and how both attempt to perpetuate the asymmetric relationships between the West and the Middle East that were the product of colonialism.

Priyadarshini (2003) continues this examination of the business press, looking at the *Economist*'s representation of the Indian political economy in the 1990s. Her study focuses on the metaphors of wild animals (tigers, dragons, and elephants) routinely used to describe burgeoning Asian economic systems. Arguing that *animalization* or rendering colonized cultures as wild beasts has been a recurrent colonial trope, Priyadarshini (2003) analyses the *Economist*'s portrayal of the Indian economy as a "tiger economy" in three separate articles. She makes an interesting distinction in her analysis between first-level and second-level metaphors. First-level metaphors carry an immediate and straightforward image, whereas second-level metaphors carry more latent pictures and images that can only be discerned on closer analysis. Thus, a first-level metaphorical analysis would lead us to believe that the tiger metaphor is mostly positive—emphasizing the power and majesty of the tiger. A second-level analysis, however, indicates that tiger economies can also be read as wild, ferocious, dangerous, and out of control. With the help of a detailed analysis, Priyadarshini shows how the notion of the tiger economy is used to reduce Asian economic and cultural circumstances to biological ones, thus preserving the hierarchy between the civilized West and the uncivilized non-West.

The theme of representation continues to receive attention in Echtner and Prasad's (2003) study of the promotion of Third World countries as tourism destinations. Echtner & Prasad primarily contextualize the tourism industry in colonial relations, pointing out that tourism operators are located in and promote these destinations to people from the West or the First World, and that tourists to the Third World are overwhelmingly from the Western world while Third World visitors to the West are likely to be much smaller in number. Having established an asymmetric and historically colonial institutional context, Echtner and Prasad (2003) examine 223 tourism brochures promoting a range of Third World countries. They examine both the language and visual images of the brochures from a postcolonial perspective and conclude that the representation of Third World destinations remains disturbingly tied to a set of nostalgic colonialist images. Their analysis draws attention to the predominance of three myths—the myth of the unchanged, the myth of the unrestrained, and the myth of the uncivilized, which shapes the discursive representations of Third World destinations.

The myth of the unchanged (corresponding largely to Said's notion of orientalism), squarely located Third World destinations in a glorious and opulent past tacitly encourages present-day tourists to relive the exotic journeys of colonial traders, explorers, and treasure hunters. The myth of the unrestrained depicts Third World destinations (like Fiji and Jamaica) as luxuriant paradises and encourages tourists to shed their inhibitions and to sensuously indulge themselves in the natural beauty and charms of the natives. Echtner and Prasad further argue that the myth of the unrestrained in some ways re-creates a romanticized vision of colonial exploitation. Finally, the myth of the uncivilized (depicting Kenya and Namibia) focuses on untamed nature and primitive cultures, and is also a modernized version of the colonial fantasy of the jungle expedition and the last frontier. Overall, this piece of research demonstrates the tenacity of colonial discourse and raises questions about the kind of influence it carries in shaping broader attitudes and expectations about the Third World.

It would be a mistake to conclude that the postcolonial tradition is interested mainly in questions of representation and the analysis of documents and texts. Some postcolonial researchers have clearly been interested in studying colonial imprints on contemporary institutions such as museums (Harrison, 1997; Prasad, 2003). Harrison's ethnography of an American state museum's efforts to jettison its overtly imperialist ideology and transform itself is an excellent example of such field studies. Harrison argues that museums had an important role in colonial societies because they were one important way in which these societies came to know and interpret (albeit in a limited way) those peoples who were part of their empire or imperialist domain. Thus, museums frequently mirrored the rules, structures, and values of the colonial milieu particularly around themes of containment, objectification, and reduction. The state museum studied by Harrison was no stranger to this imperialist ideology that was evident in its representation of indigenous peoples and native cultures. Her study looks at the attempt of a new museum director to revise the museum's vision so that it was more in keeping with the wider society's postcolonial ethos. Harrison (1997) uses interviews and analyzes museum exhibits to arrive at an understanding of the institutional processes that prevented a genuine transformation from taking place. Her study helps us understand how the museum's identity as a respectable state bureaucracy and guardian of Western heritage influenced its adoption of representational techniques that only reproduced the objectification and reduction of native cultures.

Altogether, the postcolonial tradition compels recognition of global (frequently imperialist) dynamics into management and organization studies, thus contextualizing contemporary workplaces within wider political situations. Although the tradition's early connections to literature and literary theory make it particularly amenable to studying what are commonly understood as "texts" (e.g., press reports, tourism brochures), it is equally relevant for examining institutional processes and cultural events within organizations. Above all, the postcolonial tradition restores a stronger sense of historical cultural awareness to our understanding of contemporary organizations and is useful in identifying patterns of hierarchical reproduction that are grounded in colonial dynamics. Thus, postcolonialism has enormous potential when it comes to looking at current trends on globalization—notably such phenomena as transnational worker migrations, the formation and effect of Export Processing Zones (EPZs), the cultural and economic effects of transnational organizational takeovers, and the ramifications of new ideologies such as market fundamentalism and the Washington Consensus.

Figure 14.1 **Highlights of the Postcolonial Tradition**

Philosophic influences: Mahatma Gandhi, Ho Chi Minh, Leopold
Senghor, Franz Fanon, Albert Memmi,
Aime Cesaire

Major figures: Edward Said, Gayatri Spivak, Ashish Nandy,
Homi Bhabha, Robert Young, Arjun Appadurai

Central concepts
- Colonialism and neocolonialism
- Imperialism
- Eurocentrism
- Hybridity and creolization
- Representation
- Colonial discourse
- Primitivism
- Orientalism
- Tropicalization

Key practices
- Interdisciplinarity
- Colonialism as a constant backdrop
- Colonialism as a practice rather than a metaphor
- Commitment to cultural pluralism
- Dialectics of domination and resistance

Exemplary research
- "The Context of Third World Tourism Marketing" (Echtner & Prasad, 2003)
- "Museums as Agencies of Neocolonialism in a Postmodern World" (Harrison, 1997)
- "Accounting for the Banal" (Neu, 2003)
- "The Colonizing Consciousness and Representations of the Other" (Prasad, 1997)

15

Conclusion

Tradition, Improvisation, and Quality Control

A final chapter in a book like this one ideally provides some summary reflections, caveats, cautionary remarks, and comments on the field. This book has outlined what I believe to be the major traditions influencing much of qualitative research on work and organizations in contemporary society. This is not meant to indicate, however, that the book is a completely comprehensive treatment of the field. Entire scholarly traditions have been excluded (e.g., action research, cultural studies, and queer theory), and some traditions have only received partial treatment (e.g., institutional theory) under the rubric of structuration and praxeology. Obvious limitations of time, space, and personal expertise have restricted the scope of the book in many ways.

The book's main intent has been to present the sheer variety of possibilities present while doing qualitative research and to offer researchers a diverse array of epistemological and methodological options. The book was also intended to problematize the use of interviews, observation, and document analyses as *starting points* in qualitative research. Instead, it underscores how these data collection methods would be put to different uses within different scholarly traditions. For instance, field observations conducted within a dramatist tradition would be directed at uncovering the central dramatic narratives that are most meaningful to actors in a given social situation, whereas observation by a historical materialist would focus on understanding the exploitative dynamics and class struggles present in any event or social process. The same obviously holds true for interviews and textual analyses. A feminist researcher's interview protocol is likely to look very different from a semiotician's interview protocol, even when they are studying the same phenomena and the identical situation or event.

Thus, a central message of the book relates to the importance of becoming familiar with any tradition in its entirety (i.e., assumptions, inclinations, debates, writing styles) for the purpose of conducting high-quality research. In other words, data collection techniques and data analyses cannot be *abstracted* or *removed* from the broader intellectual tradition within which the researcher is working. At this point, however, another major caveat is in order. The discussions of the different traditions in this book offer no more than a relatively detailed *introduction* to each tradition and are by no means exhaustive. Researchers are strongly advised to delve more deeply into the tradition in which they have most interest by reading original texts, commentaries, debates, and other pieces of fieldwork done within the tradition. In short, no single chapter here will turn the reader into an expert on any particular tradition. All it can do is to give the reader a feel for and a flavor of a given tradition, and a sense of what it means to work within it. The somewhat exhaustive bibliography is likely to be helpful to those who want to pursue any of these traditions further.

Being exposed to a variety of traditions also offers novice researchers a range of options from which to choose. In many ways, the choice of a tradition to work within is a highly personal one, involving a series of aesthetic, ethical, and methodological preferences. Researchers who are fascinated by the minute details of everyday life, for instance, might want to work within the ethnomethodological tradition, whereas those who are drawn to macro-analyses of social institutions might want to explore historical materialism or structuration. Also, as mentioned in the first chapter, the book offers a meta-phorical map of potential research pathways and destinations. This is important because in my experience, novice researchers spend far too much time in the field without having much focus or direction. Too many researchers spend an inordinate amount of time at the exploratory stage of research, especially when the principal method of data collection is observation.

Let me be quite clear here. I am not suggesting that a certain amount of exploratory research is not useful. What I am suggesting is that without any kind of focus or direction, participant observation in particular can be both confusing and overwhelming. It is hard to absorb the full range of interactions taking place in any organizational site, and it is even harder to figure out what one should be paying attention to or noting down without a theoretically driven focus. Having some idea of the different traditions can give researchers a better sense of the genre of questions they would like to ask and the broad directions they might want to follow.

Throughout the book, I have made sustained efforts to discuss actual research pieces in the different traditions and to highlight what I consider to be "exemplary" pieces of fieldwork in each tradition. In my many years of working with doctoral students, I have found these to be most useful. I would therefore urge researchers to take the trouble to read through existing fieldwork in the traditions that interest them. There are few better ways of learning the *craft* of qualitative research than by looking at other well-crafted pieces themselves. Most of these pieces are exemplary because they pay attention to diverse dimensions of doing research—the formulation of the research problem, its connection to existing literature, the choice of a theoretical framework, an awareness of underlying assumptions, the selection of a suitable site or set of subjects, the collection and analysis of data, and the final presentation of the findings. I would once again emphasize how important it is to pay attention to all of these aspects and not to assume (as many researchers do) that extensive periods of time spent in the field or a vast number of interviews are themselves indicators of good qualitative research.

Traditions and Improvisation in Qualitative Research

In speaking about the different research traditions, I am often asked two interrelated questions that might be worth addressing here. The first is: How closely should one follow a particular tradition? The second is: Does working in any tradition curtail a researcher's own originality and imagination? The answers to both questions are obviously far more complex than a simple yes or no.

How closely should a researcher follow a tradition? To begin with, I would like to stress that in my viewpoint, the value of scholarly traditions lies in their ability to *inspire* and *guide* researchers rather than to *police* them. For example, if one is drawn to looking at the social world as a stage, the dramaturgical tradition can help the researcher further clarify and extend this premise by exploring notions such as face-work, stigmas, and impression management. It can also help shape the contours of the research project by suggesting specific directions and avenues. In short, if a researcher has an affinity for the dramaturgical world-view, the tradition also offers him or her ways of operationalizing these ideas and styles of presenting them.

Unlike many conventional statistical methods and research designs such as cluster analyses or repeated measures design, the traditions discussed in this book are much more fluid and less tied to strict protocols of data gathering and analysis. The question about closely following a tradition is therefore not easily answered. In general, I would advocate that a researcher become both familiar with and comfortable in the tradition(s) of her choice. Once a certain level of theoretical and methodological comfort is reached, the researcher can draw on those elements of the tradition that work best for him or her and that are most suitable for the fieldwork at hand.

Having said this, I would still maintain that working in a particular tradition should mean something more than a loose appropriation of central ideas and terminology. As a journal reviewer, I am sometimes confronted with articles claiming to be engaging in hermeneutics, which, however, do little more than a surface exploration of conventional organizational texts. To me, this is at best something of a lost opportunity. Working in the hermeneutic tradition can offer incredible insights when it comes to probing texts and is helpful in connecting texts to the social contexts in which they were produced. Hermeneutics also helps a researcher be more reflexive when it comes to understanding her or his own relationship to the texts being examined. In this case, therefore, delving deeply into a tradition would be more likely to result in the production of high-quality research.

The second question raised here asks about the dangers of traditions stifling the researcher's creativity and imagination. The main thing to remember here is that working within a tradition is not to be confused with blindly *imitating* a style of work and writing. Just as in any artistic or literary tradition, no two research pieces within the same tradition are identical. Although they may be driven by identical ontological assumptions and may share an interest in the same organizational and cultural dimensions, they typically pose different questions, examine different field sites, and work with different kinds of subjects. As an illustration, let us briefly return to the chapter on historical materialism. If one looks at the examples of fieldwork discussed in this chapter, one is struck as much by the differences as by the similarities among them. Thus Collinson's (1988) study of factory workers is significantly different from O'Connor's (2001) portrayal of Ordway Tead, or Bertaux and Bertaux-Wiame's (1981) materialist ethnography of French artisan bakers. The first study connects masculinity to control relations on the shopfloor, the second places the discourse of industrial democracy in a historical context, and the third offers explanations for the resilience of French family bakeries in the wake of industrial expansion and takeovers in the European food industry. Yet, all three studies are still bound by many common assumptions about the nature of social segmentation and conflict, and the value of historical analysis.

In other words, research traditions do not stifle creativity or imagination because of the endless possibilities of *improvisation* within them. In many ways, doing research within a particular research tradition is similar to composing a melody within a particular harmonic scale. Just as the notes are limited, so are the ontological and epistemological assumptions, the central concepts, and so on. The important point to keep in mind is that one pursues research directions that are personally exciting and one builds research narratives that are interesting and relevant, within the parameters of certain conceptual building blocks. Traditions are not and should never be used as instruments of standardization.

All of this talk about innovation and creativity inevitably begs the question of improvising by melding and blending different scholarly traditions. This is both possible and feasible, provided one pays careful attention to the assumptions undergirding the different traditions. If one were to look carefully at many of the traditions discussed in this book, it would very quickly become apparent that they themselves are frequently the products of blended traditions. Critical hermeneutics, for instance, is born out of the marriage of hermeneutics and critical theory, while Giddens' structuration grew out of his interest in both historical materialism and ethnomethodology, and postcolonialism emerged out of the uneasy discussions between Marxism, poststructuralism, and various national liberation movements. A number of feminists are also prone to such theoretical improvisation, given their orientation toward ontological and epistemological flexibility in the pursuit of praxis.

The work of Aihwa Ong (1987) in many ways exemplifies fieldwork at the intersection of different traditions. Ong studied Malaysian electronic chip factories in the 1980s, with a view to understanding how women workers in these factories lived and refashioned their culture and self-images in the wake of their recent encounters with late capitalism. Though offering a range of insights on the emergence of indirect resistance, Ong's (1987) study also defies easy classification into any one of the scholarly traditions discussed in this book. She draws on the notion of contradiction from Marxism, gender identity from feminism, discipline from poststructuralism, and institutional binaries from postcolonialism to provide a potent explanation of cultural transgression by women workers. She particularly focuses on a series of recurring dramatic events in these factories—the "possession" of these women by ancestral spirits that brought entire assembly lines in the country to a grinding halt.

At the time of these spirit possessions, a number of managerial interpretations were present. These interpretations typically dismissed these events as hysterical reactions to factory life by superstitious rural women, or viewed them as devious acts of subversion directed against the companies that hired them. Ong, on the other hand, offers a far more nuanced explanation drawing on feminist, Marxist, postcolonial, and poststructural traditions. She suggests that in the vocabulary of spirit possessions, one can find the *unconscious* roots of an "idiom of protest" against capitalist forms of control and discipline. Her study is a powerful example of work that draws on multiple traditions and keeps them in productive tension with one another rather than superficially synthesizing them.

Quality Control: Individual Initiatives

Questions of standards and quality control surface regularly in discussions of qualitative research, partly because the application of standards is by no means clear or conclusive. Here again the tradition in which one is working can be helpful in furnishing standards according to which one might do one's research. Certainly individual researchers can do a lot on their own to make sure that their work is of a high caliber. First, researchers need to make sure that research questions are conceptually aligned with theoretical assumptions and that the questions asked are meaningful to the tradition in which they are working. Thus, research questions dealing with matters of social and cultural meaning are entirely appropriate to the ethnographic and hermeneutic

traditions, whereas questions relating to social conflict, power, and domination are best informed by any of the critical traditions. In other words, researchers need to be aware of and demonstrate the connections between their
empirical interests and the intellectual traditions that they are drawn to.

Intellectual traditions also shape the direction and focus of the research
project. Researchers need to be conscious of this consideration as well. The
question of focus is important and should not in general be left to chance or
accident, for it determines who is talked to and who is not (e.g., part-time
workers rather than corporate board members), what kinds of questions are
posed, what activities are observed closely (e.g., meetings rather than informal conversations), and how one interprets individuals' words and actions in
organizations. More than anything, a timely awareness of the intellectual tradition in which one would like to work also prevents a researcher from walking in "blind" into a field site and making random and aimless observations.

By now, many readers have probably grasped that I have serious reservations about walking "blind" into a site, or adopting what is often called a
"blank slate" approach to qualitative research. This is indeed the case for
several reasons. First, such an approach assumes that a researcher is capable
of approaching a site without theory, which is simply not ever the case. It
makes far more sense to have a relatively informed idea of the kind of social
dynamics that one is interested in before walking into a site. There is nothing,
after all, to stop one from altering one's interest once some preliminary observations have been made. But at least such a change of mind has a clear
intellectual grounding and base for altering one's focus. Beginning to study
any empirical situation without any idea of focus or direction is not only
confusing and pointless, it is also theoretically sloppy and ill informed. One
can still spend a few days or hours at the site of one's choice as a part of a pilot
study in the very early days of formulating one's research. But I would not
recommend a research strategy that believes in prolonging an atheoretical
contact with the field for a long period of time.

Once an intellectual tradition has been selected, researchers would do well
to acquaint themselves with the *styles of representation* found within that
tradition. Unfortunately, too many social scientists pay insufficient attention
to writing styles and the art of presenting one's research, resorting instead to
a somewhat dry and detached style of presentation and analysis. Here again,
the different traditions can be sources of inspiration when it comes to adopting a narrative style. Any tradition has its own vocabulary and presentational
style, and researchers are well advised to study these closely. Ethnographers
and hermeneuticians, for instance, favor rich textual flavors and often insert
themselves into their discussions, whereas semioticians can be more detached
and formal in their presentation styles, and historical materialists can even be

somewhat polemic in tone. Newer traditions such as postmodernism and poststructuralism are stylistically subversive, often deliberately breaking with linguistic and literary conventions, and ensuring that these stylistic disruptions are highlighted in the text. In any event, researchers cannot afford to ignore these questions of narrative style when presenting their research.

Quality Control: The Gatekeepers

In most academic fields, research quality is guaranteed by external reviewers who are typically knowledgeable experts in relevant areas. Relatively younger and intensely interdisciplinary fields such as management and organization studies, however, cannot always depend on having sufficient experts in multiple qualitative research traditions serving as important gatekeepers. This is particularly the case with the North American segment of management and organization studies, which has, until relatively recently, been dominated by the disciplines of industrial and organizational psychology and economics. As a result, the predominant view of scholarship and science has also been influenced by models from these two disciplines. Not surprisingly, the actual practice of research has been largely limited to following experimental designs and survey-based research concerned mostly with hypothesis testing through the *measurement* of multiple social and psychological phenomena.

Even though qualitative research has made some kind of a breakthrough in the last two decades, it still occupies a relatively marginal position within "leading" management journals such as the *Academy of Management Journal* and the *Administrative Science Quarterly*. Even more regrettable is the lack of awareness of multiple qualitative traditions on the part of reviewers, who insist that different genres of qualitative research mimic conventional positivism, albeit with alternate data collection techniques such as interviews and participant observation. These reviewers persist in raising questions about interrater reliability, generalizability, and replication in situations in which they have no place at all because of the researcher's interest in interpretation, historical analysis, or cultural critique. Put differently, some gatekeepers of prestigious management journals introduce distinctly inappropriate criteria that can actually be detrimental to producing good qualitative work. If we used an artistic metaphor here, we could liken it to insisting on applying the tenets of realism and representational art in judging surrealism, modern abstraction, or even impressionism.

Anyone who has submitted qualitative research to mainstream American journals or who has served as reviewers or on editorial boards will have experienced some of what I am talking about. The problem is relatively serious because the caliber of qualitative research is often diluted in an effort to placate reviewers who have only perfunctory knowledge of many nonpositivist traditions but who nevertheless insist on evaluating the work in accordance with positivist conventions. In many cases, these reviewers call for a simplification of research findings when the goal is actually to present the complexity of several organizational situations. Sometimes reviews can object to a more literary style of presentation even when the tradition that the researcher is working in (e.g., dramatism) calls for a certain kind of narrative expression. Therefore, when submitting qualitative research to such journals, researchers should be prepared to defend alternative analyses and writing styles to reviewers who have little knowledge of these traditions.

Despite these obstacles, superior qualitative research continues to be published even in mainstream American management journals. It is important for researchers to make sure that they defend their work on sound theoretical grounds and to be prepared to educate reviewers in some of the intricacies of doing qualitative work. It remains important that we conduct qualitative research in accordance with the teachings of the well-known traditions rather than compromise it so that it meets the conventions of positivist research.

Fortunately, a number of European journals such as the *Journal of Management Studies, Human Relations,* and *Organization Studies* are staffed with reviewers who are well versed in multiple qualitative traditions and who can therefore offer useful and constructive advice on how to conduct qualitative research. In addition, a number of American scholarly outlets in related fields such as sociology, anthropology, and communication studies are also recognizably at the forefront of qualitative research and encourage fieldwork from diverse intellectual traditions. If one is serious about producing high-quality nonpositivist scholarship, it is important to select publication outlets that would be relevant in terms of making meaningful contributions and having audiences that would appreciate and understand one's work.

Finally and most importantly, books and book chapters remain excellent publication outlets. Not only do books offer the space required to do justice to the density and complexity of much of qualitative fieldwork, but both books and book chapters also foster a more creative narrative style that is integral to several qualitative traditions. Many mainstream journals on the other hand remain stylistically committed to the deductive hypothesis testing model of research, where far greater attention is paid to developing the hypothesis and far less attention is paid to a detailed presentation and discussion of findings. Tailoring hermeneutic, dramaturgical, postmodern, or other qualitative research traditions to this model of writing is quite meaningless and is only likely to detract from the overall craftsmanship of qualitative research. Researchers are therefore urged to carefully consider publication outlets if they are serious about producing high-quality nonpositivist work.

One also continues to hope that editors and reviewers of the more mainstream journals will take the trouble to acquaint themselves with the many qualitative research traditions that are currently present in so many other academic disciplines and to become genuinely open-minded in their conceptions of what might be considered solid research. Without such a willingness, the field of management and organization studies in North America runs the risk of being intellectually stagnant and stuck within the straightjacket of normal science. A concerted effort by qualitative researchers to be faithful to their own qualitative traditions and to resist the standardization of positivism can go a long way in making management and organization studies more lively and relevant to the wider social world.

The Joys of Crafting Qualitative Research

Our discussions of qualitative research have emphasized its theoretical and practical complexity, the amount of effort expended in data collection, the creativity required in presenting the research, and the problems involved in dealing with reviewers who are not always well versed in many qualitative traditions. In short, any reader of this book should be in no doubt about the quantum effort required in the crafting of qualitative research. This should not, however, prevent researchers from appreciating the sheer joy and excitement of conducting qualitative research in many of the traditions discussed in this book.

First, the immense interdisciplinarity of many of these traditions, exposing scholars to a range of perspectives, standpoints, and theoretical considerations is exhilarating. Thus there is the sheer joy of encountering new and different ways of conceptualizing and understanding our organizational worlds. Ideas from the fine arts, the humanities, and the social sciences enhance our ways of engaging with work and organizations, and can introduce a level of creativity and expressiveness that is largely absent in more conventional management studies. This is undoubtedly a source of personal enjoyment for those of us who delight in experimenting with new ideas and narrative styles.

Many of the qualitative traditions are also immensely rewarding to individuals who enjoy working with a variety of *details*. Ethnography, dramatism, critical theory, and many other traditions call for fine-grained attention to detail when it comes to documenting how people construct workplace identities, make decisions in organizations, establish social relations, exercise power and influence at work, and, in general, produce and perform their life stories in organizations. For those who relish working with such details, there is an almost sensual quality to working in traditions that are interested in observing and commenting on the intricacies of organizational arrangements.

Another joy in working in many of the qualitative traditions comes from establishing meaningful contacts with people who are either the "subjects" of one's research or are connected to the research project in multiple ways. In other words, qualitative research often calls for a higher degree of personal involvement and direct engagement with people's lives and problems. In addition, for those who want their research to have a more direct social relevance, the critical and *post* traditions offer myriad opportunities to critique contemporary social structures and envision alternative institutional formations. Thus, in many ways, a number of the qualitative traditions offer the excitement of intellectual vigor without the seclusion of the ivory tower. For those of us who love the challenge of academic discourses but want to remain a part of the so-called real world, qualitative research may well be the answer.

And finally, the traditions discussed in this book help us examine important and interesting life questions that cannot easily be addressed by the positivist tradition for the simple reason that many qualitative traditions are actually absorbed by the irrationality, complexity, and paradoxicality of organizational worlds, without seeking to exclude much of it as "noise" or to reduce it to sterile and formulaic representations of the social world. For those of us with an interest in the messy realities of organizations, with a desire to be creative and imaginative but with a willingness to be theoretically and empirically disciplined, the qualitative research traditions can offer a world of excitement, engagement, and enjoyment.

References

Aboulafia, M.Y. (1996). *Making markets: Opportunism and restraint on Wall Street.* Cambridge, MA: Harvard University Press.

Aboulafia, M.Y., & Kilduff, M. (1988). Enacting market crisis: The social construction of a speculative bubble. *Administrative Science Quarterly, 33,* 177–93.

Acker, J. (1990). Hierarchies, jobs, bodies: A theory of gendered organizations. *Gender and Society, 4,* 139–58.

Acker, J. (1992). Gendering organizational theory. In A. Mills & P. Tancred (Eds.), *Gendering organizational analysis* (pp. 42–66). London: Sage Publications.

Acker, J. (1994). The gender regime of Swedish banks. *Scandinavian Journal of Management, 10,* 117–30.

Adorno, T.W. (1951). *Minima moralia: Reflections on a damaged life.* London: New Left Review Books.

Adorno, T.W. (1969). *The authoritarian personality.* New York: W.W. Norton.

Adorno, T.W. (1991). *The culture industry: Selected essays on mass culture.* London: Routledge.

Adorno, T.W., & Horkheimer, M. (1972). *Dialectic of enlightenment.* New York: Herder & Herder.

Alexander, J.C. (1995). *Fin de Siecle social theory: Relativism, reduction and the problem of reason.* London: Verso.

Alleyne, B.W. (1999). Cultural politics and globalized infomedia: C.L.R. James, Theodor Adorno and Mass Culture Criticism. *Interventions: International Journal of Postcolonial Studies, 1,* 361–72.

Althusser, L., & Balibar, E. (1971). *Reading capital.* London: New Left Review Books.

Alvesson, M. (1987). *Organization theory and technocratic consciousness: Rationality, Ideology and quality of work.* Berlin: Walter de Gruyter.

Alvesson, M. (1990). Organization: From substance to image. *Organization Studies, 11,* 373–94.

Alvesson, M. (1993). *Cultural perspectives on organizations.* Cambridge: Cambridge University Press.

Alvesson, M. (1994). Critical theory and consumer marketing. *Scandinavian Journal of Management, 10,* 291–313.

Alvesson, M. (2002). *Postmodernism and social research.* Buckingham, UK: Open University Press.

Alvesson, M., & Deetz, S. (2000). *Doing critical management research.* London: Sage Publications.

Alvesson, M., & Due Billing, Y. (2002). Beyond body counting: A discussion of the social construction of gender at work. In I. Aaltio & A.J. Mills (Eds.), *Gender, identity and the culture of organizations* (pp. 72–91). London: Routledge.

Amin, S. (1974). *Unequal development.* New York: Monthly Review Press.

Aparicio, F.R., & Chavez-Silverman, S. (1997). Introduction. In F.R. Aparicio & S. Chavez-Silverman (Eds.), *Tropicalization: Transcultural representations of Latinidad.* Hanover, NH: University Press of New England.

Apfel-Marglin, F., & Marglin, S. (Eds.) (1996). *Decolonizing knowledge: From development to dialogue.* Oxford: Clarendon Press.

Appadurai, A. (1990). Disjuncture and difference in the global economy. *Public Culture, 2,* 15–24.

Appadurai, A. (1996). *Modernity at large: Cultural dimensions of globalization.* Minneapolis: University of Minnesota Press.

Aredal, A. (1986). Procrustes: A modern management pattern found in a classical myth. *Journal of Management, 12,* 403–14.

Aristotle (1976). *Nicomachean Ethics.* Harmondsworth: Penguin.

Arnold, S.J., & Fischer, E. (1994). Hermeneutics and consumer research. *Journal of Consumer Research, 21,* 55–70.

Asad, T. (Ed.) (1973). *Anthropology and the colonial encounter.* London: Ithaca Press.

Ashcroft, B., Griffiths, G., & Tiffin, H. (1989). *The empire writes back: Theory and practice in post-colonial literatures.* London: Routledge.

Atkinson, P., & Hammersley, M. (1994). Ethnography and participant observation. In N.K. Denzin & Y. Lincoln (Eds.), *Handbook of qualitative research* (pp. 248–61). Thousand Oaks, CA: Sage Publications.

Axtell, J. (1981). *The European and the Indian: Essays in the ethnohistory of Colonial America.* Oxford: Oxford University Press.

Baert, P. (1998). *Social theory in the twentieth century.* New York: New York University Press.

Bannerjee, S. (2003). The practice of stakeholder colonialism: National interest and colonial discourses in the management of indigenous stakeholders. In A. Prasad (Ed.), *Postcolonial theory and organizational analysis: A critical engagement* (pp. 255–79). New York: Palgrave/Macmillan.

Baran, P., & Sweezy, P. (1966). *Monopoly capital.* Harmondsworth: Penguin.

Baritz, L. (1974). *The servants of power.* Westport, CT: Greenwood Press.

Baritz, L. (1990). *The good life: The meaning of success for the American middle class.* New York: Harper & Row.

Barker, J.R. (1993). Tightening the iron cage: Concertive control in self-managing teams. *Administrative Science Quarterly, 38,* 408–37.

Barley, N. (1983). *Adventures in a mud hut: An innocent anthropologist abroad.* New York: Vanguard Press.

Barley, S.R. (1983). Semiotics and the study of occupations and organizational cultures. *Administrative Science Quarterly, 28,* 393–413.

Barley, S.R. (1988). The social construction of a machine: ritual, superstition, magical thinking and other pragmatic responses to running a CT scanner. In M. Lock & D. Gordon (Eds.), *Knowledge and practice in medicine: Social, cultural and historical approaches* (pp. 497–540). Boston: Kluwer Academic Publishers.

Barrett, M., & Walsham, G. (1999). Electronic trading and work transformation in the London insurance market. *Information Systems Research, 10,* 1–22.

Barthes, R. (1953). *Writing degree zero.* New York: Hill & Wang.

Barthes, R. (1972). *Mythologies.* London: Jonathan Cape.

Bate, S.P. (1997). Whatever happened to organizational anthropology? A review of the field of organizational ethnography and anthropological studies. *Human Relations, 50,* 1147–75.

Baudrillard, J. (1975). *The mirror of production.* New York: Telos.

Baudrillard, J. (1983). *Simulations.* New York: Semiotext(e).

Baudrillard, J. (1984). *The evil demon of images.* Armandale, Australia: Power Institute.

Baudrillard, J. (1988). The year 2000 has already happened. In A. Kroker & M. Kroker (Eds.), *Body invaders: Panic sex in America.* Montreal: New World Perspectives.

Baudrillard, J. (1990). *Fatal strategies.* London: Pluto.

Bauman, Z. (1978). *Hermeneutics and social science: Approaches to understanding.* Aldershot, UK: Gregg Revivals.

Bauman, Z. (1989). *Modernity and the holocaust.* Ithaca, NY: Cornell University Press.

Bauman, Z. (1992). *Intimations of postmodernity.* London: Routledge.

Bayoumi, M., & Rubin, A. (2000). Introduction to *Orientalism*. In M. Bayoumi & A. Rubin (Eds.), *The Edward said reader* (pp. 63–67). New York: Vintage.

Becker, H. (1982). *Art worlds*. Berkeley: University of California Press.

Belenky, M.F., Clinchy, B.M., Goldberger, N.R., & Tarule, J.M. (1986). *Women's ways of knowing*. New York: Basic Books.

Bell, D. (1973). *The coming of post-industrial society*. New York: Basic Books.

Bell, D. (1976). *The cultural contradictions of capitalism*. London: Heinemann.

Benford, R.D., & Hunt, S.A. (1992). Dramaturgy and social movements: The social construction and communication of power. *Sociological Inquiry, 62*, 36–55.

Benschop, Y., & Dooreward, H. (1998a). Six of one and half a dozen of the other: The gender sub-text of Taylorism and team-based work. *Gender, Work and Organization, 5*, 5–18.

Benschop, Y., & Dooreward, H. (1998b). Covered by equality: The gender subtext of organizations. *Organization Studies, 19*, 787–805.

Benschop, Y., & Meihuizen, H.E. (2002). Reporting gender: Representations of gender in financial and social annual reports. In I. Aaltio & A.J. Mills (Eds.), *Gender, identity and the culture of organizations* (pp. 160–84). London: Routledge.

Benson, J.K. (1983). A dialectical method for the study of organizations. In G. Morgan (Ed.), *Beyond method: Strategies for social research* (pp. 331–46). Beverly Hills, CA: Sage Publications.

Benz, S. (1997). Through the tropical looking glass: The motif of resistance in U.S. literature on Central America. In F. Aparacio & S. Chavez-Silverman (Eds.), *Tropicalizations: Transcultural representations of Latinadad* (pp. 51–66). Hanover, NH: University of New England Press.

Berger, P.L., & Luckman, T. (1967). *The social construction of reality*. New York: Doubleday.

Berman, M. (1983). *All that is solid melts into air: The experience of modernity*. London: Verso.

Bernard, J. (1981). *The female world in a global perspective*. Bloomington: Indiana University Press.

Bernstein, R. (1985). *Beyond objectivism and relativism: Science, hermeneutics and praxis*. Philadelphia: University of Pennsylvania Press.

Berreman, G. (1962). *Behind many masks: Ethnography and impression management in a Himalayan village*. Society for Applied Anthropology Monograph 4. Ithaca, NY: Cornell University Press.

Bertaux, D., & Bertaux-Wiame, I. (1981). Artisanal bakery in France: How it lives and why it survives. In F. Bechofer & B. Elliot (Eds.), *The petite bourgeoisie: Comparative studies of the uneasy stratum* (pp.155–81). New York: St. Martin's Press.

Bessis, S. (2003). *Western supremacy: The triumph of an idea?* London: Zed Books.

Best, S., & Kellner, D. (1991). *Postmodern theory: Critical interrogations*. New York: Guilford Press.

Bhabha, H. (1984). *The location of culture*. London: Routledge.

Bhabha, H. (1990). *Nation and narration*. London: Routledge.

Bittner, E. (1965). The concept of organization. *Social Research, 32*, 230–55.

Blumer, H. (1969). *Symbolic interactionism*. Englewood Cliffs, NJ: Prentice Hall.

Boden, D. (1990a). The world as it happens: Ethnomethodology and conversation analysis. In G. Ritzer (Ed.), *Frontiers of social theory: The new synthesis* (pp. 185–213). New York: Columbia University Press.

Boden, D. (1990b). *The business of talk: Organizations in action*. Cambridge, MA: Polity Press.

Boissevain, J. (1990). Ethnic entrepreneurs and strategies. In R. Waldringer, H. Aldrich, & R. Ward (Eds.), *Ethnic entrepreneurs* (pp. 42–58). Newbury Park, CA: Sage Publications.

Boje, D. (1991). The storytelling organization: A study of story performance in an office-supply firm. *Administrative Science Quarterly, 36*, 106–26.

Boje, D. (1995). Stories of the storytelling organization: A postmodern analysis of Disney as Tamara-Land. *Academy of Management Journal, 38*, 997–1035.

Borman, E.G. (1982). Fantasy and rhetorical vision: Ten years later. *Quarterly Journal of Speech, 68*, 288–305.

Borman, E.G. (1983). Symbolic convergence: Organizational communication and culture. In L. Putnam & M.E. Paconowsky (Eds.), *Communication and organizations: An interpretive approach* (pp. 99–122). Beverly Hills, CA: Sage Publications.

Bottomore, T. (Ed.) (1983). *A dictionary of Marxist Thought.* Cambridge, MA: Harvard University Press.

Boulding, E. (1976). *The underside of history.* Boulder, CO: Westview Press.

Bourdieu, P. (1977). *Outline of a theory of practice.* Cambridge: Cambridge University Press.

Bourdieu, P. (1984). *Distinction: A social critique of the judgement of taste.* Cambridge, MA: Harvard University Press.

Bourdieu, P. (1986). The forms of capital. In J.G. Richardson (Ed.), *Handbook of theory and research for the sociology of education* (pp. 241–58). New York: Greenwood Press.

Bourdieu, P. (1989). The corporatism of the universal: The role of intellectuals in the modern world. *Telos*, 99–110.

Bourdieu, P. (1990). *The logic of practice.* Palo Alto, CA: Stanford University Press.

Bourdieu, P. (1991). *Language and symbolic power.* Cambridge, MA: Polity Press.

Bourdieu, P., Chamboredon, J., & Passeron, J. (1991). *The craft of sociology: Epistemological preliminaries.* New York: Walter de Gruyter.

Bourdieu, P., & de Saint Martin, M. (1974). Scholastic excellence and the values of the educational system. In J. Eggleston (Ed.), *Contemporary research in the sociology of education* (pp. 338–71). London: Methuen.

Bourdieu, P., & Wacquant, L. (1992). *An invitation to reflexive sociology.* Chicago: University of Chicago Press.

Bowles, S., & Gintis, H. (1976). *Schooling in capitalist America.* New York: Basic Books.

Brantlinger, P. (1988). *Rule of darkness: British literature and imperialism, 1830–1914.* Ithaca, NY: Cornell University Press.

Braverman, H. (1974). *Labor and monopoly capital: The degradation of work in the twentieth century.* New York: Monthly Review Press.

Bristor, J.M., & Fischer, E. (1993). Feminist thought: Implications for consumer research. *Journal of Consumer Research, 19*, 518–36.

Broms, H., & Gahmberg, H. (1983). Communication to self in organizations and cultures. *Administrative Science Quarterly, 28*, 482–95.

Bronner, S.E., & Kellner, D.M. (1989). Introduction. In S.E. Bronner & D.M. Kellner (Eds.), *Critical theory and society: A reader* (pp. 1–21). New York: Routledge.

Bulbeck, C. (1998). *Re-orienting Western feminisms: Women's diversity in a postcolonial world.* Cambridge: Cambridge University Press.

Burawoy, M. (1979). *Manufacturing consent: Changes in the labor process under monopoly capitalism.* Chicago: University of Chicago Press.

Burgelman, R. (1994). Fading memories: A process theory of strategic business exit in dynamic environments. *Administrative Science Quarterly, 39*, 24–56.

Burke, K. (1969a). *A grammar of motives.* Berkeley: University of California Press.

Burke, K. (1969b). *A rhetoric of motives.* Berkeley: University of California Press.

Burrell, G., & Hearn, J. (1989). The sexuality of organization. In J. Hearn, D. Sheppard, P. Tancred-Sherrif, & G. Burrell (Eds.), *The sexuality of organizations* (pp. 1–28). Newbury Park, CA: Sage Publications.

Burrell, G., & Morgan, G. (1979). *Sociological paradigms and organizational analysis.* Portsmouth, NH: Heinemann.

Burris, B.H. (1989). Technocracy and gender in the workplace. *Social Problems, 36*, 165–80.

Calas, M., & Smircich, L. (1991). Voicing seduction to silence leadership. *Organization Studies, 12*, 567–602.

Calas, M., & Smircich, L. (1992). Rewriting gender into organizational theorizing: Directions from feminist perspectives. In M. Reed & M. Hughes (Eds.), *Rethinking organization: New directions in organization theory and analysis* (pp. 227–53). London: Sage Publications.

Calas, M., & Smircich, L. (1993). Dangerous liaisons: The feminine-in-management meets globalization. *Business Horizons*, March/April, 71–81.

Calhoun, C. (1993). Habitus, field and capital: The question of historical specificity. In C. Calhoun, E. LiPuma, & M. Postone (Eds.), *Bourdieu: Critical perspectives* (pp. 61–88). Chicago: University of Chicago Press.

Callinicos, N. (1989). *Against postmodernism: A Marxist critique*. Cambridge, MA: Polity Press.

Campbell, C. (1987). *The romantic ethic and the spirit of modern consumerism*. Oxford: Basil Blackwell.

Caplan, P. (1989). Introduction. In P. Caplan (Ed.), *The cultural construction of sexuality* (pp. 1–30). London: Routledge.

Carby, H.V. (1985). On the threshold of woman's era: Lynching, empire and sexuality in black feminist theory. In H.L. Gates (Ed.), *"Race," writing and difference* (pp. 301–16). Chicago: University of Chicago Press.

Carchedi, G. (1977). *On the economic identification of social classes*. London: Routledge & Kegan Paul.

Carchedi, G. (1983). Class analysis and the study of social forms. In G. Morgan (Ed.), *Beyond method: Strategies for social research* (pp. 347–66). Beverly Hills, CA: Sage Publications.

Cassell, P. (1993). Introduction. In P. Cassell (Ed.), *The Giddens reader* (pp. 1–37). Stanford, CA: Stanford University Press.

Chatterjee, P. (1989). *Nationalist thought and the colonial world: A derivative discourse*. London: Zed books.

Cesaire, A. (1950). *Discourse on colonialism*. New York: Monthly Review Press.

Chakrabarty, D. (2000). *Provincializing Europe: Postcolonial thought and historical difference*. Princeton, NJ: Princeton University Press.

Chia, R. (1996). *Organizational analysis as deconstructive practice*. Berlin: Walter De Gruyter.

Childers, J., & Hentzi, G. (1995). *The Columbia dictionary of modern literary and cultural criticism*. New York: Columbia University Press.

Chua, B. (1977). Delineating a Marxist interest in ethnomethodology. *The American Sociologist*, *12*, 24–32.

Cicourel, A. (1968). *The social organization of juvenile justice*. New York: John Wiley & Sons.

Cicourel, A. (1974). *Cognitive sociology: Language and meaning in social interaction*. Harmondsworth: Penguin.

Clark, M. (1985). *Michel Foucault: An annotated bibliography*. London: Garland.

Clegg, S.R. (1990). *Modern organizations: Organization studies in a postmodern world*. London: Sage Publishers.

Clegg, S.R. (1994). Power relations and the constitution of the resistant subject. In J.M. Jermier, D. Knights, & W. Nord (Eds.), *Resistance and power in organizations* (pp. 274–325). London: Routledge.

Clegg, S.R. (1996). Postmodern management. In G. Palmer & S.R. Clegg (Eds.), *Constituting management: Markets, meanings and identities* (pp. 235–66). Berlin: Walter de Gruyter.

Clegg, S.R., Pitsis, T.S., Rura-Polley, T., & Marosszeky, M. (2002). Governmentality matters: Designing an alliance culture of inter-organizational collaboration for managing projects. *Organization Studies*, *23*, 317–37.

Clifford, J. (1988). *The predicament of culture: Twentieth-century ethnography, literature and art*. Cambridge, MA: Harvard University Press.

Clifford, J. (1997). *Routes: Travel and translation in the late 20th century*. Cambridge, MA: Harvard University Press.

Clifford, J., & Marcus, G.E. (Eds.) (1986). *Writing culture: The poetics and politics of ethnography*. Berkeley: University of California Press.

Cohen, A. (1981). *The politics of elite culture: Explorations in the dramaturgy of power in a modern African society*. Berkeley: University of California Press.

Cohen, I.J. (1989). *Structuration theory: Anthony Giddens and the constitution of social life.* London: Macmillan.

Cohn, C. (1987). Sex and death in the relational world of defense intellectuals. *Signs: Journal of Women in Culture and Society, 12,* 687–718.

Collins, R. (1985). *Three sociological traditions.* New York: Oxford University Press.

Collins, R. (1990). Conflict theory and the advance of macro-historical sociology. In G. Ritzer (Ed.), *Frontiers of social theory: The new synthesis* (pp. 68–87). New York: Columbia University Press.

Collinson, D.L. (1988). Engineering humor: Masculinity, joking and conflict in shopfloor relations. *Organization Studies, 9,* 181–99.

Collinson, D.L. (1992). *Managing the shopfloor: Subjectivity, masculinity and workplace culture.* Berlin: Walter de Gruyter.

Colton, C.W. (1987). Leisure, recreation, tourism: A Symbolic interactionism view. *Annals of Tourism Research, 14,* 345–60.

Comstock, D.E. (1982). A method for critical research. In E. Bredo & W. Feinberg (Eds.), *Knowledge and values in ethical and educational research* (pp. 370–90). Philadelphia: Temple University Press.

Connor, S. (1989). *Postmodernist culture: An introduction to theories of the contemporary.* Oxford: Basil Blackwell.

Cooke, W. (2003). Managing organizational culture and imperialism. In A. Prasad (Ed.), *Postcolonial theory and organizational analysis: A critical engagement* (pp. 75–94). New York: Palgrave/Macmillan.

Cooley, C.H. (1918). *Social process.* New York: Scribners.

Coombes, A.E. (1994). *Reinventing Africa: Material culture and the popular imagination in late Victorian and Edwardian England.* New Haven, CT: Yale University Press.

Cooper, D., & Essex, S. (1977). Accounting information and employee decision making. *Accounting, Organizations and Society, 2,* 201–17.

Cooper, R. (1989). Modernism, postmodernism and organizational analysis 3: The contribution of Jacques Derrida. *Organization Studies, 10,* 479–502.

Cooper, R., & Burrell, G. (1988). Modernism, postmodernism and organizational analysis. *Organization Studies, 9,* 91–112.

Costello, C. (1987). Working women's consciousness: Traditional or oppositional. In C. Groneman & M.B. Norton (Eds.), *To toil the livelong day: America's women at work* (pp. 37–48). Ithaca, NY: Cornell University Press.

Craib, I. (1992). *Modern social theory: From Parsons to Habermas.* New York: Harvester Wheatsheaf.

Crapanzano, V. (1977). On the writing of ethnography. *Dialectical Anthropology, 2,* 69–73.

Cronin, C. (1996). Bourdieu and Foucault on power and modernity. *Philosophy and Social Criticism, 22,* 55–85.

Crotty, M. (1998). *The foundations of social research.* London: Sage Publications.

Culler, J. (1976). *Saussure.* Hassocks, Sussex: Harvester Press.

Culler, J. (1982). *On deconstruction: Theory and criticism after structuralism.* Ithaca, NY: Cornell University Press.

Czarniawska, B. (1997). *Narrating the organization: Dramas of institutional identity.* Chicago: University of Chicago Press.

Czarniawska, B. (1998). *A narrative approach to organization studies.* Thousand Oaks, CA: Sage Publications.

Dahrendorf, R. (1959). *Class and class conflict in industrial society.* Stanford, CA: Stanford University Press.

Dalby, L.C. (1983). *Geisha.* Berkeley: University of California Press.

Dalton, M. (1959). *Men who manage: Fusions of feeling and theory in administration.* New York: John Wiley & Sons.

Darby, P. (1997). *At the edge of international relations: Postcolonialism, gender and dependency.* London: Cassell.

Davies, M. (1983). *Third world–second sex: Women's struggles and national liberation.* London: Zed Books.

De Beauvoir, S. (1957). *The second sex.* New York: Vintage.

De Man, P. (1971). *Blindness and insight: Essays on the rhetoric of contemporary criticism.* New York: Oxford University Press.

Deetz, S. (1992). *Democracy in an age of corporate colonization: Developments in communication and the politics of everyday life.* Albany: State University of New York Press.

Deleuze, G., & Guatarri, F. (1983). *Anti-Oedipus.* New York: Viking.

Denhardt, R.B. (1981). *In the shadow of organization.* Lawrence, KS: Regents Press.

Derrida, J. (1976). *Of grammatology.* Baltimore, MD: Johns Hopkins University Press.

Derrida, J. (1978). *Writing and difference.* London: Routledge & Kegan Paul.

Derrida, J. (1981). *Positions.* Chicago: University of Chicago Press.

Derrida, J. (1988). *Ear of the other: Otobiography, transference, translation.* Lincoln: University of Nebraska Press.

Dews, P. (1986). *Habermas, autonomy and solidarity.* London: Verso.

Dezalay, Y. (1995). "Turf battles" or "class struggles": The internationalization of the market for expertise in the "professional society." *Accounting, Organizations and Society, 20,* 331–44.

Diamond, I., & Quinby, L. (1988). *Feminism and Foucault.* Boston: Northeastern University Press.

Dilthey, W. (1976). *Selected writings.* (Edited by H.P. Rickman). London: Cambridge University Press.

DiMaggio, P., & Powell, W.W. (1983). The iron cage revisited: Institutional isomorphism and collective rationality in organizational fields. *American Sociological Review, 48,* 147–60.

DiMaggio, P., & Powell, W.W. (1991). Introduction. In W.W. Powell & P. DiMaggio (Eds.), *The new institutionalism in organizational analysis* (pp. 1–38). Chicago: University of Chicago Press.

Dingwall, R. (1976). Accomplishing profession. *Sociological Review, 24,* 331–49.

Dirks, N. (2001). *Castes of the mind: Colonialism and the making of modern India.* Princeton, NJ: Princeton University Press.

Docherty, T. (1993). Postmodernism: An introduction. In T. Docherty (Ed.), *Postmodernism: A reader* (pp. 1–31). New York: Columbia University Press.

Donaldson, L. (1985). *In defense of organization theory: A reply to the critics.* Cambridge: Cambridge University Press.

Dreyfus, H., & Rabinow, P. (1982). *Michel Foucault: Beyond structuralism and hermeneutics.* Brighton: Harvester Press.

Du Gay, P. (1996). *Consumption and Identity at Work.* London: Sage Publications.

Echtner, C., & Prasad, P. (2003). The context of Third World tourism marketing. *Annals of Tourism Research, 30,* 660–82.

Eco, U. (1976). *A theory of semiotics.* Bloomington: Indiana University Press.

Eco, U. (1984). *Semiotics and the philosophy of language.* London: Macmillan.

Edwards, R. (1979). *Contested terrain: The transformation of the workplace in the twentieth century.* New York: Basic Books.

Ehrenreich, B. (2001). *Nickel and dimed: On not getting by in America.* New York: Metropolitan Press.

Eisenstein, H., & Jardine, A. (1985). *The future of difference.* New Brunswick, NJ: Rutgers University Press.

Elmes, M.B., & Costello, M. (1992). Mystification and social drama: The hidden side of communication skills training. *Human Relations, 45,* 427–45.

Engels, F. (1945). *The conditions of the working class in England.* Leipzig: Otto Wigand.

Engels, F. (1902). *The origin of the family, private property and the state.* Chicago: Charles Kerr.

Escobar, A. (1995). *Encountering development: The making and unmaking of the Third World.* Princeton, NJ: Princeton University Press.

Evans, B. (1999). The ethnographic imagination in American literature: A genealogy of cultures, 1865–1930. Unpublished Ph.D. dissertation, University of Chicago.

Everett, J. (2002). Organizational research and the praxeology of Pierre Bourdieu. *Organizational Research Methods, 5,* 56–80.

Ewen, S. (1976). *Captains of consciousness: Advertising and the social roots of consumer culture.* New York: McGraw-Hill.

Ezzamel, M., & Willmott, H. (1998). Accounting for teamwork: A critical study of group-based systems of organizational control. *Administrative Science Quarterly, 43,* 358–96.

Fals-Borda, O., & Rahman, A. (Eds.) (1991). *Action and knowledge: Breaking the monopoly with PAR.* New York: Apex.

Fanon, F. (1961). *The wretched of the earth.* London: Penguin.

Fanon, F. (1967). *Black skin, white masks.* New York: Grove Press.

Feldman, S.P. (2000). Management ethics without the past: Rationalism and individualism in critical organization theory. *Business Ethics Quarterly, 10,* 623–43.

Ferguson, K.E. (1984). *The feminist case against bureaucracy.* Philadelphia, PA: Temple University Press.

Feyrabend, P. (1987). *Farewell to reason.* London: Verso.

Filby, I., & Willmott, H. (1988). Ideologies and contradictions in a public relations department: The seduction and impotence of living myth. *Organization Studies, 9,* 335–49.

Filmer, P. (1972). On Harold Garfinkel's ethnomethodology. In P. Filmer, M. Phillipson, D. Silverman, & D. Walsh (Eds.), *New directions in sociological theory* (pp. 203–21). London: Collier-Macmillan.

Finch, J. (1983). *Married to the job.* London: Allen and Unwin.

Fine, G.A. (1992). Symbolic interactionism in the post-blumerian age. In G. Ritzer (Ed.), *frontiers of social theory* (pp. 117–57). New York: Columbia University Press.

Fink-Eitel, H. (1992). *Foucault: An introduction.* Philadelphia: Pennridge Books.

Fiol, C.M. (1989). A semiotic analysis of corporate language: Organizational boundaries and joint venturing. *Administrative Science Quarterly, 34,* 277–303.

Fiol, M.C. (1991). Seeing the empty spaces: Towards a more complex understanding of the meaning of power in organizations. *Organization Studies, 12,* 547–66.

Firestone, S. (1970). *The dialectic of sex: The case for feminist revolution.* New York: William Morrow.

Fishman, P. (1978). Interaction: The work women do. *Social Problems, 25,* 399–406.

Flax, J. (1990). *Thinking fragments: Psychoanalysis, feminism and postmodernism in the contemporary west.* Berkeley: University of California Press.

Fletcher, J.K. (1999). *Disappearing acts: Gender, power and relational practice at work.* Cambridge, MA: MIT Press.

Flyvbjerg, B. (2001). *Making social science matter: Why social inquiry fails and how it can succeed.* Cambridge: Cambridge University Press.

Fondas, N. (1997). Feminization unveiled: Management qualities in contemporary writings. *Academy of Management Review, 22,* 257–82.

Fonow, M.M. (1997). Women of steel: A case of feminist organizing in the United Steelworkers of America. *Canadian Women's Studies, 18,* 117–22.

Forester, J. (1985). Critical theory and organizational analysis. In G. Morgan (Ed.), *Beyond method: Strategies for social research* (pp. 234–46). Beverly Hills, CA: Sage Publications.

Forester, J. (1992). Critical ethnography: On fieldwork in a Habermasian way. In M. Alvesson & H. Willmott (Eds.), *Critical management studies* (pp. 46–65). London: Sage Publications.

Foster, M.L. (1974). Deep structure in symbolic anthropology. *Ethos, 2,* 334–55.

Foucault, M. (1972). *The archaeology of knowledge.* London: Tavistock.

Foucault, M. (1973). *Madness and civilization: A history of insanity in the age of reason.* New York: Random House.

Foucault, M. (1974). *The order of things: An archaeology of the human sciences.* New York: Vintage.

Foucault, M. (1975). *The birth of the clinic: An archaeology of medical perception.* New York: Vintage.

Foucault, M. (1977a). *Discipline and punish: The birth of the prison.* London: Allen Lane.

Foucault, M. (1977b). *Language, counter-memory, practice.* London: Blackwell.

Foucault, M. (1979). *The history of sexuality.* London: Allen Lane.

Foucault, M. (1981). *Power/knowledge.* New York: Pantheon.

Frake, C.O. (1983). Ethnography. In R.M. Emerson (Ed.), *Contemporary field research* (pp. 60–67). Boston: Little, Brown.

Francis, J.R. (1994). Auditing, hermeneutics and subjectivity. *Accounting, Organizations and Society, 19,* 235–69.

Fraser, N. (1989). *Unruly practices: Power, discourse and gender in contemporary social theory.* Cambridge, MA: Polity Press.

Freire, P. (1970). *The pedagogy of the oppressed.* New York: Herder & Herder.

Friedan, B. (1963). *The feminine mystique.* New York: Dell.

Friedman, S.S. (1998). *Mappings: Feminism and the cultural geographies of encounter.* Princeton, NJ: Princeton University Press.

Fukuyama, F. (1989). The end of history. *The National Interest, 16,* 3–18.

Gabriel, Y. (1991). Turning facts into stories and stories into facts: A hermeneutic exploration of organizational folklore. *Human Relations, 44,* 857–75.

Gadamer, H.G. (1960). *Truth and method.* New York: Seabury Press.

Gandhi, L. (1998). *Postcolonial theory: A critical introduction.* New York: Columbia University Press.

Gane, M. (1986). Introduction. In M. Gane (Ed.), *Towards a critique of Foucault* (pp. 1–14). London: Routledge & Kegan Paul.

Gane, M. (1991). *Baudrillard: Critical and fatal theories.* London: Routledge.

Garfinkel, H. (1967). *Studies in ethnomethodology.* Englewood Cliffs, NJ: Prentice Hall.

Garfinkel, H. (1974). On the origins of the term "ethnomethodology." In R. Turner (Ed.), *Ethnomethodology* (pp. 15–18). Harmondsworth: Penguin.

Gavey, N. (1989). Feminist poststructuralism and discourse analysis: Contributions to feminist psychology. *Psychology of Women Quarterly, 13,* 459–75.

Geertz, C. (1973). *The interpretation of cultures.* New York: Basic Books.

Giddens, A. (1973). The class structure of advanced societies. London: Hutchinson.

Giddens, A. (1976). *New rules of sociological method: A positive critique of interpretive sociologies.* New York: Harper and Row.

Giddens, A. (1979). *Central problems in social theory: Action, structure and contradiction in social analysis.* London: Macmillan.

Giddens, A. (1982). *Profiles and critiques in social theory.* Berkeley: University of California Press.

Giddens, A. (1984). *The constitution of society: Outline of the theory of structuration.* Cambridge, MA: Polity Press.

Giddens, A. (1990). *The consequences of modernity.* Stanford, CA: Stanford University Press.

Giddens, A. (1991). *Modernity and self-identity: Self and society in the late modern age.* Cambridge, MA: Polity Press.

Giddens, A. (1992). *The transformation of intimacy.* Cambridge, MA: Polity Press.

Gilligan, C. (1977). In a different voice: Women's conceptions of self and morality. *Harvard Educational Review, 47,* 481–517.

Gilroy, P. (1987). *There ain't no black in the union Jack.* London: Hutchinson.

Giroux, H. (1983). *Theory and resistance in education: A pedagogy for the opposition.* South Hadley, MA: Bergin & Garvey.

Gitlin, T. (1983). *Inside prime time.* New York: Pantheon.

Glaser, B., & Strauss, A. (1967). *The discovery of grounded theory: Strategies for qualitative research.* New York: Aldine Publishing.

Goffman, E. (1959). *The presentation of self in everyday life.* Garden City, NJ: Anchor Books.

Goffman, E. (1961). *Encounters.* Indianapolis, IN: Bobbs-Merrill.

Goffman, E. (1963a). *Behavior in public places: Notes on the social organization of gatherings.* New York: Free Press.

Goffman, E. (1963b). *Stigma: Notes on the management of spoiled identity.* Englewood Cliffs, NJ: Prentice Hall.

Goffman, E. (1977). The arrangement between the sexes. *Theory and Society, 4,* 301–31.

Goke-Pariola, A. (1993). Language and symbolic power: Bourdieu and the legacy of Euro-American colonialism in an African society. *Language and Communication, 13,* 219–34.

Golden-Biddle, K., & Locke, K. (1993). Appealing work: An investigation of how ethnographic texts convince. *Organization Science, 4,* 595–616.

Golding, D. (1991). Some everyday rituals in management control. *Journal of Management Studies, 28,* 569–83.

Goldman, P., & Van Houten, D. (1977). Managerial strategies and the worker: A Marxist analysis of bureaucracy. *The Sociological Quarterly, 18,* 108–25.

Gopal, A., & Prasad, P. (2000). Understanding GDSS in symbolic context: Shifting the focus from technology to interaction. *MIS Quarterly, 24,* 509–46.

Gopal, A., Willis, R., & Gopal, Y. (2003). From the colonial enterprise to enterprise systems: Parallels between colonization and globalization. In A. Prasad (Ed.), *Postcolonial theory and organizational analysis: A critical engagement* (pp. 233–54). New York: Palgrave Macmillan.

Gorman, R.A. (1982). *Neo-Marxism: The meanings of modern radicalism.* Westport, CT: Greenwood Press.

Gottfried, H. (1994). Learning the score: The duality of control and everyday resistance in the temporary-help service industry. In J.M. Jermier, D. Knights, & W.R. Nord (Eds.), *Resistance and power in organizations* (pp. 102–27). London: Routledge.

Gouldner, A. (1954). *Patterns of industrial bureaucracy.* New York: Free Press.

Gramsci, A. (1971). *Selections from the prison notebooks of Antonio Gramsci.* London: Lawrence & Wishart.

Gregory, K. (1983). Native-view paradigms: Multiple cultures and culture conflicts in organizations. *Administrative Science Quarterly, 28,* 359–76.

Greimas, A.J. (1966). *Structural semiotics.* Lincoln: University of Nebraska Press.

Habermas, J. (1970). *Towards a rational society.* London: Heinemann.

Habermas, J. (1972). *Knowledge and human interests.* London: Heinemann.

Habermas, J. (1974). *Discourses of modernity.* London: Heinemann.

Habermas, J. (1976). *Legitimation crisis.* London: Heinemann.

Habermas, J. (1984). *Theory of communicative action. Volume I: Reason and the rationalization of society.* London: Heinemann.

Habermas, J. (1990). The hermeneutic claim to universality. In G.L. Ormiston & A.D. Schrift (Eds.), *The hermeneutic tradition* (pp. 245–72). Albany, NY: SUNY Press.

Hall, S. (1982). The rediscovery of "ideology": Return of the repressed in media studies. In M. Gurevitch, T. Bennet, J. Curran, & J. Woolacott (Eds.), *Culture, society and the media* (pp. 56–90). London: Methuen.

Hall, S. (1990). *Culture, media, language.* London: Unwin Hyman.

Hamilton, D. (1993). Traditions, preferences and postures in applied qualitative research. In N. Denzin & Y.S. Lincoln (Eds.), *Handbook of qualitative research* (pp. 60–69). Thousand Oaks, CA: Sage Publications.

Hammond, T., & Oakes, L. (1992). Some feminisms and their implications for accounting practice. *Accounting, Auditing, Accountability Journal, 5,* 52–70.

Hannerz, U. (1987). The world in creolization. *Africa, 57,* 546–59.

Harken, R., Mahar, C., & Wilkes, C. (1990). The basic theoretical position. In R. Harken, C. Mahar, & C. Wilkes (Eds.), *An introduction to the work of Pierre Bourdieu: The practice of theory* (pp. 2–18). London: Macmillan.

Harris, R. (1987). *Reading Saussure: A critical commentary on the Cours de Linguistic Generale.* London: Open Court Publishing.

Harrison, J. (1997). Museums as agencies of neocolonialism in a postmodern world. *Studies in Cultures, Organizations and Societies, 3,* 41–65.

Hartsock, N. (1983). The feminist standpoint: Developing the ground for a specifically feminist materialism. In S. Harding & M.B. Hintikka (Eds.), *Discovering reality: Feminist perspectives on epistemology, metaphysics, methodology and philosophy of science* (pp. 216–30). London: D. Reidel.

Hassan, I. (1987). *The postmodern turn: Essays in postmodern history and culture.* Columbus: Ohio University Press.

Hassard, J. (1990). Ethnomethodology and organizational research: An introduction. In J. Hassard & D. Pym (Eds.), *The theory and philosophy of organizations* (pp. 97–108). New York: Routledge.

Hassard, J. (1994). Postmodern organizational analysis: Toward a conceptual framework. *Journal of Management Studies, 31,* 303–24.

Hearn, J., & Parkin, W. (1983). Gender and organizations: A selective review and a critique of a neglected area. *Organization Studies, 4,* 219–42.

Heidegger, M. (1962). *Being and time.* London: SCM Press.

Held, D. (1980). *Introduction to critical theory.* London: Hutchinson.

Heritage, J. (1984). *Garfinkel and ethnomethodology.* Cambridge, MA: Polity Press.

Hewitt, J. (1988). *Self and society.* Boston: Allyn & Bacon.

Hirschman, E. (1990). Secular immortality and the American ideology of affluence. *Journal of Consumer Research, 17,* 31–42.

Hochschild, A. (1983). *The managed heart: The commercialization of human feeling.* Berkeley: University of California Press.

Hodder, I. (1993). The interpretation of documents and material culture. In N. Denzin & Y.S. Lincoln (Eds.), *Handbook of Qualitative Research* (pp. 393–402). Thousand Oaks, CA: Sage Publications.

Holman, R.H. (1980). Clothing as communication: An empirical investigation. In J.C. Olson (Ed.), *Advances in Consumer Research* (pp. 372–77). Ann Arbor, MI: Association for Consumer Research.

Holstein, J.A., & Gubrium, J.F. (1993). Phenomenology, ethnomethodology and interpretive practice. In N. Denzin & Y.S. Lincoln (Eds.), *Handbook of qualitative research* (pp. 262–65). Thousand Oaks, CA: Sage Publications.

Holvino, E. (1996). Reading organizational development from the margins: Outsider within. *Organization, 3,* 520–33.

hooks, bell (1989). *Talking back: Thinking feminism, thinking black.* Boston: South End Press.

Horkheimer, M. 1947. *Eclipse of reason.* New York: Oxford University Press.

Hossfeld, K. (1993). "Their logic against them": Contradictions in sex, race and class in Silicon Valley. In A.M. Jagger & P. Rothenberg (Eds.), *Feminist Frameworks* (pp. 346–58). New York: McGraw Hill.

Howard, R.J. (1982). *Three faces of hermeneutics.* Berkeley: University of California Press.

Howe, I. (1970). *The decline of the new.* New York: Harcourt, Brace and World.

Husserl, E. (1960). *Cartesian meditations: An introduction to phenomenology.* The Hague: Martinus Nijhoff.

Hutcheon, L. (1989). Circling the downspout of empire: Postcolonialism and poststructuralism. *Ariel, 20,* 150–62.

Ibarra, H. (1992). Homophily and differential returns: Sex differences in network structure and access in an advertising firm. *Administrative Science Quarterly, 37,* 422–47.

Illich, I. (1973). *Tools for conviviality.* London: Fontana.

Inglis, R. (1979). Good and bad habitus: Bourdieu, Habermas and the condition of England. *Sociological Review, 27,* 353–69.

Irigiray, L. (1974). *Speculum of the other woman.* Ithaca, NY: Cornell University Press.

Jack, G., & Lorbiecki, A. (2003). Asserting possibilities of resistance in the cross-cultural teaching machine: Re-viewing videos of others. In A. Prasad (Ed.), *Postcolonial theory and organizational analysis: A critical engagement* (pp. 213–32). New York: Palgrave/Macmillan.

Jackall, R. (1988). *Moral mazes: The world of corporate managers.* Oxford: Oxford University Press.

Jackson, B. (1996). Re-engineering the sense of self: The manager and the management guru. *Journal of Management Studies, 33,* 571–90.

Jackson, B. (2001). *Management gurus and management fashions.* London: Routledge.

Jacob, E. (1987). Qualitative research traditions: A review. *Review of Educational Research, 57,* 1–50.

Jacques, R. (1996). *Manufacturing the employee: Management knowledge from the 19th to the 21st centuries.* London: Sage.

Jameson, F. (1992). *Postmodernism, or the cultural logic of late capitalism.* London: Verso.

Jaros, S. (2000). .Labor process theory: A commentary on the debate. *International Studies of Management and Organization, 30, 25–39.*

Jay, M. (1973). *The dialectical imagination.* Boston: Little, Brown.

Jencks, C. (1989). *What is post-modernism?* London: Academy Editions.

Jermier, J. (1988). Sabotage at work: The rational view. *Research in the Sociology of Organizations, 6,* 101–34.

Jhally, S. (1987). *The codes of advertising: Fetishism and the political economy of meaning in the consumer society.* London: Francis Pintner.

Kanter, R.M. (1977). *Men and women of the corporation.* New York: Basic Books.

Kaufman, A., Zacharias, L., & Karson, M. (1995). *Managers vs. owners: The struggles for corporate control in American democracy.* New York: Oxford University Press.

Keller, E.F. (1985). *Reflections on gender and science.* New Haven, CT: Yale University Press.

Kellner, D. (1990). The postmodern turn: Positions, problems and prospects. In G. Ritzer (Ed.), *Frontiers of social theory: The new synthesis* (pp. 255–89). New York: Columbia University Press.

Kendall, J.E. (1993). Good and evil in the chairman's 'boiler plate': An analysis of the corporate visions of the 1970s. *Organization Studies, 14,* 571–92.

Kets de Vries, M., & Miller, D. (1987). Interpreting organizational texts. *Journal of Management Studies, 24,* 233–47.

Kilduff, M. (1993). Deconstructing organizations. *Academy of Management Review, 18,* 13–31.

Kincheloe, J.L., & McLaren, P. (1994). Rethinking critical theory and qualitative research. In N. Denzin & Y. Lincoln (Eds.), *Handbook of Qualitative Research* (pp. 138–57). Thousand Oaks, CA: Sage Publications.

Kling, R. (1992). Audiences, narratives and human values in social studies of technology. *Science, Technology and Human Values, 17,* 349–65.

Knights, D., & Willmott, H. (1990). Exploring the class and organizational implications of the UK financial services. In S. Clegg (Ed.), *Organization theory and class analysis* (pp. 345–66). Berlin: Walter de Gruyter.

Koester, J. (1983). The Machiavellian princess: Rhetorical dramas for women managers. *Communication Quarterly, 30,* 165–72.

Kondo, D. (1990). *Crafting selves: power, gender and discourses of identity in a Japanese workplace.* Chicago: University of Chicago Press.

Kroker, A., & Cook, D. (1988). *The postmodern scene: Excremental culture and hyper-aesthetics.* London: Macmillan.

Kuhn, T.S. (1970). *The structure of scientific revolution.* (2nd ed.). Chicago: University of Chicago Press.

Kumar, K. (1995). *From post-industrial to post-modern society: New theories of the contemporary world.* London: Basil Blackwell.

Kunda, G. (1992). *Engineering culture: Control and commitment in a high-tech corporation.* Philadelphia: Temple University Press.

Lakatos, I. (1965). Falsification and the methodology of scientific research programs. In I. Lakatos & A. Musgrove (Eds.), *Criticism and the growth of knowledge.* Cambridge: Cambridge University Press.

Larrain, J. (1979). *The concept of ideology.* Athens: University of Georgia Press.

Larrain, J. (1983). *Marxism and ideology.* London: Macmillan.

Lasch, C. (1977). *Haven in a heartless world: The family besieged.* New York: Basic Books.

Lash, S. (1988). Discourse or figure? Postmodernism as a regime of signification. *Theory, Culture and Society, 5,* 311–36.

Latour, B. (1987). *Science in action: How to follow scientists and engineers through society.* Cambridge, MA: Harvard University Press.

Lechte, J. (1994). *Fifty key contemporary thinkers.* London: Routledge.

Lee, A. (1994). Electronic mail as a medium for rich communication: An empirical investigation using hermeneutic interpretation. *MIS Quarterly, 18,* 143–57.

Leidner, R. (1991). Serving hamburgers and selling insurance: Gender, work and identity in interactive service jobs. *Gender and Society, 5,* 154–77.

Lemert, C. (1979). Structuralist semiotics. In S. McNall (Ed.), *Theoretical Perspectives in Sociology* (pp. 96–111). New York: St. Martin's Press.

Lemert, C. (1997). *Postmodernism is not what you think.* Oxford: Basil Blackwell.

Lengermann, P.M., & Niebrugge-Brantley, J. (1990). Feminist sociological theory: The near-future prospects. In G. Ritzer (Ed.), *Frontiers of social theory: The new synthesis* (pp. 316–44). New York: Columbia University Press.

Levi-Strauss, C. (1963). *Structural anthropology.* New York: Basic Books.

Levi-Strauss, C. (1966). *The savage mind.* Chicago: University of Chicago Press.

Linstead. S. (2000). Comment: Gender blindness or gender suppression? A comment on Fiona Wilson's research note. *Organization Studies, 21,* 297–303.

Loomba, A. (1998). *Colonialism/postcolonialism.* London: Routledge.

Lukacs, G. (1923). *History and class consciousness.* London: Merlin.

Lyman, S.M., & Scott, M.B. (1975). *The drama of social reality.* New York: Oxford University Press.

Lynch, M., & Woolgar, S. (Eds.) (1990). *Representation in scientific practice.* Cambridge, MA: MIT Press.

Lyotard, J.F. (1984). *The Postmodern Condition: A Report on Knowledge.* Manchester: Manchester University Press.

Lyytinen, K. (1992). Information systems and critical theory. In M. Alvesson & H. Willmott (Eds.), *Critical Management Studies* (pp. 159–80). London: Sage.

Maines, D.R. (1988). Myth, text and interactionist complicity in the neglect of Blumer's macrosociology. *Symbolic Interaction, 11,* 43–57.

Mangham, I.L., & Overington, M.A. (1987). *Organizations as theater: A social psychology of dramatic appearances.* New York: John Wiley & Sons.

Mann, M. (1986). *The sources of social power.* New York: Cambridge University Press.

Manning, P.K. (1989). Signwork. *Human Relations, 39,* 283–308.

Manning, P.K., & Cullum-Swann, B. (1994). Narrative content and semiotic analysis. In N.K. Denzin & Y.S. Lincoln (Eds.), *Handbook of Qualitative Research* (pp. 463–78). Thousand Oaks, CA: Sage Publications.

Marcuse, H. (1964). *One-dimensional man.* London: Routledge & Kegan Paul.

Marcuse, H. (1966). *Eros and civilization: A philosophic inquiry into Freud.* Boston: Beacon Press.

Marcuse, H. (1989). From ontology to technology: Fundamental tendencies of industrial society. In S.E. Bronner & D.M. Kellner (Eds.), *Critical theory and society: A reader* (pp. 119–35). New York: Routledge.

Marglin, S. (1974). What do bosses do? The origins and functions of hierarchy in capitalist production. *Review of Radical Political Economics, 6,* 24–52.

Margolis, S. (1989). Postscript on modernism and postmodernism. *Theory, Culture and Society, 6,* 5–30.

Marshall, B. (1994). *Engendering modernity: Feminism, social theory and social change.* Boston: Northeastern University Press.

Martin, J. (1990). Deconstructing organizational taboos: The suppression of gender conflict in organizations. *Organization Science, 1,* 339–59.

Martin, P.Y. (1988). Rethinking feminist organizations. *Gender and Society, 4,* 182–206.

Martin, R. (1988). Sowing the threads of resistance: Worker resistance and managerial control in a paint and garment factory. *Humanity and Society, 10,* 259–75.

Martindale, D. (1981). *The nature and types of sociological theory.* Boston: Houghton Mifflin.

Marx, K. (1963). *The eighteenth brumaire of Louis Bonaparte.* Hamburg: Meissner.

Marx, K. (1964). *The economic and philosophic manuscripts.* Hamburg: Meissner.

Marx, K. (1977). *Capital.* New York: Vintage.

Marx, K. (1973). *Die Grundrisse: Foundations of the critique of political economy.* Harmondsworth: Penguin.

Marx, K., & Engels, F. (1948). *The Communist Manifesto.* New York: International Publishers.

Mautner, T. (Ed.). (1996). *A dictionary of philosophy.* London: Basil Blackwell.

May, T. (1996). *Situating social theory.* Buckingham, UK: Open University Press.

McCall, L. (1991). Does gender fit? Bourdieu, feminism and conceptions of social order. *Theory and Society, 21,* 837–68.

McCarthy, T. (1978). *The critical theory of Jurgen Habermas.* Cambridge, MA: MIT Press.

Mead, G.H. (1934). *Mind, self and society.* Chicago: University of Chicago Press.

Mead, G.H. (1977). *On social psychology.* Chicago: University of Chicago Press.

Megill, A. (1985). *Prophets of extremity: Nietzsche, Heidegger, Foucault, Derrida.* Berkeley: University of California Press.

Mehan, H. (1979). *Learning lessons: Social organization in the classroom.* Cambridge, MA: Harvard University Press.

Memmi, A. (1967). *The colonizer and the colonized.* Boston: Beacon Press.

Memmi, A. (1968). *Dominated man: Notes toward a portrait.* London: Orion.

Meyer, J.W., & Rowan, B. (1977). Institutionalized organizations: Formal structure as myth and ceremony. *American Journal of Sociology, 83,* 340–63.

Mick, D.G. (1986). Consumer research and semiotics: Exploring the morphology of signs, symbols and significance. *Journal of Consumer Research, 13,* 196–213.

Miliband, R. (1969). *The state in capitalist society.* New York: Basic Books.

Miller, J.B. (1986). *Toward a new psychology of women.* Boston: Beacon Press.

Millet, K. (1970). *Sexual politics.* New York: Avon.

Mills, A.J. (1987). Duelling discourses: Desexualization versus eroticism in the corporate framing of female sexuality in the British airline industry, 1945–1960. In P. Prasad, A.J. Mills, M. Elmes, & A. Prasad (Eds.), *Managing the organizational melting pot: Dilemmas of workplace diversity* (pp. 171–98). Thousand Oaks, CA: Sage Publications.

Mills, A.J. (1988). Organization, gender and culture. *Organization Studies, 9,* 351–69.

Mills, C. Wright (1956). *The power elite.* New York: Oxford University Press.

Mills, S. (1997). *Discourse.* London: Routledge.

Mir, R., Mir, A., & Upadhyaya, P. (2003). Toward a postcolonial theory of organizational control. In A. Prasad (Ed.), *Postcolonial theory and organizational analysis* (pp. 47–74). New York: Palgrave/Macmillan.

Mirchandani, K. (2003). Challenging racial silences in studies of emotion work: Contributions from anti-racist feminist theory. *Organization Studies, 23.*

Mishra, V., & Hodge, B. (1994). What is Post(-)colonialism? *Textual Practice, 5,* 399–414.

Mohanty, C.T. (1988). Under Western eyes: Feminist scholarship and colonial discourses. *Feminist Review, 30,* 242–69.

Moore, H. (1999). *A passion for difference.* Cambridge, MA: Polity Press.

Morgan, G. (1992). Marketing discourse and practice: Towards a critical analysis. In M. Alvesson & H. Willmott (Eds.) *Critical Management Studies* (pp. 136–58). London: Sage.

Morris, G.H., & Coursey, M. (1989). Negotiating the meaning of employees' conduct: How managers evaluate employees' accounts. *The Southern Communication Journal, 54,* 185–205.

Morrow, R. (1994). *Critical theory and methodology.* Thousand Oaks, CA: Sage Publications.

Moulettes, A., & Prasad, P. (2001). Crossing cultures: A postcolonial reading of an organizational encounter. Paper presented at the 2nd biannual Critical Management Studies Conference, July, Manchester, U.K.

Muecke, S. (1992). *Textual spaces: Aboriginality and cultural studies.* Sydney: University of New South Wales Press.

Mullins, N. (1973). *Theories and theory groups in contemporary American sociology.* New York: Harper & Row.

Mumby, D.K., & Putnam, L.L. (1992). The politics of emotion: A feminist reading of bounded rationality. *Academy of Management Review, 17,* 465–86.

Murray, J.B., & Ozanne, J.L. (1991). The critical imagination: Emancipatory interests in consumer research. *Journal of Consumer Research, 18,* 129–44.

Nandy, A. (1995). *The savage Freud and other essays on possible and retrievable selves.* Princeton, NJ: Princeton University Press.

Neu, D. (1992). Reading the regulatory text: Regulation and the new stock issue process. *Critical Perspectives on Accounting, 3,* 359–88.

Neu, D. (2000). "Presents" for the Indians: Land, colonialism and accounting in Canada. *Accounting, Organizations and Society, 13,* 268–88.

Neu, D. (2003). Accounting for the Banal: Financial techniques as softwares of colonialism. In A. Prasad (Ed.), *Postcolonial theory and organizational analysis: A critical engagement* (pp. 193–212). New York: Palgrave/Macmillan.

Neu, D., Friesen, C., & Everett, J. (2003). The changing internal market for ethical discourses in the Canadian CA profession. *Accounting, Auditing and Accountability Journal* (forthcoming).

Norris, C. (1982). *Deconstruction: Theory and practice.* London: Methuen.

Norris, C. (1987). *Derrida.* London: Fontana Press.

Oakes, L.S., & Covaleski, M.A. (1994). A historical examination of the use of accounting-based incentive plans in the structuring of labor-management relations. *Accounting, Organizations and Society, 19,* 579–99.

Oakes, L.S., Townley, B., & Cooper, D.J. (1998). Business planning as pedagogy: Language and control in a changing institutional field. *Administrative Science Quarterly, 43,* 257–92.

O'Connor, E.S. (2001). Back on the way to empowerment: The example of Ordway Tead and industrial democracy. *Journal of Applied Behavioral Science, 37,* 15–32.

Ong, A. (1987). *Spirits of resistance and capitalist discipline: Factory women in Malaysia.* Albany: State University of New York Press.

Orlikowski, W.J. (1993). CASE tools as organizational change: Investigating incremental and radical changes in systems development. *MIS Quarterly, 17,* 309–40.

Orlikowski, W.J. (2000). Using technology and constituting structures: A practice lens for studying technology in organizations. *Organization Science, 11,* 404–28.

Ostrander, S. (1999). Gender and race in a pro-feminist, progressive, mixed-gender, mixed-race organization. *Gender and Society, 13,* 628–42.

Overington, M.A. (1977). Kenneth Burke and the method of dramatism. *Theory and Society, 4,* 131–56.

Packard, V. (1957). *The hidden persuaders.* New York: Penguin.

Palmer, R.E. (1969). *Hermeneutics.* Evanston, IL: Northwestern University Press.

Paules, G.F. (1991). *Dishing it out: Power and resistance among waitresses in a New Jersey restaurant.* Philadelphia: Temple University Press.

Pentland, B. (1995). Grammatical models of organizational processes. *Organization Science, 6,* 541–56.

Perera, S., & Pugliese, J. (1998). Parks, mines and tidy towns: Enviro-Panopticism, "post" colonialism and the politics of heritage in Australia. *Postcolonial Studies, 1,* 69–100.

Perinbanyagam, R.S. (1982). Dramas, metaphors and structures. *Symbolic Interaction, 5,* 259–76.

Pfeffer, J. (1981). Management as symbolic action: The creation and maintenance of organizational paradigms. In L.L. Cummings & B.M. Staw (Eds.), *Research in Organizational Behavior, 3,* 1–52. Greenwich, CT: JAI Press.

Phillips, N., & Brown, J.L. (1993). Analyzing communication in and around organizations: A critical hermeneutic approach. *Academy of Management Journal, 36,* 1547–76.

Poster, M. (1984). *Foucault, Marxism and history: Mode of production versus mode of information.* Cambridge, MA: Polity Press.

Poster, M. (1989). *Critical theory and poststructuralism: In search of a context.* Ithaca, NY: Cornell University Press.

Poster, M. (1990). *The mode of information: Poststructuralism and social context.* Chicago: University of Chicago Press.

Poulantzas, N. (1975). *Classes in contemporary capitalism.* London: New Left Review Books.

Poulantzas, N. (1978). *State, power, socialism.* London: New Left Review Books.

Powell, G. (1988). *Women and men in management.* Newbury Park, CA: Sage Publications.

Power, M. (1991). Educating accountants: Towards a critical ethnography. *Accounting, Organizations and Society, 16,* 333–53.

Power, M. (1994). The audit society. In A. Hopwood & P. Miller (Eds.), *Accounting as social and institutional practice* (pp. 299–316). Cambridge: Cambridge University Press.

Power, M., & Laughlin, R. (1992). Critical theory and accounting. In M. Alvesson & H. Willmott (Eds.), *Critical Management Studies* (pp. 113–35). London: Sage Publications.

Prasad, A. (1997). The colonizing consciousness and representations of the other: A postcolonial critique of the discourse of oil. In P. Prasad, A. Mills, M. Elmes, & A. Prasad, *Managing the organizational melting pot: Dilemmas of workplace diversity* (pp. 285–311). Thousand Oaks, CA: Sage Publications.

Prasad, A. (2001). Understanding workplace empowerment as inclusion: A historical investigation of the discourse of difference in the United States. *Journal of Applied Behavioral Science, 37,* 51–69.

Prasad, A. (2002). The contest over meaning: Hermeneutics as an interpretive methodology for understanding texts. *Organizational Research Methods, 5,* 12–33.

Prasad, A. (2003). The gaze of the other: Postcolonial theory and organizational analysis. In A. Prasad (Ed.), *Postcolonial theory and organizational analysis: A critical engagement* (pp. 3–46). New York: Palgrave/Macmillan.

Prasad, P., & Elmes, M. (2005). In the name of the practical: Unearthing the hegemony of pragmatism in the discourse of environmental management. *Journal of Management Studies* (forthcoming).

Prasad, A., & Mir, R. (2002). Digging deep for meaning: A critical hermeneutic analysis of CEO letters to shareholders in the oil industry. *The Journal of Business Communication, 39,* 92–116.

Prasad, A., & Prasad, P. (1993). Reconceptualizing alienation in management inquiry: Critical organizational scholarship and workplace empowerment. *Journal of Management Inquiry, 2,* 169–83.

Prasad, A., & Prasad, P. (1998). Everyday struggles at the workplace: The nature and implications of routine resistance in contemporary organizations. *Research in the Sociology of Organizations, 15,* 225–57.

Prasad, A., & Prasad, P. (2001). (Un)willing to resist? The discursive production of local workplace opposition. *Studies in Cultures, Organizations and Societies, 7,* 105–26.

Prasad, A., & Prasad, P. (2002a). The coming of age of interpretive organizational research. *Organizational Research Methods, 5,* 4–11.

Prasad, P. (1993). Symbolic processes in the implementation of technological change: A symbolic interactionist study of work computerization. *Academy of Management Journal, 36,* 1400–29.

Prasad, P. (1997). Systems of meaning: Ethnography as a methodology for the study of information technologies. In A. Lee, J. Liebenau, & J. DeGross (Eds.), *Information systems and qualitative research* (pp. 101–18). London: Chapman & Hall.

Prasad, P. (2003). The return of the native: Organizational discourses and the legacy of the ethnographic imagination. In A. Prasad (Ed.), *Postcolonial theory and organizational analysis: A critical engagement* (pp. 149–70). New York: Palgrave/Macmillan.

Prasad, P., & Caproni, P. (1987). Critical theory in the management classroom: Engaging power, ideology and practice. *Journal of Management Education, 21,* 284–91.

Prasad, P., & Prasad, A. (2000). Stretching the iron cage: The Constitution and implications of routine workplace resistance. *Organization Science, 11*, 387–403.

Prasad, P., & Prasad, A. (2002). Casting the native subject: Ethnographic practice and the (re)production of difference. In B. Czarniawska & H. Hopfl (Eds.), *Casting the other: the production and maintenance of inequalities in work organizations* (pp. 185–204). London: Routledge.

Pratt, M.L. (1992). *Imperial eyes: Travel writing and transculturation.* New York: London.

Preston, A., Wright, C., & Young, J.J. (1996). Imag[in]ing annual reports. *Accounting, Organizations and Society, 21*, 113–37.

Priyadarshini, E. (2003). Reading the rhetoric of otherness in the discourse of business business and economics: Toward a postdisciplinary practice. In A. Prasad (Ed.), *Postcolonial theory and organizational analysis: A critical engagement* (pp. 171–92). New York: Palgrave/Macmillan.

Propp, V. (1968). *The morphology of the folktale.* Austin: University of Texas Press.

Rabinow, P. (1977). *Reflections on fieldwork in Morocco.* Berkeley: University of California Press.

Rafaeli, A., & Sutton, R.J. (1991). Emotional contrast strategies as means of social influence: Lessons from criminal interrogators and bill collectors. *Academy of Management Journal, 34*, 749–75.

Reich, C. (1972). *The greening of America.* Harmondsworth: Penguin.

Reichard, G. (1934). *Spider woman: A story of Navajo weavers and chanters.* New York: Macmillan.

Reinharz, S. (1983). Experiential analysis: A contribution to feminist research. In G. Bowles & R. Duelli Klein (Eds.), *Theories of women's studies* (pp. 187–201). London: Routledge & Kegan Paul.

Reskin, B., & Padovic, I. (1994). *Women and men at work.* Thousand Oaks, CA: Pine Forge Press.

Richon, O. (1985). Representation, the despot and the harem: Some questions around an academic orientalist painting by Lecomte-du-Nuoy. In F. Barker, P. Hulme, M. Iverson, & D. Loxley (Eds.), *Europe and its others* (vol. I) (pp. 1–13). Colchester: University of Essex Press.

Ricoeur, P. (1971). The model of the text: Meaningful action considered as text. *Social Research, 38*, 529–62.

Ricoeur, P. (1981). *Hermeneutics and the human sciences: Essays on action, language and interpretation.* Cambridge: Cambridge University Press.

Ricoeur, P. (1991). *From text to action.* Evanston, IL: Northwestern University Press.

Riley, P. (1983). A structurationist account of political culture. *Administrative Science Quarterly, 28*, 414–37.

Ritzer, G. (1983). *Sociological theory.* New York: Alfred A. Knopf.

Ritzer, G. (1996). *The McDonaldization of society.* Newbury Park, CA: Sage Publications.

Rock, P. (1979). *The making of symbolic interaction.* London: Macmillan.

Rofel, L, (1992). Rethinking modernity: Space and factory discipline in China. *Cultural Anthropology, 7*, 93–114.

Rorty, R. (1979). *Philosophy and the mirror of nature.* Princeton, NJ: Princeton University Press.

Rosaldo, R. (1993). *Culture and truth: The remaking of social analysis.* Boston: Beacon Press.

Rosen, M. (1988). You asked for it: Christmas at the bosses' expense. *Journal of Management Studies, 25*, 463–80.

Rosen, M. (1991). Coming to terms with the field: Understanding and doing organizational ethnography. *Journal of Management Studies, 28*, 1–28.

Rosen, M., & Astley, W.G. (1988). Christmas time and control: An exploration in the social structure of formal organizations. *Research in the Sociology of Organizations, 6*, 159–82.

Rosenau, P.M. (1992). *Post-modernism and the social sciences: Insights, inroads and intrusions.* Princeton, NJ: Princeton University Press.

Rossi, I. (1974). *From the sociology of symbols to the sociology of signs.* New York: Columbia University Press.

Roszak, T. (1969). The making of a counter culture. New York: Doubleday.

Rowlinson, M., & Hassard, J. (1993). The invention of corporate culture: A history of the histories of Cadbury. *Human Relations, 46,* 299–326.

Roy, D. (1960). Banana time: Job satisfaction and informal interaction. *Human Organization, 18,* 156–68.

Said, E. (1978). *Orientalism.* New York: Vintage Books.

Said, E. (1989). Representing the colonized: Anthropology's interlocuters. *CriticalInquiry, 15,* 205–25.

Said, E. (1994). *Culture and imperialism.* New York: Vintage.

Sapir, E. (1949). *Language: An introduction to the study of speech.* New York: Oxford University Press.

Sapir, E., & Hoijer, H. (1967). *The phonology and morphology of the Navajo language.* Berkeley: University of California Press.

Sarup, M. (1993). *An introductory guide to poststructuralism and postmodernism.* Athens: University of Georgia Press.

Saussure, F. (1966). *The course in general linguistics.* New York: McGraw-Hill.

Schlosser, E. (2001). *Fast food nation: The dark side of the all-American meal.* New York: HarperCollins.

Schwartzman, H.B. (1993). *Ethnography in organizations.* London: Sage Publications.

Scott, W.G. (1992). *Chester I. Barnard and the guardians of the managerial state.* Lawrence: University Press of Kansas.

Seron, C., & Ferris, K. (1995). Negotiating professionalism: The gendered social capital of flexible time. *Work and Occupations, 22,* 22–47.

Sherry, J.F. (1990). A sociocultural analysis of a midwestern American flea market. *Journal of Consumer Research, 17,* 13–30.

Shibutani, T. (1967). Reference groups as perspectives. In J.G. Manis & B.N. Meltzer (Eds.), *Symbolic interaction: A reader in social psychology* (p. 30). Boston: Allyn & Bacon.

Shilling, C. (1993). *The body and social theory.* London: Sage Publications.

Silko, L.M. (1977). *Ceremony.* New York: Vintage.

Silverman, D., & Jones, J. (1973). Getting In: The managed accomplishment of "correct" outcomes. In J. Child (Ed.), *Man and organization: The search for explanation and social relevance* (pp. 63–106). London: George Allen & Unwin.

Sim, S. (1999). *Derrida and the end of history.* Cambridge, UK: Icon Books.

Simmel, G. (1950). *The sociology of Georg Simmel.* Glencoe, IL: Free Press.

Smart, B. (1985). *Michel Foucault.* London: Routledge.

Smith, D. (1979). A sociology for women. In J. Sherman & E. Torton-Beck (Eds.), *The prism of sex: Essays in the sociology of knowledge* (pp. 43–61). Madison: University of Wisconsin Press.

Smith, D.E. (1987). *The everyday world as problematic: A feminist sociology.* Milton Keyes: Open University Press.

Smith, P. (1987). What lies behind the statistics? Trying to measure women's contributions to Canadian agriculture. In *Women in Agriculture* (pp. 123–207). Ottawa: Report of the Canadian Advisory Council on the Status of Women.

Solomon, M.R. (1983). The role of products as social stimuli: A symbolic interactionist perspective. *Journal of Consumer Research, 10,* 319–29.

Spivak, G.C. (1991). *The post-colonial critic: Interviews, strategies, dialogues.* London: Routledge.

Spurr, D. (1993). *The rhetoric of empire: Colonial discourse in journalism, travel writing and imperial administration.* Durham, NC: Duke University Press.

Stablein, R. (1996). Data in organization studies. In S.R. Clegg, C. Hardy, & W.R. Nord (Eds.), *Handbook of Organization Studies* (pp. 509–25). London: Sage Publications.

Stam, R. (1995). Eurocentrism, polycentrism and multicultural pedagogy: Film and the quincentennial. In R. De La Campa, E.A. Kaplan, & M. Sprinker (Eds.), *Late imperial culture* (pp. 97–121). London: Verso.

Steffy, B.D., & Grimes, A.J. (1986). A critical theory of organization science. *Academy of Management Review, 11,* 322–36.

Steiner, G. (1971). *In Bluebeard's castle.* New Haven, CT: Yale University Press.

Stone, K. (1974). The origins of job structures in the steel industry. *The Review of Radical Political Economics, 6,* 61–97.

Strauss, A., Schatzman, L., Ehrlich, D., Bucher, R., & Sabshin, M. (1963). The hospital and its negotiated order. In E. Friedson (Ed.), *The hospital in modern society* (pp. 42–61). New York: Free Press.

Stryker, S. (1968). Identity, salience and role performance: The relevance of symbolic interaction theory for family research. *Journal of Marriage and the Family, 30,* 558–64.

Sugiman, P. (1992). 'That wall's comin' down': Gendered strategies of worker resistance in the UAW Canadian region, 1963–1970. *Canadian Journal of Sociology, 17,* 1–27.

Sutton, R.I., & Callahan, A.L. (1987). The stigma of bankruptcy: Spoiled organizational image and its management. *Academy of Management Journal, 30,* 405–36.

Swan, E. (1994). Managing emotion. In M. Tanton (Ed.), *Women in Management.* London: Routledge.

Swartz, D. (1997). *Culture and power: The sociology of Pierre Bourdieu.* Chicago: University of Chicago Press.

Tedlock, B. (1991). From participant observation to the observation of participation: The emergence of narrative ethnography. *Journal of Anthropological Research, 47,* 69–74.

Thayer, L. (1982). Human nature: Of communication, of structuralism, of semiotics. *Semiotica, 41,* 25–40.

Thompson, H. (1994). *Hell's Angels: A strange and terrible saga.* New York: Random House.

Thompson, P. (1993). Postmodernism: Fatal distraction. In J. Hassard & M. Parker (Eds.), *Postmodernism and organizations* (pp. 183–203). London: Sage Publications.

Thompson, W. (1983). Hanging tongues: A sociological encounter with the assembly line. *Qualitative Sociology, 6,* 215–37.

Thornton, S. (1996). *Club cultures: Music, media and subcultural capital.* Hanover, NH: University Press of New England.

Tienari, J., Quack, S., & Theobald, H. (2002). Organizational reforms, "ideal workers" and gender orders: A cross-societal comparison. *Organization Studies, 23,* 249–79.

Tinker, T., & Niemark, M. (1987). The role of annual reports in gender and class contradictions at General Motors, 1917–1976. *Accounting, Organizations and Society, 12,* 71–88.

Tom, A. (1993). Children of our culture? Class, power and learning in a feminist bank. In M.M. Feree & P.Y. Martin (Eds.), *Feminist organization: Harvest of the new women's movement* (pp. 165–79). Philadelphia: Temple University Press.

Torgovnick, M. (1990). *Gone primitive: Savage intellects, modern lives.* Chicago: University of Chicago Press.

Townley, B. (1993). Foucault, power/knowledge and its relevance for human resource management. *Academy of Management Review, 18,* 518–45.

Turner, B. (1986). Sociological aspects of organizational symbolism. *Organization Studies, 7,* 101–15.

Turner, S. (1983). Studying organization through Levi-Strauss's structuralism. In G. Morgan (Ed.), *Beyond method: Strategies for social research* (pp. 189–201). Beverly Hills, CA: Sage Publications.

Turner, V. (1969). *The ritual process.* Ithaca, NY: Cornell University Press.

Urraca, B. (1997). A textbook of Americanism: Richard Harding Davis's *Soldiers of fortune.* In F.R. Aparicio & S. Chavez-Silverman (Eds.), *Tropicalizations: transcultural representations of Latinidad.* Hanover, NH: University Press of New England.

Useem, M. (1979). The social organization of the American business elite and participation of corporate directors in the governance of American institutions. *American Sociological Review, 44,* 553–72.

Uzzell, D. (1984). An alternative structuralist approach to the psychology of tourism marketing. *Annals of Tourism Research, 11,* 79–99.

Van Maanen, J. (1973). Observations on the making of policemen. *Human Organization, 32,* 407–18.

Van Maanen, J. (1988). *Tales of the field: On writing ethnography.* Chicago: University of Chicago Press.

Van Maanen, J. (1995). An end of innocence: The ethnography of ethnography. In J. Van Maanen (Ed.), *Representation in Ethnography* (pp. 1–35). Thousand Oaks, CA: Sage Publications.

Van Maanen, J., & Kunda, G. (1989). Real feelings: Emotional expression and organizational culture. *Research in Organiztional Behavior, 11,* 43–103.

Vaught, C., & Wiehagen, W.J. (1991). Escape from a mine fire: Emergent perspectives and group behavior. *Journal of Applied Behavioral Science, 27,* 452–74.

Vidich, A.J., & Lyman, S.M. (1994). Qualitative methods: Their history in sociology and anthropology. In N.K. Denzin & Y. Lincoln (Eds.), *Handbook of qualitative methods* (pp. 23–59). Thousand Oaks, CA: Sage Publications.

Walby, S. (1990). *Theorizing patriarchy.* Cambridge, MA: Polity Press.

Walter, L. (1990). The embodiment of ugliness and the logic of love: The Danish redstocking movement. *Feminist Review, 36,* 103–26.

Weber, M. (1949). *The methodology of the social sciences.* Glencoe, IL: Free Press.

Weber, M. (1968). *Economy and society.* New York: Bedminster Press.

Weedon, C. (1997). *Feminist practice and poststructural theory.* Oxford: Basil Blackwell.

West, C. (1984). *Routine complications: Troubles in talk between doctors and patients.* Bloomington: Indiana University Press.

West, C., & Zimmerman, D. (1987). Doing gender. *Gender and Society, 1,* 125–51.

Westley, F.R. (1990). Middle managers and strategy: Microdynamics of inclusion. *Strategic Management Journal, 11,* 337–51.

Westley, F.R., & Vredenburg, H. (1996). Prison or ark? The drama of managing the modern zoo. *Studies in Cultures, Organizations and Societies, 2,* 17–30.

Whittington, R. (1992). Putting Giddens into action: Social systems and managerial agency. *Journal of Management Studies, 29,* 693–712.

Whyte, W.F. (1955). *Street corner society.* Chicago: University of Chicago Press.

Wiggeshaus, R. (1994). *The Frankfurt school: Its history, theories and political significance.* Cambridge, MA: MIT Press.

Williams, R. (1980). *Problems in materialism and culture.* London: Verso.

Williamson, J. (1978). *Decoding advertisements.* London: Martin Boyars.

Willmott, H. (1984). Images and ideals of managerial work. *Journal of Management Studies, 21,* 349–68.

Willmott, H. (1993). Strength is ignorance, slavery is freedom: Managing culture in modern organizations. *Journal of Management Studies, 30,* 515–52.

Wilson, F. (1996). Research note: Organization theory, blind and deaf to gender? *Organization Studies, 17,* 825–42.

Wolcott, H.F. (1995). Making a study more ethnographic. In J. Van Maanen (Ed.), *Representations in ethnography* (pp. 79–111). Thousand Oaks, CA: Sage Publications.

Wray-Bliss, E. (2002). Interpretation–appropriation: (Making) an example of labor process theory. *Organizational Research Methods, 5,* 81–104.

Young, E. (1989). On the naming of the rose: Interests and multiple meanings as elements of organizational culture. *Organization Studies, 10,* 187–206.

Young, R.C. (1995). *Colonial desire: Hybridity in theory, culture and race.* London: Routledge.

Young, R.C. (2001). *Postcolonialism: A historical introduction.* London: Blackwell.

Zantop, S. (1997). *Colonial fantasies: Conquest, family and nation in precolonial Germany, 1770–1870.* Durham, NC: Duke University Press.

Zimmerman, D. (1969). Record-keeping and the intake process in a public welfare agency. In S. Wheeler (Ed.), *On record: Files and dossiers in American life* (pp. 52–70). New York: Russell Sage Foundation.

Index

About the Author

Pushkala Prasad (Ph.D., University of Massachusetts, Amherst) is the Zankel Chair Professor of Management for Liberal Arts Students at Skidmore College in Saratoga Springs, New York. Prior to her present appointment, she was the Chair Professor of Public Administration at Lund University in Sweden. Dr. Prasad has also held full-time faculty positions at Clarkson University, the University of Calgary, and the Helsinki School of Economics in Finland. In 1997, she was a visiting scholar at the MIT Sloan School of Management. Her research interests include workplace resistance, the computerization of work, workplace diversity, postpositivist research, discourse analyses, and organizational legitimacy. She has published widely in reputed journals such as the *Academy of Management Journal, Organization Science, Human Relations, Studies in Cultures, Organizations and Society,* and *Research in the Sociology of Organizations.* She is also a coeditor of *Managing the Organizational Melting Pot: Dilemmas of Workplace Diversity* (1997) and has edited several journal special issues on topics such as "Critical Theory in Management Education" (*Journal of Management Education*) and the "History of Workplace Empowerment" (*Journal of Applied Behavioral Science*). She has begun researching the acquisition of social legitimacy in the tobacco, beef, gun, fur, and chemical industries.

Professor Prasad's work has been widely recognized in the scholarly community. She was named University of Calgary's Outstanding New Scholar in 1995 and received the Western Academy of Management's Ascendant Scholar Award in 1997. She is currently listed in *Who's Who in the Management Sciences.* Her research has also been generously supported by government grants and private foundations such as the Alberta Energy Corporation, the Social Sciences and Humanities Research Council of Canada, the Swedish Quality of Worklife Foundation, and the Bank of Sweden's Tercentenary Foundation.